LANDING IT

LANDING IT

My Life On And Off The Ice

SCOTT HAMILTON

with Lorenzo Benet

KENSINGTON BOOKS
http://www.kensingtonbooks.com

KENSINGTON BOOKS are published by

Kensington Publishing Corp.
850 Third Avenue
New York, NY 10022

Library of Congress Card Catalogue Number: 99-071666
ISBN 1-57566-466-6

First Printing: October, 1999
10 9 8 7 6 5 4 3 2 1

Printed in the United States of America

To my mother, Dorothy McIntosh Hamilton.
You were with me every step of the way.

Contents

Acknowledgments

The greatest blessing in life is to have many people touch you in a way that makes your life better. I have been truly blessed, and it started at the very beginning. I was in need of a family and I got a great one. I was in need of health and I was given the best medical care available. I needed help in school and found it everywhere. When I started to skate, I had coaches who taught me the fundamentals and did so in a way that nurtured my newfound love of skating. When money ran short, I was given another lease on life from two of the finest people I have ever known.

Every lesson from every coach could be considered a brick in building something strong and lasting. Each competitor taught me how to test myself and gave me memories that grow richer with the passing of each season. The opportunities that came from my Olympic successes were generous and the quality of the workplace was a healthy, supportive environment that pushed me to heights I could only dream of. Each and every person I met over the years showed me something that I could apply to everyday life. During my fight with cancer, I received an incredible amount of support that made an amazing difference in my healing. For all of the kindness and help, I can never express my gratitude adequately.

For the friendship, support and love from the people who have been the closest to me over the years, I would like to express my sincerest thanks and appreciation.

Thanks to my family, Dorothy, Ernie, Sue and Steve, who sacrificed more than their fair share at every level of my development.

To Frank and Helen McLoraine, for believing in me and through your love and support, making sure I had the opportunity to compete, grow and learn.

To Karen for loving me no matter what.

To Don Laws for seeing something in me no one else did.

To Bob Kain for your friendship and picking up the pieces every time I had a major crisis.

To Dr. Henry and Helen Landis for accepting me as one of their own.

To Bob and Barbara Camp, I loved being one of your chickens.

To Sarah Kawahara and Jef Billings for MAKING my professional life.

To Kevin Albrecht for your friendship and all that you have done to reinvent my career.

To all of you reading this for being generous in your support and the kindness you show each time I run into you in airports, restaurants and everytime I take the ice. I couldn't and wouldn't do anything without you.

Scott Hamilton

I would like to thank Scott Hamilton, a calm and strong soul, for his loyalty, trust and humor; Tracy Bernstein for her encouragement and guidance; and Frank Weimann, whose support was much appreciated.

For their unyielding faith and patience during the time I was devoted to this book. I owe a debt of gratitude to my family, Aimee, Hannah and Lorenzo, Jr. Aimee, your contributions were invaluable.

I also want to thank my oldest sister, Shaun. I don't think I'd be half the person I am today without the example you set for me growing up. Thanks for being strong for all of us.

Lorenzo Benet

Introduction:
The Competition of My Life

It's August 9, 1997, and I'm back on the ice for the first time in five months. My new skates are killing my feet, and my legs feel heavy and stiff. The bitter cold air is searing my throat, so it won't be long now before my toes turn numb. As I stroke across the ice, my heart pounds faster and my breathing grows harder. My body is throbbing in sync with the music blaring across the rink.

I'm in agony, but it feels awesome.

I'm alive.

Back in March, I was diagnosed with cancer and was ordered to stop skating by my doctors. I underwent chemotherapy, and just six weeks ago, had what was once a malignant tumor surgically removed from my abdomen. I should be lying on a beach in Malibu today, resting. Not skating around an ice rink.

Yet here I was. Some people urged me to take the year off, kick back and let my body heal. I was turning thirty-nine in a couple of weeks, and until last spring had been skating nonstop for thirty years. But slowing down is not my style, especially not when I was in the biggest competition of my life: me versus cancer.

I was determined to beat this illness, and that meant skating again, showing everyone I could regain my old form. If I took a year off, it would mean this insidious disease had defeated me. Even though it was gone from my body now, cancer still owned me if I couldn't do what I do best of all, and that's skate. I was not going to let cancer take that away.

I became very competitive with cancer. Obviously I had to fight to keep the disease from spreading and destroying me, but the aggression I felt flowed through every vein, every facet of my being—the emotional, physical and mental. Thirteen years ago, I won an Olympic gold medal by being the best all-around skater in the world. On some days I might not have finished first in compulsory figures, but my freestyle was strong enough to keep me on top. On other occasions, if my free skating was subpar, my figures kept me in the game. The key was to be prepared on all fronts, and that became my approach toward cancer. So skating had to play a vital role in my recovery, as essential as the chemotherapy and surgery.

That was why on this sun-drenched Southern California day, I was indoors working out in an ice rink a good fifty degrees colder than the temperature outside. I decided on my first day back to break in a new pair of skates. That way I would keep myself from doing something foolish, like attempting a triple Lutz. Funny thing was, in my head I felt I could go out and do it.

But man, after I'd spent an hour in skates, the initial wave of euphoria had disappeared. I needed to limber up and my body just didn't want to cooperate. My choreographer, Sarah Kawahara, asked me to try a spin and I did three turns, got dizzy and lost my balance. My incision from the surgery burned from all the pulling and bending. Near the end of the session, I skated two laps around the rink and had to slow down because I was ready to collapse. This was unfair, I thought. I deserved to get in at least five laps before passing out on the ice, for Pete's sake.

That first day back was tougher than I had imagined. My muscles were so sore after practice I could barely get in my car to drive back to the hotel. It was devastating to my body and my ego. As gentle and patient as Sarah was, I was frustrated and embarrassed.

The second day was better. I was doing some single Axels and holding my spins a little longer. By the fourth day, I did several double toe loops and Salchows. Patience and positive thinking were the keys. If I tried to rush back and failed, I might start thinking I'd never be able to skate again. The triple jumps would come in time.

Each day, I gained a little more stamina and confidence. I tried to use everything around me for motivation. Though Sarah and I had one surface of ice to ourselves, there was a second rink next door. Sometimes the young skaters, mostly little girls in pigtails and skating dresses, wandered over to watch me skate. They giggled and whispered, waved and smiled. In their faces I saw all the great people who included me in their prayers and took the time to send me get-well cards and letters. It's not something I ever aspired to, but circumstances had made me a symbol of hope and inspiration for other cancer victims. And I wanted to succeed for them. I wanted to skate this year to show other cancer survivors that they could regain their old form, too. I could not let them down. If I didn't ask my body to do something, I'd never get an answer, so I just kept on pushing.

On my last day working with Sarah, I tried to do a run-through of a new program we were putting together. With each crossover, my arms sagged a little more until my hands were down to my hips. I was too weak to hold them up. I was getting ready to stop when Sarah cut the music and called me over.

"Scott, you have to treat every practice from this point on like a performance—no matter how terrible you feel. Don't stop early; I don't care how tired you get or how ugly you think you look on the ice. Don't quit."

I could handle that. For as long as I could remember, I had been going nonstop, first as an amateur competitor, then as a professional. I was fortunate that I could draw on that work ethic now, when I needed it most. As I skated back to my starting position, there was only one thing on my mind: I will win.

Chapter One

The Pain that Won't Go Away

At first, it felt like a stress-related ulcer—nothing that a week off at the end of the "Stars on Ice" tour and a few rounds of golf in Hawaii couldn't cure. Or so I thought.

But the antacids wouldn't make the pain go away. The massage therapy made me wince. It was just after the 1997 new year, and I still had three months of touring ahead. How was I going to make it through the season feeling this miserable?

Though some victims of testicular cancer, the disease I was diagnosed with, experience swelling in the testicles, I didn't have those symptoms, at least nothing that was conspicuous to me. People who saw me perform in January mentioned that I was looking thin and pale, but that was from a bout of the flu that hit me in December and just never seemed to leave my body. The pain that was really bothering me was deep inside, and no amount of treatment was making any difference.

In February and early March, the symptoms got worse. I'm a fair eater, a meat and potatoes guy with a decent appetite, but I started skipping meals altogether. My performances started to get shaky, partly due to a sore back. There is nothing worse for someone with a bad back than travel. Airports and airplanes are inhospitable places, since the seats are uncomfortable, the flights often bumpy and there is no place to lie down. In 1992, Todd Eldredge threw out his back before the Albertville Olympics, nursed himself back to health, only to reaggravate the injury on the plane ride over to France. He was in pain for the entire competition and finished tenth. I didn't want to leave the tour, but the air travel wreaked havoc on my body, especially since we were on the move four to five times a week. The last leg of the tour is even worse because reaching smaller markets required taking two flights a day with long layovers between stops. So I rented myself a tour bus that came with a TV, shower, refrigerator, washer, dryer and plenty of room to stretch out. Though I missed the camaraderie of traveling with the cast, the bus gave me a chance to catch up on my rest and relieve the pain in my back.

On Thursday, March 13, I rolled into my hometown of Bowling Green, Ohio, a place that brings back many memories. It was there where I was raised and learned to skate, the thing that gives me more joy and happiness than anything else. Over the years, I had frequently returned home to skate in local ice productions to raise money for the skating club or for cancer research in my mother's memory. This time I was stopping through as a favor to a friend, Sam Cooper, the man responsible for building the rink where I learned to skate. He was giving a dinner in my honor to raise money for the Bowling Green State University precision iceskating team. The town fathers made me honorary mayor for the day, and my first official act was to eliminate income taxes. Too bad for everybody my term expired at midnight.

The next day I boarded my bus and headed north on Interstate 75 to East Lansing, Michigan, our next tour stop. I loved performing there. It's a classic college town, home to Michigan State University, and one of the original dates from the first full "Stars" season in 1987–88.

I was feeling refreshed and optimistic. The sun was out and there was a bite in the air that told you spring was just a month or two away. For the past week, I had been skating better than I had all winter, and my stamina was excellent, despite the pain. The visit home had been a great reprieve. But as Bowling Green's quiet residential streets and church steeples faded in the distance and were replaced by the vast soybean fields and farm silos of the Ohio countryside, I could sense this damn ache in my belly creeping back to the surface.

On Saturday, March 15, I woke up feeling sluggish and drank a pot of coffee, which didn't kick-start my day the way it usually did. Then a few hours before the show, my body staged a revolt. That day at practice, my back went out and I couldn't jump. I got off the ice early and went to see the company's physical therapist, Martina Chmelova-Gyokery. She had a massage table set up in a room at the arena. She worked my back muscles, and then I rolled over so she could apply some pressure to my abdominals. Perhaps if she could loosen my stomach muscles it would relieve the tension in my back. Her hands dug into my abs and I winced. I felt like I had been punched in the stomach.

"Scott, there's a tight mass in there," she said, relaxing her fingers for a moment. I said nothing and just stared at the ceiling. I'll shake it off, I thought.

"This isn't muscular. You need to have this checked out," she said. My heart was beating a little harder when I got up from the massage table. The concern in Martina's voice and the worried look on her face scared me a little. I went to look for our tour manager, David Baden. I told him what Martina had said and asked him if he would mind calling ahead to our next tour stop, Peoria, Illinois, and making an appointment for me to see a doctor at a local hospital. Then I went to catering to get something to eat. I grabbed a salad, a handful of rolls and a cup of coffee, and then sat down with Kurt Browning and Paul Wylie, my two good friends from the tour. We commiserated on the lousy ice conditions and how badly the practice had gone for all of us. For some reason, the ice was too thin and the paint from the hockey stripes was coming up to the surface. Catching your blade on paint is something like hitting a patch of grass on a ski slope—your leg stops but the rest of your body keeps going. Makes performing a triple Lutz in front of several thousand people quite a challenge. Only I knew the ice wasn't the only reason I was having a bad day.

With my dinner half-eaten, I excused myself from the table and went for a walk. I always carry a headset and portable CD player with me, so I popped in an Edwin McCain disc and tuned out the world for the next couple of hours. I needed some time alone to get in a mental zone. I didn't want to repeat my pathetic performance at practice in the show.

It was one of those nights where just about everybody skated poorly. Bad ice will do that sometimes. I tripped a couple of times and missed many of my jumps. Kurt made some miscues, and Jayne Torvill and Christopher Dean decided not to skate their second number because the ice was too dangerous.

During intermission, I tried to convince myself that the ice had more to do with my lackluster effort than my bad back, which was stiffening up considerably. The crowd, as always, was great. They cheered wildly even though it wasn't one of our better efforts. But applause is no cure for bad skating. We're all too proud and competitive to accept anything less than our best. If I skate lousy, I'm in a funk for the rest of the night. I had missed a triple Lutz and that ruined it for me. Well, by the end of the night, everyone had something to gripe about, except for Paul, who has this uncanny ability to thrive on terrible ice. You never know with Paul—sometimes he even complains when the ice is great! Go figure.

After the show, I was changing in the dressing room and my back went into spasms. Lightning bolts were streaking down my legs to the ends of my feet. I sat down once to take off my skates but didn't sit down again because I was afraid I might not get up. On my way to the shower, I shuffled across the floor, slightly bent over at the waist like an old, old man. If you had thrown me a cane and a smock, I could have played Yoda in the *Star Wars* movie, except with the skin complexion of Casper the ghost. That was how feeble I looked.

Later, outside the dressing room, I ran into Kristi Yamaguchi. She saw I was in pain and gently grabbed my arm.

"Scott, what's the matter?"

"I got gas," I said jokingly, trying to mask the pain. "The Maalox isn't doing any good."

She smiled and told me I'd be okay. For the past month, I had been getting words of encouragement because people knew something was wrong, but now the words were accompanied by worried glances. As I boarded my bus for the overnight trip to Peoria, David tapped me on the shoulder. "It's all set for tomorrow," he said. "Thanks," I replied. I was relieved a doctor was finally going to check this out.

The next day, I was feeling much better after a breakfast of French toast and coffee. For a moment, I considered skipping the hospital appointment, but David had pulled all sorts of strings to get me in on short notice, so I decided to go. Kurt was having breakfast with us. "Hey, man, it's no fun going to the hospital alone," he said.

Boy, was that ever an understatement. As a child I'd suffered from a mystery illness that stunted my growth and played havoc with my digestive system. I was in and out of hospitals for six years, getting poked, probed and prodded more times than a defective car on an assembly line. So I knew exactly what Kurt was talking about. Hospitals can be terrible places to be alone.

"Kurt," I said with a grin, "I know your idea of a good time is going to the hospital. Come with me."

When I walked into Peoria's St. Francis Medical Center with Kurt and David, a familiar feeling of dread came over me. Those hallmarks of hospitals everywhere—bright fluorescent lights, polished floors, the smell of disinfectant, waiting rooms filled with vases of paper flowers and stacks of worn-out magazines—are enough to make me ill. A nurse guided us into an exam room and I changed into a hospital gown. It wasn't until months later that I realized that if you put one gown on forward and one on backward, they're not nearly as humiliating to wear. Kurt and David waited with me until we were greeted by Dr. John Carrol, an emergency room physician. "What seems to be the problem?" he asked.

Dr. Carrol listened as I explained my symptoms—an ulcerlike feeling in the stomach, chronic back pain, loss of appetite. He ordered a battery of tests. A nurse came in and took my blood pressure and drew some blood. Then they wheeled me in for the first of two CAT scans. I sat down and a small X-ray tube circled my body 360 degrees and recorded detailed cross-sectional slices of my entire body. Kurt and David had sat in the waiting room all morning, so when they returned from lunch, I told them to get the heck out of there.

Besides, if the news was bad, I didn't want anyone around. In many respects I'm the biggest pessimist in the world. Before I go out to skate, I always tell everyone within earshot that this is the night I'm going to blow up and have my worst performance ever. It's a ritual of mine: I go into a minor panic; psychologically I prepare for disaster, actually imagine myself falling, and then go out and give it my best shot. I guess I stay on my feet when it counts because in my head, I've already hit the ice and gotten it out of my system. And if I do mess up, I can't say I didn't warn myself. But that wasn't the only reason I felt uncertain. There was no denying that the pain was getting progressively worse, and Martina's concern the day before was still fresh in my mind. So before meeting with Dr. Carrol, I prepared for the worst.

When he returned from lunch, he took me into an exam room and asked me to take a seat. He flipped on a bright display panel and inserted a sheet of film, the results of the CAT scan. The image was black and white, making it hard to tell one internal organ from the other. "Look here," he said, making a circle with a pointer in an area around the general vicinity of my intestines. There was an unrecognizable blob there, and my first thought was, "Man, it's big."

Dr. Carrol's next words were calm and methodical. "The CAT scan has identified a large mass in your abdomen."

Silence. I swallowed hard and squinted to get a better look at the film.

"If it were me," he said in a concerned tone of voice, "I would take care of this situation immediately."

Something was being left unsaid. "What is it?" I asked nervously.

"It's a tumor—and it's either benign, or it's lymphoma or some other kind of malignancy, so you need to get it checked out."

In other words, I might have cancer.

Even though I had tried to mentally prepare myself for bad news, there was no damming up the flood of emotions roaring through my body. Shock and disbelief. Frustration that my body was betraying me as it had when I was a child. And, oh, yes, fear. I had just left Bowling Green, and memories of my mother's three-year battle with breast cancer ending with her death in 1977 were fresh in my mind. I had visited her grave site and could vividly recall those last months of her life as the cancer robbed her spirit and drained the life from her body. After she died, a fan sent me a woven cotton wristband, the kind sailors wear at sea for good luck. I wore that band on my left wrist for years and always rubbed it with my right hand just before I stepped on the ice to compete. It was a signal to my mother, my guardian angel, that I was skating in an important event and that I needed her energy and spirit for support. The band was gone, but as I sat in that sterile exam room with Dr. Carrol absorbing the grim news, I wanted to reach over and start making that small circular motion on my wrist. I remained calm, but if my body could have reflected my emotions, I would have been flat on my back like a boxer who had just absorbed a knockdown punch.

I must have appeared to be in a fog, because Dr. Carrol was kind enough to offer me a ride to my hotel. On the drive back he was comforting and reassuring, and strongly urged that I get checked out by an oncologist. I was quiet, alone with my thoughts. When he dropped me off, I thanked him and went to my tour bus to make a game plan. I was a little scared, but I didn't want to burden anyone with this until I got more information. The practice bus was leaving soon for the 4 P.M. workout and I knew that if I got on, I might give something away. I decided to wait and go to the rink alone.

Away from the hospital, I started to consider the alternatives. Though there was a "mass" inside of me, perhaps it was benign. That possibility did exist. Maybe it was some kind of infection that could be treated with antibiotics, I thought. But where had it come from? Had I given this thing to myself because of my breakneck schedule and all the stress I was under? Between commentary jobs with CBS, pro competitions, television appearances and the sixty-city "Stars" tour, this had been one of the most insane years of my life.

Whatever the cause, I needed to get more tests, but I was no expert when it came to picking cancer specialists. I grabbed my cell phone and dialed Bob Kain, a close friend who lives and works in Cleveland. He's my former agent and cofounded "Stars on Ice" with me in 1986. When I got Bob on the line, I skipped the small talk and got right to the point:

"Bob, I think I've just been diagnosed with cancer."

"Oh, my God," he said.

Once the initial shock wore off, Bob went into action.

"First, are you skating in the show tonight?"

"Yeah, I'm going to skate."

"All right," Bob said. "I'm going to set up an appointment for you first thing tomorrow at the Cleveland Clinic. It's one of the best cancer centers in the country. That's where you're going. I want you here first thing in the morning and I promise we'll get this sorted out."

I had tremendous trust in Bob, and I was familiar with the Cleveland Clinic because my father underwent a heart bypass operation there. I knew I would be in good hands.

"See you tomorrow," I said and clicked off the phone.

My thoughts turned to the show that night and how I was going to maneuver around my friends. Even though everyone knew I was at the hospital all day, I'm not the type to put my problems out for everyone to dwell on. Paul, Kurt, Kristi, Ekaterina Gordeeva and Rosalynn Sumners had been touring with me for years and know me like a brother. I consider them all family. How could I keep them from reading the concern in my eyes? I remembered something I had heard from comic Mack Dryden, a friend and cancer survivor himself. "When you tell someone you have cancer," he said, "you give it to them." So I would not share my misfortune with the cast just yet, not until I knew for sure what was inside of me.

At around 4 P.M., I left for the arena. I had missed the workout, so I knew there was going to be talk. In the dressing room, Paul Wylie was relentless in his concern and curiosity. He could tell I was a little down and kept asking me if I was okay. Finally he changed the subject. He was thinking about buying a Porsche Boxster—a car I wanted to purchase myself—and asked my opinion. Everything I had been suppressing threatened to erupt, but I fought to control the emotion in my voice when I replied. "You have to do it now," I told him. "You only live once and life is very short." He laughed and gave me a friendly pop in the stomach with his fist. "Oww," I yelped. Poor Paul. He could see that I was in some pain. "Are you all right?" he asked.

"I don't know," I said. "It's a long story. I can't talk about it right now."

I went outside in the hallway between dressing rooms and saw Kristi doing some stretching exercises. She, too, asked me about my hospital visit earlier in the day. "Yama, I'm fine," I said. But I could tell she noticed I averted my eyes. I walked away quickly, wondering if she could see how nervous I was. I hated lying to her like that.

One by one, my friends on the tour approached me to share their concern. I felt awkward. I'm supposed to be the rock everyone leans on, not the other way around. I sensed I was bringing people down, and that was the last thing I wanted to do before a show. So I disappeared. I walked out into the empty Peoria Civic Center, a 9,500-seat arena, sat in the stands and nursed a bottle of water. Pairs skaters Denis Petrov and Elena Bechke were warming up their routine on the ice below, and all I could hear were the sounds of two pairs of steel blades slicing and grinding across the ice. Though we played the large arenas in New York, Chicago and Los Angeles, I liked the smaller places like this because I could see the top row from the ice.

Suddenly it dawned on me that even though the verdict was still out on the extent of my illness, this was probably my last performance of the year—at the very least. Sick or not, I had to go out and skate the best show I had in me. At least now I knew the source of the pain, and that relaxed me a bit. My back was actually feeling pretty good. Then one of the crew came out and yelled "Doors!" That was the signal to all the skaters on the ice that the crowd was filing in and it was time to go backstage. I got up from my chair and went to get changed into my costume. I had a show to skate.

In the opening number, the cast skated out into the darkness as one at a time we were introduced to the crowd. Then Michael Kamen's guitar concerto, a hard rock anthem, kicked in, and my skating instincts took over. We took turns under the spotlight, and I hit a triple toe and two double Axels cleanly. Later in the first half, I performed my solo, "Figaro," a parody of the classic from the opera *The Barber of Seville*. You might have thought I was in no mood to be funny on a night like this, but making the crowd laugh gave me a jolt of adrenaline and put me back in control of my environment, even if it was only for a few minutes. I didn't make one mistake in the program.

I was skating so well it seemed to put everyone backstage at ease. But at intermission, I decided to tell David and Deb Nast, another manager of the tour, what was going on. I was going to be leaving for Cleveland after the show and I couldn't vanish without explaining why to someone in charge. I also could count on David and Deb to update the cast and crew of any future developments.

In the second half, I continued skating well. In my last number of the night, a solo to "I (Who Have Nothing)," I hit an opening triple Lutz. I had one last triple ahead of me—the Salchow. As I went into it, I realized a clean landing would mean I'd skated a perfect show—no missed jumps. But I got caught up in the moment and doubled it. That was all right. A guy with a possible tumor in his belly was entitled to one mistake. Though the night had special significance to me, it was lost on the crowd through no fault of their own. Near the end of the number, I looked into the audience and saw a lady sitting in a front-row seat holding a mirror to her face. She was touching up her makeup during my performance. I smiled and thought, "I guess she has someplace important to go after the show."

Kurt met me as I got off the ice. "Good one, man. Not bad for a guy who spent all day in the ER."

Back at the hotel, I was feeling pretty good and I had a beer in the lounge with Kristi, Rosalynn, Paul and Lea Ann Miller. I told everyone I was going to Cleveland that night for some more tests, but didn't elaborate. I promised to meet back up with the cast in time for the next show, just two days away in Dayton, Ohio. It was optimistic thinking on my part, but not out of the realm of possibility, I kept reminding myself. Paul kept after me. "So what kind of tests did they do?" he asked. He had been accepted to Harvard Law School, and I could tell that night that he had a fine future as an interrogator. Every time we changed the subject, he directed the conversation back to my hospital visit. Paul is very religious, and what I didn't understand at the time was that he wanted more information so he could start praying for me. Before we packed it in for the night, Kristi gave me a big hug. "We love you and we're here for you," she told me.

After they went back to their rooms, I climbed aboard my bus and lay down to rest. I was spent. The trip to the hospital, the show, my deceptive behavior, had left me worn out. I had a long trip in front of me—461 miles across Interstate 80, through Illinois and Indiana and into northern Ohio. We'd pass through the city of Toledo, where I was born, and continue east toward Cleveland, bypassing Interstate 75 and Bowling Green, just twenty miles to the south.

"Let's get going," I said to my driver, Keith Cummings. At that moment my cell phone rang. It was Karen calling from home to find out how I skated in the show. We had been living together for seven years, and I knew the minute I started talking she would know something was wrong. I was at a loss over what to say. How do you break it to someone that you might have cancer?

I froze for a couple of seconds and then gathered myself. "I went to the hospital today for some tests," I began deliberately. "I had a CAT scan. There's a tumor in my stomach. I'm going to Cleveland to see a specialist."

"Oh, no, Scott," she sympathized. "I'll be on a plane first thing in the morning."

I wasn't sure that was the best idea. Karen and I were struggling in our relationship. All my traveling was taking a terrible toll on us, and I didn't think it would be fair to burden her like this, at least not until I knew more. "No," I said. "It may be something I can take care of quickly. Let me get some more information before you come."

Karen let out a sigh of frustration. Obviously I had upset her by putting her off. Here she was willing to drop everything for me, and I was keeping her at arm's length.

"I'll be there tomorrow," Karen repeated.

This time I didn't put up any resistance. "You're right," I said contritely. "I'll see you tomorrow."

I felt guilty, but to be honest I was relieved she had insisted on coming. As independent as I am, I didn't really want to face this alone. In a crisis, we've always been there for each other. Why should anything be different now?

Karen needed to go pack so we hung up. I sat down in back of the bus and just stared out a window at the passing city lights of Peoria. Soon we were driving through the countryside and were surrounded by darkness. I wondered if I would be able to get any rest, but by the time Keith maneuvered the bus across the Indiana state line into my home state, it was early Monday morning and the emotion of the previous twenty-four hours had long given way to exhaustion. I was sound asleep.

Chapter Two

It All Started When
I Was Born

The irony didn't escape me on my bus trip to Cleveland. I was back in Ohio, ailing and checking into a hospital, a routine I became very familiar with as a child. And there was a mystery to my new illness, just as there had been when I was three years old and suddenly stopped growing.

I wasn't always sick. I was a healthy baby boy when my parents brought me home to Bowling Green from a Toledo adoption center. My mother, Dorothy, doted on me. She was an elementary schoolteacher, and had majored in home economics in college, an ideal background for someone who dreamed of raising a large family. Though she wasn't a blood relative, people say we looked alike. She was short, only five feet and one-quarter inch tall—when you're small, you always count the quarters and the halves—and had a high forehead, just like me. Yet my clearest and fondest memory of my mother is her laughter, which creased her whole face and almost made her eyes disappear. As she got older and heavier, she became a celebration of round, especially when she smiled.

My mother met my father, Ernie, on a blind date at the University of Massachusetts. She was a junior and he was a sophomore majoring in botany. He was an only child and she was the oldest of two girls, but they both came from families with deep colonial roots. His bloodline went back to Alexander Hamilton, the American revolutionary statesman who was killed in a duel with political opponent Aaron Burr. My mother's famous ancestor, John Adams, managed to avoid an untimely death and was elected the second president of the United States.

While Dad towered over Mom by a good ten inches, they were drawn together by a common love: teaching. After they were married in 1951, they moved to New Brunswick, New Jersey. My father wanted to be a college professor, and for the next five years, he worked toward a Ph.D. in plant ecology at Rutgers and drove tanks in the army. Like a good soldier, he became a traditional, hard-nosed teacher—strict, methodical and demanding.

In the classroom, my father had a scholarly look: rumpled sports coat, a pair of black horn-rim glasses wrapped around matching long sideburns. But his congenial face and friendly grin disguised a fierce temper. At home, there was no negotiating with him. He was the disciplinarian in the family and I sidestepped him whenever I could. When I wanted something, I went directly to my mother. I loved my dad, and as he got older, he mellowed considerably. The laid-back Ernie my skating friends got to know, the guy we affectionately called "Big Ern," didn't materialize until I was in my late teens, after he had quit smoking and put on twenty-five pounds. That was not the father I knew as a child. When I acted up or got into some mischief, he sometimes would explode and I'd run and hide behind my mother.

Once in a while when I'm signing an autograph on tour, I'll run into one of his old students. "Your father was my professor," someone will say.

"I'm sorry he was so hard," I'll respond. And then we have a good laugh together. Fortunately for my dad, none of his students were descendants of Aaron Burr.

My mother was the nurturing one, at home and in the classroom. She came from a family of teachers. Her father, Everett, taught industrial arts, and her mother, Helen, taught second grade. My mother's younger sister, Marjorie, also grew up to become a teacher. It was a family tradition and an honorable profession, one I might have followed my parents into had I not continued in skating.

What most impressed me about my mother was her open heart and drive to grow and learn. When I was ten, she returned to school and received a master's degree and eventually became an associate professor herself, teaching family relations in addition to home economics. I can remember when she was fighting cancer in the mid-1970s, her students at Bowling Green watched her lose her hair and listened to her frank discourses on death and dying. My mother harbored no secrets. Once she told her class, "We're all dying of this terrible disease called time. Make the most of the days you have."

When I meet up with her old students, I remind them they were the luckiest people in the world to have taken a class with her.

Two years before I was born, my father accepted a teaching job at Bowling Green State University and he moved himself, my mother, and my then three-year-old sister, Susan, into a three-bedroom tract home on

State Street. The neighborhood was surrounded by parks and ball fields and was just a 10-minute walk from campus. Sue started nursery school and my mother found a job teaching first grade. But my parents' dream of raising a large family was put on hold. My mother was unable to get pregnant.

In the three years after Sue was born, she suffered two miscarriages. Then in 1956, she carried a pregnancy to term and gave birth to a baby boy, Ernest Everett Hamilton. Eight hours after delivery, my mother was resting in bed when an indignant nurse burst into her hospital room cussing and berating one of the doctors. My mother was still a little groggy and couldn't make out what she was complaining about. Then the nurse spoke up.

"Here I am, the delivery nurse, and no one bothered to tell me that your baby died," she said.

That made two of them, because no one had bothered to inform my mother either.

After that horror, my mother didn't want to get pregnant again. But my parents didn't give up on building a family. They decided to adopt and put in an application with Lucas County Child and Family Services in Toledo.

I was born on August 28, 1958. I was a little guy right out of the box, a mere five pounds, seven ounces, and nineteen-and-a-half inches long. Six weeks later, my mother, father and Sue picked me up from the adoption center and drove me back to Bowling Green.

I was given the corner bedroom and slept in a family heirloom, a crib built by my maternal grandfather. I was a good baby, ate well and slept a lot. But I guess I wouldn't have won any beauty contests. With my big head and small body, Sue thought I was the funniest-looking thing she had ever seen. She even suggested to my mom that they take me back to the adoption center and exchange me.

For me, the mischief started at six months, when I somehow managed to climb out of my crib. Sue found me hanging on the rail, and Dad responded by building a grid that fit over the top, so I slept in a cage. Once I started walking, I was Godzilla in diapers. I knocked over glasses, banged my head on walls, drew on the dining room table with crayons, decorated my parents' white bedspread with red nail polish, destroyed my sister's artwork and tore up my father's papers. In short, I did anything for attention. I even erected a fort in a cupboard over the refrigerator and hid in there from my parents.

The only person allowed in my fort was my imaginary friend, the happy cowboy. My maternal grandmother, Nana Helen, and I had a game.

She'd ask me, "How big is the happy cowboy?" And I'd take the hat off my head and hold it up as high as I could. "This tall," I'd say.

My mother nicknamed me "Scooter," because I was constantly on the move. Once when I was two, my father was working on the roof and went inside the house to get a drink, mistakenly leaving the ladder up. Standing in the kitchen, he heard the pitter-patter of little feet running across the tiles. "That's one heck of a big squirrel up there," he told my mother. When he went back outside to take a look, he nearly fainted at the sight of me peering over the ledge. Then he flipped.

The neighborhood was filled with kids, many of them sons and daughters of other professors at the university. Next door were the Brents and the Terrels. Across the street were the Gonyers and the Hallbergs. Jane Hallberg was my kindergarten teacher.

In many ways, Bowling Green was like small towns everywhere. My parents and their friends used to joke that there must have been some unwritten city code that if you built a church, you had to build a bar and a pizza parlor. And if you built a pizza parlor you had to build a church and a bar. The dominant plant in town was a ketchup factory, and when the wind was blowing just right, there was no escaping the scent of cooking tomatoes. But what made this community special was the university. It drew people from other cultures who otherwise never would have set foot in Bowling Green. And my parents got to know these kids because my father served as an academic adviser for foreign exchange students.

A Kenyan student, Jim Karugu, used to come by our house when I was in nursery school. Our favorite thing to do was take long walks through the neighborhood. I pointed out the trees and cars and he taught me basic Swahili. The word "Jombo" meant "hello," so Sue and I took to calling him Jombo Jim. His father was a tribal chief, and Jim would go on to become a lawyer and a politician. But for me, he was the first black person I got to know up close. One Christmas, my parents gave a party for a group of exchange students and neighbors, and Jim brought over a set of bongo drums. I did everything I could to get my hands on those drums, but my mother wouldn't let me near them. That didn't stop me from trying to get everyone's attention. I bounced from guest to guest, trying to make people laugh by putting on my sister's shoes or placing tambourines on top of my head. I was a ham from early on, and Jim found me the most amusing of all.

My mother was thankful for my exposure to Jim because there were otherwise few minorities living in Bowling Green. There was only one African-American child in my nursery school class, and she aroused my curiosity. I remember coming home from school one afternoon and telling my mother how different she was from the rest of the girls.

"What makes her so different?" my mother asked.

I said, "Some days she comes to school wearing three pigtails and other days she has four. The other girls just have two."

My mother chuckled and let out this big sigh of relief because what had caught my attention was the number of her pigtails, not the color of her skin.

In 1962, my parents adopted a second son, Steven, who was born in February of that year. A new face in the house was not the only change going on at home. I was getting sick all the time, coming down with bronchitis and other respiratory infections. While I was eating plenty at mealtimes, my parents noticed I was having trouble digesting my food and was severely constipated. My ribs showed and my abdomen was noticeably distended. Most alarming was that it appeared I had stopped growing.

Because of my chronic cough, my mother and I were making frequent trips to the doctor's office, and from these experiences an unshakable bond formed between us. She became my tireless medical advocate.

Sometime after my fourth birthday, our family doctor referred me to a pediatrician in Toledo for a thorough physical. My mother drove me to his office and I went through a battery of tests. A nurse injected me with a needle and drew a vial of blood from my arm. I was crying and clinging to my mother when the doctor came in to conduct an exam of my pelvis. Somehow, with my mother's help, he pried me loose from her chest and had me lie down on an exam table. As I held my mother's hand, his fingers explored my abdomen, pushing and digging as he looked for abnormalities in my intestines and colon. The doctor also performed an enema to open my bowels. After that experience, I didn't care what they found, as long as I wouldn't have to go through that again. The pediatrician suspected I had malabsorption syndrome, an inability to absorb nutrients from the intestines into the bloodstream. But he recommended more tests and more doctors. I was referred to the pediatric clinic at Ann Arbor's University Hospital for a consultation with a nutritionist.

Nothing changed much over the next two years. I didn't grow much and continued having problems going to the bathroom. My mother and I drove back and forth to Ann Arbor for follow-up visits. Life was an endless parade of dreary waiting rooms, injection needles and stethoscopes. Sometimes I resisted and threw major tantrums to keep from going to the doctor. I remember once screaming until my face turned red, and when my mother still managed to get my shoes on, I held my breath until I turned blue. My favorite trick was just lying still, facedown, to keep my mother from getting me dressed. I just wanted to stay home and do normal things: draw pictures, play with trucks and run outside.

I was in first grade when our family doctor had me admitted to Riverside Mercy Hospital in Toledo. I weighed thirty-three pounds, putting me below the third percentile for six-year-old boys. There were dark circles under my eyes and a perpetual frown pasted across my face. But when it was time to go, I calmly got in the car with my mother, the fight pretty much drained out of me by now. She drove me to Toledo and stayed with me for three days at the hospital, sleeping in a bed next to mine.

My father stayed home to care for Sue and Steve. Not having my mother around was tough on my brother and sister. The only two dishes that Dad could cook were fried Spam and spaghetti. Sue was only eleven, and while she gave cooking a gallant try, she had trouble making a bologna sandwich without a recipe book.

In Toledo, I underwent another physical and more tests. The results suggested I had the symptoms of chronic malnutrition. But the diagnosis this time was celiac malabsorption and the prescription a gluten-free diet, the same kind people with cystic fibrosis follow. When I got home, all flour-based treats like cookies, cakes and bread were off-limits.

My first day back at school, my mom packed rice cakes and gluten-free yogurt. A relative sent her some recipes and she learned how to bake gluten-free bread and delicious jelly rolls from rice flour, which I took with me to birthday parties. It was frustrating, but my mom tried to smooth things over. "You get to bring your own food because you're special," she said.

The sacrifices might have been worth it if I had grown or gained weight, but my condition got worse. Six months after coming home from Mercy Hospital, I was admitted to University Hospital in Ann Arbor. My mother packed our bags for a three-day stay, though she wasn't there the whole time. Since the hospital was only a ninety-minute drive from home, she could teach and then get up there by late afternoon to spend the night with me.

When we checked in, I smelled that familiar odor of disinfectant and immediately asked my mother if we could go home. She stayed with me the entire first day, holding my hand and rubbing my head as I underwent a physical and diagnostic workups.

As a small boy, I never understood the terminology and the doctors spent most of their time explaining everything to my mother. But they tested for everything; lactose and glucose tolerance; sweat chlorides to check for cystic fibrosis; fat absorption tests for malabsorption syndrome. I also underwent colon exams, which I despised because they required me to undergo an enema.

This was an aspect of my medical care I have a difficult time discussing. But the reality was that from the time I was a small boy until age nine, occasional enemas were needed at home and the doctor's office to pass the food I was eating. It was brutal growing up like that, and I can't even remember how often or for how long this was going on because I've blocked it out of my mind. I get ill just thinking about it.

On my second day at University Hospital, a doctor inserted a weighted piece of string down my throat to my stomach to test my digestive process. I had to keep it down for hours before the results came in, and they allowed me to go to the playroom with the other children in the ward. When I wasn't looking, a small boy came up to me and got his toy airplane tangled in the string protruding from my mouth. He panicked and started pulling on the airplane with both hands. I was gagging and trying to call for help until he finally let go. It was an accident, but since no one saw what happened, the doctors and nurses presumed I had tried to yank it out myself. As a precaution, they tied me up in a straitjacket and put me in my bed until the testing was complete. My mother wasn't there and I was terrified at being strapped down. I never forgot that.

When the test was over, I got up from my bed without saying a word and walked down the hall and into a bathroom right by the nurses' station. I sat down on the tiled floor and burst into tears, as loud as I possibly could. The noise echoed out into the corridor, and a nurse came running in to pick me up. I wanted everyone to hear me, just to let them know how unhappy I was.

At the end of my stay, the doctors gave my mother the usual diagnosis—malabsorption syndrome. But this time they concluded that my body was allergic to both milk and gluten, and prescribed a diet that eliminated both food groups.

"Scott," she explained during the car ride home, "we're going to be changing your diet again. I know you like milk and ice cream, but the doctors feel your body can't handle it. It's one of the reasons you're not growing and having trouble going to the bathroom."

"Aww." I groaned. "That's not fair." Now when I went to a party, I couldn't have cake or ice cream. I immediately started to wonder what was left to feed me. I didn't take this well, but I passively accepted my fate.

There was one piece of news my mother didn't share with me. Before picking me up from my hospital room, she had met with one of the university doctors in her office. They had a frank discussion and she offered a grim prognosis. If my body continued rejecting the nutrients from my food at the current levels, my condition could grow critical.

"Your son needs to put on some weight," she said. "I know you're not starving him. But at the rate he's going, I don't know if he'll last more than six months."

My mother never told me about this until years later, but in the months ahead, I seemed to pick up on the concern and worry that lingered around me. One day I got into my sister's room and made a mess of her closet. When she got home, she jumped all over me.

"Don't worry," I said defensively. "I won't be around much longer."

"You don't know what you're talking about," she replied, and proceeded to pound away at me for my trespassing.

When my mother and I returned home from Ann Arbor, it was to a new home we had recently purchased in a development on Brownwood Street in Bowling Green. My father had recently gotten tenure, and buying the house was his way of rewarding himself for all his hard work and dedication. It had everything in a home my father could ask for, even an extra room to store his collection of vintage train sets. He used to spend hours in his train room constructing miniature buildings and railroad bridges from toothpicks. We also had a large living room and backyard for parties and cookouts. In the winter, my parents held a weekly Monday night drinking club, when they served their homemade orange blossom drinks to neighbors and my father's university colleagues. A lot of our friends from State Street also bought homes on the same block on Brownwood, which made for a nice transition after the move.

Another added bonus was the small apartment off the kitchen, which my father's parents, Ernest and Olga Hamilton, moved into when they came to live with us. Ernest had a bad heart and my grandmother needed help caring for him. But Olga was a godsend to my parents, particularly since my mother worked full-time and spent a lot of time with me away at the hospital. She cooked, cleaned and did the laundry. She had grown up in her mother's bakery and learned how to make wonderful pies.

Every morning, she whipped up a batch of cornmeal mush, eggs and bacon for breakfast, and then stood watch to make sure all the kids cleaned their plates. Grandpa Ernest, a quiet and introspective man, loved golf and painting. He was a gifted commercial artist who designed everything from matchbook covers to billboards. I heard him raise his voice only once. I was eleven at the time, and had run away from home. Grandpa was the one who came looking for me, and he gave me a tongue-lashing I'll never forget.

My maternal grandparents, Everett and Helen McIntosh, lived in Weymouth, Massachusetts, but they were frequent visitors to Bowling Green. We called Everett "Grandaddy." Strong and full of vitality, he dreamed enough for all of us. Despite my health problems, his wish for me was to grow up and play baseball. He raised two daughters, and I think there was a part of him that coveted parenting a boy. A die-hard Red Sox fan, he met us at the front door holding a bat and glove on the day my parents brought me home from the adoption agency. At his home near Boston, every radio and TV in the house was tuned in to the Sox on game day. He bought me my first baseball uniform, a Red Sox outfit that was about three sizes too big for me.

Every time he came to visit, we'd play catch. "C'mon, Scotty, get your uniform on; we're going out," he'd say.

I'd run into my room, put on my baggy uniform and cap, and we'd head over to the ball field to watch the older boys play baseball. I could throw and hit well for a small kid, just not for much distance. Grandaddy, though, never let me get discouraged. He always urged me to go out and try my best. When I got older and took up skating, it took him a little longer than the others to appreciate my accomplishments. Old dreams die hard, but he eventually became one of my biggest boosters.

Nana Helen was a very straitlaced Bostonian. She always wore a dress, high-heeled shoes and tasteful costume jewelry. My mother dressed just like her to go to work or go shopping. My sister had to wear her Sunday best, too, even for a trip to the bank with my mother. Nana was strong-willed and set in her ways. Once when I was seven, we went to visit Grandaddy and Nana at their vacation home in Maine, and I arrived with a mop of hair on my head. "It's too long," Nana informed me, and she immediately took me to the barber and ordered a buzz cut. When my mother saw what she had done, she was reduced to tears. Of course by the next day, she was laughing and telling everyone it was the funniest thing she had ever seen. All I needed was a white T-shirt and an earring and I could have been Mr. Clean.

My illness certainly played a part in my mother's tendency to overprotect and spoil me. My suffering made her feel guilty, and I sensed it and sometimes took advantage of her. One summer, we were visiting my mother's sister in Salem, Massachusetts, and the two families went out to dinner. I decided on the spot that I wanted a hot fudge sundae before my hamburger and French fries, and my mother, who sometimes broke ranks from my nondairy diet, actually let me order one. My Aunt Marjorie, whose two sons were now demanding ice cream, rolled her eyes in disgust.

While I felt protected and secure at home, it was a struggle keeping up with the other kids at school. My mother started me early in kindergarten, just days after my fifth birthday. I had some success because she had taught me to read at an early age and I loved drawing pictures, but most of all, I relished playing outdoors.

In first grade at Kenwood Elementary, I felt sluggish most of the time. That was the same year I was admitted to Mercy and University hospitals. The antihistamines I took to battle chronic congestion made me drowsy and lethargic. Because my mother was paranoid about my getting sick, cold days were especially frustrating. When the temperature outside dropped below freezing, my teacher, Grace Bell, would pull me aside and gently tell me I was staying inside during recess. I didn't care how cold it was; I wanted to bundle up and go outside with the other kids. Instead I sulked indoors, reading or playing with toys.

Since for part of the year I couldn't drink milk, I brought a six-pack of Coke to school each Monday and gave it to Mrs. Bell. In the winter, she set the cans outside on the windowsill to keep them cold. I needed the cola to keep up my energy, and it was the one thing I could eat or drink that made the other kids jealous. Still, my schoolwork suffered, which was reflected in my average grades. Mrs. Bell was very patient and didn't make me try to keep pace with the other kids.

Besides being one of the youngest in the class, I was at a disadvantage because I was always the smallest, usually by an entire head. On my first day of second grade, my teacher, Virginia Draney, felt so bad for me because I could barely see over my desk, she ran into one of the first-grade classrooms and borrowed a smaller table and chair so I could do my class work in comfort. That was pretty embarrassing.

My health was still an issue when I entered third grade. My teacher took one look at me and almost had a nervous breakdown. I was rail thin, my cheeks were sunken, and I had a bluish pallor to my face and dark circles under my eyes. I was a walking corpse. Diane Hunter called home to find out what was going on.

"Dorothy, are you sure he's going to last the year?" Mrs. Hunter asked.

"He'll be okay," my mother promised. "Just treat him like the other kids."

That was one of the things I admired about Mrs. Hunter—she didn't baby me at all. Early in the school year, I was looking for some attention from the other kids and chugged a warm, twelve-ounce can of Coke in about five seconds. Pretty darned impressive, I thought to myself as the class goaded me on. Just as Mrs. Hunter stepped into the room, I let out a wicked, loud belch, and broke the class up. Mrs. Hunter let me have it.

She took me in the hallway and chewed me out. "That's disgusting," she said. "You probably think you're really cute because you're getting all this attention for something gross like that."

I was speechless, yet she taught me a good lesson. Just because I was sickly didn't mean I was exempt from the rules. I was upset with Mrs. Hunter that day, but years later I can appreciate the fact she didn't cut me any slack. I was acting like a pampered kid and she showed me I had to stay on the same page as the rest of the class.

I would never give up going for laughs, though. It was a way to carve out a place for myself in an uncomfortable and judgmental environment. I used my small size to my advantage. By being the runt of the litter, I was treated like a team mascot. Some of the girls took it upon themselves to look after me, and some of the boys went out of their way to protect me, including the biggest and toughest kid in class, Abel Trevino. Abel had long hair, a muscular build and a reputation among the kids that preceded him. Sometimes he appeared out of nowhere like a comic book superhero to bail me out.

Once when I was in third grade, a fourth grader walked by me and gave me the shoulder during recess. I knew immediately what was coming and started backing away.

"Hey, you bumped into me. Why'd you do that, punk?"

"I'm sorry," I said, but as I turned around to get away I felt this hand grab the collar of my shirt. Suddenly my body was going in reverse and all the voices around me that had been hooting and hollering a moment ago grew silent. There was murmuring, the kind you hear just before the first punch is thrown in a boxing match. Only this was no match at all. The kid was twice my size and I was about to get my head kicked in. I closed my eyes and put my arms over my head; then suddenly I was free.

"Leave him alone," the voice ordered. It was Abel to the rescue. The fourth grader backed off and I was saved again by the mighty Abel. Years later when I ran into him in Bowling Green, I shook his hand and told him I never forgot what he did for me.

It was always the older kids who gave me problems. If there was a nickname for being small, I've heard it: peewee, shrimp, sissy, peanut, dwarf. I heard that junk all the time. Being adopted also led to some unwanted attention. One kid in the neighborhood used to make fun of the fact that my birth parents had to give me up. It was cruel, the meanest thing you can say to an adopted child. My mother came up with a line to use in these situations: "My parents got to pick me out and your parents had to take whatever they got."

The sad fact about being small was that there was not a whole lot you could do about it. When it came time to pick a team, chances are you got chosen last, just as I was when the neighborhood organized a baseball game. That killed me because I loved the game so much. But what was I going to do? Get in a fight to prove I was tough? What would that accomplish?

The best offense and defense for me were my personality, charm and humor. I mastered the art of getting along with people, a skill I use to this day while skating on tour and working in television. You may not be best friends with everyone, but you get along with everyone. You accept people for who they are. As time passed, I developed friendships in Bowling Green with people from all walks of life—farmer kids, burnouts, athletes and intellectuals. And when I got into a sticky situation, there always seemed to be someone there to help me out.

It wasn't a conscious effort on my part to make friends with kids just to keep from getting pounded on. It just kind of worked out that way. I remember in junior high one afternoon, I borrowed a bike from school to take a ride to grab a burger. People at school were always borrowing each other's bikes. And it was no big deal as long as they were promptly returned. But when I came back a half hour later, I discovered the bike belonged to an older kid who was not happy to see me on his two-wheeler. He was huge, a whole head taller than I, and wider than a tree.

"I'm sorry," I said over and over.

But he was unmoved. "I don't have time to go get my lunch because you took my bike," he said.

The tone of his voice and his body language made it clear I now had to pay for this transgression. I started backing away and he put a baseball mitt-size paw around my neck, stopping me in my tracks. In one motion, he threw me to the ground, and then kicked me a couple of times. Suddenly I heard the back door to my science teacher's class slam open and four of my neighborhood pals came outside.

"Is there a problem out here?" one of them shouted.

The big kid went ballistic. "This midget stole my bike and I'm gonna thrash him."

My friends approached the bully and gently pointed out that the bike was returned undamaged, that I had admitted I made a mistake and I was profusely sorry.

"Lay off," they ordered. He got on his bike and rode away. I was sitting there thinking, "Man, I'm so lucky I befriended these four jocks." I felt like I had just been rescued by the Fantastic Four.

Deep down, I wished I could be like the Incredible Hulk, who got huge and menacing when he needed to kick some butt. I longed to grow a foot and gain twenty-five pounds overnight so I could take care of myself in these situations. But my growth rate remained stagnant and my health actually took a turn for the worse.

In October 1967, I was in terrible shape. I stood three feet, eleven inches tall and tipped the scales at a meager forty-eight pounds. I was in fourth grade and felt like a pygmy. Earlier in the year, doctors had conducted another series of sweat chloride tests and they had come back positive, suggesting I had cystic fibrosis. The more conclusive DNA tests used today weren't available at the time, so this was all the doctors had to go on. I was sickly and fatigued. My parents were so afraid I might die they admitted me to Wood County Hospital in Bowling Green.

During the four-day stay, they inserted a nasal gastric tube in my right nostril and slid it down to my stomach, and attached the other end to a bottle of food supplement, called Probana, that hung from an IV tree. The Probana reminded me of liquid chalk but it was a hydrolyzed form of protein that would help me gain weight and correct some vitamin deficiencies. Feeding me by the tube, they could nourish me with twelve hundred to fifteen hundred calories a day to go along with another thousand calories I was getting from regular meals.

When I was discharged, the force-feedings continued at home. Since it was cumbersome to take the tube in and out of my body, we kept it in, capping the loose end with a nylon coupling, taping it across my face and back behind an ear. Good thing I wasn't dating at the time. Here I wanted desperately to fit in and yet I had to wear the thing to school every day.

At home, my mother kept the flow of Probana on slow drip, which could make a feeding last one to two hours. It was bad enough having a tube sticking out of my nose, but the time it took to sit through a feeding was unbearable. My mother always joked, "Okay, it's time to plug in." I knew what that meant.

One day when I was alone, I got so sick of watching this stuff drip with the speed of a leaky faucet that I opened the valve all the way to increase the flow of liquid. I called these "quick feeds," and they left me feeling bloated with indigestion, but I kept on doing them because it got the drudgery over quickly—in under ten minutes.

Over the next several weeks, my parents monitored my weight and height closely. They set up a height grid in the basement of our house and measured me constantly. When you ask my brother about his most lasting image of me as a child, he'll tell you the picture etched in his mind is of me standing under a measuring tape, this thin little waif with a bloated belly and a ridiculous-looking feeding tube stuck to his face. Nevertheless, the Probana supplement seemed to help. I gained eight pounds over the next eight weeks.

Our new family doctor, Andrew Klepner, was skeptical of the recent cystic fibrosis diagnosis and was not a fan of my special diets. He had been urging my parents to have me start eating normal food again, without any success. At his recommendation, my parents took me to Children's Hospital in Boston, the top pediatric unit in the country. There he requested a full cystic fibrosis workup and to have my colon tested for paralysis.

It turned out to be my best hospital stay in memory. I was examined by Dr. Henry Shwachman, a Harvard Medical School professor and an expert in cystic fibrosis and gastrointestinal disorders. Children's was a beautiful setting. I remember my room looked out over a snow-covered garden filled with trees and pathways where families could sit or walk with their kids. My parents drove in each day from my Aunt Marjorie's house in Salem to spend time with me. Dr. Shwachman was a cordial man with a soft touch and an easygoing manner. While hospitals can be sterile and lonely places, Children's provided warmth and security.

Years later when I returned to Boston to skate in a fund-raiser for Children's Hospital after the 1984 Olympics, Dr. Shwachman was there sitting in a front-row seat watching me skate. He had suffered a stroke and was unable to speak. He didn't have much longer to live, but looking into his eyes, I could see the gentle man I remembered as a little boy.

During my four-day hospital stay, he ruled out cystic fibrosis once and for all. He also believed my intestinal problems were the result of a secondary, not a primary disorder. He suspected that a disease he had discovered, called Shwachman's Syndrome, a pancreatic enzyme deficiency that affects digestion, could be the culprit. But he couldn't conclusively diagnose what had ailed me all these years. So he advised my parents to take me home and let me live as normal a life as possible.

I returned to Bowling Green and continued with the nose-tube feeding and the gluten- and dairy-free diets. Though I was ready for a change, which was heartily endorsed by Dr. Klepner, my mother and father felt that if they took me off the diets cold turkey, it might be fatal. While I couldn't change their minds about that, there was one thing they were willing to do: take me skating.

My interest in the sport had been sparked the month before we left for Boston. Dr. Klepner and his family came by the Brownwood house to take Sue ice-skating at the new rink the university had opened earlier in the year. Dr. Klepner decided to stay behind to visit with my parents. As his wife, their daughter and Sue were getting ready to leave, he said, "Why don't you take Scott along with you?"

"I don't want him going," my mother interrupted.

"But I want to," I said.

"Just let him go," Dr. Klepner advised. "There are three people there to keep an eye on him."

My mother was probably reluctant to allow me on skates because of my single previous experience on ice. When I was four, I was skating on a frozen driveway and fell backward, cracking my head on the ice. To this day I always warn beginners to keep their weight forward. It's fine to fall on your knees, it's fine to fall on your hands, but the second your feet get out in front of you and you go off your heels, you can fall on your tailbone and hit the back of your head. That can cause a concussion.

I was pretty excited about this outing. When we arrived at the rink, I ran ahead and burst through the doors. I remember the odor of fresh paint and the din of about fifty kids and adults who were gliding in a counterclockwise circle around the ice surface. Rock music blared from the loudspeakers. Mothers with worried expressions on their faces watched from a row of bleachers. It was a public session in full force. I noticed the ice was clean and white and everyone was smiling and having a good time. I put on a pair of rental skates and hit the ice in full stride, immediately falling on my rear. My sister grabbed me under the armpits and hauled me back on my feet. "Fall forward," she warned me. "And make sure you get on all fours before standing up. It's easier to balance that way."

Skating was a struggle at first. I clung to the boards and stayed close to Sue, who had started taking lessons in the fall. I had a few more bad spills and there were tears, but I didn't quit. Heck, I banged my head on the ice on many occasions, which probably explains my kooky personality today. But even on that first day, I saw that all the other kids, even the bigger, athletic ones, were having just as much trouble as I. For once I was on an equal footing with everyone else.

The fact that a rink ever got built at all in Bowling Green was a minor miracle. Thanks to the perseverance of athletic administrator Samuel Cooper and university president William Jerome, the regents were convinced to construct the ice arena over a science center. Sam, who happened to be a close friend of my father's, argued successfully that athletic facilities were in short supply for the students. A regulation-size rink, he said, could accommodate physical education classes for up to fifty students at a time.

When the doors opened in June 1967, the building also housed a smaller-size ice surface where several skaters at a time could practice compulsory figures on individual patches of ice. There was also a curling rink and a large space in back of the main rink for a multipurpose area used by the tennis and track teams.

Sam wanted a first-class operation, so the university recruited a pair of national figure skating coaches, the husband-and-wife coaching team of David and Rita Lowery from Troy, Ohio. They set up the hockey program, a skating school for students and residents, a precision skating team and the Bowling Green Figure Skating Club.

David had been a Canadian pairs champion, and Rita was a Scottish dancer who had toured with "Holiday on Ice" in Europe. They arrived that spring with eight national-level skaters. Rita would become my first coach, but private lessons were still months away for me.

After the Christmas holiday, I started bugging my mother to take me skating again. My second time out, I noticed I was staying on my feet longer and moving faster than most of the other kids. I'd watch these lumbering teenagers have trouble balancing on these little blades, and then I'd glide right by them. My coordination and close proximity to the ice gave me an advantage. But just being a little better than some of the older kids was all it took to hook me in.

With each trip to the rink, my parents noticed my mood would brighten considerably. So in February 1968, my mother signed me up for Saturday group lessons with Rita Lowery. I was in a class with about eight other kids, and Rita taught us the basic skills—forward stroking, one foot glides, forward and backward swizzles and how to turn from forward to backward.

Rita knew how to make me laugh even when things weren't going my way. On that first day of class, I fell and cried out loud. She glided over to where I was sitting on the ice, turned around, spread her feet apart, and then bent over at the waist to look at me between her legs. "Look," she said. "Everybody's upside down." I cracked up through the tears because I thought that was a silly thing for an adult to do.

The weekly class lessons weren't enough. I kept pestering my mother to take me on Sundays and after school when she had the time. I progressed quickly. My mother monitored my group lessons with Rita closely and enjoyed her rapport with young people. After the class was over, Dorothy asked Rita to start giving me one fifteen-minute private lesson a week.

We began working on forward and backward crossovers and posture and positioning. Then we progressed to bunny hops, a simple forward jump that requires no turns, and waltz jumps, a forward jump with a half turn.

There was another reason I liked coming back to the rink each week:

girls. Tammy Edwards was my first crush, the first of many, I might add. She had blond hair and blue eyes and I melted away like a miniature snowman on a hot day when she came near. The most I could ever manage to get out of my mouth was "Hi." One day I was showing off, went off the heels of my skates and landed on my tailbone and head. She glided over to me and said in a sweet, consoling voice, "Are you okay?" I looked up at her and had to bite my lip to keep from crying. My vision was blurry, and my head was spinning. "I'm fine, I'm fine," I kept saying. I was determined not to let that girl see a tear.

In May, Rita and David cast me in the first annual "Ice Horizons" show. I was one of the racers in an ice production of *Hans Brinker and the Silver Skates*. My job was to complete one furious lap around the rink with twenty other kids and then fall down and slide before crossing the finish line. It was a small role, but a very big deal to me. I had been on skates for only a few months, and while my skills were still raw, I was one of the faster little kids at the rink.

On show night, the entire family came to watch, and the stands were packed with friends and family of the skaters. My mother made me a Dutch boy costume, which I enjoyed wearing for the night. The little bit of makeup one of the skating moms put on my face, I could have done without. But when the moment arrived, it was a rush flying around the rink and getting a laugh from the crowd. After my performance, I left my costume on for the night as I sat with a group of other skaters to watch the older kids perform their solo numbers. We cheered when they hit their jumps and yelled for them to keep going after a fall. No matter what happened, we applauded for everybody. I started imagining the day I could do a double jump and a sit spin. After that night, I wanted to be good enough someday to step out on the ice alone, and have complete command of the crowd. I remember thinking that would be the ultimate.

I continued skating through the spring and summer, and Rita had me working on single jumps, a spiral and two-foot spins. Though I loved to free skate, there was another part of the sport I needed to practice, called compulsory figures. They developed edge control, balance and turning skills on a single skate over a small piece of ice called a "patch." By early summer, I was taking one figures lesson and a freestyle lesson with Rita each week.

In July, I took a short break from skating and we went on a family vacation with Dr. Klepner and his family. Our destination was Put-in-Bay, an island retreat on Lake Erie where my father spent part of each summer teaching college-level biology. We stayed in a cottage and went boating, swimming and played ball. I ran and jumped with abandon, and everyone around me speculated that skating had something to do with my new-found energy. One morning, we were having breakfast with Dr. Klepner and he asked me a funny question.

"Scott," he said, "if you could eat whatever you want, what would it be?"

My eyes lit up at the thought, and I didn't hesitate in my answer. "A peanut butter sandwich, doughnuts and a bowl of ice cream."

Dr. Klepner turned to my mother. "I know what you're thinking, Dorothy, but I have my bag with me in case anything goes wrong. Go out and buy whatever he wants."

My mother did and when she returned, I had the feast of a lifetime for lunch. Guess what? I didn't keel over from the food. My mom put away the Probana for the week. I drank milk and ate cookies, and didn't get sick or have an allergic reaction at all.

"See," Dr. Klepner told my mother. "I told you so."

Chapter Three

Being Sick, Being Well

I had a heck of a party on my tenth birthday. It wasn't big or fancy; just a cookout with family and a few kids from the neighborhood. My father manned the grill and cooked hamburgers, hot dogs and corn on the cob. Then there was dessert. For once, no jelly rolls or corn bread for me. I took my seat at the head of the picnic table and after everyone sang "Happy Birthday," my mother cut me a piece of chocolate cake the size of Rhode Island and dished out a bowl of vanilla ice cream topped with hot fudge and whipped cream. I don't think Willy Wonka had it as good.

As we kids gorged ourselves, my mom stood by the barbecue with my dad and Dr. Klepner. "Look at Scotty," she said, laughing. "I don't think there's a happier boy on the planet right now."

She was absolutely right. Later that night, my mother was inspired to write a letter to Dr. Shwachman while I sat in the living room watching TV with my brother and sister. We were all tired from the long day and I was on the verge of falling asleep. My mother came over to the couch and sat next to me.

"Scotty, I want to show you something."

She'd written that I was gaining weight and getting taller, and that my appetite had doubled since our December visit to Boston. I no longer had to use a feeding tube and my diet was returning to normal.

Nobody could say for sure what prompted the change in my health and attitude, but my mother speculated that skating had something to do with it. She noticed that the cold, damp air at the ice rink helped my breathing, and the more I skated, the more confident I got. Maybe it was a coincidence, but when I stopped skating for more than a few days the old symptoms would return, and then vanish once more after I resumed.

By the end of 1968, I was virtually free of the health problems that had dogged my childhood. Exactly what role skating played is still a mystery. I wasn't cured the first day I walked into a rink, or even after a few months. The way my illness was sometimes portrayed in the media, it's as though skating miraculously healed me. I can just imagine what some people are thinking: that I was led into a rink in a wheelchair and lying on a bench were the most beautiful pair of rental skates on earth, the silver blades glistening and the boots all shiny and polished. Then to the gasps of the crowd, I unplugged the feeding tube from my nose, put on the skates, and rose and walked onto the ice.

Of course, it didn't happen like that at all. To set the record straight, the skates were too big and they hurt my feet. Glass slippers they weren't.

Still, I believe skating had something to do with making the disease go away, though I suspect its contribution to my health was more mental than physical. The more I gave to skating, the more it gave back to me in the form of emotional and physical strength.

I believe good health is tied to the emotional spirit as well as the physical. I've noticed that people who laugh are healthier than people who feel stressed. Growing up, it was hard keeping up with the bigger kids, but when I put on a pair of skates, the psychological lift I got was enormous. By the time school started in the fall of 1968, I was getting to be a pretty good little skater. I could stroke around the rink fast, do crossovers, skate backward, zigzag and turn. I could complete a couple of single-rotation jumps and some spins. Something just came over me when I walked into an ice rink. I felt confident and self-assured. I felt ten feet tall.

One afternoon, a kid from the Brownwood neighborhood showed up at the rink to skate in the public session. He used to hassle me because I couldn't hit a baseball or kick a football very far, yet there he was stumbling and falling all over the ice. I couldn't resist skating up to him and giving an unsolicited demonstration. I skated circles around him, forward, then backward. I had this big smile on my face and I could see he was embarrassed. He was one of the better athletes in the neighborhood and didn't like being shown up by someone who was less gifted.

We didn't exchange any words. As I skated away, I felt awesome. Watching this kid struggle did more for me than all those bottles of liquid Probana combined. There was a lesson in this. Once, when I was in seventh grade, our gym teacher made us run up and down the block several times. I had forgotten my sneakers and decided to run in bare feet. I came in second in the class, even though I felt so tired and cramped I nearly quit. What I learned that day, as I did at the ice rink, was that if you don't give up you can pass others who have, even if they are stronger and have more natural talent.

Part of the credit has to go to Coach Rita, who not only had the ability to lay a solid foundation for my skating future, but also made skating a blast. She taught me fundamentals, but it was never work with her; it was play. She was beautiful, charming and I was amused by her proper Scottish accent. At some rinks, the pros don't let the kids play crack the whip, chase or tag. But these games develop skills, as long as skaters aren't reckless. I learned how to stop on a dime, how to turn quickly and how to maneuver edges to make your body go in different directions, and it made a difference in my development and my love for the sport.

By the fall of 1968, I was taking four lessons a week with Rita—two in freestyle and two in school figures. I was what they called a low test skater; short on fundamental skills and years away from contending for national and world titles. There's a hierarchy based on what freestyle and figures test you've passed: juvenile, intermediate, novice, juniors and seniors, and I was still below the juvenile level.

It was clear early on that compulsory figures, which required enormous patience and discipline, would be my biggest obstacle to success. Tracing a series of identical loops and figure eights on a small portion of ice was tedious and boring. Figures demanded fine edge control, and all I wanted to do was fly across the rink.

I remember my first patch lesson well because I got a very public lesson in etiquette. Rita was late so I decided to warm up. When I got on the ice, I noticed the older skaters gliding in circles in slow motion, carving lines in the ice with their blades. A few others had large metal scribes (a long compasslike circle maker) they were using to create their figure-eight circles. The coaches stood in the middle of the ice, inspecting the figures being traced into the surface. The rink was completely silent, totally unlike the public sessions, when we played rock music and show tunes. Since I didn't know better, I stroked around the ice as if it was a freestyle session. As I zipped by a more experienced skater, Lynda Grinke, she looked up, startled and confused.

"What are you doing?" she said.

And knucklehead me, I skidded to a stop right in the middle of her nice clean patch, ruining it completely. What I had done was the equivalent of taking a black Magic Marker and scribbling over someone's drawing in art class. Everybody looked at me like I was a buffoon. I was totally embarrassed and it was one of the few times I can recall Rita getting angry with me.

It was the kind of start from which there would be no recovery. Rita and I began our lesson, yet instead of methodically tracing the figures on one foot, I developed a habit of impatiently skating through them as fast as I could, frustrating Rita to no end.

During this period, I also became a master of the twenty-minute skate change. Unlike freestyle skates, patch skates aren't designed for jumping and therefore they don't have toe picks that allow you to dig and turn in the ice.

Between freestyle and patch sessions, then, we all had to change skates—as quickly as possible. But somehow, someone always had a deck of cards and managed to get a game of Spit or Hearts going. Or the girls would start playing jacks and we'd join in. I was easily distracted, especially before a patch session. Sometimes I'd be in the middle of a game and my mother would come over, grab me by the arm and physically point me in the direction of the ice.

Back then, of course, compulsory figures accounted for 60 percent of your total score at the higher-level competitions. As boring as they were to practice, failing to learn them doomed your skating existence. It would take me eight years to pass the nine figures tests required to compete as a senior. In all, there were forty-one separate figures to perfect, and many had to be traced with each foot. They ranged from the basic forward outside figure eight to the difficult left back paragraph loop. Rita and I spent as much time on compulsory figures as we did on jumps and spins, which drove me nuts. During the school year, my mother started waking me up at 5 A.M. to bring me to the rink so I could skate a freestyle and a patch session before class.

Rita tried to help; boy, did she ever try. One morning while attempting to complete the three-circle tracing that formed the serpentine figure, I convinced myself that if I could get a little speed behind me, I'd get through it fine. I forgot to work the edges of my blades and the toes of my feet. Rita got impatient.

"No, no, no," she said. "Slow down; it's patch, not free skating. It's like playing the piano—you have to know what finger to use on the scale. Scott, what did you do in school first? Write a sentence or learn the ABCs? Figures are your ABCs."

I looked up into the bleachers where my mother was sitting, wrapped up tight in an overcoat and scarf. The look on her face said, "Listen to Rita; she knows what she's talking about." However, Rita's pep talks and warnings didn't kick in right away.

"The judges are really strict," Rita warned. "You won't pass your first test with these figures."

I looked down. The circles I had just traced were uneven and crooked. She was right, but I was a stubborn boy who had his own way of doing things and his own ideas about what made a great skater. I had two idols at the rink: Jimmy Disbrow and Kevin Bupp. Jimmy was an eighteen-year-old senior pairs skater with his partner, Katie Walker. I didn't look up to him because he did great compulsory figures; what I admired was his great flow across the ice and his big jumps. He rotated in the air fast, which was exactly what I wanted to do. Jimmy had a double Axel, a triple Salchow and a triple loop—at a time when top male skaters were competitive with the double Axel and one triple. It's amazing how much the sport has progressed—those jumps are now the minimum requirements for competitive novice lady skaters.

I was good pals with Rita's son, whose name was also Scott. He and I were competitors, including for Jimmy's attention.

"Jimmy," I'd call out. "Check out my toe loop."

Jimmy would pay me a compliment and then Scott would skate by and yell, "Jimmy, look at mine, look at mine!"

Jimmy was a great inspiration to me for another reason. He'd had polio as a child and started skating to strengthen his legs. In this respect, we had a lot in common, because skating became our escape from a sickly childhood.

After his skating days were over, Jimmy stayed in the sport, becoming a world judge and traveling with American skaters to fifteen international competitions, including a job as team leader for the 1998 U.S. Olympic Figure Skating Team. He is now the president of the United States Figure Skating Association, the sport's governing body in this country. But what I will always remember him for is showing me how to turn a single Lutz. For the Lutz, a skater leaps backward from the outside edge of the left skate, using the right toe pick to propel off the ice. After a single revolution in the air, the skater lands on the right foot skating backward. The key is the takeoff, and Jimmy taught me how to keep my left skate on its outside edge. Years later, my opening triple Lutz became my signature jump and I never missed it in the long program.

Kevin Bupp, my other idol, was a senior skater but not the jumper Jimmy was. His forte was making people laugh and entertaining a crowd. He had a Jim Carrey–type appeal—funny, good-looking, yet not overpowering. He was a natural comedian who could also sing and play the piano. And his entertaining ability carried over onto the ice. I've always been drawn to people who were funny, and Kevin had the best sense of humor, and the talent to take it with him on the ice. So in my first year of skating, I decided my goal was to jump like Jimmy and capture an audience like Kevin. That would be an unbeatable combination. School figures were just going to have to wait.

Figures wasn't the only new discipline I had to learn. One morning I came in for a lesson and Rita had a surprise for me. During my warmup, she waved over a young girl.

"She's going to be your dance partner for the day," she explained. "I want you to try dance because it will give you a sense of musical appreciation and teach you something about moving to music."

I was not very excited but I didn't have much say in the matter. I started taking dance a couple of times a week with two partners, Bonnie Marshall and Leslie Reynolds. Later, I competed with Kim Kortier and Edwaa Smith. Though dance was not my thing, there was a shortage of males at the rink who were even willing to try, so I got drafted. It's still a problem today finding American boys to take up the dance discipline. Most just aren't interested. It has gotten so bad in the United States that the parents of girls who dance competitively are adopting Russian male ice dancers so their daughters will have someone to skate with. I remember spending entire weekends in 1969 taking one little girl after another through her preliminary dance tests, which required each skater to earn passing grades in three separate beginner dances. Most of the girls were taller than I and not as fast. One of my test partners, Calla Urbanski, was eight years old and close to me in size. She would go on to become a U.S. pairs champion skating with Rocky Marvel. But on the day she took her dance test, she was petrified and stiff as a board. When she got on the ice, I took her hands and told her to relax. I had done about 150 dances to the same canasta tango, and was at my wits' end. Calla was frantic. "I can't relax," she moaned, "I can't." But she managed to get moving and passed. At the end of the day, there was a reward for the patience and hard work I put in taking all those girls through their dance tests. I received a token gift certificate, which was all I was allowed to get under the USFSA rules. Rita promised the experience would pay off in other ways over time. Dance helps your edge control and body movement, areas I needed a lot of work in.

In the spring of 1969, I skated in my first Tri-State Free Skating Competition, which drew the top young competitors from the midwest. Though I was only forty-nine inches tall and weighed just fifty-one pounds, I was getting stronger and having some success in some of the local skating competitions around Bowling Green. However, Tri-State was a step up, since the best regional skaters in the area competed there.

My mother drove me to Port Huron, Michigan, for the competition while my father stayed behind to keep an eye on Steve and Sue. When we arrived at the rink, she gave me a kiss and wished me luck. Then Rita took me by the hand and we went outside to warm up with a series of stretches and jumping jacks. I was an hour early, so I had some forty-five minutes before putting on my skates. My mom went to sit with some other parents whose kids were in the competition. The Bowling Green Skating Club had a sizable contingent there.

There were no figures in this event for low test skaters like me, just a free skate. Rita and I had spent the last two months working on my program, a ninety-second routine that opened with three half-revolution waltz jumps and included a Lutz, toe loop, loop, a spiral and a combination spin. I didn't have an Axel. It would take almost two years of practice to get that jump, which is difficult for most beginners to perfect because it requires you to take off going forward and turn one-and-a-half revolutions in the air.

In the preliminary boys' group, age thirteen and under, there were six of us vying for three medals. When my group went out to warm up, it hit me that this competition was different. The stands were packed and people were calling out the names of skaters, more voices than I had ever heard before. Each time someone yelled out, "Scotty!" I pushed a little harder. I liked skating fast, so I raced out in front and lit around the rink in a flash before going into my jumps. Rita said leading the pack would show off my speed and make a good impression on the judges, many of whom were seeing me for the first time. When the warm-up was over, I went back to the boards, put my warm-up jacket back on and stood anxiously by Rita, watching the others skate as I waited my turn.

"Remember," she said before I went out on the ice, "always smile during your performance. Smiling makes it appear to the crowd that what you're doing is easy, even though we both know it's not."

I nodded, but I was feeling nervous. Since many of the low-level judges are new to the discipline and don't know the skaters in these preliminary events, it wasn't unusual for the winner to get a fourth, even a last, to go with a few firsts and seconds. But Rita told me not to worry about the judges' marks—just to go out and skate my best and everything else would take care of itself. I was still nervous. I thought I would relax after a few seconds of skating but the nerves didn't go away. Somehow I managed to skate clean. Rita gave me a hug when I came off the ice, and then my mother came running down from her seat in the stands to give me another embrace.

Rita had other students to tend to, so I went to hang out with some friends. We all gravitated to the bulletin board where the results would be posted. When the official brought over the score sheet, everyone pressed forward to get a closer look. I couldn't see over the crowd of people. "Scotty got first!" somebody yelled. I craned my neck and spotted my name at the top of the list. It was my first victory ever.

A cascade of emotions pour forth in those first few minutes after the scores are displayed. The winners are jumping for joy and accepting congratulations. Those who missed a place on the podium might be crying or getting some comforting words from coaches and parents. You can overhear the complaints about the judging, or even worse, a frustrated mother or father rudely wondering why a certain skater beat their little boy or girl.

I was ecstatic. I won a blue ribbon with a plastic medal attached to the center. I held it aloft for all to see as I posed for a picture atop the podium, the second- and third-place finishers a step below. There was no better place than being on top, I thought.

A month later, the Bowling Green Skating Club held its second annual "Ice Horizons" production. A year ago, I had played a racer in the crowd, and now I was doing a solo, skating in a jack-in-the-box costume to a number Rita had choreographed for me.

What a day it was! That morning, the local Bowling Green paper, the *Sentinel-Tribune*, ran a story about me that was picked up later by the national wire services. "Boy Beats Death Prediction," the headline read. "Skating Uplifts Life of Miracle Child."

The day before, while Rita gave me a lesson, my mother sat with the reporter in the stands, explaining how lucky I was to be alive. "Actually, both my husband and I have to pinch ourselves every once in a while just to prove everything is real. . . . He's not supposed to be here, you know," she told him. After I was finished practicing, a newspaper photographer came over and took a shot of me wearing my patch jacket. When that newspaper hit our steps the next morning, I opened it up to the sports page and saw my picture in the paper. There I was, a far cry from the ghostly little kid skating around with a tube sticking out of his nose. Only a year had gone by, and now the newspaper was publishing a story about me! It was unbelievable.

On the day of the "Ice Horizons" show, my main concern was how to get through the night without having to put on any makeup. I was hiding out all night. The skating moms packed it on so thick I felt like a girl. To make matters worse, I had to wear it around the rink for hours until show time. I hated the stuff. It's the one thing I hate about show skating, even today. Years later, at a competition in Sun Valley, Idaho, Brian Boitano joked that I looked like a corpse on the ice. I don't care, and I still won't wear makeup in a competition. I'd rather go out there looking like a ghost than cover my face with rouge, mascara and lipstick. Okay, I did use some mascara for a while, but not to make my eyes stand out. I dabbed it on my bald spot to cover it up. Worked pretty good, too, enough that Kurt Browning and Viktor Petrenko have used it. Of course, it's not an issue for me anymore—there isn't enough mascara on the planet to cover the spot I have now.

Since I was one of the youngest soloists in the show, I was among the first to skate. The number began with a big box moving to center ice, where everyone expected it to stop. Only it didn't; it kept on moving. Then it spun around a few times and I popped out of the top and skated my solo. It was my first in a long line of gimmick numbers. The crowd ate it up. During the ovation after my performance, I looked up in the stands and saw my mother and father beaming. Ernie had spent the last couple of weeks volunteering to build the sets and props for the show, and Dorothy was now working as the test chairwoman for the Bowling Green Figure Skating Club. Skating was becoming a family affair.

Except for my sister, Sue. Skating, while relatively easy for me, came to Sue a lot harder. Earlier in the year, we were playing follow the leader during a public session. I did a toe loop jump and then turned around to watch her. Sue didn't complete the rotation and when she came down on the ice, her blade went out from under her and she crashed hard, breaking her arm. She was screaming in pain and a skate guard had to carry her off the ice. When my mother arrived to take Sue to the hospital, Sue was sitting in the skate shop icing down her arm. "Mom," I said, "Sue went up all right but she sure came down wrong."

As my skating flourished, Sue's time at the ice rink dwindled. While she did a little ice dancing and took dance tests until her senior year in high school, there just wasn't enough money for two serious skaters in the family.

One weekend, my mom and dad took me to Port Huron, Michigan, for a competition, and we stayed over a couple of nights because I was in several events. Sue had the house to herself and, like any rebellious teenager might, she threw a party. I don't think she ever got caught for that one, but she was constantly at odds with my mother. Sue had a lot of responsibility and wanted more freedom. She was getting more involved politically and even went to the campus protests over the Vietnam War. But since both our mother and father worked and Mom was studying for a doctorate in education at Bowling Green, many of the baby-sitting chores fell to Sue.

Saturday nights could get loud if Sue missed her curfew. One night when she got home, my mother hit the roof.

"That's it," Mom yelled. "You're grounded all next week."

"I'll do whatever I want," Sue shot back. "I'm sick and tired of you and Daddy telling me what to do."

Watching my parents' lives orbit around mine was frustrating to her. For the first nine years of my life, it was because I was sick most of the time. Then my skating took over. "Everything's Scotty, Scotty, Scotty," she used to say.

I didn't make it any easier on her. Once when she was baby-sitting, we got into a fight and I ran away six miles to the rink, my place of refuge. Sue and my dad's father, Ernest, who was living with us at the time, went looking for me. When they eventually found me, Grandpa lost his temper and really bellowed at me. It was the only time I ever heard him raise his voice. He was generally quiet all the time, spending his days watching golf and working on his painting projects. But on that day he went berserk, and in retrospect, I can't say I blame him.

I learned something from my sister's arguments with my mother. I decided the best way to get what I wanted was not to follow Sue's confrontational style. I'm still a nonconfrontational person; I learned the best way for me to get something was to charm people and then pick and choose my spots when it came time to take a stand. That time for me came in the late fall of 1969, when I demanded to play organized hockey.

Being a male figure skater was no easy task in a Middle America town like Bowling Green, where the boys are bred to play football, basketball and baseball. I was in the minority and getting all sorts of heat from the guys. I usually heard it coming off the ice and walking past the hockey players who were getting ready to skate. "Hey, Hamilton, why do you want to skate like a girl?" I remember them saying.

I ignored the insults, or tried to crack a joke. What made it harder for me was that I actually wanted to play hockey myself, but my mother was dead against it. I was a speed freak and loved all things fast. I had a minibike that I would take out into the woods behind our house to race around the trails. I was proud of that bike because I actually took out a loan from a bank to pay for it. My monthly payments were $9.32, and I earned the money doing a paper route and household chores. Grandaddy Everett used to scold me all the time because I rode it too fast. "Slow down, Scotty," he'd yell. That only made me want to go faster. I think he was afraid I was going to damage my throwing arm.

So I was drawn to hockey. But no matter how many times I begged my mother to let me play, I'd get the same answer. One morning, as my mother was driving me to a skating lesson with Rita, I brought it up again.

"Scotty, we've gone over this enough. It's too rough and takes up too much time," my mother complained. Left unsaid was the enormous cost for another pair of skates, pads, a helmet, sticks.

"Okay," I replied. "Then I'm not figure skating anymore."

After that morning lesson, I went on strike. For the next three days, I took forever to change into my skates, didn't work hard in practice, stopped listening to Rita, and just did a lot of standing around on the ice. One afternoon I draped the stalls in one of the bathrooms with toilet paper in protest. The rink manager was complaining about me and my mother was getting furious. Finally, after three days of this, she caved in and let me give hockey a try.

That winter, I played in the BG Squirts division for the Bruins, which was one of four teams in the league. The season was all of one month and four games long, which made it tolerable for my mother. My end of the deal was that I had to make up any time lost from figure skating, and I didn't miss a beat. Even during hockey season, I was spending about three hours a day on the ice. I was skating a forty-five-minute patch and a forty-five-minute freestyle session in the morning and then again after dinner.

My first game left my mother a nervous wreck. I was excited and it didn't bother me that the other players were bigger. Since I could skate faster than most of the taller kids, I kept one step ahead of any potential head-hunters, though my mom covered her eyes anytime I got near the puck. I learned fast to pass the thing whenever I got possession or else somebody was going to take my head off. I was terrible, but after the game while we were walking to the car, my mother gave me a hug. "Nice going, Scooter," she said. "Now all we have to do is find a uniform that fits you."

True, my jersey hung down to my knees, but I didn't care. I gradually improved and learned to pass the puck well, though I wasn't much of a scorer—two goals in three years. One year I believe I led the team in assists because every time I touched the puck I looked to get rid of it. It was that or get checked into the boards. I was much better at figure skating. During a Youth Hockey Night, I got an assist in the first period, then changed into a costume and a pair of figure skates to perform an exhibition between periods.

The major drawback in playing hockey was my size. I took some pretty hard hits, and my parents were panicked that I was going to get a concussion or a broken limb. I was carried off the ice a couple of times. I had to do something to defend myself. In one game, I took a pass from a teammate and was rushing up the ice when an opposing player took his stick and slashed me across the back of my legs. It was a cheap shot, so I retaliated a minute later with a cross-check, knocking him to the ice. The referee saw that one. As I skated to the penalty box, I looked up at my mother and father in the stands; I couldn't tell if they were proud of me or if they were upset.

In my third and final season of youth hockey, in my very last game, I went into a corner to chase down a loose puck, and looked up just in time to see my friend, Doug Black, lining me up for a hit. He had that look on his face that said, "You are about to get nailed." And I was. He tattooed me. I was crushed against the boards and actually heard something crack as I slithered to the ice. I remember lying there feeling woozy, looking up at the blurry scoreboard and all these dark faces I couldn't make out because the overhead lights were in my eyes. Somebody was asking if I was okay, so at least I knew I was still alive. It actually felt pretty nice lying there, so I didn't feel like getting up right away. Not only did I need help walking off, but my neck was stiff. My parents took me to the emergency room. The doctor said I was suffering from whiplash and he fitted me with a neck brace.

My parents had seen enough. When we got home, my mother and father sat me down.

"Scott," my mother said, "I think it's time to reconsider playing hockey."

For a minute I felt like crying. I was thinking, "Darn it, I should have protected myself from Doug's hit." One of my coaches, who was small too, had a couple of techniques, like a hip check to take another player's legs out from under him. That was legal, but he also said I should use my stick as an impaling device in emergencies. But the truth was, I couldn't have done that to Doug, or any other kid, for that matter. I had decided in that instant that I was going to take the hit and I paid for it. I was in the wrong place at the wrong time, but that happens a lot in hockey.

"Mom, I can protect myself better next time," I argued. My words were halfhearted. I knew they were right, but there wasn't any urgency to make a decision since the season was over.

As time went by, it was no contest between figure skating and hockey. I knew I could succeed at figure skating, and I was never going to be a great hockey player. Even though I quit, I accomplished what I set out to do. I didn't stop because I was a poor player. I left because I was much better at something else. And by trying, I won some respect from the guys.

I think I knew I was destined to skate when Kenwood School honored me with the Baron Award, which is given annually to a sixth grader who shows promise in the arts. I was to receive it on the last day of school, only it was supposed to be a surprise. My big plan for the day was to play a prank on my teacher. Some friends and I took Magic Markers and drew all over our faces. The next thing I knew, we were hauled off to the principal's office. "What are you doing?" he yelled, knowing I was to receive a surprise award that afternoon. I had to spend the next half hour in the boys' room scrubbing my face raw with soap and water. At the assembly I sat unsuspecting, until my name was announced. I was psyched and sprinted up onstage. When I accepted my award I turned around toward the audience, and people sitting up close started laughing and pointing. Then I remembered: my friend had written "Hi there" across my forehead and I had forgotten to wash it off because my bangs were in the way.

By this time, I was on my third coach. I had lost Rita in 1969 when she and David left to head up a rink in Buffalo, New York. With all the university and community obligations, our rink was becoming ill-suited as a training center for advanced figure skaters. We kept on losing ice time to public sessions and hockey, which could generate more money for the rink. So the Lowerys decided to move on.

We were all sad to see them go, and for a while I was in limbo as my parents tried to decide who would coach me next. During the transition period, I took lessons from a couple of young pros, Phyllis Hendrix and Mark Beck, until my parents finally settled on a coach named Giuliano Grassi. He was an established pro who commuted between Fort Wayne and Bowling Green. He trained one of my rivals, Brian Maier, and his sister, Jill, and I got to become good friends with them. Mr. Grassi came to Bowling Green on weekdays to work with me. Then my mom and I traveled to Fort Wayne on weekends for lessons. That was a good two-and-a-half-hour trip one way.

Mr. Grassi was an old-world Italian and didn't put up with any of my nonsense, on or off the ice. Taking from him, skating was work, work, work and no play. I found myself at odds with him sometimes, and his temper and my tendency to fool around did not make a good match. During patch sessions, he demanded absolute silence, and if I talked to another skater, he chewed me out. Many coaches display a rigid style because they want skaters to absorb the passion they have for their craft. But I was still a kid who also wanted to play tag on the ice with my friends. Decades later, I ran into Mr. Grassi while rehearsing for a show at a rink where he taught. It was so funny watching him work with his students because he was laughing and smiling. The Grinch had become a marshmallow. I thought, "Where was this guy when I was a kid?"

I got my double Salchow with Mr. Grassi and passed my first figures test—no small task, since I failed on my first two tries. I still thought figures were too boring for my blood, but I learned that the only thing worse than actually practicing figures was failing them in front of three judges, my coach and my mother. After my second ill-fated attempt, I wanted to quit on the spot. I pouted for a few days and didn't go to the rink. Unless I improved, however, my skating career would be over before my eleventh birthday, so I kept on working at them.

I stayed with Mr. Grassi for only ten months. My mother switched coaches in the middle of a competition, right after I finished the figures portion of the juvenile event at the 1970 Eastern Great Lakes regionals. It's highly unusual to change coaches in the middle of a competition, but the split had been brewing for some time. My mother felt Mr. Grassi was giving my friend Brian more attention than me and that Mr. Grassi's temper got the best of him sometimes. She decided I needed a softer touch. In all fairness to Mr. Grassi, Brian was there first. He was a hometown boy from Fort Wayne, which was where Mr. Grassi taught most of the time, so I could see how I would be second banana.

My mother had a successor all lined up. His name was Herb Plata, a German pro who had recently moved to Bowling Green. He took over for Mr. Grassi immediately. I won the freestyle, pulling up from third in figures to first overall.

Winning regionals was significant because it was my "nationals." I defeated the top skaters from seven other states, but I couldn't go any further until I advanced to a higher level. Only the top three intermediate, novice, junior and senior skaters go on to the second round, which was the Midwestern Sectionals competition, which then feeds its top three winners in the novice, junior and senior categories into the U.S. nationals, along with the medalists from Eastern and Pacific Coast Sectionals.

I took to Mr. Plata immediately. He was an ice show star, and in my mind the most exciting skater to hit Bowling Green since Kevin Bupp, who had moved on to the "Ice Follies." When I watched Mr. Plata reel off twenty-five Arabian jumps in a row, I was mesmerized. "That's how good I want to be someday," I told my mom after I saw him skate for the first time. Once a German junior national champion, he had charisma and style on the ice, all the things I thought were cool in a skater.

Under Mr. Plata, I got the rest of my double jumps through the Lutz and passed my second figures test. He taught me solid technique, skills I would take with me for the rest of my life. But compulsory figures were turning out to be my albatross. I failed my third test four times before passing it a week before the 1971 Eastern Great Lakes regionals. That allowed me to advance a level, from juvenile to intermediate. I won figures at that competition, so at least the work was paying off. And I placed first overall. In fact, at every level I ever skated, I never lost a regionals competition. I went to midwesterns that year for the first time, and placed third. Maybe next year, I thought, if I was able to move up to novice, I could actually make nationals.

The following season we went on the road for competitions in New York, Michigan and Toronto. In those days you had to travel far to find competitions. It's not like today, with events at every rink. As you move up the skating ranks, it's good to get exposure so judges from different parts of the region know who you are. My mother and I made most of these trips together by car. Lake Placid, New York, was a special trip because the competition was held in the same arena where they staged the 1932 Olympics. Not only did other kids come all the way from Bowling Green, but I'd see my friends who skated in Troy and Fort Wayne. We'd practice together, but after skating I'd spend most of my time with my mother.

It was in Lake Placid where I received my first dose of meddlesome judging. I was still an intermediate and came in second to a skater named Ray Belmonte, who is now a doctor. Although I skated well, one judge marked me way down. Mr. Plata got permission from the referee to speak with him.

"Why did you mark Scott so low?" Mr. Plata asked.

"Your student shouldn't be doing so many doubles in his program," he admonished. "The person who won had a spread eagle and Scott didn't." This particular judge felt that at my level, I should have had more singles in my program to show proper technique, which made no sense whatsoever. I learned a valuable lesson. It was important to listen to what the judges had to say, but there was no way you could please an entire panel all the time. Each judge has different tastes, and what I now understood was that there would be times I would receive unfair marks. Of course, Mr. Plata and I would digest the critiques from judges and apply the feedback as much as possible. To hear comments about music selection, choreography and certain disciplines, like jumps and spins, was useful, but we didn't accept the observations as gospel. Sometimes you had to go with your gut, and this was something I would keep with me for my entire skating career.

While Mr. Plata was a fine coach and an inspiration, he suffered through many physical and personal problems, bad ones that sometimes interfered with his job. He had a chronic bad shoulder that popped out on him constantly. Unfortunately, he tried to alleviate the pain with alcohol. My mother was so concerned, she invited him to stay in our home after my paternal grandparents moved away to Florida. We helped him find a surgeon to put his shoulder back in place and that seemed to help him for a while. But the drinking resumed.

I could always tell when he'd had too much to drink. His eyes would be swimming and there were occasions when he actually disappeared during lessons, stepping off the ice and never returning. Sometimes I smelled alcohol on his breath. Even at competitions, he'd drink himself into oblivion and we'd hear about it the next day from another coach or parent.

Drinking can be a big problem for tour skaters, and Mr. Plata had spent a lot of years on the road with "Holiday on Ice." I learned much later that traveling with a show could either destroy a skater or provide him with a chance to see and understand the world. While the hours are long and the pace is hard, skaters are pumped up after a show, and drinking becomes a way to pass the time and socialize.

During the 1972 season, the Bowling Green Figure Skating Club hosted its first Eastern Great Lakes regionals event. I had moved up to Novice and won my category. Midwesterns were held in Minneapolis that year, and my parents and I drove to Minnesota with the hope I would place in the top three so I could gain a berth to nationals, which was in Southern California. The novice event takes place early in the week before junior and senior competition gets under way. We had one day to practice, and then the figures competition was held the next afternoon. Despite the fact that I was having so much trouble passing figures tests, I usually came up with my better efforts when it counted. I finished third, putting me in position to make it to nationals if I stayed in the top three after the free skate. I was excited about being in the hunt. We had dinner in the hotel and my mother was in a good mood. It had been a tough year with Mr. Plata, but it all seemed to be coming together for me at the right time.

"Now are you glad you gave up hockey?" she kidded.

My performance the next day was not one of my better ones. I missed a couple of elements and fell to fourth place overall, missing an invitation to nationals by one place. In an odd quirk of the judging system back then, I came in fourth even though I finished third in each event. That could happen when skaters ahead of you in figures dropped in the freestyle and someone below you in figures jumped over you in the free skate. It was a disappointing loss and I knew it spelled trouble for Mr. Plata. His drinking, combined with my lackluster free skate, left my parents very frustrated. They were investing so much time and money in my skating, and while I was improving, they felt I deserved better.

It was a long drive back to Bowling Green. The trees were barren and the farm fields lay fallow after the fall harvest. Another season had come to an end and winter was closing in. As my mother and father talked about my situation, it was clear there were a number of things holding me back besides coaching problems. For one, ice time at the campus rink, while suitable for low test skaters, was inadequate for novice competitors like me with designs on competing internationally, which was precisely the reason Rita and David Lowery had left. I needed more patch and freestyle sessions to be competitive, and that ice time just wasn't available. On the drive home I could sense that for me, too, a certain season was coming to an end, just like the countryside all around us.

After we got home, my mother contacted Nancy Meiss, a Cincinnati judge whom she had known for many years, and who was a big supporter of mine. Nancy was very candid, and my mother really liked that about her. She agreed that a change was called for; if I was going to get to the next level, I needed a coach who understood the next level. In Minneapolis, my mom had been impressed with Slavka Kohout, the main coach at the Wagon Wheel training center in Rockton, Illinois. I had skated there the year before at midwesterns, and Slavka was an internationally recognized coach who trained Janet Lynn and Gordie McKellen, two skaters on the verge of making the 1972 Olympic team. My mother wanted Slavka to take me on as a student and asked Nancy to set up a meeting. We would have to wait a couple of months, since Slavka would be busy with nationals, the Olympics and the world championships.

In the spring, my mother drove me to Rockton to try out with Slavka. I did my program and a few jumps. She also took a look at my figures. Slavka was too busy to take on another student, but she liked what she saw enough to refer me to another Wagon Wheel coach, Pierre Brunet. He had coached the 1960 Olympic champion Carol Heiss and Canadian legend Donald Jackson. And he was a French-born champion, the 1928 and 1932 Olympic pairs champion with his partner and wife, Andrée Joly. He was in his seventies at the time and commanded everyone's respect.

Monsieur Brunet, as he liked to be called, agreed to take me on as a student. I had no reservations about leaving home. I was only thirteen years old, but I knew I wanted to keep skating, and that was the most important thing in my life. During the short time I had spent in Rockton, I was excited about the possibility of training there, even though it would be tough on my folks. It was a sacrifice we had to make if I was to continue skating. We agreed that I would spend the summer and fall in Rockton, and I would return to Bowling Green during the winter, right after nationals. I would spend the rest of the winter and spring there, training and going to school.

So when school let out, we packed up the Mercury, and my mom drove me to Illinois. I think she was relieved that I would be able to continue skating at a topflight training rink. I would be working with the best coaches in the country and working out with other high test skaters with big aspirations. And I would have all the ice time I needed.

It was odd, but in the four years since I had taken up skating it had gone from being a cure for my illness to something much larger in significance for me and my parents. I didn't mind leaving home if it meant I could skate more. I had no idea where skating was going to take me; all I knew was I didn't want to stop.

Chapter Four

On My Own

When I left home in 1972, skating took on a new place in my life. The other students I trained with became my brothers and sisters, and my coaches became parental figures. My morals, values and approach to everyday existence would be influenced by this sport and the people in it. It was the start of living life out of a suitcase, of skating becoming the centerpiece in my life. It's very much how I live my life today.

My new home was the Wagon Wheel Ice Palace in Rockton, Illinois, situated in the country 100 miles northwest of Chicago and just south of the Wisconsin border. In its heyday, Wagon Wheel was a vacation retreat for the city-dwellers from the southern part of Illinois. There was golfing, horseback riding, tennis, bowling and swimming. Guests had four restaurants to chose from, and families could take their kids to a zoo or a ride on a minitrain circling the grounds. The owner also built two indoor skating rinks and then recruited some of the top coaches in the country to run the skating program, including Slavka and my coach, Mr. Brunet. They in turn attracted some of the best skaters in the country to train there.

I lived in a dormitory shaped like a horseshoe. I shared a small room with four other skaters, three of whom were eighteen. I settled into a steady routine. In the morning, I'd wake up and eat a breakfast of eggs and pancakes in the kitchen area prepared by one of the dormitory mothers, and then we'd head to the rink with sack lunches. Part of the afternoon was reserved for school, and then we'd head back to the dorm for dinner. One of the moms made terrific Italian dishes, so I gorged myself on pasta, cheese and sauce all summer long.

On my first practice, I got to meet Janet Lynn, and I had the privilege of skating with her daily in her final year as an amateur. She was a huge star: Olympic bronze medalist, four-time national champion, best free-style skater on the planet. The only reason she didn't win the gold in Sapporo was her fourth-place finish in school figures, which prevented her from pulling ahead of eventual winner Beatrix Schuba of Austria, and Canada's Karen Magnussen. Despite a fall on a flying sit spin, nobody was even close to her in the free skate. Janet won the night, as always.

For the 1973 season, the skating officials added the short program and changed the breakdown of the total score to 40 percent for figures, 20 percent for the short and 40 percent for the long. The new rules seemed tailor-made for Janet, who could now capitalize even more on her free skating ability.

I remember I was putting on my patch skates and she sat down next to me and said hello. Wagon Wheel was a musty old barn of a rink. But Janet, I would come to learn, had a way of lighting up even the darkest and coldest midwestern winter morning. I don't think there has been another skater other than Sonja Henie who was as worshiped and loved as Janet Lynn. Ask most skaters now who the greatest of all time was, and they'd say Janet Lynn. Peggy Fleming and Dorothy Hamill would likely pick Janet Lynn. All I could think of at the moment was "I'm just this little nobody from Ohio, and Janet Lynn is actually talking to me."

After I calmed down, we talked for a little while about my skating and she said, "If you take nothing else from this conversation, remember this: anything you do in your career can never be taken away from you. Every day is new and whatever you accomplish only adds to what you've done in the past. So you can't lose; you can only gain."

I've never forgotten those words. Some thirty years later, I saw Janet during a visit to Detroit. "Stars on Ice" was playing the Palace at Auburn Hills, and Janet lives nearby, so on the day of the show she invited me over to her house for lunch and I got to see two of her five children, Michael and Peter, and her husband, Rick, who worked for the FBI. We reminisced about old times over peanut butter and jelly sandwiches in her kitchen. As I watched her play with her kids, I thought of something Jo Jo Starbuck once told me. Janet, she said, had a choice: she could have made a fortune as a professional ice skater, or she could raise her own kids at home and shop at garage sales. She chose family over career. On that visit, I could see she was meant to be a mother. We spent part of the afternoon talking about the decline of the family structure and the importance of one-on-one interaction between parents and children.

During a lull in the conversation, I said, "Janet, I have never forgotten the advice you gave me on my first day at Wagon Wheel."

Then she lit up the room with her megawatt smile, just like she used to when we trained together.

During my first few days in Rockton, I was disappointed that Janet's coach had passed me off to Mr. Brunet instead of teaching me herself. Miss Kohout, as she was called, preferred teaching women, though she did make an exception to work with Gordie McKellen and Chris Kales, another high test skater. I saw the results she was getting with her skaters and was envious. That feeling lasted about a week.

One morning, I was on a freestyle session alongside a student of Slavka's, Jackie Dean. Jackie was not having a good day. During a lesson with Slavka, Jackie made the fatal error of stopping in the middle of a long program run-through, and that was something you just did not do. Slavka demanded competition intensity at all times. If you made a mistake, you never quit skating. You finished the program. Jackie didn't really stop— she fell and didn't get up as fast as Slavka would have liked, and Slavka made her pay.

"Stop the music," Slavka yelled to a skater standing by the record player. Jackie was already back on her feet and skating into her next move, but when the music stopped she jerked her head around and there was this terrified look in her eye.

"Get back to your beginning position," Slavka said. By now most of the skaters knew what was coming, yet didn't dare let on they were watching.

"But I've got to catch my breath," Jackie said.

The music came on and Slavka waved her arm. "Go," she said sternly.

Jackie started the program again, fell again and Slavka made her start over one more time. Every time she made a mistake, Slavka cut the music and made her start over. This went on for twenty minutes. By the end of the lesson, Jackie was spent. Slavka was determined to drive home a point: her skaters don't make mistakes, and if they do, they don't stop in the middle of a program. They skate from start to finish, preferably without error.

I turned pale watching this go on. Today, I doubt a coach could get away with that without being sued. But make no mistake about it: Slavka's skaters came into competition prepared. They were ready and they never quit. But I was thanking the skating gods I was taking from Mr. Brunet. Slavka intimidated me, and I'm not sure I could have handled being coached by her.

Not that Mr. Brunet was putty in my hands. Far from it. He was a perfectionist, one of those coaches who wouldn't end a lesson until he was certain a student knew he was getting something from it. Half-hour lessons could stretch to more than two hours, and I don't think he ever got paid for all the time he put in. When I began working with him, it was like starting over from scratch. We started each practice with a series of warm-up calisthenics he said he learned in the French Foreign Legion. They included a series of hops, squats, jumps and balance exercises. His specialty, however, was figures.

Much of what I learned from him in this area, I didn't apply until years later, when I was a more advanced senior skater and more intense about perfecting my figures. That was when his lessons finally started to make sense. Mr. Brunet was strong on technique—the position of your shoulders, arms and hips should be in relation to the blade on your skate and the line in the ice. One of his favorite expressions on a patch lesson was "little toe, little toe, little toe," then "big toe, big toe, big toe." What he meant was to roll my skate all the way to the ball of the foot to get the correct amount of pressure on the front edge of the blade.

When he was repeating, "little toe, little toe, little toe," I'd press up on my little toe and go right into a forward loop and then I'd lean back on the edge to come out of a circle. Then I'd be on a forward inside loop and he'd be chanting, "big toe, big toe, big toe."

Later, when I took from Carlo Fassi, another great figures coach, he had his own way of communicating "rhythm." When I was doing a loop and he would say, "in, in, in," in my head I heard Mr. Brunet saying, "big toe, big toe, big toe." That was when some of Mr. Brunet's lessons began kicking in. I was able to take the technique taught to me by Mr. Brunet and apply it to Carlo's rhythm technique.

Mr. Brunet liked things done his way. Time was of no consequence to him. He used to sharpen skates by hand, using stones instead of a sharpening wheel. It took him longer, but that way he could make the perfect edge. I had a bad habit of never wearing skate guards on my blades, which was a problem at an old rink like Wagon Wheel because all the rubber matting was hammered down with nails that jutted above the surface. I remember during my first week he caught me walking around without guards.

"Where are your guards?" he demanded.

"I don't know," I answered lamely.

"I spent an hour and a half sharpening your blades and you're walking around on these nails and tacks?" he yelled. "You find your guards. You walk on your toes until you find your guards."

And I went looking for them, on my tiptoes, of course.

Skaters at Wagon Wheel worked hard and we played hard. At thirteen, I was one of the youngest skaters in the training program, and it was my first time ever away from home. That alone left my mother a nervous wreck. Good thing she didn't know half of what was going on. I got some quick lessons in life from my roommates, who were not the best of influences. I shared a large room with three guys in their late teens. A half hour drive away was the Wisconsin state line and with it, a legal drinking age of eighteen. I spent a lot of nights alone at the dorm. While my roommates were out barhopping, I was the designated fibber who covered for them during room check. Sometimes they returned totally smashed, so I grew up a little quicker than most kids my age.

It was difficult in the beginning because I was homesick and called Bowling Green almost every day, and it would take more than a month for me to make the adjustment. One thing about living away from home— you need good supervision and someone looking out for your well-being and diet. The food at Wagon Wheel was excellent, but I found it hard to resist the temptations of peer pressure, especially around the older guys. Teenagers by nature like to experiment, and I was no different, so there were times I had a can of beer or a cigarette, which wasn't the best thing.

Eventually, I was moved into a separate room with my younger roommate, skater Charlie Carapazza, who was fifteen. One afternoon, a good friend of mine from Bowling Green, Bob Hyduke, paid us a visit at the dorm. He and his parents were vacationing in Wagon Wheel and they had all gone out to dinner the night before, at which Bob got acquainted with a certain vending machine in the men's room. Charlie and I looked at the condoms and said, "Cool, let's make some water balloons."

After we ambushed some girls in the dorm, we put on bandannas, loaded up some squirt guns and went outside to conduct raids on the resort. The kiddie train was our primary target. When it was parked in the station, we sprinted by and squirted the passengers, and then made a fast getaway.

We were full of stupid ideas that day. After the attempted train robbery, we went and hid out like fugitives. One of the guys pulled out a cigarette and lit it up. When it was my turn to take a puff, I wouldn't inhale.

"C'mon Scott, do it," urged Bob and Charlie.

When the smoke went into my lungs, I doubled over and heaved. My head started to spin and I got very sick. Still, I thought I was pretty darn cool, until the next day, when Mr. Brunet made a surprise room inspection. No doubt he had heard we were misbehaving. His search was pretty thorough, enough that it was obvious he was looking for something. As he rummaged through our drawers, Charlie and I stood at attention, like a couple of soldiers at boot camp. Guess what he found? Our unused water balloons, of course.

Mr. Brunet held one up for a closer look and grimaced. It reminded me of a couple of years earlier in Bowling Green, when I had gotten nabbed for throwing firecrackers. I was hiding out on the roof of the ice rink, picking off unsuspecting skaters in the parking lot below. The prank nearly got me arrested. Fortunately, the campus police just took my name. My parents grounded me for a week, however.

The powers at Wagon Wheel came down much harder. I went home two weeks after the incident and was told I wouldn't be allowed back in the dorm unless my parents found me a chaperon. Charlie was given the same conditions. I returned to Rockton accompanied by Sue, who had celebrated her honeymoon at Wagon Wheel earlier in the summer with her husband, James Michael Sanders. He was in the navy and had gone overseas, so Sue moved into the Wagon Wheel dorm and shared a room with me. She wasn't thrilled with the idea of baby-sitting her thirteen-year-old brother, but her presence had the desired effect; my appetite for trouble dwindled considerably with my sister around to give my mother daily reports. But I was still no angel. I was a freshman attending the local high school, Hononega, and had a separate group of friends there. The curfew at my dorm was 9:30 P.M. on Friday nights, which meant I couldn't meet up with my friends to go see Hononega's football games. So I sneaked out. Dorm security was always on the lookout for an open window to see who was violating curfew, so it wasn't long before I was on a first-name basis with all the security people. Half the time, I was escaping from my room just for the sake of busting out. That was the thrill. Obviously I wasn't very good at it.

Sue made some friends, even joined some of the older skaters on their forays into Wisconsin, but some of the more acerbic skaters were kind of rough on her. They would pull pranks like inviting her to go swimming and then not showing up. Sue stuck it out for five months and then joined her husband overseas after the 1973 competitive season was over.

While I did have some success during my first season at Wagon Wheel, my skating was erratic. The extra time and attention devoted to school figures paid off at once. Competing as a novice, I won the Eastern Great Lakes regional competition in Columbus, Ohio, and earned first-place scores from all five judges in figures. I also won midwesterns in Denver, and earned an invitation to the 1973 U.S. National Championships in Minneapolis. My undisciplined training habits and my inexperience caught up with me at nationals. For some reason, officials scheduled the novice men's competition on the night of the senior ladies' final. When I went out for my warmup, I looked into the stands and they were packed with fifteen thousand fans waiting to see Janet Lynn in her final amateur performance. I was just one of those skaters who had a hard enough time going from jump to jump and ending on time with the music, and now I had to skate in front of more people than I had ever seen in my life. Not surprisingly, I fell five times in the freestyle event and finished last in a field of nine.

Janet Lynn won nationals for a fifth time and then flew to Czechoslovakia for worlds. This was her last year and everyone was expecting her to win the world title. But something totally unexpected happened. Janet fell in the short program, the very event that seemed designed for her, and she finished second overall. But wherever Janet finished had no bearing on her contribution to the sport—which was monumental.

Gordie McKellen won his first national title that year and finished seventh at worlds. He was the undisputed king of Wagon Wheel, and my idol. Though Gordie was four years older than I, we did have one thing in common: we were both short. My height would top out at five feet, three-and-a-half inches, and Gordie was a few inches taller. He was also built. Not only did he skate, he played high school football, which was unheard-of in the skating world.

There was nothing conventional about Gordie. He did only one runthrough a day—a hard one in the Wagon Wheel annex. This rink had a low ceiling, and every time the Zamboni made the ice, the place filled up with carbon monoxide. It was so bad everyone waited ten minutes for the air to clear before skating. Not Gordie. He would jump on the ice and go right into a run-through amid the Zamboni exhaust, which hung over the freshly made ice like mist over a pond. It stank, but Gordie decided skating hard in the fumes made him tougher and built stamina. For sure it beat skating his program twice in a row. We all tried it, because Gordie being Gordie, he had to be right. And none of us could take it. We'd come off the ice hacking and coughing.

One time Gordie was working on his program and he raised his arm dramatically above his head. "That's radical," I thought. I had never seen another male skater do that. When a guy raised his arms above the shoulder at Bowling Green, it was skating sacrilege. Only the girls did that.

But if Gordie could do it, and he was the major stud at Wagon Wheel, it had to be okay. The other skaters talked about it for the rest of the day; then we all went out on the next freestyle and started trying it ourselves.

Gordie was always a trendsetter. Later, when he adopted boot covers and flashy shirts with showbiz flair, the rest of us followed suit. What I liked most about his skating style was his crowd appeal and strong jumps. In many ways he was ahead of his time. He was the first skater I ever saw do a triple Axel. He showed me how to combine humor and drama in a performance and how to take control of an audience. He did it in practice, and then I got to watch him do it in front of large audiences at nationals. I saw and felt the effect it had on crowds, and that was an experience I never forgot.

He also could make an entrance off the ice. I remember this one barbecue where everyone was playing lawn Frisbee and jumping on the trampoline. There was music and good food and a lot of laughs. Then Gordie shows up in his green rally sport Camaro with the racing stripe. You could hear his car approaching from a mile away, and by the time Gordie pulled up to the house, everything had stopped and someone was putting on Neil Diamond, Gordie's favorite singer. When he walked in, people swarmed around and the girls all seemed to swoon and giggle. I said to myself, "Whoa, it's like Frank Sinatra walking into a room and everyone stops to pay their respects." This guy was the king. Maybe someday I could be as good, and the king of my own rink.

He knew I looked up to him and I think he liked that. He never hesitated to confide in me, even about his girl problems. There was this one girl he was unsure about, so he asked me to come along with them on a date. We went to a drive-in movie—the three of us—and I ended up playing on a swing set with his date while he sat in his car drinking a couple of beers and watching the movie.

I put him on a pedestal, yet Gordie always had a way of bringing himself back to earth. One of his favorite stories was of his first Olympic practice in Sapporo, Japan. He was feeling as if he could do no wrong. Flying around the rink, which was surrounded by a sheet of unbreakable glass, he decided to turn a triple toe loop without even setting up for the jump, the kind of thing you do when your body is spiked with adrenaline. He stuck his jump and then decided to hotdog a little on the landing, holding it extra long so everyone could see he was the man. But he made a miscalculation, and when he turned around, he skated right into the glass and knocked himself over. The king was on his backside, and Gordie still laughs about the incident to this day.

For all the inspiration Gordie provided, I was not a workhorse in my Wagon Wheel days. I remained in novice for the 1974 season, and had another disastrous nationals in Providence, Rhode Island. I fell all over the place and finished ninth out of ten. Mr. Brunet was beside himself. "I don't know what we're going to do; this is not good," he said. I could sense the disappointment in his voice.

Part of the problem, if you could call it a problem, was that I was growing. I had shot up almost six inches in a year and a half. In the summer of 1973 my knees were hurting from the growth spurt, and I grew out of my clothes. I also wrecked my ankle jumping out of my bunk bed, and that injury kept me off the ice for weeks.

From Providence, I went home to Bowling Green with my mother and father and stayed there for the rest of the winter and spring. I skated on my own and attended Bowling Green High. While I was kept in the dark about the financial sacrifices my family was making so I could skate, there was no hiding the fact that my parents had sold the Brownwood home and moved into a smaller house on Liberty Hi Road on the outskirts of town.

Like many skating families, they had decided they would do and spend whatever it took to support my skating, even if it meant sacrificing the needs of my brother and sister. They all gave up a lot, and that included the symbol of my father's success, the Brownwood house, which they sold after I moved to Wagon Wheel. The one consolation was that the new place had more land—four acres. My mom and dad explained that we were moving because Dad wanted a large lot to plant a one-acre vegetable garden. What they kept private was that the $40,000 in equity they gained from the sale went toward my skating bills, which were running about $8,000 per year.

Coming home, however, was always a nice respite. My dad had his vegetable garden and a small pond he stocked with bluegill and largemouth bass, which was a terrific swimming hole on hot days. In the late summer, I'd come home for minivacations and go outside with a bucket of water and a knife and sit in our strawberry patch eating berries right off the vine. I did the same with green beans. I'd pick them, wash them and eat them. We grew cantaloupe, corn, tomatoes, zucchini and watermelon, giving away a lot to friends and canning the rest for the winter.

The only bad part about a one-acre garden is tending it. I got very familiar with a rake and a hoe. I used to complain about the weeding because it killed my back, but Steve and I would do it. Steve, actually, did a lot more work than I.

My brother and I were competitive growing up, and although I was three-and-a-half years older, he was always bigger than I, ever since he was five years old. He was a tough little guy. When he was a toddler, he stepped on a toothpick hidden in our carpet and it pierced the skin between his first and second toes. All we could see was a little end sticking out, yet he never showed an ounce of pain. As my mother was getting ready to take him to the hospital, Steve reached down and pulled it out himself. Another time, he was bitten by a German shepherd, which was bad enough. But the doctor gave him a series of rabies shots in his stomach using a huge needle. He said it wasn't so bad the first week, but the second week of shots did hurt. Ouch.

I used to pick on him, but around the time I left for Wagon Wheel, when I was thirteen and he was ten, I knew my days of pushing him around were numbered. Even when Steve was little, he was big and strong and eventually grew to six feet in height. I was fast and wiry, but it was just a matter of time before he could take me. So I tried to stop bothering him and treated him with more respect.

A few days after returning from Providence, I got carried away during a wrestling match with Steve. I gave him a hard pinch on his chest and he jumped up and chased me out of the house. He tackled me and threw me to the ground, holding me down with his legs on my arms. It was over. He had this huge grin on his face, the kind that said, "Don't ever mess with me again, brother. Or else."

Steve had it tough while I was away. He was responsible for mowing our huge lawn with a small tractor and spent a lot of time in the garden helping my father plant, weed and harvest. Although we never talked about it, I sensed he resented that I wasn't around to help. He was burdened with a lot of responsibility with none of the rewards. I got to skate and he was mowing the lawn every week and taking care of the dogs and the geese that made their home in our backyard pond. We wouldn't get close until I was much older, after my amateur skating career was over and he had completed a stint in the U.S. Coast Guard.

After school got out in June, my mother drove me back to Wagon Wheel. In Rockton, there were many changes under way at the rink. Mr. Brunet fell ill and had to take a medical leave from teaching. There was a tragic side to my coach, a part of him he never let on to his students. He had married his pairs partner, Andrée, in 1929 and they had had one child, a son named Jean-Pierre. By the mid-1940s, Jean-Pierre was blossoming as a skater; he was a novice pairs champion for the U.S. and filled with promise. But in 1948 he died in an auto accident, and people around Mr. Brunet say he never really recovered from that tragedy. All the time I was training with Mr. Brunet, his wife Andrée was very sick, which took a lot more out of him. Mr. Brunet also suffered from a chronic shoulder injury and was in constant pain. There was a lot of anguish and heartache in his life.

In Mr. Brunet's absence, a coach and choreographer from the East Coast was recruited to work with some of his and Slavka's students, including me and Gordie. Her name was Mary Ludington, a onetime Ice Follies skater who was recently separated from Ron Ludington, a prominent pairs and dance coach who would go on to coach Kitty and Peter Carruthers to an Olympic silver medal. The rink also brought in another coach from Los Angeles, Evy Scotvold, who taught Gordie's biggest rival, Terry Kubicka.

With Mr. Brunet, I improved my figures and got my double Axel. Taking from Mary, I became the beneficiary of her superb choreography skills. We didn't see eye-to-eye on my training habits, though. I thought one run-through a day was plenty, just like Gordie. Mary wanted me doing double run-throughs. Stamina work was hard for me, and my mother told Mary my childhood illness probably had something to do with it. Still, Mary kept after me.

I moved up to the junior level at the start of the 1975 season, and after winning regionals I moved on to midwesterns, which were held at Wagon Wheel. I entered the free skate in fourth place and needed to pull up one spot to make nationals.

On the night of the long program, the crowd was pulling for me because it was my home rink. I was feeling high-strung and jittery. I couldn't stop moving and I thought Mary was going to have a coronary if I didn't calm down. As I got ready to go on the ice, I looked up in the stands and the place was packed. I never remembered it being so hot. Mary tried to calm my nerves. "Everything's going to be okay. You're going to do fine," she said.

Before my long program, Gordie and his girlfriend, Kath Malmberg, the number two ladies' skater in the country at that time, approached me in the warm-up area. There was commotion all around us and people calling out my name, but Gordie and Kath had my complete attention.

"Whatever happens, we love you, Scott," Kath said. She gave me a hug and then Gordie grabbed my arm. "Just go out and skate well."

That gesture really fired me up. "There are a lot of people behind me," I thought. "I'm not going to disappoint them." I went out, hit my double Axel, skated clean and moved up to third place. A month later at nationals in Oakland, I fell a couple of times and finished seventh out of nine. Yet I came away from the experience feeling optimistic about my future. I told Mary later, "I think I'm starting to get the hang of this."

After nationals, I went home to Bowling Green to take a break and finish up my junior year of high school. In February we had a birthday party for Steve, who had turned thirteen. Later that night, my mother and father took me into the living room. They had been quiet all week and now they seemed almost ashen.

"Scott," my mother said. "I have cancer."

I was stunned, and even more shocked to learn that she and my father had kept it a secret from me for almost four months. Back in November, Mom had felt two lumps on her breast and the doctors had diagnosed malignant melanoma. She had surgery immediately—a modified radical mastectomy where the doctors removed the lymph nodes in the left arm, and part of her left breast. Then she underwent chemotherapy, which made her very sick. But I didn't know about any of this. Everyone had kept quiet around Steve and me during the Christmas holiday, and I didn't suspect a thing when I later saw my mother in Oakland for nationals.

I didn't really grasp just how serious the situation was. It was never explained to me that her illness was life threatening, and the sense I got from my mother was that she was feeling fine and in control. Clearly they were protecting me from the truth. I knew my skating was central to my mother's life, and the last thing she wanted to do was burden me with any distractions.

That winter my mother continued with the chemotherapy program, and she spent a lot of time at home sick in bed. She bought a wig after her hair fell out and wore it outdoors and around the house. Dad was awesome helping her out, and Steve and I chipped in around the house. My mother tried to stay upbeat. We spent a lot of time talking about my skating and the next year's programs. Each day when I came home from practice, we always talked about what jumps I was working on and my goals for the upcoming season. She found solace in the activities of everyone around her.

Unhappy with her treatment program, Mom contacted the National Cancer Institute and was referred to Massachusetts General Hospital in Boston. In June, after I returned to Rockton to resume training, my mother went to Weymouth for her parents' fiftieth wedding anniversary. Her mom and dad were also kept in the dark, since Nana Helen tended to get overly emotional at bad news. Mom and Aunt Marjorie did their best to cover up her illness. Because she was feeling sick during the reception, Mom spent part of the afternoon seated at a table monitoring the guest book. Then without her parents finding out, she went to Mass General to have a melanoma tumor removed. When she returned to Bowling Green, she began commuting with Dad to Columbus to undergo a new chemotherapy treatment.

In Wagon Wheel, I was undergoing an attitude adjustment. Mr. Brunet had scaled back on his teaching, and it made more sense for Mary to work with me full-time. Slavka was also gone. She had married television skating commentator Dick Button and left the area. I moved out of the dorm and into the home of one of the skating families, who lived near the rink. My parents felt I would benefit more in a family setting away from the bustle of the dorm.

Since Mary's strength was in choreography, Evy Scotvold helped her with some of her students, including me. His strong suit was jumps and figures, but he also had a disciplinarian style that Mary felt I could benefit from. Working with Evy was a whole different experience compared to Mr. Brunet. Evy was known for his energy and toughness. He doesn't coddle his skaters; he works them hard and tells them exactly what he's thinking. Evy and Mary would eventually marry and one day work as a team to guide Paul Wylie and Nancy Kerrigan to Olympic silver medals. But at Wagon Wheel, they were young and ambitious coaches on the cusp of making it big.

Evy's prize student was Terry Kubicka, a senior man who had finished second to Gordie at nationals the past two years. His skating style was the exact opposite of Gordie's, the ultimate showman. Terry had a ton of athletic talent and could land all his triples through Lutz. At practice each day, Terry did multiple run-throughs and always hit his jumps. I was in awe of his back flip and delayed double Axel—he would jump in the air and instead of rotating immediately, he would hold back for a moment, and then rapidly execute the turns. It takes tremendous athleticism to pull it off. It came as no surprise to me when I heard Terry was one of Brian Boitano's all-time favorite skaters. They were very similar in their ability to jump and train.

Watching his main rival work day after day was too much for Gordie to bear. It drove him crazy, and Slavka wasn't around to lean on anymore. Training with Kubicka and dealing with Slavka's departure drove away whatever love Gordie had for competitive skating. He was miserable, so after he won his third nationals and finished fifth at the world championships in 1975, Gordie retired. Besides, I know he wasn't looking forward to nationals the following year, since it was going to be held in Colorado Springs. Gordie despised skating in altitude, and the Broadmoor arena was a mile high. While it's a shame he quit the year before the Olympics, Gordie was just ready to turn pro and tour with an ice show. He was destined to be an entertainer and that was what he did best. He and Kurt Browning are the two best show skaters I've ever seen.

Many great skaters from that era didn't get much recognition because they didn't win an Olympic title, and Gordie was one of them. But the U.S. Figure Skating Association certainly appreciated his contribution to the sport by inducting him into the Hall of Fame in 1998.

The biggest change for me in 1975 had nothing to do with coaching or living away from the dorm. It was supposed to be my last year in skating. My parents were on the verge of bankruptcy. The money from the house was gone, my mother couldn't work and more than half of my father's $16,000 salary was eaten up by my skating bills.

They had broken the news to me shortly before I left for Rockton in June.

"We can only pay for it one more year," Dad told me. "Your mom can't teach; she's got to concentrate on getting better. But she wants you to skate one more year."

I loved to skate, but I agreed it made perfect sense. My mom took priority now. I sat there thinking that I should have known how tight the money situation was. I knew we were poor compared to most skating families. Several months earlier at midwesterns, I had wanted my mother to come to the competition party with me and socialize with the other Wagon Wheel parents, but she didn't want to go because she had nothing to wear. And she didn't have the money to go out and buy a nice dress. My mother was very self-conscious about her appearance and she was afraid she would embarrass us with her bare-bones wardrobe. I begged her to go, and she agreed, but only for my sake. At the party, I could see in her eyes she was hurt and embarrassed. It was even tougher at nationals matching wardrobes with the other mothers. Although none of these people would ever make anyone feel bad about how they dressed, Linda Fratianne's mother, Virginia, was a striking woman. So was Mrs. Babilonia, Tai's mom. Mrs. McKellen was always dressed to the nines. At competitions, the stands were always filled with women in designer dresses, furs and diamonds. My mother's plain blouses and skirts paled in comparison. My father's voice brought me out of my trance.

"After nationals next year, you can come home, finish up high school here, and start up at Bowling Green in the fall of 'seventy-six," he said.

My parents had it all mapped out for me. Funny thing was, I didn't feel angry or sad over the news. While I would have preferred to go on skating, I wasn't exactly setting any rinks on fire, figuratively speaking. If I couldn't skate any longer, it was no big deal. I was the seventh-ranked junior in the country, and had a long way to go before I could contend at the senior level. As for their plans for me to go to college, well, I was never much of a student, but it seemed like a pretty cool lifestyle. I could live on campus, teach at the rink, and maybe become a schoolteacher.

During my fourth year at Wagon Wheel, something came over me. I didn't kick back and go through the motions. I actually skated with a sense of urgency. Now that I knew I was a short-timer, my intensity and desire doubled. I worked my tail off and got hungry. It wasn't just about skating well enough to stay on my feet and get through my program any-more. I got hungry to win.

Mary and Evy were the perfect coaches to exploit my new attitude. Mary scolded with the gentle caress of a satin glove, while Evy had the tact of a grizzly bear. It was good cop, bad cop. What drove me crazy about Evy was that he meted out his punishment quietly. I could respond to yelling, and apply the criticism, yet when Evy gave me the silent treat-ment, I felt desperate and frustrated. He could be the greatest guy in the world one day, and mean the next. No one ever knew which Evy was going to show up at the rink. On the other hand, I was a results guy and I saw the success Evy had with Terry Kubicka. Maybe there was something to the tough-love tactics after all.

I had a big breakthrough the week of Midwestern Sectionals in Den-ver, Colorado. One day at practice, Evy and I were working on the triple Salchow, and I landed it for the first time. Easy. Somehow, my body just got it and I hit three in a row. Well, after the first one, I was jumping up and down like a crazy man.

"Calm down," Evy snapped. "Don't ever show emotion. If you land something, ho-hum it. Always let your competitors think that you do this all the time. Never cut them any slack."

After the lecture, he nodded toward the ice. "Now go do another one."

I turned around, circled the rink once, and then glided into my jump, leaping off a left back inside edge, three rotations, and landing on a right back outside edge. Clean again. Man, I couldn't believe it. I wanted to do a somersault right there, but this time I kept my cool. I pretended I did it all the time.

The plan was to insert my triple Salchow in the long program. My mother was against it because I had only just gotten the jump, but Mary told her not to worry. There was no harm putting it in. On the night of the free skate, I ran into Evy and Mary at the hotel and they told me to meet them later after dinner and we'd all go over to the arena. I went to my room and waited by myself. I was nervous, pacing back and forth, feel-ing the precompetition anxiety that tied my stomach in knots. Fortu-nately I could walk out on the balcony and see Evy and Mary eating dinner in the restaurant below. I felt better knowing they were nearby.

When I checked on them a few minutes later, they were gone. Where were they? I was feeling sick to my stomach. I surveyed the parking lot and saw Evy getting into his car. I assumed they were going to drive around to the front of the hotel and pick me up. I grabbed my skate bag, went downstairs and waited in the lobby for ten minutes. They never showed.

My old friend from Fort Wayne, Brian Maier, was skating in the competition, so I called his mother and asked for a ride to the rink. My event was going to start in less than a half hour, and I was frantic. Mrs. Maier rushed downstairs. We hopped in her car and sped over to the rink. When we arrived, Evy was waiting in the lobby, furious at me. "Where the hell have you been!" he yelled.

While Evy was dressing me down, I spied Gordie watching this unpleasant scene unfold. He was in Colorado coaching Kath, his future wife. Gordie came over to try to calm us down. I reminded Evy that he had promised to pick me up, but he wouldn't hear of it. He said it was my fault. I should have yelled at him from the balcony or chased him down in the restaurant. Finally I went to change, and when I was out of Evy's sight, I just broke down sobbing. Gordie was there, trying to console me. "It's going to be okay," he kept saying.

I just looked up at Gordie and started rambling. "No, that's it. I've had it. But I'm a man. I can deal with this. Just to hell with him."

"Scott," Gordie said, grabbing me by both shoulders. "Get yourself together. You're on the ice in like two minutes."

I composed myself, changed into my costume and skates and went out for my warm-up. I was supposed to win this competition, and indignant or not, I wanted to skate well and hit my triple Salchow. I knew I needed that jump for nationals, which were coming up in three weeks in Colorado Springs. Two guys from California who would surely be there—Robert Waggenhoffer and Mark Cockerell—each had two triples in their programs. I went for it that night and missed it terribly, just as my mother had feared. I came down right on my butt and hit so hard I didn't feel like getting up. I got right back on my feet—I was a skater from Wagon Wheel, after all—and finished out the program strong. Despite the fall, I won midwesterns, and that was a big confidence booster for me going into nationals.

I went back to Wagon Wheel and resumed training. Sometimes I couldn't get a break with Evy. When I left for Christmas vacation, I skipped a morning patch session to pack my bags. On my way to the airport, I stopped by the rink to say good-bye to everyone. I walked up to Evy and stuck out my hand and wished him a happy holiday. He just turned and walked away, clearly steaming because I had missed practice. That was how we parted for the holidays. I was off to Bowling Green and wasn't going to see him again until nationals, but it never mattered what the circumstances were; he wanted to let me know who was boss. This tough-love approach was something Evy's father, a hockey coach, had used to motivate Evy when he competed. So he used the same approach with his skaters.

There were times I felt he was unfair, yet for every slight there was an incredibly generous gesture that made up for it. Evy could motivate me with a casual wink or a nod. When a skater got that much from him, he knew it was the equivalent of one hundred "good jobs" from another coach. That look of satisfaction on his face made me feel that I had accomplished something, like the day I got my triple Salchow. Sure I was being manipulated, but it seemed to be working.

Colorado Springs, the site of the 1976 nationals, was about a two-hour drive from Denver. The competition was held at the famous Broadmoor arena. I came to town feeling strong and consistent, and I was in the best shape of my life. Mary and Evy had gotten me doing double run-throughs during the season for the first time in my skating career.

The makeover carried over from the rink to my appearance. In the week leading up to the competition, Mary decided I should perm my hair and go for the same look as Terry Kubicka and British champion John Curry. "You look like a blond-haired cue ball," she said. My life was one unending bad hair day and I was resistant to the idea, but Evy promised to make my life miserable if I didn't get it cut, so I did it. I wound up with an Afro so peculiar-looking that Mary, I learned later, wanted to wash it out. I figured if it was good enough for John Curry, who would win the gold medal in a few weeks at the '76 Olympics, it was fine for me.

During the week of practice, I was landing my triple Salchow only 50 percent of the time. As far as I knew, this was going to be my last nationals, and I felt distracted and depressed that I wouldn't be skating anymore. I started out the week skating to a fourth place finish in figures, and then I got a huge break. Reggie Stanley, the favorite to win the junior title, placed first after figures but pulled out of the competition with a sprained ankle. It was a piece of good fortune because had he managed to stay on his feet the rest of the way, he was far enough ahead that he probably would have won. His coach, however, didn't want to risk further injury and Reggie withdrew, throwing the championship up for grabs.

I skated a clean short program, and jumped into second place after two events. I was behind Los Angeles skater Mark Cockerell and, while in position to place for the first time ever at nationals, I was down in the dumps because my career was coming to an end. My mother picked up on my downcast spirit. The day before the long program, we had breakfast at the hotel. "I've got some great news," she said. "You're going to be able to keep skating. You don't have to quit." I pressed for details but she wouldn't say anything more. "I'll explain everything after the competition," she said. "Don't mention a word of this to anybody."

I promised not to breathe a word. It was terrific having a new lease on my skating life.

The following night during the warm-up for the free skate, Evy called me over. "Don't warm up the triple Salchow; just do three nice doubles."

Mark skated first. I didn't watch but he hit a triple Salchow and a triple toe loop. Mark and I would become great friends, and in 1984 we both made the Olympic team. But in Colorado Springs, we were two relatively anonymous junior skaters trying to make names for ourselves.

With Mark hitting two triples, I would need to land my Salchow to have a chance at winning. When I took the ice, my mother and father were nowhere in sight. They didn't like watching me skate at these big competitions; it made them too nervous. On this night they were pacing in a corridor beneath the stands as my name was announced to the crowd. At the last minute, a friend talked them into taking a seat.

For my long program, I was skating to *Carmen,* and as the first strains of music filled the rink, I was still on a high from the news that I wouldn't have to quit. I thought, "It's meant to be." I hit my triple Salchow and both double Axels and won the junior national title.

At the competition party later in the week, I still hadn't come off my cloud. I hung out with a group of close friends, including a Boston pairs skater named Peter Carruthers, who was adopted like me. He skated with his adopted sister, Kitty. My mother and father also went to the party. This was their moment, too, as it was for my coaches, Mary and Evy, who could lay claim to coaching the junior and senior men's champions, since Terry had won the senior title and with it a berth on the 1976 Olympic figure skating team. Mary was especially excited as she went looking for my parents, because she had some great news for them. She was aware of our financial problems and had lined up a sponsor to cover my expenses so I could continue skating at Wagon Wheel.

That night, when my mother and father approached Evy and Mary, they held out their hands. "This is good-bye," my mother said softly.

Then she broke the news she had kept from me all week. I was leaving Wagon Wheel to begin training at the Colorado Ice Arena under Carlo Fassi, all expenses paid by an anonymous donor.

Mary was hurt and my parents were so sorry. Though Mary tried to explain she had just obtained a sponsor for me herself, my mom and dad had already committed to Carlo and my new sponsor. I was told the same day and had mixed emotions. I was thrilled that my skating career was saved, but sadly, it came at Evy and Mary's expense. Switching coaches is never easy. It's a harsh reality of the skating world, and good people get hurt. I know my mother had my best interests at heart. My new sponsor had financed Dorothy Hamill's skating career, and Carlo was arguably the top coach in the world. He was teaching both Dorothy and John Curry. He had coached Peggy Fleming to an Olympic gold medal in 1968 when I was still toiling in rental skates. There was security in that picture. My mother had a fatal disease and she went with the team she felt was best for my future, a future that she suspected might not include her.

Chapter Five

Breaking Through

Now I knew why my mother had been acting strange all week, as if she had something to tell me but couldn't get the words out. Her arm was in a sling because she had recently had a radical mastectomy. She actually didn't need it to support her arm; she wore it to keep people at a safe distance so they wouldn't bump into her. My mother was in a lot of pain. Because of her condition and all the traveling, I expected her to be tired when she arrived in Colorado. But she was unusually content all week, like a cat with a canary.

It turns out she had been in touch with Nancy Meiss, and asked for her help in finding me a sponsor—someone who would cover all my skating and living expenses so I could keep training and my parents could get back on their feet financially.

Nancy knew of a Chicago couple, Helen and Frank McLoraine, who had sponsored Dorothy Hamill. Frank, an attorney, and Helen, an investor, were limited partners in Denver's Colorado Ice Arena, where I had just won midwesterns a month earlier. The top pro and general partner there was Carlo Fassi, who had come to America in 1961 after the tragic plane crash at the world championships wiped out the U.S. figure skating team and many of our country's top coaches. Now he was on the verge of guiding two skaters to Olympic gold, Hamill and John Curry.

When Nancy contacted Carlo and mentioned my name, he was interested in taking me on, and thinking ahead—all the way to the 1984 Olympics. Carlo had guided many skaters to the top of the podium, but never an American man. It was the one thing in his distinguished career he had yet to accomplish. Carlo liked the idea of teaching me and told Nancy to get in touch with the McLoraines.

Though Helen and Frank had never met me, Nancy and Carlo put in a good word, and the McLoraines agreed to meet with my mother and father. My parents borrowed some money from my grandparents so they could fly to Chicago and then make a connection to Colorado Springs to watch me skate at nationals. They met the McLoraines during the stop over at O'Hare Airport. Over lunch, my parents talked about my career and recent progress and explained to the McLoraines they were in dire financial straits.

Carlo wanted me, which was enough for the McLoraines. But my parents made a great impression on them, and Frank and my mother especially hit it off. "He reminded me so much of Grandaddy," she told me later, comparing Frank to her father, Everett. "He was funny and so kind."

Frank, whom I called Big Mac (he was five feet, ten inches tall and weighed 200 pounds), had an infectious laugh, and people were drawn to him like moths to a lamp. He was like the Jimmy Stewart character in *It's a Wonderful Life,* a big giver with a million friends who would do anything for him.

When my mother arrived in Colorado Springs, she wanted to give me the good news right away. But Carlo swore her to secrecy. He didn't want me getting distracted.

The day after my parents gave the news to Mary and Evy, I was feeling awkward because they would be putting me on the ice for an exhibition I was scheduled to perform. At nationals, it's a tradition that senior medalists and the novice and junior champions perform the day after the competition ends. It's considered an honor and a reward after a long week of hard work, a relaxed moment a skater can share with his coach and family without all the tension of competing. Evy and Mary made it easy for me, however. They were gracious to me and kept a polite distance. I knew they were hurting. They had given me so much, and I felt disloyal.

But my mother and father's decision made sense. Mom felt she was living on borrowed time, and one of her goals was to provide me with a secure skating environment. In her estimation, the combination of the McLoraines, whom she grew to love, and Carlo, who had a great track record, was unbeatable. Evy and Mary knew my mother was up against a life-threatening illness, and I believe they understood that any decision she made was done on my behalf, and was no reflection on them.

After nationals, I flew back to Wagon Wheel, packed up my room and stopped by Hononega High to tell the principal my plans. The school didn't want to give me any credit for the year because I was leaving in January and wasn't going to finish out the semester there. One administrator told me, "We cut slack to all the skaters and you're spoiling it for the rest of them."

"I have to leave," I explained. "I'm not dropping out. I'll be attending school in Bowling Green and Denver if I have to."

I left Rockton with the situation still unresolved. At home, I enrolled in Bowling Green High and explained my situation to the assistant principal. After reviewing my records, he told me I could make up the second quarter with three weeks of intense study. I hit the books—hard—and made up the schoolwork.

After I moved to Denver in February, I flew to Chicago to spend a few days with Frank and Helen, whom I met briefly in Colorado Springs. They lived in a big cozy house on a lake in the suburb of Winnetka. They had a massive yard and an indoor swimming pool. It was the largest house I had ever set foot in, but Frank and Helen made me feel instantly welcome, like a member of the family. Frank was a golfer and he introduced me to the game, which is now my favorite diversion. One day he grabbed a nine iron and took me outdoors in the freezing cold to show me how to swing a club. We went swimming in his indoor pool, and on Sunday morning, we got up at 5:30 A.M. and drove to Big Mac's favorite bakery for butterscotch coffee cakes.

On Monday we went to downtown Chicago for the Saint Patrick's Day Parade, bought a couple of green shakes from McDonald's and had dinner at Frank's favorite restaurant, Hackney's Hamburgers. We would be back many times over the years and I always ordered the same thing—a French dip sandwich with fried mushrooms.

In Denver I lived with a skating family, the Hills, and bought my first car, a used Volkswagen Bug. I loved that car. I hung a cord from the rearview mirror and called it my "pickup line." I completed the second semester of school at John F. Kennedy High, but in the end I was still a credit short of earning a diploma, so Bowling Green High floated me a physical education credit. Since I was a junior national champion, that wasn't too hard to swing. Kennedy High agreed to transfer my credits to Bowling Green, and I returned home for June commencement, graduating with the class of 1976—right on time. I was very proud of that accomplishment, and so were my parents.

That spring, I was invited to skate in the Colorado Ice Arena's annual exhibition, "Show Time on Ice," starring Dorothy Hamill and John Curry, the newly crowned Olympic champions. Dorothy was emerging as the star of the games and she had a huge contract with "Ice Capades." She was represented by a famous Hollywood manager, Jerry Weintraub, and she was breaking new ground for figure skaters. In a few short months, she had gone from being an ice-skating star to an international celebrity. Every girl at the rink—and across the country—cut her hair like Dorothy's. She had even been featured on the cover of *Time* magazine wearing a costume with a sweetheart neckline. Unfortunately, in the picture you could see her bra sticking up from beneath her outfit, and America's sweetheart took a lot of good-natured kidding for that.

The night of the show, a skating friend of Dorothy's, June Clark, threw a Kahlua party. I went with a new friend from the rink, Brent Landis, a local hockey player whose parents had rented a room to Dorothy while she was training with Carlo. We hung around for a while and then decided to leave. We walked into a bedroom to grab our coats, and there were Dorothy and her boyfriend, kissing. Stunned and embarrassed, I should have just left the room. Instead I blurted out the first thing that came to mind. "Is that the bra you wore on the cover of *Time* magazine?"

"Yes, it is," Dorothy said evenly. "Now good night."

Brent and I got our coats and left. Good thing Dorothy was retiring and about to join an ice show; I'm not sure I could have faced her every day at the rink after that blunder.

A couple of days later, I had my first lesson with Carlo. He was very serious and all business. We wouldn't become good friends until years later, long after I had finished training under him. Carlo commanded a lot of respect. His reputation was second to none in the skating world. He surrounded himself with a great team, including his choreographer wife, Christa, who complemented his expertise in compulsory figures. I would need every bit of his influence and talent to challenge the best skaters in the country. Terry Kubicka had retired after the '76 world championships, which left Charlie Tickner, David Santee and Scott Cramer as the frontrunners for the 1977 U.S. men's title. Scott trained at the Broadmoor in nearby Colorado Springs, a rival rink to the CIA. We would get to know each other very well over the next couple of years.

The most important thing Carlo gave me was a true understanding of compulsory figures. I learned to trace them with rhythm and timing and improved my control so I could retrace figures within a fraction of the first tracing. I also enjoyed the international feel to Carlo's rink. It was much different from Wagon Wheel. Carlo attracted skaters from all over the world—Finland, Japan, Great Britain, Canada and Italy.

Robin Cousins, the British champion, came all the way from England to work with him. Robin was having a hard time getting any respect from international judges for his figures, until he started training with Carlo. His marks and placements improved each year, and he would go on to win the Olympic gold medal in 1980. Carlo used to drive him crazy sometimes. On freestyles, he'd ask me to demonstrate jumps for Robin because I had good technique. It made me feel pretty good, but it drove Robin up a wall.

Carlo's other talent was his ability to lobby international judges, who respected him a great deal. This was where Carlo's European roots put him at an advantage over his American counterparts. He could speak their language, often literally. At a competition, he could get a judge's ear and say, "Watch this skater; he's really improved." That judge then passed the word and that's how he got things done. Having Carlo in your corner was sometimes good for two or three places at competition time.

I received immediate dividends from my association with Carlo. On May 22, 1976, a date I'll always remember, I passed my eighth figure test—the one that qualifies you to compete internationally as a senior—on the first attempt, and Carlo had a lot to do with it.

For my eighth test, I first needed to complete twelve figures—six tracings on each foot. I had a great panel. Two of the three judges were a very passive husband-and-wife judging team who would pass a skater simply for showing a basic command of the figures. The third judge was Jean Goldstein, who had a reputation for being scrupulous and hard-nosed. She wouldn't hesitate for a minute to fail anyone who didn't deserve a passing mark. She was tough, but fair. Carlo probably assumed I had it in the bag because the first two judges were lenient, and all you need is two out of three. However, I got passing marks from all three. Jean put me over by three-tenths of a point, which was pretty good for her. Then came the freestyle test—a five-minute program in altitude. In those days, senior men had to skate five-minute-long programs, which could be a painful spectacle to watch if the skater showed up to the event out of shape. (The International Skating Union lowered the time to four-and-a-half minutes after the 1981 season, where it remains today.) During my test, I was gasping for air the entire time, but I completed the basic elements—including a triple toe loop and Salchow—and survived.

For passing my freestyle and figures tests, I earned gold medals in both disciplines. It's a major milestone, like getting your Ph.D. in grad school. I called my mother, who was in the hospital again for treatment, this time at the Arthur C. James cancer clinic in Columbus.

"Scotty, I'm so proud of you," she said. "All the hard work has paid off. I'm so happy." I could tell from the tone of her voice that she was tired. Then I heard her sobbing.

"Are you okay?" I asked.

"I feel great," she replied.

I skated well in my first international meets, placing second in Oberstdorf, West Germany, and third in Saint Gervais, France, where I celebrated my eighteenth birthday with an all-nighter. The next morning, I was on a plane to New York, and Nancy Meiss, who had judged my event, wanted to go over my marks. All I felt like doing was crashing, but to avoid being rude, we talked the whole trip back. Once we landed at JFK, we went our separate ways. I changed to a plane heading for Chicago to spend some time with the McLoraines, and fell asleep the second it lifted off the runway. When I woke up, the plane was sitting on the tarmac in Kansas City. I had slept through the Chicago stop and left the McLoraines waiting at the gate! I caught another plane back and then took a cab to their house.

Before returning to Denver, Helen and I went to Columbus to visit my mother, who was in the hospital again. I hadn't seen her in almost two months, and her health and appearance were deteriorating. She was thin and gaunt and didn't have her usual energy. She still had the same remarkable smile, though. I sat holding her hand as I told her about my trip to Europe. I imagined that this was what it must have been like for her years ago, when I was a sick little boy confined to a hospital bed.

"The doctors are going to operate again," she said. "They want to remove a cyst."

Another surgery? I could tell she was crestfallen. "It'll be okay," I said. "Remember, you can always count on an Ohio State doctor leaving a scar in the shape of a football."

My mother laughed. It was a familiar sound. I could almost close my eyes, listen to her cheerful voice and pretend all was well. It wasn't.

Melanoma is an insidious cancer that comes and goes in the body as it pleases. Just when it appeared my mother was turning a corner and getting better, the cancer would show up somewhere else. She went from having tumors removed from her skin to losing her left breast. She had gone through chemo, radiation and several surgeries, including a hysterectomy. It was looking very bad for her, but I tried to stay optimistic. It was hard to admit what was happening because I loved her more than anyone.

She was such a fighter. Near the end of my visit, she told me she was feeling good today because a young couple she was counseling earlier in the year had gotten back together after breaking their engagement. Even while she was sick, and entitled to conserve her energy, my mother tried to touch as many lives as she could. In this case, the bride had been diagnosed with cancer and had a double mastectomy. Her fiancé wasn't the problem, my mother explained; it was the woman. Because she felt unattractive and unworthy of her fiancé, she didn't want to go through with the wedding. My mother knew what that felt like and somehow rebuilt the woman's self-esteem.

"The wedding is back on," she said.

"What a wonderful gift you gave them," I told her.

To share and connect with people suffering through emotional turmoil, while she was fighting for her own life, was incredibly generous.

My mother was completely open with her students about her troubles, and I think her honesty and integrity drew people to her. She was teaching a marriage and family relations class, and her cancer experience was a frequent catalyst for discussions on larger issues, like death and dying. She had her situation in perspective and never hesitated to share her ordeal if it could help other people.

Helen and I left the hospital and went to an ice rink nearby to say hello to an old coach, Mr. Grassi. I hadn't seen him in ages. I knew he was in town because he had been visiting with my mother. They had long since patched up their differences, which seemed so small compared to what my mother was enduring now.

"Scott," Mr. Grassi said, "your mother is so proud of you. The one thing she said she wanted to see you accomplish was becoming a senior, and you did it."

I knew my mother had bigger dreams for me. When I was a little boy still training in Bowling Green, a reporter from the *Sentinel-Tribune* asked me if I had ever dreamed of going to the Olympics.

I hemmed and hawed a little. It's one of those questions skaters don't usually ask other skaters. It's not good etiquette.

"Yeah, I want to skate in the Olympics," I told him. "But I don't think I'm good enough to get there."

My mom was watching nearby and she made a face at me and shook her head. "Uh, maybe I will get there," I said, changing my answer. "But I probably won't win. Maybe I'll get second or third." Now if only crack the whip was an Olympic event, I was thinking, I'd definitely win the gold.

When I returned to Denver, I had trouble getting back into training. It wasn't Carlo's fault; I just couldn't duplicate the intensity of the year before. I skated poorly at midwesterns and finished third—barely. After I accepted my bronze medal, Charles DeMore, the president of the USFSA, approached me and warned, "You damn well better skate good at nationals."

People were expecting a lot more from me than I had to give. Instead of bearing down and training hard, I had spent the fall building a reputation as a party boy. Now that I was eighteen and legal, I started exploring Colorado's 3-2 beer bars. Brent Landis and I had a favorite hangout, a disco called After the Gold Rush. We'd get all decked out in our Jordache jeans and wide-collared rayon shirts, and hit the town in Brent's Camaro. While I was no John Travolta, I knew how to have a good time. I wasn't messing around with drugs or anything, just beer. Still, my reputation preceded me. Veterans like Charlie Tickner, who trained at another rink in Denver, thought I had a bad attitude. He was warning the up-and-coming skaters to keep their distance. Charlie once pulled aside a young Paul Wylie, who trained with me at the CIA, and warned him: "Don't be like Scott. He's wasting all his talent by partying all the time."

I spent most of my weekends at Brent's house. He lived on a lake and his parents owned a speedboat. When Carlo got wind that I was water-skiing, he told me to knock it off. Instead, we were just more careful about what we said around the rink. I started calling water-skiing "power swimming," and power swimming was fine by Carlo.

Approaching the 1977 U.S. National Championships in Hartford, I didn't heed Mr. DeMore's warning. Part of the problem was that I had low expectations. It was my first year in seniors and I was aiming for a top-seven finish, at best. But I lost sight of the importance of simply skating well.

It was looking good for me after figures; I was somehow in fifth—a shock beyond shocks. That meant I had some solid politics going for me. Thank you, Carlo. I didn't think at the time I had figures that would put me in the top five, but as I said before, having Carlo in your corner was often good for two or three places. I was beginning to think something special might happen. My mother had made the trip from Bowling Green to see me compete, and I wanted to skate well for her. I could tell she was tired and expending a lot of energy. She would come to practice and then go back to the hotel to rest. It was all she could do to get to the rink.

But my desire to skate well for her wasn't enough to overcome my poor training habits from the past year. And it caught up with me. In the short program, I made mistake after mistake and didn't do much better in the long. I dropped all the way down to ninth. I was pathetic. My mother tried to lift my spirits. "It's your first year in seniors," she said, trying to play down my bad performance. "There's a lot going on right now. You'll be back next year."

I went back to Denver in a funk. In Bowling Green, the prognosis for my mother was bleak. Then she had a terrible setback. Our family doctor, Andrew Klepner, was diagnosed with cancer himself and died after only three weeks. My mother was able to spend some time with him before he passed away, but her system could not handle the shock. Her spirit sank, along, I believe, with her will to live.

I went home to see her in March. She was taking medication now and resting at home, feeling better than she had in a while and reminiscing about the old days when I skated in Bowling Green. As she spoke, my mind was wandering a little. I was thinking about her illness and my own shaky medical history. I had just met someone who was adopted and was looking for his birth parents. It piqued my curiosity because I was interested in my own past.

"Mom, can I ask you something?" I said.

"Sure." She nodded.

"I wonder who my birth parents are?" Before I even finished the sentence, I could tell from the look on her face that I had hurt her feelings. The last thing in the world I wanted to do was offend her.

"Is there something we've done? Have Dad and I let you down in any way?" she said quietly.

I fell silent and regretted bringing the subject up. "We've tried to give you everything," my mother went on. "We love you and have sacrificed for you."

"I know, Mom. I'm sorry. I didn't mean anything by it."

"It's okay," she said, trying to make me feel better. "Can I tell you what I think makes someone a parent? It's the person who changes a child's diapers; feeds him; takes him to school; helps him with his homework; hugs him when he cries and offers advice and perspective. A parent is there to hold a child when he needs stitches and washes his hands when they're dirty. A parent is someone who is there for a child every day."

"You're right," I said. The conversation about the identity of my birth parents ended right there. It was clear to me now. I had just one mother, and I was looking right at her. And as the years went by, I never would pursue my birth parents. I would come to believe what my mother did; that just because you bring someone into the world doesn't make you a parent.

A couple of days later, Mom felt well enough to make a trip to Fort Wayne to watch me perform in an exhibition. It was the city she used to drive me to every weekend for lessons with Mr. Grassi. After she returned home, she had another setback and was back in the hospital in Columbus, this time for ten days before she was well enough to return home.

I went back to Denver to train and then came back to Bowling Green in early May. Mom was in critical condition and the doctors were urging her to do another round of chemotherapy. She refused. Now it was just a matter of time.

Helen McLoraine flew in with her mother for a visit. On May 9, Helen's mom celebrated her birthday at my house, and later on they went to the hospital to see Dorothy. They walked into her room and there was a large chocolate cake on her food tray. My mother was smiling. She had asked some friends from the university's home economics department to bake her a cake so that she could give it to Helen's mom on her birthday. Helen was overwhelmed by the gesture. That was my mom, considerate of others even when she was feeling her worst.

On the night I performed in the annual "Ice Horizons" show, my mother wanted to come watch me skate one more time. She begged the doctors to let her go in an ambulance but they wouldn't allow it. My father videotaped the entire show and then we took it over to the hospital to play back for her. But she wasn't strong enough to watch the whole performance. Before it was over, I looked over at Mom and she was sound asleep.

The next day I went back to the hospital and she was feeling better. We talked briefly about a new romance, a skater named Jamie Armbruster. My mother loved hearing about my love life. It made her happy that I trusted her enough to confide in her about my girl problems. Half the time she could tell what I was thinking before I said it. Jamie lived in Perrysburg, Ohio, near Bowling Green and some thousand miles away from Denver. We hardly ever got to see each other, and I didn't know whether we should break up or try to keep up a long-distance relationship.

"What should I do?" I said. "She's in high school up here. I'm always training and traveling."

My mother smiled. "Follow your heart, Scott. Do what you think is right." I could tell she was very tired. I sat with her for a while longer and she began to doze off, so I left the room. Sadly, it turned out to be our last conversation.

As the week went on, Mom became more disoriented, and she eventually lapsed into unconsciousness. Family and friends had been making the pilgrimage to Bowling Green to see her. Sue and her husband Michael came to town, so Steve and I took turns sleeping on the living room couch. My father was in bad shape. There was a side of him coming out that I had never seen before, a hopeless and devastated side. One afternoon we went for a walk and he started opening up about Mom. I don't think he felt comfortable talking to Steve, who was only fifteen, or Sue, who had been away from home now for several years. He knew how close I was to her, and that was a bond we shared. As he spoke there were tears in his eyes.

Since I was away from home most of the time, I was sheltered from my mother's pain and suffering, but my father saw it, felt it, from up close. He lived for her and cared for her day and night, and now he was so frustrated over not being able to help her. He took her to the hospital, helped her recuperate from surgery, spent countless nights with her in the hospital. But when she was in pain, all he could do was watch helplessly. He felt bad that Steve had to bear the brunt of his absence. And now these difficult times were coming to a rapid close. I was worried about him.

On May 18, my father came home shortly before midnight. He had stayed by her side for most of the week and needed some rest. I drove over to the hospital with Michael and Steve to sit with her. She was asleep and on all sorts of pain medication. I couldn't really look at her so I sat in a chair and looked around the room, decorated with get-well cards and drawings done by my niece and nephew, Tammy and Tim. She was only forty-eight years old, and I didn't want to remember her like this.

We left the hospital at 3 A.M. and went home. I fell asleep on the couch. When I woke up, the sun was out and I could hear tractors plowing the soybean fields behind our house. I looked up and saw Michael. "Your mother's gone," he said. I nodded and quietly replied, "Okay," and then turned away. I lay there for a long time, relieved that her suffering was finally over and depressed that I'd never be seeing her again. I regretted that I hadn't been around more the past couple of years so I could have spent more time with her when she was well.

Finally I got up, got dressed and walked outside to sit by the pond, I don't know for how long. I was in my own world for three days. It was as if a wall had been erected around my body. Helen called to check up on me but I didn't feel like coming to the phone.

Aunt Marjorie, Uncle Bill and my cousins came to town for the funeral. The memorial service was held at the First Presbyterian Church and it was jammed with mourners: neighbors, friends from the university and the skating club. As my mother wished, we cremated her remains and buried her in Memorial Gardens cemetery, just a ten-minute walk from the Liberty Hi house.

I don't think I can describe how brutal it was watching my mother die of cancer. Like my father, I felt helpless watching her strength and vitality, her love and generosity, succumb to disease. She was tortured. I don't know how else to put it. Twenty-two years after her death, I still can't put her loss behind me. I've met a lot of people who have accomplished amazing things, yet I have never come across anyone who exhibited her strength. She persevered through the death of a child, raised a family while going back to school, and gave it everything she had during her two-and-a-half-year fight with cancer.

But I gained something from the experience, too. She showed me how to reach for something extra when the logical decision is to give up. Most of all, she taught me to take responsibility for my ability. I had a special talent, only I was running around acting like I didn't know it, like I didn't give a damn. The time had now come to maximize my gift and not let it go to waste. My mother had worked hard and suffered much to keep me in skating. It was an awful burden to put on myself, but a part of me felt her death would be in vain if I didn't accomplish something in the sport. She had unwavering faith in my talent and my ability, more than I did at that time. Only after she died did I start believing in myself.

Winning juniors was one thing; the senior level demanded another level of commitment. I was the ninth-ranked senior in the country and needed to leap at least six spots to make the world team, which would represent the U.S. at the next world championships. Other than going to the Olympics, this is what every competitor shoots for. If I was going to make the top three, it would take an all-out effort; no more half-speed run-throughs or cutting short practices. And if I didn't make a move soon, I could kiss good-bye any chance of making the 1980 Olympic team.

A couple of days after my mom died, I had called Carlo and told him to get ready for my return to Denver. I was going to give him the best of the best and start fulfilling my potential. "I'm going to be everything my mom wanted me to be; I owe her that," I said. Carlo's clout in the sport was unmatched and his knowledge of school figures unquestioned. He could get me where I wanted to go, if I got some help with my free skating. I had a triple Salchow and a triple toe loop, but I needed another triple jump, and more consistency under pressure. I had to stop falling all over the place.

When I got back to Denver, my mind was made up to change my work ethic. I had left the Hills and moved into an apartment the previous summer, but I decided I would be better off living with a family again. So I moved into the home of a Bowling Green childhood friend and his father, Doug and Norman Bassett. I needed some stability in my environment, and living alone at this time wasn't conducive for an all-out assault on the ice. I needed support, and Doug and Norman were there for me. But when I resumed my workouts at the CIA, Carlo wasn't ready to work with me, nor did he seem to have the time. I don't think he was writing me off, but I didn't feel I was a big priority of his. He had a huge stable of skaters, and that didn't sit well with me because I needed more attention. Eventually he sent me all the way to Canada—Hamilton, Ontario—for my new programs.

It turned out to be a blessing. I spent several weeks training with coach Ronnie Shaver and choreographer Neil Carpenter. Neil is an amazing talent. He not only choreographed my short and long programs for the 1978 season, but later gave me two of my classic show programs, "Short People" and "The Chicken." Ronnie helped me work on my jumps, including a triple Lutz, which started getting very consistent while I was in Canada.

I never trained harder than that summer. When I got back to Denver, I worked out daily with another senior skater, Mahlon Bradley, Brad for short. He had a serious rivalry going on with a California skater named John Carlow, Jr. Brad and I interacted like a boxer and a trainer a week before a heavyweight fight. He'd be huffing and puffing through the last thirty seconds of a five-minute run-through and I'd yell, "Right now, John Carlow's already doing his second run-through and it's clean." That got him to push harder. When I did my run-through, we switched hats.

I was developing a rivalry with Scott Cramer, who skated seventy miles away at the Broadmoor Club in Colorado Springs. Scott had finished second at the Hartford nationals, so I had quite a mountain to climb to catch him. Although Charlie Tickner, the reigning national champion, also trained in Denver, I conceded that I couldn't catch him, nor could I overtake David Santee, a member of the '76 Olympic team who trained in Chicago and finished third in Hartford. My goal wasn't to be the national champion at this time, but to make the world team, which meant I had to place in the top three. I figured out early that Charlie and David were almost untouchable and veritable locks to make the 1980 Olympic team. They had the experience and the talent, along with solid politics. The skater I somehow had to displace was Scott Cramer. So whenever I needed a kick in the pants, all Brad had to do was mention Scott's name and I'd get my second wind.

By late August, I needed a mental holiday and a change of scenery. All over the country, there are summer skating programs where students can go and train on different ice and get a break from the usual routine. One of those places was the North American Training Camp, which holds its weeklong training sessions every August in Lake Placid, New York. Carlo was one of the top coaches in the program, along with Peter Burrows, Ron Ludington and Canadian pro Kerry Leitch.

Carlo took me there in 1977, and since he was the host coach in charge of camp operations, he asked a coaching friend of his from Philadelphia to look after me—Don Laws.

"I remember you from 'seventy-six nationals at Colorado Springs," I said when Don and I met. "You were Reggie Stanley's coach. I owe you a huge debt of gratitude for pulling him out of the competition."

Don laughed. He wasn't doing me any favors by resting his skater. He just didn't want his student to ruin his ankle.

Despite the name, these camps weren't about "training"; they were really designed for skaters to bond with other skaters and absorb the views of different coaches. The camp attracted talent from all over North America. Best of all, there were a ton of girls there.

I don't know if the camp organizers in Lake Placid were aware, but the schedule was custom-made for holding late-night parties. We arrived early each morning at 5:30 A.M. for patch sessions at the Lake Placid Olympic arena and the Gus Lussi rink, named after the legendary coach who trained Dick Button. Then there would be a long break during which most of us would eat and catch up on our sleep. At 5 P.M., we'd show up for the nighttime freestyle sessions and skate until 8 P.M. Then it was party time. We went out dancing, drove cars up and down the horse trails and hung out in a creepy old abandoned house everyone said was haunted. Then we'd head back to the dormitory and hang out until it was time to hit the sack.

One night I didn't fall asleep until 4 A.M. and was due on the ice in an hour and a half. When I got to the rink, I regretted the previous night's activities. The last thing I wanted to do was skate around in circles. That morning, we were doing rockers, a three-circled figure that requires 180-degree body turns and numerous head turns to follow the tracings. A half hour into the patch, I was exhausted to the point of double vision, and boy, was I sorry I had eaten breakfast.

I barely noticed when Don Laws and five other coaches came over to examine my figures. I was about to begin tracing the figure and was looking anemic when Don said, "Do you want to show me a rocker?"

I felt like answering, Do you want to see eggs and cereal all over the ice? "No, not really, Don."

He nodded and shrugged. "Okay," he said and they moved on to the next patch. Years later, I found out that he was in worse shape than I was that morning. I had spent the night whooping it up with skaters, and he had spent it partying with the coaches.

When I returned to Denver, it was back to the grind, but I felt rejuvenated by the Lake Placid experience. My skating had turned a serious corner over the summer. I was doing double run-throughs and hitting my triple Lutz in the short and long program. Not many other competitors had the jump. Carlo was very pleased with my progress. At the regionals I felt great. The competition was held at the CIA, and I was going to at-tempt to become the first American to land a triple Lutz in the short pro-gram. The great thing was that I was trying it in my home rink, where I had made the jump hundreds of times on the exact same piece of ice be-fore doing it in competition. When I hit it, Carlo jumped up and down and started yelling—he always got animated when his skaters did well. Landing the triple Lutz (in combination with a double toe) was a huge boost and gave me great confidence going into the Midwestern Section-als in Chicago. Because the top three American men from the year before were going head-to-head at this event, this was one of the most intense competitions anywhere in the world that year. I was up against all the previous year's medalists: Charlie Tickner, Scott Cramer and David San-tee. David was the favorite, since he was competing on home turf.

Ninth at nationals the year before, I was miles behind these guys. But I really felt I could make a move if I could hit my Lutz and stay on my feet. Not many of the top men could hit the jump consistently, and it set me apart from the rest of the pack. Of course, hitting it in practice meant nothing. I had to do it in competition up against the best, and that was the opportunity before me in Chicago.

Frank and Helen put me up at their house, and my father flew in from Bowling Green to stay with us. My dad had promised my mom before she died that he would take her place and never miss a major skating event I was participating in. We shared a room at the McLoraines' and he kept me up every night with his snoring, which I can laugh about now. Actu-ally, I didn't let it bother me. I was focused on the task before me and had a knack for blocking out any potential distractions. Frank was great all week. He'd drive me to practice and give me pep talks. He wasn't very knowledgeable about skating, but he knew the right buttons to push. "Skate the ice; don't worry about anything else. Don't get nervous; just take what the ice will give you." He was full of positive energy and I fed off it.

I finished fifth in figures—not a bad start, but I still had a ways to go to crack the top three. There was no room for error. The next day, before the short program, Frank and I went out to lunch at our usual spot—Hackney's Hamburgers—and I ordered the usual, fried mushrooms and a French dip sandwich. Then we went back to Winnetka and I took a nap. That night I skated first, a big disadvantage since judges may hold down your marks to leave "room at the top" for the other contenders. But I had the short program of my life, including landing my breakthrough triple Lutz in a combination with a double toe. Out of the corner of my eye I could see Carlo jumping up and down after I hit the combination. Win-

ning that short—beating Charlie Tickner, who would go on to win the
world title later in the season—was the biggest accomplishment of my
career to that point. The next day I was feeling so superstitious I didn't
want to do anything different, so we went back to Hackney's for more
deep-fried mushrooms. I absolutely gorged myself on mushrooms that
week, until they were sprouting out of my ears.

By winning the short, I threw the competition into chaos. As I was
getting ready for the long program, skating officials in Chicago were on
the phone with the USFSA in Colorado Springs, deciding what would
happen if I placed in the top three. Would that mean that a member from
last season's world team would not make it to nationals this year? Carlo
loved that I was throwing a wrench into the works. They ruled that all
world team members—Charlie, Scott and David—would receive auto-
matic byes to nationals, regardless of placement. They also would take
the top three nonworld team skaters in order of finish.

Skating to a long program set to the music of *Lawrence of Arabia*,
Aspen and *Star Wars*, I hit the triple Lutz again and took third place in
the event, finishing third overall behind Charlie and David. Scott
Cramer was fourth, a significant setback for him. After his long program,
he did something I had never seen before. He remained on the ice, defiantly waiting for his scores and staring down the judges. He was not
happy with the outcome. Chicago midwesterns would always be remembered as my opening salvo to the skating community: there was a new
skater on the block, and he was pretty darn good. As I stood on the
podium for the medal ceremony, John LeFevre, an executive with the
USFSA, hung a bronze medal around my neck and congratulated me.
"You had us scrambling pretty good last night," he said.

I had a three-week layoff before nationals in Portland, Oregon, and it
took a while for my new status to sink in. Suddenly I had the arsenal to
compete with the best skaters in the country, and a spot on the world
team was within reach. There were so many unanswered questions.
Could I hold myself together for three competitions in a row? Would a
national panel of judges recognize my new attitude and ability and reward me if I skated well in Portland?

I kept up my intensity in Denver and took the energy to nationals. In
February, the weather in the Pacific Northwest was forbidding: dark,
gloomy, cold and rainy. But I was in such a zone I didn't let it bother me.
I was focused and confident, and in my best shape in two years. I was feeling prepared as ever, and then I went to watch the junior men compete.
Out there on the ice, there was this skinny little boy who was turning
heads. I remembered him from a year ago, when he had a beautiful triple

toe. Now he showed up at Portland—with a stunning triple Lutz, the jump I had just managed to get at age nineteen. What got my attention—everyone's attention—was that this boy was just fourteen years old, a phenom in the making. I hadn't even made the world team yet and I realized that if I did, it was probably going to take everything I had just to stay far enough ahead of him so he wouldn't be a threat. After all, I had just jumped six places from the year before, and so could he. I was going to have to keep my eye on that Brian Boitano kid.

I repeated my solid performances from midwesterns—I was third in the short, hitting the Lutz combination again—and third in the long. Placing third overall, I made the world team. Even better, I beat my Colorado rival for the second time in a row, Scott Cramer, who finished fourth.

Until this year, I wasn't sure if Scott had known who I was. I was so far down in 1977 he probably didn't think I was a threat. Getting my Lutz changed all that. Scott had wonderful triple toe loops that he could do in combination with just about any jump, and big dynamic landings; he didn't have the Lutz. He also had a biting sense of humor. We had a mutual friend, Billy Schneider, who trained in Denver and at Scott's rink, the Broadmoor. So things got said that got back to me, and things I said got back to him. And by the time we reached Portland, it was pretty tense. We were civil, but barely speaking.

As I was waiting for the medal ceremony, I went back to the dressing room and saw how much losing his place on the world team meant to Scott. He was really, really upset. A small group of skaters—Tai Babilonia, Randy Gardner, and Michael Botticelli, a pairs skater from Boston—were consoling him. I felt bad. As much as I wanted to represent the U.S. in Ottawa, I was even happier about beating Scott. "He ought to go to worlds, because all I wanted to do was beat him," I thought. "I'm happy enough with that."

I didn't know it at the time, but my rivalry with Scott was about to take one of those turns where I would never feel sorry for him again.

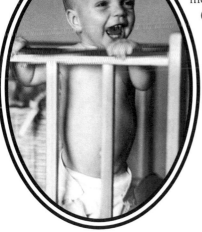

Already a handful at age 1. My parents had to put a top on that crib to keep me from climbing out.
(Hamilton family)

My mother, Dorothy, and I in our backyard. (Hamilton family)

My very first attempt at skating. I fell on the back of my head and wouldn't skate again for another five years.
(Hamilton family)

Grandaddy dreamed of making me a ballplayer. I could hit, just not for much power.
(Hamilton family/IMG)

The Hamilton family at Christmas in 1962. (Marjorie Ives)

Even when I was in kindergarten, my mother always took great pains to dress me in my Sunday best for my school picture. I liked bow ties because my father wore them. (Marjorie Ives)

Everyone cool in skating had a patch jacket, which let people see everywhere you'd ever competed.
(Cliff Boutelle/IMG)

In retrospect I'm glad I didn't give up figure skating for hockey. Here I am in 1969 as a member of the Ice Hawks.
(Cliff Boutelle/IMG)

In my third Ice Horizons show in 1970, I was the ring master of a circus and jumped through a fire hoop. (Cliff Boutelle/IMG)

Skating in Wagon Wheel in 1972. (Phil Martin)

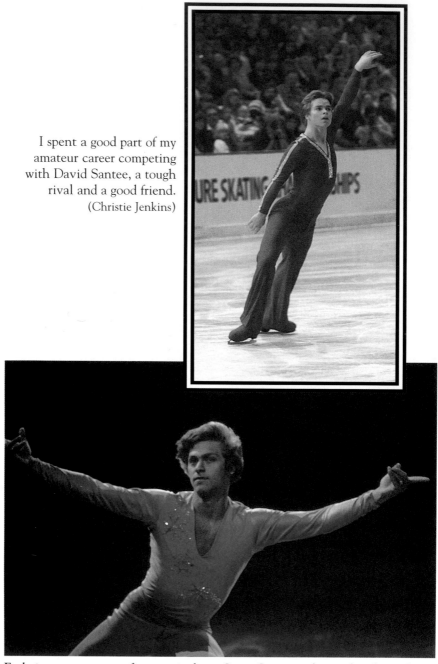

I spent a good part of my amateur career competing with David Santee, a tough rival and a good friend. (Christie Jenkins)

Early in my career, my fiercest rival was Scott Cramer, who vied with me for the last spot on the 1980 Olympic team. (Christie Jenkins)

Norbert Schramm, showing the flair that made him popular with audiences everywhere, competing at the world professional championships in 1984. (Christie Jenkins)

A master at choreography and showmanship, Robin Cousins was tough to beat at the world professional championships. (Christie Jenkins)

Carrying the American flag in the opening ceremonies was a highlight for me at the 1980 Winter Olympics. (Eric Schweikardt/*Sports Illustrated*)

I finished fifth at the '80 Olympics, setting the stage for the next four years. (Heinz Kluetmeier/*Sports Illustrated*)

Skating to "Georgia on My Mind" in 1982, I wore a stars and stripes costume because I wanted to let the European community know I was proud to be an American. During that time, I felt I was at a disadvantage being from the United States because most international panels had at least six European judges. (Laura Keesling)

I won my first
world title
in 1981,
edging out
David Santee.
(Domo/Steven Sutton)

Kitty Carruthers and I
on one of our many
getaways to the New
Jersey Shore in 1980.
(Kitty Conrad)

Waterskiing in Colorado in 1982. Carlo Fassi forbade waterskiing on my days off, so my buddies and I referred to it in code: we called it "power swimming." (Laura Keesling)

Wearing my woven bracelet in memory of my mother. (Laura Keesling)

Practicing figures with my coach,
Don Laws, in 1983.
(Laura Keesling)

Performing my long program at
the 1983 nationals in Pittsburgh.
It was the last time I wore my
beaded blue costume.
(Christie Jenkins)

On the podium with two good friends at the 1983 Nationals, Brian Boitano and Mark Cockerell. (Manuel Millan/*Sports Illustrated*)

With Helen McLoraine and my father at the 1984 Olympics in Sarajevo. (Personal collection)

Doing a Russian split in my long program at the 1984 Olympics. Pretty limber for someone who never took ballet. (Duomo)

I never missed a triple Lutz in my long program—this one is at the 1984 Olympics. (Duomo/Steven Sutton)

I carried the flag in my second Olympics, too, this time during a victory lap around the Zetra arena after winning the gold. (Duomo)

Celebrating on the medal
stand in Sarajevo with
Brian Orser, left, and
Jozef Sabovtik, right.
(Duomo/Paul J. Sutton)

Bringing the gold medal
back to my hometown
with the help of the
USFSL Denver Gold
cheerleaders.
(Tom Masamori/*Denver Post*)

Chapter Six

Roller Coaster Years

At my first world championships in Ottawa, I skated to an eleventh-place finish, not bad for my first time out. Considering that a year earlier I was watching the competition from home after finishing ninth at nationals, this was a quantum leap for me.

I wished it had been enough to get me an invitation to skate on the "Tom Collins Tour of World and Olympic Figure Skating Champions," a sixteen-city spring tour that showcased the best figure skaters in the world. The money wasn't huge—about fifty dollars a show—but it was a dream come true for an elite skater.

Competitors spent eleven months a year training and living on tight budgets. A few weeks out on the road with Tommy meant staying in first-class hotels, all the catered food we could eat and a thirty-dollar-a-day per diem. Best of all we got to skate for the fun of it before large and enthusiastic crowds, and somebody always threw a party after a show. Tommy's tour was as good as it got.

Tommy got his start skating in "Holiday on Ice" back in 1949, but later gravitated to the production side of the business. In the early 1970s, he came up with the idea to get all the top skaters from nationals and worlds on one tour and barnstorm arenas across the country. In my day, the show was on the road for only a few weeks, but today his tour, since renamed "John Hancock Champions on Ice," goes out in winter and summer, reaching almost ninety cities.

Though I didn't get invited to skate full-time on the 1978 tour, I was asked to perform in the show's last stop at the Broadmoor World Arena in Colorado Springs. It was a nice reward for the year.

On show night, I was the first skater after intermission. In the first half,

I waited backstage anxiously, pacing back and forth. Scheduled to skate after me were Charlie Tickner, David Santee, Linda Fratianne, Jan Hoffman of East Germany and two of Carlo's students, Robin Cousins and Susanna Driano of Italy. With that lineup, I wanted to make a good impression.

Finally, intermission came and went. "You're on in one minute," the stage manager yelled out. As I stood in the aisle, my view of the arena was blocked by a curtain. When I turned around, I saw Scott Cramer approaching. He was skating in the show, too, and he started making small talk with me. On the surface, I tried to be friendly with Scott, but our rivalry was so intense now it was at the point of no return. I had displaced him from the world team and he wanted that spot back. We had our eyes squarely on the 1980 Olympics in Lake Placid, and we both realized that probably only one of us would make it. David and Charlie, who had been around a lot longer than either of us, had the inside track on two of the three slots on that Olympic team. It was going to come down to either me or Scott.

As I was preparing to go on, Scott said something that made my head spin around. "It looks like I'm going see a lot more of you from now on," he said, ever so coyly.

"What are you talking about?" I asked, a little confused.

"Oh, I'm just going to be seeing a lot of you pretty soon," he said.

"What do you mean?" I was getting annoyed. Just as my name was being announced over the loudspeaker, Scott blurted out what he was getting at. "I'm going to start taking from Carlo."

There was no time to absorb what he had just told me. As I glided to my spot, my legs felt wobbly and my arms felt heavy, like a couple of 747 wings attached to a Piper Cub. When my music began, it was all I could do to get through my number. I was a mess, falling three times and cursing to myself as I tried to keep my composure. When I got off, I walked past the cast and crew and went straight to the dressing room. I changed into my street clothes, hustled out into the parking lot and drove back to Denver. I left so fast I forgot to thank Tommy and didn't even get paid for the show, something I needle Tommy about to this day. He still owes me fifty bucks. The whole drive home I was thinking, "How could this be happening? How could this be true?"

The next day I got a call from Carlo, and he asked me to come over to his house for a meeting. This was it; he was going to tell me he was teaching Scott. I drove over wondering what his rationale was going to be. As he sat me in his living room, he handed me a cup of coffee and then launched into his explanation.

"The combination this year for the short is going to be a double flip–triple toe," he said. "Scott's going to be very strong and I'd rather have him in the rink with you than dumping you off the team, so you're going to be skating together this year. I'll treat you equally. Don't worry about it."

I knew Scott could do the double flip–triple toe in his sleep, while my jumping style made it hazardous to my health. And so did Carlo. I wondered if he was giving up on me and taking his best shot with Scott.

"But Carlo, one of the reasons I made it this year was because I wanted to beat Scott," I said.

"I think if I teach you both, you'll both have a better shot at being on the podium together next year," he argued.

I didn't like it. I was convinced that Charlie and David were locks to make the world team next year, and that left Scott and me scrambling for the last place. How could Carlo lobby for both of us? Wouldn't he have to make a choice? Because I was Carlo's student first, I felt I deserved to be his highest priority. But I had a feeling all bets were off and I was on the verge of being dumped.

As the year went on, I came to the conclusion that Carlo's decision to take on Scott was politically motivated. He had once worked at the Broadmoor World Arena and wanted to do so again. It was the home rink for one of the most powerful clubs in the world, the Broadmoor skating club, with the clout to draw the national and world championships to Colorado Springs on a regular basis. The United States Figure Skating Association is also headquartered there, and I sensed that Carlo wanted to return to the power center. A position at the Broadmoor better suited his stature as world and Olympic coach. Of course, that meant he had to get on the good side of Thayer Tutt, the president of the Broadmoor Hotel, which included oversight of the Broadmoor World Arena. Now Thayer was married to the two-time U.S. ladies' champion Yvonne Sherman Tutt, a world judge, and the Tutts were friends of Scott Cramer's parents, Les, a prominent surgeon, and Annette, both of whom were judges and very active in the Broadmoor skating club. Thayer treated Scott like a son.

The Cramers are nice people who are still very active in skating. As Scott's parents, they supported him unconditionally and did everything they could to help him succeed. They wanted the best for him. It wasn't personal, but I was an obstacle in Scott's path. And his success, unfortunately, was contingent on my failure. I don't feel the Cramers' motivation to switch to Carlo was meant to hurt me directly, but clearly they wanted Carlo in their son's corner.

So I didn't blame Scott for going to Carlo. It was the right thing for him to do. But while I was friends with everyone else I skated with, I couldn't be friends with him. Once Carlo took him on, the stakes got even higher, and peaceful coexistence was impossible. Paul Wylie, another one of Carlo's students at the time, used to liken our rivalry to the one shared by Ilie Nastase and Jimmy Connors, on a smaller scale, of course. But make no mistake about it, Scott brought out my worst competitive instincts.

In May, Scott started coming to the CIA to work with Carlo once or twice a week. If Scott's motivation was to discredit my standing with Carlo, it worked brilliantly. All spring and summer, Carlo straddled the fence—does he support this Scott or that Scott? Which way was he leaning? An ugly situation was in the making.

To make matters worse, my worst fears about the double flip–triple toe came to fruition when I ripped my ankle to shreds trying to learn the darned combination. Since I wasn't crossing my feet when I turned the triple toe back-to-back, my feet were side by side coming out of the jump. One day my foot stuck in the ice and my body kept rotating, twisting my right ankle badly. I was in a cast for six weeks. The only blessing was that I didn't have to go to the rink and watch Scott hit the combination.

My ankle healed and in late summer I went to a skating camp in Squaw Valley, California, the picturesque ski resort in the Sierra Nevada Mountains where the 1960 Winter Olympics were held. I spent a couple of weeks training with Charlie Tickner, who had won the world title five months earlier in Ottawa. Charlie trained at Denver's South Suburban rink, just a few miles from the CIA, and we had become good friends. He was a champion and I looked up to him. I was feeling pretty good in California, and started trying triple Axels, and I was landing them clean. "Wait until Charlie sees this," I thought.

At that time, the jump wasn't needed to contend for world titles, and I had never bothered to perfect it. Besides, doing them irritated my ankle, so I eventually stopped fooling with them. But the Axel felt great in Squaw Valley. On the next freestyle session, I raced by Charlie and nailed a triple Axel in his face. He laughed and shook his head, and then started cussing me out in a good-natured way. I just smiled back at Charlie, who was a good sport.

Now even though Charlie was a competitor of mine, there wasn't nearly the intensity in our rivalry as the one I had with Scott. In fact, there was no rivalry with Charlie because I was not a serious threat to him. He was the number one guy and had a track record that made him nearly invincible. Instead of getting in my face, he went about his business with a quiet confidence that I admired. Dethroning Charlie was the furthest thing from my mind. I looked up to him and someday hoped to have what he had—a U.S. and world title.

Back in Denver, I hunkered down and began training hard. I had to make up for lost time from the ankle injury. I was all business at the rink and still remained estranged from Scott. At every practice, he seemed to go out of his way to do the double flip–triple toe combination in my face, and it started to wear on me. His triple Salchows were consistent too. Hitting five triples in a row was no problem for him. I never did get used to his working with Carlo, and preferred it when he wasn't around.

Artistically, many thought Scott was a cross between Gordie McKellen and Toller Cranston, the great Canadian champion. Scott tried blending Toller's avant-garde style and Gordie's show-skating techniques, but he often went back and forth between them. So I nicknamed him "Scott McKranston," which obviously got back to him.

One day at the start of the 1979 season, I went home after practice and began sorting through my mail. To my surprise there was a letter from Scott. It said our situation had gotten out of hand and that the competition between us should stay on the ice. "Back-stabbing has no place in the sport," he wrote. I'm reading this thinking, "Hmmm, is this a peace offering?" Then I got to the end of the letter, where he signed his note "Scott McKranston."

This required a return salvo and I had just the ammunition. Scott had once gone through Billy Schneider's address book, and sarcastically jotted down "Great Skater" next to my name. So I decided to write Scott back.

Dear Scott,

You're right about keeping the competition on the ice. See you at midwesterns.

Sincerely,
Scott, Great Skater

Nothing seemed to be going right during the 1979 season. First Carlo took on Scott. Then I started having trouble with the short program jump combination and hurt my ankle. Midwesterns were coming up and it promised to be another brutal competition. Charlie, David, Scott and

I, the top four skaters in the country, were going head-to-head again in another sectional. This time it was playing out on Scott's home rink, the Broadmoor, which did not bode well for me.

As expected, Charlie won midwesterns, Scott taking a solid second, with a third in figures, first in short, second in the long. David was third and I was fourth. I was fourth across the board in every event, and I came away feeling discouraged. My worst fears were coming true.

A month later I flew to Cincinnati, Ohio, for the U.S. nationals. It was an important competition, since the 1980 Winter Olympics were just a year away. The time for skaters to make their mark was now. During the week, I felt the momentum swing toward Scott. He was hitting his short program combination in practice and I was not. Carlo had many students in the event, so when he wasn't around to help, I relied on Don Laws to give me pointers. But no matter what Don said or did, I sensed those dreaded defeat clouds forming over my head.

I got off to a bad start in the short program, performing a double flip–double toe instead of the planned triple toe. David Santee did the same thing. I was in fourth after the short, Scott was in second with David positioned between us. The only chance I had of cracking the top three was beating David in the long program. David skated brilliantly and received a standing ovation. I skated my best, landing all my triples, including the Lutz and got the second standing ovation of the night. But when it was over, I finished fifth in the long program and fourth overall. David hung on to third.

I was upset for a number of reasons. I had skated well in the long, and Scott had not. Still, the judges held him up. Did I think Carlo might have had something to do with the results? I'm always going to wonder. But I'm not going to hold him responsible. It was obviously Scott Cramer's nationals. He beat me in practice all week and came in a solid second. I screwed up my short program and was penalized for it by being marked down in the long. From a judging standpoint, I can see why I was dropped. They wanted to send someone to worlds who could nail that double flip–triple toe combination, and Scott was their man. David was having trouble with the combination too, but he saved himself with a great long program. Before I left Cincinnati, a couple of judges came up to me and apologized for dumping me in the long program. "We had to make some tough choices. Just keep working hard and you'll be there again," they said.

I was bitter but I did learn something. You can skate great and lose, and you can skate lousy and win. It's an old cliché but true: all you can control is what you do, not what anyone else does. Still, when I left Cincinnati, I was emotionally spent and dejected. The McLoraines were upset with Carlo and not happy with the arrangement. I thought my career was unraveling before my eyes a year before the Olympic games. The loss in Cincinnati left no question in my mind that I didn't fit into Carlo's plans. Scott was his man now, and a coaching change seemed imminent, especially after working with Don at nationals.

The McLoraines also picked up the good rapport between Don and me. Over the past couple of years, they had become my surrogate parents. They tried to provide the love and support my mother would have. It was more than paying the bills. They came to all my shows and competitions, and though I didn't know it at the time, they always provided a plane ticket for my father so he could travel to see me skate without dipping into his salary.

Helen and Frank met with Don and gave him a big endorsement. I trusted them implicitly, but it was still my call. "Whatever you want to do," Helen told me in Cincinnati, "we're behind you."

I knew I wanted to make a switch. My only hesitations were that I was grateful to Carlo for saving my skating career . . . and there were potential reprisals if I left him. He was that powerful. Out of respect and loyalty, I wasn't about to make a break without giving him one more chance to keep me as his student. He had saved my skating career when my parents were flat broke, so I owed him that. The world championships were a week away when I asked Carlo if I could meet with him after a session. When the session ended, we met on the ice.

"Carlo, I just want you to know I've really been disappointed about the year and how it went."

"Yeah, I know, I know," he said.

I thanked him for everything he'd done. "Without your help, I wouldn't have made it to worlds last year. We've had three years together, good times and bad."

I paused for a moment, swallowed hard, and chose my next few words very carefully. "Here's my situation. The McLoraines said they would continue to support me no matter what. I have this opportunity to be coached by Don, if for some reason you have decided you don't want me around or can't give me the attention I need."

I let out a sigh of relief. There, I had said what needed to be said. Now the rest was up to Carlo. He had plenty of wiggle room to lobby me to stay. Carlo is ordinarily a very animated person, but he seemed unusually sullen at that moment. My stomach must have rolled over twice waiting for his answer. His next few words were important because they would tell me exactly what he was thinking. Finally he said, "Well, Don's a very good friend of mine. If you went to Don I wouldn't be upset and I wouldn't try to hurt you."

Carlo's answer was very clear, not so much for what he said, but what he didn't say: "I think you should stay. We can work together to make you a better skater." He didn't even say: "Let's talk about this." Instead, his not so subtle reply was, "Move on." I shook his hand and then skated over to his wife, Christa.

"Good-bye," I said.

"No, no, no. Don't leave, please don't leave."

"If Carlo would have said that to me, I'd stay," I told her resignedly. "I wouldn't even think twice. I'm sorry, Christa, I have to go. As much as I love you, there is no other way. Without Carlo's support, this place can't offer me anything. His interest lies with Scott."

I spent a couple of days saying good-bye to friends and making arrangements to move. Then I packed up my orange MG and drove home to Bowling Green to spend some time with my father before going on to Philadelphia to work with Don. Carlo took Scott Cramer to the world championships in Vienna, Austria, while I watched them on TV from home. Scott finished an impressive fifth.

Years later, I would look back and understand that Carlo's honesty was the best thing that ever happened to me. Not only did he give me his blessing and allow me to move on, but his rejection inspired me to work even harder on my skating. As I explained to Christa, part of me wanted him to beg me to stay. I wanted to hear him say that I was making a huge mistake going to Don. He gave me up without a fight, and for that reason I was hurt. Now I had something to prove to Carlo next time I saw him at the 1980 nationals in Atlanta. I was going to show him he had chosen the wrong Scott.

Chapter Seven

Carrying the Colors

After I arrived in Philadelphia in April, it rained for three-and-a-half weeks straight. I moved in with Robert and Barbara Camp, whose daughter Evelyn was a skater. They owned a large house in suburban Philadelphia, with plenty of room for one more.

Driving in the rain was awful. On my first morning of practice, the dashboard on my MG was leaking like a sieve. I ran out in the pouring rain, saw that my interior was soaked, and went back into the house to get some bath towels. I laid two of them over my legs and sped to practice, and I still got soaked.

Because the Philadelphia Skating Club and Humane Society rink in Ardmore was closed for repairs, Don and I would be skating in Valley Forge. When I walked into the building, Don was already on the ice, ready to go to work. I changed into my skates and went out to find a patch to make my figures.

"Good morning," Don said. "Are you ready to go to work?"

"Yes, I am," I said.

"Good. Now I want you to know that I'm well aware of your party-boy reputation. When you're on the ice with me, you work. Whatever you do off the ice is your business, but don't let me catch you. If you want to go out with your friends and stay out until five in the morning, go right ahead. But you will do a long program run-through the next morning and it had better be clean. And you can come and go anytime, but the door swings both ways, my friend. That's all I have to say. Now let's see a rocker."

He was speaking in a light tone of voice, but I got the message. I wasn't living up to my potential. He was close to Carlo and I'm sure they'd had plenty of conversations about me. While I was starting to develop some flair on the ice, my jumps, spins and figures still needed improvement if I ever hoped to make the Olympic team. Don was smart enough to know he couldn't drill it into me. It had to come from within.

My new coach was a Washington, D.C., native and had been coaching in Philadelphia since 1959. He was training several junior- and senior-level skaters, including Lori Nichol, who would go on to become a choreographer for Michelle Kwan. With his debonair smile and snow white hair, Don earned a special nickname from pairs skater Kitty Carruthers: the Silver Fox. The description was perfect. Don was tall and dapper, and smooth as silk around the ladies. I once told a writer, "I'd like to look like Don just once in my life, and see what I could get away with."

A month after we began working together, Don invited me to come along with him to a Professional Skaters Guild of America coaches convention in Atlanta. As president he was speaking and wanted to use me as a demonstrator in one of his on-ice seminars.

I was doing some different triple jumps for the coaches one morning when Don asked me to try a triple Axel. I hit five of them, every one of them better than the one I landed in front of Charlie Tickner the summer before. Though today the triple Axel is a mandatory jump for a senior man, they were a rare commodity in 1979. Vern Taylor of Canada had landed the first triple Axel in competition only the year before, at the 1978 worlds in Ottawa. And no American would start landing them with any regularity in competition for another few years. That day I went through them like butter. Don and I actually discussed working more on the jump, but since it aggravated my ankle we stopped. With my triple Lutz, a jump many senior men at the time couldn't do consistently, if at all, I was already ahead of the pack. Today the top men need six different triples to be competitive, and a quad or two, but we were figuring that three to five triple jumps would be plenty for the next few years. The triple Axel would have to wait.

On the night of the PSGA dinner, Don got up to speak before a packed hotel ballroom. I was feeling pretty heady after my triple Axel exhibition earlier in the day. "I've taken on a new pupil," he told the crowd. "And this pupil, from this day forward, will not resort to ice show comedy and will present himself and train himself in a manner that will be more beneficial to his skating career."

Wow, I thought. So that's the reputation I have to overcome. The other coaches in the room knew exactly who he was talking about. I was sitting at Don's table, and all eyes seemed to turn to me and my embarrassed reaction. I obviously had some work to do to start being taken seriously as a competitor.

Don's plan that first year was to whip me into top shape. I had slacked off the year before and needed some tough love. Not only did I work harder in practice, I put a moratorium on going out during the week. Those days were all behind me.

Living with the Camps made the adjustment easier. Barb Camp was a mother hen and I was one of her "chickens." She had five children of her own, and all but one had grown up and moved away. She treated me like a son. She loved doing mom things—cooking, shopping, mending my outfits. She was very nurturing and made me feel at home. It was an aspect of my life that had been missing since my mother died, and Barb, like Helen, helped fill the void.

For dinner, Barb frequently cooked my favorite dish: boneless breast of chicken with rice and mushrooms. We ate it so much that her husband, Bob, started to complain. "We're not having that chicken stuff again, are we?" he'd say before dinner each night. I'd gleefully reply, "Yeah, we are." Bob sometimes got so frustrated he ordered food from a pizza joint where I had a part-time job working as a delivery boy.

I kept a pretty low profile. The only complaint about me we ever got from the neighbors was about my noisy MG, which needed a new exhaust system. Each morning as I was leaving for practice, I had a tendency to wake up the entire neighborhood when I started up my car.

One afternoon I came home and Barb had clearly gotten an earful from a neighbor.

"We've got to do something about your car," she said. "The neighbors are starting to think there's a love affair of some sort going on inside the house, and the person who's leaving at 5 A.M. is making their getaway."

The only thing I was doing at that time of the day was entertaining the Camps' two golden retrievers, Gus and Heidi, who needed to be let out each morning to do their business. Only Gus wouldn't go outside unless Heidi went first, so half the time I was dragging Heidi by the collar, hoping Gus would stop crying and follow her outdoors to relieve himself.

Gus was amazing—he could hold five tennis balls in his mouth at the same time, and if you dared try to take one away, Gus snarled at you as if you were a burglar. In thunderstorms, however, he was a pussycat. I was once home alone in an electrical storm and the power was knocked out of the house. It was pitch-black, and Gus spent the entire time sitting underneath a chair whimpering like a baby.

Compared to my Denver days, Philadelphia was domestic bliss. I really thrived living with a family again and having someone look after me like Barb. With less responsibility, I could bear down and focus on my training. My nightlife was comparatively subdued. I became a big fan of The

Incredible Hulk TV show and filled my room with Hulk memorabilia, including a piggy bank. What can I say? It was a vicarious thrill watching a small guy like Bill Bixby get angry and transform into this massive green menace to beat up on bad guys.

I was all about skating that spring, focusing on one thing only: getting ready for nationals next year in Atlanta—the winners of which would go on to compete in the Olympics. I was happy to be away from Denver and not training with Scott any longer. It was probably better for both of us to be in separate rinks with separate coaches. Life was going almost too smoothly, and I started to get nervous. But the last thing I expected was losing another person close to me.

On June 7, I was in Squaw Valley at a training camp with Don when I got a call that Frank McLoraine had died. Don and I immediately flew to Chicago to be with Helen and attend his funeral. I was devastated. Frank was like a father figure to me, and a mentor to scores of his friends and acquaintances.

Helen had told me he became ill after returning from a trip to China the previous year, but I had no idea he was that sick. He was suffering from a degenerative blood disease, and Helen said they never really did get a satisfactory explanation for the cause of death. Frank wasn't the type of man to talk about his ailments. I remember during a visit to Chicago earlier in the year, a friend of his bumped into us while we were having lunch. "Frank, you look ill. Have you seen a doctor?" Big Mac's response was curt. "Yes, and he saw me."

Frank was popular and beloved by everybody. I think he believed he had to be strong for everybody else. Perhaps that's why he kept his illness a secret. If people had known how sick he was, all his friends would have been overwhelmed with grief, and I don't think Frank could have handled the fallout. It's not his way, and it just would have worn him out to have everyone feeling sorry for him. In some ways, I handled my cancer the same way. Though I let people know I was sick and that my disease was curable, I didn't allow them access to what was going on inside my mind and body. I turned down every interview request. I decided I needed to handle it on my own and didn't want to discuss it publicly until I had something positive to say. Otherwise I'd be exploiting the situation. It's ironic, but Frank was very private about his illness around people he was close to, and so was I. The public knew almost as much as some of my friends and family. The difference between Frank and me was the aftermath. Had he lived, I'm sure he still would have not shed any light on his illness. He only emphasized the positive.

Frank's family gave him a traditional Irish viewing, which lasted two days and drew hundreds and hundreds of people. Frank was a trustee of DePaul University and a member of the visiting committee at the University of Chicago Law School, his alma mater. It seemed as though he knew everyone in town. I went to the wake with Don, but I was so distraught I sat by myself in a chair in back of the funeral home. Don came over and sat down next to me.

"Are you okay?" he asked.

I shook my head no. "Why do all the people close to me have to be taken away?"

It was starting to gnaw at me. First Dr. Klepner, then Mom. In August 1977, three months after my mother died, her father, Grandaddy Everett, also passed away. And now Frank. What was going on?

At the funeral Helen treated me like a member of the family. I sat next to her during the service and was in awe of the number of people in attendance. How could one man have touched so many lives? The answer was easy: he was the type of person everyone could look up to, but not feel intimidated by, because he put on no airs and gave you all his attention. He was gregarious and enjoyed every minute of his life. He made people laugh and was incredibly approachable. I sat there thinking how Helen and Frank complemented one another so well. He could walk into a room and just take over with his humor and personality. In contrast, Helen was quiet and introspective. She would sit back, assess a situation and ask questions. She cared for him so much. What would she do without him now?

I was quiet on the flight home to Philadelphia. I didn't feel much like skating but I had no choice. The 1980 season was approaching fast, and we had to get my short and long programs ready. My first competition was in September at an important international event, the "Norton Skate" at Lake Placid, since renamed "Skate America." The USFSA wanted as many of its top American skaters there as possible, since judges from different nations would be scoring the competition. This gave the event huge international implications. Don and I knew U.S. skating officials would be watching the outcome closely, so despite the fact that it was early in the year, we wanted to be in peak form going into the "Norton Skate." Once again, I would go up against Scott Cramer and David Santee. This time around there was another person in my corner besides my coach and extended family—my girlfriend, Kitty Carruthers.

Kitty and I had met in 1976 while skating in a Jimmy Fund cancer benefit at Boston's Northeastern University. Like me, Kitty and her brother, Peter, were adopted. Physically they were a mismatch. He was ten inches taller and fifty pounds heavier than Kitty. Her heritage was

Lebanese; his was Dutch-English. But they had a nice dramatic presence. Kitty had amazing charisma and a huge smile, and hit the landings cleanly on the throw jumps better than anyone.

After the Jimmy Fund show, Kitty and I went out with a group of people and cruised around Boston. For the longest time that was how we did everything together—in a pack. We met again at the 1978 nationals in Portland, and I'd see her each summer at the North American Training Camp. But now they trained in Delaware at the Skating Club of Wilmington with pairs coach Ron Ludington, who won four U.S. pairs titles and an Olympic pairs bronze medal in 1960 skating with his sister, Nancy.

From the beginning I had a crush on Kitty, and whenever I saw her I'd just melt. And I knew I had a fighting chance because she laughed at my jokes, even the stupid ones. After my move to Philadelphia, we got to be closer friends, since she trained only an hour away.

There was so much to like about Kitty. Of course, she was beautiful— dark hair, dark eyes, striking smile; sportswriters used to refer to her as Cleopatra. But what I admired was her grit and toughness on the ice, balanced by kindness and loyalty off the ice. Pretty soon we were spending every weekend together.

The New Jersey shore was a favorite destination of ours. We'd visit the boardwalk, hang out in the arcades and go to concerts. It was hot in Philadelphia and Delaware in the summertime, and the shore was a nice getaway. Kitty loved to sunbathe, so we'd spend hours lying on the beach.

During the week, I trained early in the morning while they skated at night. We'd talk on the phone after lunch and spend part of the conversation egging one another on. If I had a good morning at practice, I'd tell Kitty, "Hey, I did a clean long today."

There would be a discernible pause as Kitty put down the receiver and called out to her brother, "Peter, we're doing a clean long tonight." We'd crack up at our competitiveness, but we fed off each other. We needed all the help we could get. I had to move up one spot to make the Olympic team, and they had to come up from seventh place to get into the top three.

Late in the summer, I finally managed to ask her out on a date. We went to the Mann Music Center in Philadelphia to see Mikhail Baryshnikov dance. From then on, I put a lot of miles on my MG driving between Philadelphia and Wilmington. I fell in love with her. I just absolutely fell in love with her.

On Fridays after my last freestyle session with Don, I'd hop in my car and head straight to Wilmington. I'd meet her at the rink and sometimes join her on a session. Then we'd go out and get something to eat. Other nights we took walks under the stars around the golf course that surrounds the skating club. (The road that winds through the course and leads to the rink was renamed "Carruthers Lane" after Kitty and Peter won their silver medal in Sarajevo.)

We'd usually end up back at the house Kitty was living in. The owner was a woman named Mrs. Sherwood, and she was always asleep when Kitty got home. We'd make a bowl of popcorn and watch old movies, and if it was Saturday, we'd tune in to Saturday Night Live. Mrs. Sherwood snored away in her bedroom. She was so loud the house practically shook. There was a nice simple quality to our relationship, uncomplicated by the pressures of winning and defending national titles. There was nothing better for me than having someone I truly cared about share my passion for skating. But that wasn't the only reason. I had dated skaters before, and Kitty was different. I knew it from the first time I met her in Boston, and at every nationals since, where I'd go out of my way to hunt her down and ask her to lunch or dinner. I think what attracted me most was her toughness. It reminded me of my mother, who was strong-willed and assertive in her own right. Kitty was my first true love, no doubt about it.

I turned twenty-one in Philadelphia, and Don took me out to celebrate my birthday. We went to Don's favorite restaurant, Horace P. Jerky's, which served a great veal Oscar. After dinner Don gave me a toast. "To a successful 1980 season," he said. Then he gave me a proposal: "We're going to drink our way from A to Z."

I was game. We started off with something called an Amaretto Sour and proceeded to work our way through the alphabet. There were some locals sitting at the bar, shaking their heads and warning us: "You're both gonna be sick."

Things got hysterical pretty fast, and while I can't remember anything after a gin and tonic, I know we each consumed a lot of drinks. Every time we knocked another down, these two middle-aged ladies watching us would chorus, "Oh, my God, look at that!" At the end of the night, I got a ride home and Don walked back to his house to sleep it off. When Don woke up, his hand was bleeding and he couldn't even remember how he cut himself. It was one of those nights.

The next day we met at our normal early morning hour at the Havertown rink, this cold, dark place I nicknamed the basement because they put on only half the lights to save on electricity. I was feeling hungover, and Don didn't look much better. I figured on an easy workout. Don had other ideas. "Okay, do your long program," he said.

I looked at him and thought, "You son of a gun. You took me out for my birthday, put me through that drinking game, and now you want me to do my long program? What a jerk."

I skated to my spot, calling him a few choice names under my breath. When the music came on, I decided I was going to show him. The "Norton Skate" was still a few weeks off, so I wasn't quite in peak form. Yet in this five-minute run-through, I hit my triple Lutz, toe loop and Salchow. I guess I was in better shape than I thought. When I finished, I was winded, but I didn't let on that I was tired. I just skated over to Don and said, "Anything else?"

"Nope," he said, "I think that'll just about do it. Good job."

In September 1979, I arrived in Lake Placid for the "Norton Skate." Besides David Santee and Scott Cramer, the field included German skater Jan Hoffman, the former world champion who would go on to win a silver medal at the 1980 Olympics. My priority now was to beat Scott. If I could handle him before an international panel of judges, I could go into the season as a favorite to make the Olympic team.

Oddly enough, the first figure of the competition was a left inside rocker, the very figure I didn't feel like tracing for Don at the North American camp two years earlier. No such problem today. I won that first figure. Jacques Favart, the president of the ISU, even remarked to Don how well I had done.

My fourth-place finish in figures was a great start, and put me in medal contention. Then I skated a clean short program, hitting my triple Salchow–double loop combination, and won. I actually beat the two Americans who had defeated me at nationals the year before, as well as Jan. No one expected this result, not even I. I must admit, I was daunted at the thought of beating a veteran like Jan, but in no way wanted to let this opportunity pass. I knew I had to finish everyone off. The trouble was, I wasn't used to being chased; I was always the chaser. By long program day, the anxiety was driving me crazy. Would I skate well? And if I did, would I get scored fairly? At the '79 worlds, Jan had placed third, Scott was fifth and David was eighth. Did I belong up here with these competitors? Don suggested I meet with Bruce Ogilvie, a sports psychologist working with the U.S. skaters.

"I'm not sure I'm supposed to be beating these guys," I told him.

"Screw 'em," Bruce said.

On the night of the free skate, Jan went out, struggled with his long program and dropped out of contention. It was no big deal for him. One bad meet early in the season would have no effect on his world standing.

Hoffman had been ranked among the top skaters in the world since 1973, so everyone knew he would be ready when it mattered most six months from now.

Then it was Scott's turn. He was in good position to pull up over Hoffman and take control of the competition. He went out and skated a nice long program, a clutch performance. After the marks came up, he and Carlo came backstage and began celebrating. I was getting ready to go on the ice and could hear them yelling, "We pulled over Hoffman, we pulled over Hoffman. We're gonna win the competition." I tried not to pay attention, but clearly they still weren't taking me seriously as a threat. Hearing Carlo and Scott act as if they had it all won was the last bit of motivation I needed. I put on my skating blinders and attacked this program as though I had something to prove. That night I opened with my Lutz, my most difficult yet most consistent jump, and didn't look back. Don liked me starting out with it because it grabs the audience by the throat. I also hit three triple toe loops and two triple Salchows. When the scores came up, I had pulled over Scott and won the "Norton Skate."

Scott was as shocked by the outcome as I was. The victory set me up for the rest of the season. In my mind, that spot on the Olympic team was now mine to lose. Something happened to me that week in Lake Placid. As much as I wanted to succeed, there had always been fear in the back of my mind that it was not meant to be, particularly after the disaster in Cincinnati. Don had spent the entire summer building my confidence and getting me in the best shape of my life. After winning at Norton—I hadn't won much of anything in almost four years—I really believed I was a good skater and deserved everything coming my way. All those ghosts and setbacks from my past seemed to vanish.

Scott may have gone into panic mode after Lake Placid. In November, he was scheduled to represent the U.S. in Japan's annual international meet, the "NHK Trophy." I was selected by the USFSA as the alternate. Three days before the competition, I was on a morning patch lesson with Don when he broke the news that Scott had pulled out of the NHK with an injury, and the USFSA wanted me to take his place.

"What should we do?" I asked, as though I had any say in the matter. I realized it was a foregone conclusion that I was obligated to go, even though we both knew I was unprepared.

"You're going," Don said.

"But Don, we're kind of in a down phase."

"It doesn't matter. You're ready and you're going."

I was furious. Although I'm certain Scott had a good reason for pulling out, I felt that he and Carlo were privately hoping I would compete there and fall on my face. David Santee was going to Japan, and if he knocked me off, it would restore Scott's position as the favorite to make the Olympic team. Man, I was feeling used.

It was a gamble, but one Don insisted we take. When I arrived in Japan, I barely had my legs under me. I was jet-lagged and not in the best of shape. I did okay in figures but skated a predictably bad short program. Rebounding in the long, I placed third in that event and pulled up to fourth overall. I didn't medal, yet I was happy for three reasons. First, I had beaten David in the long program for the second time in a row, proving that winning the "Norton Skate" was no fluke. Second, another international panel of judges had gotten to see me compete and skate well, which never hurts. And third, I came out looking like a trouper to the USFSA because I had gone to Japan on short notice and skated respectably.

In fact, the only downside to the trip was that I lost my job delivering pizzas. My boss fired me on the spot when I told him I couldn't come to work the next day because I was going to Japan. I don't think he believed me. It was no laughing matter at the time. With tips, I earned forty dollars a night and relied on the cash for spending money and putting gas in the MG.

The next month of practice leading up to nationals was intense. Earlier in the year, Don had said in passing that a skater knows he's in shape when he can do a double run-through of a long program at a 7:30 A.M. session. I never forgot it.

So on one unforgettable December morning, I did precisely that. Back-to-back run-throughs—ten consecutive minutes of skating with only a brief rest in between. Don was on another lesson, and after he realized what I had done, he skated over to me and said, "What the heck are you doing?"

He had this look of absolute panic on his face, as though I was about to jump off a building. "You said I would know I was in shape if I could do a double run-through early in the morning," I said.

"Are you crazy?" he replied. "You're gonna get hurt. It's too early in the day for that kind of thing."

We were so close now, Don didn't want anything to go wrong. I think he would have carried me by piggyback to Atlanta if it would guarantee I would arrive in one piece. He had nothing to fear, because when the time came I was in great shape.

Don and I flew down to Atlanta a couple of days before the weeklong competition got under way. All week I had great practices. I ate well and slept well. Politically speaking, my win at Norton and my decent showing in Japan had put me in good standing with the judges. You can never underestimate the power of politics in figure skating, particularly when skaters are close in ability. My hard work in the fall, combined with a week's worth of dominating practices, would make an impression on the judges. Last year, I felt Scott came into Cincinnati with a lot of momentum and he kept it up all week. I arrived feeling flat. This year I believed our roles had reversed, and people were going to notice.

Helen and my father were in town. We missed Frank, but somehow we knew he was close, sitting in a special box seat with my mother. It was as though I had two guardian angels now.

On the night I skated my short program, I was wearing a wristband a fan had given me two years before. It was a good-luck charm, a sailor brace-let of woven white fabric, something navy men wore at sea to assure them a safe return home. I thought it was cool so I slipped it on. Well, once this type of bracelet gets on your wrist, it shrinks and you can't get it off without cutting it away. But I had no intention of removing it. For some reason, the bracelet made me think of my mother. Wearing it guaranteed her presence.

Before going on the ice to compete, I rubbed the band. It was my way of signaling my mother to watch. I did the same before the long. The competition shaped up as I expected it would. Charlie and David skated strong and got first- and second-place marks. That left Scott and me vying for the final spot. I had already beaten him in figures and the short program. When I placed over him in the long, it was over. I had third and he had fourth. It was a close contest—split judging panels the whole way through. But since the Olympic and world team is made up of only the top three skaters at most, I was in and Scott was left as an alternate.

My bitter feelings for Scott subsided in the euphoria of making the Olympic team. Years later, in 1994, I would meet up with him again by happenstance. I was performing in the final show at the Broadmoor World Arena, which was being leveled to make way for new hotel rooms. After I skated, I was backstage mingling with old friends and spotted Scott across the room. He was a chiropractor now, working in the same building as his surgeon father, Les. He walked over, smiled and extended his hand. "I don't know how you do it," he complimented. "Thanks, Scott," I replied, "I don't know either."

It was a little strange running into him after all those years. We hadn't agreed on a lot of things, and I must admit I felt uncomfortable seeing him again because we were old and bitter rivals. But in his own way, he came over and acknowledged my success, and I appreciated the gesture. He went on to become a success in his field, too. He's a smart guy who didn't need skating to make a living. There was no grudge between us anymore. Rancor has a way of dissipating over time.

In Atlanta, all I felt was pure joy. I went to the competitor's party and was in a great mood all night, the complete opposite of how I felt the year before in Cincinnati, when I thought my career was coming to an end. The next day they took measurements for Olympic uniforms, and we posed for a team picture. That was very cool. What made it even more special was that Kitty and Peter had finished third and also made the team. We nicknamed ourselves the Dream Team and even had T-shirts made up to wear in Lake Placid.

On the flight home to Philadelphia, Don told me an interesting story about a couple of encounters with some judges in the aftermath of the men's event. One congratulated Don and predicted I'd be Olympic champion in 1984. The other said she was pleased to see me make the team but not to get my hopes up. I was too short to be a success internationally. I couldn't give a big enough impression on the ice.

It reminded me of the time I was a little boy and a judge put me second because I had too many double jumps in my program. It just goes to show you: don't take a judge's word as gospel.

Lake Placid, New York, held so many memories for me. I had competed in club events there as a child, attended summer camp there as a teenager and won the "Norton Skate" there last summer. Now Lake Placid was the site of the 1980 Winter Olympics. It was almost like having a home court advantage.

One of the best things about the '80 games was that I had no expectations to live up to. The *Washington Post* described me as an "Olympic nobody—just a fellow who finished a respectable third in the U.S. Olympic trials in men's singles." That suited me fine. I was just happy to be there, and my only goal was to finish in the top five and have as great a time as possible. I had made it to the Olympics—with my girlfriend, no less—and I wanted to relax and savor the whole experience.

That plan went haywire shortly after I arrived.

I had come early, a few days before opening ceremonies, to get used to the ice and hang out with my teammates. Kitty and Peter came early too because pairs was the first skating event of the games. One night, I went to see *Close Encounters of the Third Kind* with the Carrutherses, American ice dancer John Summers and Robin Cousins. Midway through the movie, John's partner, Stacey Smith, came into the theater, tapped me on the shoulder and whispered, "You're in big trouble. Meet me out in the lobby."

Stacey was a cocaptain of the skating team, and as I climbed over John and Robin to follow her, I wondered nervously what was going on. In the lobby, Stacey was waiting with pairs skater Michael Botticelli, the other cocaptain, and a few other teammates.

Stacey had this look of disgust on her face. "How could you disgrace us like that?" she asked.

I held my arms out wide and said, "What did I do?"

"You've really done it this time, Scott," Michael said.

Somebody said some team officials were on their way over to the theater to get me. After a few minutes of this, I was getting quite scared, convinced I had broken some obscure rule and gotten banned from the games. In my head, I retraced every step I had taken in Lake Placid. I hadn't missed a practice all week and had been on my best behavior.

"I haven't done anything wrong," I pleaded. By now there were about eight skaters in the lobby. I looked around and people started cracking up.

"Scott," Stacey said with a smile, "you've been elected to carry the flag in the opening ceremonies."

"Aw, c'mon," I said.

Stacey waved her hands. "No, it's true! Seriously, you're carrying the flag." Then she introduced me to Cindy Nelson, the downhill racer who had carried the colors in 1976. That was when it finally hit me. I didn't know whether to strangle somebody for the gag they'd pulled, or hug everyone in sight.

A week earlier, when we were being measured for our opening ceremony outfits, someone had mentioned that one of the athletes would be elected to carry the flag. I think I fantasized for about thirty seconds how cool it would be to bear the Stars and Stripes. Carrying your nation's flag, especially when the games are being held in your home country, has got to be one of the highest honors of the games. But the selection is made by the captains of all the U.S. teams, so why would they pick me? I was the last guy to make the team and had no chance at medaling.

What I didn't know was that Michael and Stacey had made a strong pitch for me at the captains' meeting. They talked about my childhood illness, how I almost quit because my family went broke; my mother's death and Frank's death. They recounted how I fought to make the world team in 1978, only to get dumped the next year because my coach started teaching my rival, and then reclaimed my spot on the world team this year. Apparently, the other captains agreed this represented the Olympic ideal and voted me in as flag bearer.

I skipped the rest of the movie and a group of us went to the athletes' cafeteria in the Olympic village to get a bite to eat. I was still so overcome with emotion that my hands shook as I poured some coffee and I spilled it all over my hands, scalding them. I was in pain but not enough to keep from the task at hand. I talked with Cindy for more than an hour about her experience as flag bearer and then I ran back to the dorm to call my dad, who was still in Bowling Green.

"Dad, you won't believe this. I'm carrying the flag in the opening ceremonies."

I couldn't see him, but I could tell from his voice there were tears.

"I'm at a loss for words," he said, his voice cracking. "I'm so proud of you."

It was getting a little mushy for me. "I'll see you in a couple of days," I said. "Make sure to call everyone and tell them to watch me on TV."

On the morning of February 13, the opening day of the games, I awoke in my room at the village feeling apprehensive about the responsibility lying ahead. I could barely eat any breakfast but started feeling better, as teammates were coming up and wishing me well. Then I went outside to wait for the bus to Olympic Stadium.

The transportation in Lake Placid was miserable, and the bus was an hour late, adding to my anxiety. Kitty and I rode over to the stadium together, and the whole time I was freaking out that I might do something horrible that would embarrass the country, like drop the flag or slip and fall. One screwup, I thought, and that was all anyone would remember of me for the rest of my life! It may have been a real joy and honor to carry the flag, yet the more I thought about it, the more stressed I became.

The driver stopped the bus by a snow-covered meadow outside the stadium and opened the door. The athletes filed out and we stood in the field waiting for our cue to enter. It was freezing, and the wind swirling off Whiteface Mountain made it even colder. We were all outfitted in Western-style gear: cowboy hats and suede jackets with sheepskin lining. We looked like a battalion of cattle ranchers lost on the range. Even though they took my measurements, every piece of clothing I had on was too big, which made my role even more potentially disastrous. My mittens were so large it was hard to get a grip on the flagpole. My hat was about three sizes too big and it kept slipping down my forehead. My boots were so oversize I had to wear two pairs of wool socks. Actually, that was a good thing, because they kept my feet warm in the freezing cold. Kitty and I did what we could to keep each other warm.

"This is way too much responsibility for me," I confided.

"Don't worry; you'll do great," she said reassuringly.

When it was time for me to go to the front of the line, the wind was blowing so hard I wondered if I would be able to control the flag. But once they strapped on my harness, it was easy to steady. For guidance I looked to Terrance Hanrahan, a local general contractor. He carried the U.S. placard and was a calming influence. "Just follow me," he said.

"If I start to fly away, will somebody please grab me?" I said.

As we began the march through the stadium gates, my hat was practically covering my eyes, not a good thing for the guy leading the hundred-member American team. A wrong turn would be deadly. There was a treacherous downward ramp covered with ice that served as the entrance to the stadium field. I was warned it was slippery. My doomsday headline for the day: "Skater Wipes Out while Carrying Flag into Opening Ceremonies." That I could do without.

To be on the safe side, I took baby steps down the slope and managed to stay on my feet, though each time I peeked down to check my footing, my hat slipped farther down on my face.

Once I was on firm ground in the infield, we were home free and I could start to savor the moment. I looked in the stands for my father and Helen and saw them waving. The army's skydiving Golden Knights jumped into the stadium from ten thousand feet and hit their marks. The Olympic mascot, a raccoon, bounced around the stadium in a frenzy. There was a marching band from Revere, Massachusetts, with baton twirlers leading the procession. Sure it was a low-tech production compared to Olympics to come, but I felt chills of pride and had a lump in my throat the size of a snowball. This was it. This was what I had worked for all those years—to take part in an Olympics.

As we circled the stadium briskly, I was very conscious of carrying the flag at just the angle Cindy had showed me. Vice President Walter Mondale was in the reviewing stand, and as we passed him by, I held the flag firmly at the same slight angle, honoring Olympic tradition not to dip it for any dignitary.

Earlier, the flag bearers had been instructed that when the procession was over, we were to take the flags out of our harnesses and rest the poles on the ground. But when I came to a stop and looked down the long line of athletes, nobody had put down their flags. If I put my flag down, it'll be a national disgrace, I thought to myself. I wasn't going to be the only wimp. So I held it up for the next two hours. When the ceremony was over my arms were cramped—good thing I wasn't competing in the biathlon—but the sacrifice was worth it. I spent the next several days walking around the Olympic village feeling ten feet tall.

For the rest of the week, I went to practices and stuck close to Kitty. My event wasn't starting until later in the week, but Kitty and Peter were competing on the second day of the games.

In the pairs event, the teams to watch were Americans Tai Babilonia and Randy Gardner and Irina Rodnina and Alexander Zaitsev from the U.S.S.R. Tai and Randy were defending world champions, only the second American pairs team ever to win a world title. I had known Tai and Randy since 1970, when we met and became friends at my first Golden West Championships in Culver City, California. Matched together when Tai was nine and Randy was eleven, they went on to rise rapidly through the pairs skating ranks. In 1974, when I was still a struggling novice-level skater, they finished second in seniors, and won their first of five consecutive national titles two years later. In their day, they carried the sport in this country and were the dominant skating personalities of their era.

The Russians seemed to have a stranglehold on Olympic pairs competition. Rodnina and Zaitsev had won six consecutive world championships since 1973, and the only reason they didn't compete in 1979 when Tai and Randy won was that Irina was having a baby. On top of that, Irina and her first partner, Alexsei Ulanov, had won four straight world titles starting in 1969. So coming into the 1980 Olympics, Irina had won ten world titles and two Olympic gold medals with two partners, and she wanted a third.

Tai and Randy were one of the teams standing in their way. There had been a big buildup in the media about the showdown. Ten days before the games, Randy injured a left groin muscle attempting a double flip in an exhibition. He knew he was badly hurt, but he and their coach, John Nicks, kept Tai in the dark about the seriousness of the injury because there was a chance Randy might heal in time to compete. He was coming along fine until two days before the event, when he reinjured his groin and hurt his hip. His only chance of skating was trying a painkiller, so two hours before the pairs short program, Randy was injected with xylocaine in the hope that he could perform if the leg was numbed. During the warmup, the answer came fast: he could neither jump nor spin, nor could he feel his leg. Before a worldwide television audience, they withdrew from the event. Tai was in tears. Rodnina and Zaitsev went on to win the gold, Irina's third, and then she retired from the sport.

I felt terrible for Tai and Randy. This was their moment, and it was snatched away by an unfortunate injury. No wonder Don had panicked a month ago when he saw me doing back-to-back run-throughs early in the morning. He was afraid something like that might happen to me.

Kitty and Peter had a great competition. They skated brilliantly and shocked everyone by finishing fifth, two places ahead of Americans Michael Botticelli and Sheryl Franks, who had finished second to Tai and Randy at nationals. I had never seen Kitty so happy in her life. Just a year earlier they had been seventh at nationals, and now they'd finished in

Lake Placid as the highest-ranked American pairs team. They had set themselves up perfectly for next year, when they'd be favorites to win the U.S. title.

The men's competition followed pairs. I had a good week of practices. In figures I finished eighth, so I had to make a strong move in the free skate events. Skating to "Sabre Dance," I went out and stuck my short program, hitting my triple Salchow–double loop combination cleanly. I got an incredible hand from the crowd and took fourth. Now I was in fifth place overall, so I would be in the final group of six to skate, a huge honor for me. It also put me in a good position to get in the top five. For the long, I skated to *Mutiny on the Bounty*, and made one small mistake at the end of my program on a triple Salchow. The standing ovation started with twenty seconds left in the program and got so loud I couldn't hear my music. I finished fourth in the long and fifth overall, one place behind David and two behind Charlie, who won the bronze medal. The silver went to Jan Hoffman, and Robin Cousins, my old friend from the CIA, got the gold. Robin said in his press conference later that I would be the next Olympic champion.

When Kitty and I were all finished competing, we treated the next week as vacation time. We went everywhere together—movies, concerts, dancing. The Lake Placid harbor was the hot spot with the best disco clubs, and we bumped into numerous celebrities—NFL football stars, TV actors, rock musicians and singers. Away from the excitement, we had some private time together back at the Olympic village.

Kitty and I loved watching the U.S. hockey team play. The games were extra special because I was friends with two members of the team, Kenny Morrow and Mark Wells, who played hockey at Bowling Green State University. One night I went to dinner with Helen and then sprinted over to the arena to watch the last two periods of the U.S. team's historic 4–3 victory over the Soviet Union. My tickets were way up in the bleachers with some other skaters, but between periods we sneaked down to a lower level and six of us crammed into three empty seats. When the game was over, the crowd went wild. I'll never forget the celebration, nor the image of Jim Craig standing at center ice, an American flag draped around him, as he searched the crowd for his father.

Then the games were over almost as fast as they had started. Time flew by, but for two weeks it was like Camelot in the mountains.

Between the Olympics and worlds, I visited the White House with the rest of the U.S. team. I remember walking into the building with Herb Brooks, the coach of the gold medal–winning U.S. hockey team, who was shaking his head in wonder. I'm certain he spoke for most of us when he said, "I can't believe that in my first ever visit to the White House, I'm a guest of the president."

For the athletes, this wasn't merely a meet-and-greet photo opportunity with Jimmy Carter. We all had signed a petition asking the president not to boycott the upcoming summer games in Moscow. While I understood that the country needed to respond to the Soviet invasion of Afghanistan, I disagreed with the boycott because the burden fell on a group of athletes who had trained all their lives to compete in the Olympics. Many would never get another chance. Eric Heiden, the champion speed skater who won five gold medals in Lake Placid, presented the president with the petition. It's my understanding he denied ever receiving it.

During the reception, we got a chance to meet and pose for a picture with President Carter. Though a White House photographer was on hand, I was so determined to get a good photo of me and the president, I brought along my own Instamatic camera. When it was my turn to pose with the president, I gave the camera to a friend, stood next to President Carter and kind of nudged him in the direction of my camera. "Would you mind looking over here?" I asked. I got a great photo but later felt like a total yahoo for doing that.

In late March, the world championships were held in Dortmund, West Germany. In an Olympic year, worlds is typically anticlimactic, especially nowadays when most of the Olympic medalists choose to bail out. Some are afraid to tarnish what they've won; some want to move on to other things; and others want to go out on the highest of highs. At the 1980 worlds it was different, since all the top men did show. I saw this as another chance to establish myself with the skating community.

After their great performance in Lake Placid, Kitty and Peter had exactly the same thing in mind—to use this opportunity to make another mark. To get motivated, Kitty and I made a side bet—whoever skated clean in the long got to have the other person as his or her slave for a day. Peter and Kitty were terrific again, but they made one mistake in their program and finished seventh. Poor Kitty. I had a pile of laundry in my room just for her.

There was a minor controversy swirling between me and the chairman of the international technical committee. Her name was Sonia Bianchetti, an influential Italian official who would become my nemesis over the next few years. While she was one of the early leaders in the fight to eliminate compulsory figures, her objective in Dortmund was to penalize my short program combination, a triple Salchow–double loop. The Salchow takes off from a back inside left edge. Her objection in my takeoff was that my right foot scratched the ice and assisted a little bit as it came through to transfer my weight. Many of my competitors did the same thing, yet Sonia singled me out. She informed the USFSA that if I used my right foot in the takeoff, the judging panel would deduct seven-tenths of a point from my score. That kind of penalty would knock me out of the top five, and I was determined to hold my placement from the Olympics.

This left only one solution, in Don's opinion. Three days before the short, Don informed me we were switching the combination to the riskier triple Lutz–double loop.

We tried it out and I wasn't having much luck. "I can't do it," I told Don reluctantly. "I'm only hitting it fifty percent of the time."

"You're doing it," Don snapped back. "To hell with Sonia."

No one in his right mind changes his combination jump a couple of days before competing, but that was what I did. On the night of the short program, I rubbed my wristband extra hard and landed the weakest triple Lutz–double loop ever, what skaters call "squirrelly." But it counted and I was thrilled because it was the only time I hit the combination all week outside the practice rink. I was having no luck with it on practices in the main arena, and sheer luck enabled me to pull it off. Later that night, Kitty's coach, Ron Ludington, bumped into Sonia and predictably she had a zinger. "I guess Mr. Hamilton leads a blessed life," she observed.

I didn't react negatively to *all* criticism. Dick Button was a good influence on me. In his television commentary for ABC, he always picked out something I needed to work on, and I took his advice to heart. For several years he complained about my poor spins, and I worked on speeding up my rotation and smoothing out my combination spins. Dick always said things in a way that was healthy and productive. I listened to him because whatever he said became the public perception of my skating. He was that influential.

In the long, I skated clean, finished fifth overall, and won the bet with Kitty. When I hit my last jump, I actually spent the last minute of my program thinking, "Oh, good, laundry is getting done. What else can I make her do? Polish my skates, pack my suitcase?" As I took my bow, I searched the arena for Kitty. She was sitting next to Peter, her hands covering her face. I could tell she was dreading the next twenty-four hours. When she pulled away her hands, she saw me looking at her. I gave her what I hoped was a wicked grin that said, "Yes, you are my slave."

Chapter Eight

Best Man

In May I went home to Bowling Green to skate in an exhibition. Late spring is a beautiful time of year in northern Ohio. The snow and ice have melted away. The trees and flowers are starting to bloom. At our Liberty Hi house, my father would spend hours in the backyard, seeding, planting and weeding his vegetable garden. This was his element. He was a plant ecologist and loved to research plant communities and their interaction in an ecosystem, particularly how they were affected by man. But every year at this time, my father would take a break from his garden to help out with the annual ice show at Bowling Green. He'd stop whatever he was doing and build props and sets for the production. He stayed involved with the skating club long after I left the area, and so did I.

The show wasn't called "Ice Horizons" anymore. In even years, we'd put on a benefit for cancer research in memory of my mother, and named this production "International Stars on Ice." My job was not only to skate, but to bring in guest stars, and in 1980 I asked Kitty and Peter to perform. They flew to Toledo and I picked them up in my brother's Subaru, a car we nicknamed the Beater, because when you jammed the brakes, it pulled hard to the right unless you had a tight grip on the wheel. The gearshift also had a tendency to pop out of the floor while shifting into third. It was unsafe at any speed, but always an adventure.

This visit to Bowling Green was special because I was returning as a hometown Olympic hero along with Kenny and Mark, who starred for the U.S. gold medal–winning hockey team. I was feeling confident about my skating. At Dortmund, I had held down fifth place against the best skaters on the planet for the second competition in a row. Charlie Tickner, Jan Hoffman and Robin Cousins—the only three competitors who

beat me in the long program—were all retiring. Scott Cramer was turning pro, too, leaving just David and me as the top contenders for the
1981 national championship.

The first couple of days at home were great. My father cooked up mar-
velous chicken and steak dinners and served our own preserved garden
vegetables—peas, corn and tomatoes. Later, we'd hop in the Beater and
head over to Dave's College Station, a bar owned by my friend Dave
Meek. After last call, we'd go over to Dave's house or head over to the
Big Boy restaurant for a burger. On other nights, we'd all pile into a couple of cars and take a road trip to Toledo to check out some other clubs.

Homecomings were uncomfortable in one respect—getting reacquainted with my brother, Steve. When I left to train at Wagon Wheel
in 1972, Steve was just ten years old. Though we saw each other on holidays and summer breaks, the separation kept us from developing a close
relationship. Those were tough years on Steve because my sister was gone
and raising two kids of her own, and Steve was left in Bowling Green to
deal with my family's financial hardship and my mother's illness. He was
fifteen when she passed away, and during the two years she was sick, my
father became aloof and irritable, and he stayed that way for quite a
while.

It seemed my dad stopped making time to parent him. Steve was like a
leaf that had fallen from a tree, wandering wherever the wind took him.
Later, when he bought a Camaro, he'd take it out and race around town,
picking up a few tickets along the way. He hung with an unambitious
crowd of guys who were not good influences. He obviously found the security in the group that he wasn't getting at home. He did not get the
benefit of everything my parents had to offer, and had my mother lived, it
would have been different for him.

When my skating took off after the 1980 Olympics, Steve had finished
only two quarters at Bowling Green State University and decided that
was enough for him. He took on a series of odd jobs washing cars at a
local dealership, repairing stereos, and clerking at convenience stores and
lived for his nights of cruising around in muscle cars with his pals. He did
like to tinker with his car and his stereo, showing an aptitude for mechanics that was a harbinger of good things to come.

The sad truth is that our family was never quite the same after my
mother died. As we all drifted apart, I stopped coming home on some
holidays. It wasn't always a personal choice—Thanksgiving and Christmas fall right in the middle of competition season, and sometimes it
made more sense to spend holidays with friends living nearby in Philadelphia or Denver, depending on where I was at the time.

Happily, my brother did straighten out. He joined the U.S. Coast Guard in 1985, and when he graduated from boot camp at Camp May in New Jersey, it was one of the proudest moments of my father's life. When Steve left the Coast Guard in 1991 at age twenty-nine, he went back to Ohio to study civil engineering. Best of all, Steve and my father patched up their relationship and they became very close again, just as it had been before my mother got sick. Steve was lucky. Unlike me, he got a chance to reconnect with my father in a way I never did. While Dad was devoted to my skating career—I don't think he ever missed a major competition after 1977—my career took off after the 1984 Olympics and never did slow down. Steve got to spend more time with our father after he retired from teaching and moved to Florida in 1989. Dad had more time to travel, and after Steve got out of the Coast Guard, he would often head down there to boat and fish with Dad. And the old tension that characterized their relationship a decade earlier evaporated like a puddle in a heat wave.

To celebrate my homecoming, my dad threw a party for me at the Liberty Hi house. I was having a great time until I saw Kitty. I noticed there were tears in her eyes.

"Why didn't you tell me?" she asked.

"Tell you what?"

"That you and Don are moving to Denver."

"Oh, no," I said under my breath.

A few weeks after Don and I had returned from Dortmund, he got an unexpected call from the Colorado Ice Arena in Denver. Carlo had gotten the position he coveted at the Broadmoor, leaving a coaching vacancy at the CIA. They wanted to know if Don would consider the job. Don told me it wasn't definite and to keep it to myself.

I had mixed feelings about returning to the CIA. While I liked Colorado, I knew leaving Philadelphia meant saying good-bye to Kitty, and that prospect depressed me. Our relationship was very intense, and I liked the idea of being forty minutes away by car. I wondered if our relationship could withstand the distance between Delaware and Denver. I didn't want to bring this up with Kitty until I was absolutely sure we were going. For some reason, Don had inadvertently told Kitty about the pending job offer at the party, which I thought was still up in the air. I was very upset with Don because he hadn't even told me it was for certain. Then Kitty and I got into a big fight because she felt I was withholding the information from her. I tried to explain that I didn't know until now that the move was imminent, but Kitty wasn't buying it. I was walking on eggshells for the rest of the weekend, and when we got back to Philadelphia, our relationship started to cool.

For Kitty, it was a credibility issue, and she never really trusted me again. She was offended that she didn't hear the news from me first, even though Don had sworn me to secrecy. In August—on my birthday, in fact—we packed up and moved to Denver. I was miserable. I didn't want to go but I didn't feel I could deny Don this great opportunity. On the day of my departure, I said good-bye to the Camps, who had been great to me. It was an awful day. That morning, the Camps had to put down their dog, Gus, who had been very sick with cancer. I was quiet and withdrawn, upset about Gus leaving us and me leaving Kitty. Training fifteen hundred miles away was not going to help our situation. But even though we were having problems, it wasn't over with her. Not by a long shot.

As the year wore on, my life was increasingly consumed by skating and everyone around me who was involved in it. When I returned to Denver with Don, the move proved to be a bigger adjustment than I anticipated. While Don was thrilled to be living in a new city, I was the one training in altitude for the first time in eighteen months, and it would take weeks to adjust.

Don was psyched. He had been coaching for twenty years, and now he was looking at the possibility of a world championship. I was ranked number two in the world, behind only David Santee, who had beaten me by one place both at the Olympics and worlds in Dortmund. The CIA had a great track record, having produced the last two Olympic men's champions, John Curry and Robin Cousins. Why not three in a row?

I knew I needed an ideal living arrangement to succeed. So before getting to town, I looked up my old pal Brent Landis, and asked if he and his folks could put me up for a couple of weeks until I found a place to live. Well, I never left. There was a comfort level staying with a family that I now appreciated, and the Landises offered me their finished basement, the same place Dorothy Hamill once lived. I figured you couldn't argue with that kind of history.

Getting reacquainted with Denver's mile-high altitude took some time, but the CIA looked exactly as I remembered it. A bluish gray building set on Evans Avenue on Denver's southwest side, it was cold and dreary inside, and the ice seemed more gray than white. Those first few practices were harsh. I was gasping for air after every long program run-through—and that was when I was fortunate enough to finish one. Late summer was a difficult time of year to get motivated, so Don wasn't panicking just yet.

Two months later, he was panicking.

My first international competitions of the season were coming up: Saint Ivel in England, followed by "Skate Canada" in Calgary. They were my first real tests now that I was the favorite going into them, and I think Don sensed I was mentally unprepared to compete. He couldn't have been more on the money. I was depressed and feeling homesick for Philadelphia. Kitty and I were trying to make a go of the relationship after a difficult summer, but it was tough being separated for such long stretches of time.

The Saint Ivel competition was held in a cavernous arena that also served as a public ice rink. On my first practice, I noticed the ice was a little beat—lots of subtle hills, ruts and holes. I turned my attention to the other skaters and figured out quickly who I had to contend with— Canada's Brian Pockar and Japan's Fumio Igarashi. I hadn't viewed Brian as a threat until I saw how well he was skating. He had a wonderful program that matched his style and energy. And he was a good guy. We shared cabs to and from the rink each day and got to be friends. Fumio was a more formidable jumper than Brian. He had a triple Lutz and could play to the crowd, which was unusual for a Japanese skater. They traditionally put forth business-as-usual programs with great jumping, but crowd response was a low priority. Not with Fumio. He liked the attention and knew how to work an audience.

As I expected, executing decent compulsory figures was tough because the ice was bad. But I suffered most in the short and long programs, skating badly enough that I have actually jettisoned my performances from my memory. I wasn't prepared and it was my own fault. I even blew my triple Lutz in the short, one of the handful of times in my career that I botched my most consistent jump. I managed to hit it in the long, but it was too late. Brian was on that week and I had to settle for second. He got a big boost beating me on neutral ice. It did not bode well for me a month later, when I had to meet up with Brian again at "Skate Canada," which was being staged in Calgary, Brian's hometown.

Don was quiet on the flight home and I was fuming over my half-hearted effort. But the loss in Great Britain was just the kick in the butt I needed to get in gear. There's nothing like a good whipping to light a fire under me.

Back at the CIA, I skated hard and shaped up. Don was relieved with the change in attitude. Calgary was going to be a dogfight with Brian, who would be competing on his birthday, no less. Canadians go crazy for their skaters; they practically blow the roof off a building when one of their own does well. I could just see him skating out in warm-up and ten thousand fans breaking into a chorus of "Happy Birthday." In Canada, being a superstar figure skater is like being Michael Jordan in the United States. Their male champions are treated like rock stars, and there was nowhere near the stigma of being a male skater as there was in the lower forty-eight, where our athletic ability and masculinity were routinely questioned.

The setting for "Skate Canada" was the Stampede Corral Ice Stadium, and it was going to be noisy. I would have to block that out and just let my body take control. I couldn't lose to Pockar twice in a row, even on his home turf.

Don and I arrived in Calgary on a Sunday and we got to work the next morning. I was hungry again and wanted to dominate. I won figures and the short program, but Brian was right on my heels. In the long, I hit six triples to Brian's three and won the competition. I also defeated David Santee, my main rival for the upcoming national championships. I must say, the Canadian fans were great to me. They treated me like a native son, and I loved performing there. Brian was a gracious loser in a competition I know he wanted very badly. There were no sour grapes on his part. He even invited me over to his house afterward for his birthday party.

On the way back home from Calgary, I realized that the loss in England had been just what I needed to get ready for the bigger competitions down the road—nationals and worlds. I said to Don, "You know, I needed to do that in Saint Ivel. Sometimes a loss can be more beneficial than a win." He didn't respond. The look on his face said plenty: "Spare me the drama, just be ready to skate next time."

When we got back to Denver, Don wanted to fine-tune my programs, and called in a choreographer from California—Ricky Harris. I had first worked with her in 1979 at a summer training camp in Squaw Valley, where Don put me with her one-on-one. By 1980 she was part of the team, and her goal was to give me a more dynamic look, and to get me to project more energy.

Choreographers create skating routines to music. They teach you how to move to sound and frequently draw their ideas from ballet, jazz and modern dance. Their goal is to build programs that incorporate all of the technical elements—jumps, spins and footwork. While they don't always teach you how to execute a triple jump, they can decide where a jump belongs in a program. They begin by mapping out where the jumps and spins are going to take place on the ice, and then fill it all in with steps, moves and feeling.

Most choreographers have substantial skating backgrounds. Sandra Bezic, who did Olympic programs for Brian Boitano, Kristi Yamaguchi and Tara Lipinski, went to the Olympics herself as a pairs skater with her brother Val for Canada. Typically they have more artistic flair than a skating coach, who specializes in jumps. Ricky Harris, however, was more of a dancer than a skater. And she looked the part—gorgeous, funky clothes and hats; dark, black spiky hair, long fingernails and a ton of mascara. When she walked into a room, she was like a shot of espresso. All eyes were on her. Her energy and look would just take the place over.

"I want you to think tall," she used to tell me. "When you skate, choose a face in the audience to single out and skate for that person. There will be another hundred people in the stands thinking you're looking at them."

The idea was to bring the fans onto the ice and let them participate in the performance, a philosophy I agreed with. But I wasn't completely sold on Ricky's approach, or maybe it was just the way she went about it. Don wondered if I didn't trust Ricky because she was a woman, but he forgot I'd been coached by Mary Scotvold for two years. My concern was that too much choreography might make my skating appear effeminate. I was afraid I'd look more like a ballet dancer than an athlete, and while that might work for many Russian skaters, it didn't fly with me. As it turned out, that wasn't the case. Still, Ricky took some getting used to. I remember when I first worked with her in Squaw Valley camp in 1979, she stopped me every two seconds to correct something, or lectured me about "mental imagery" or performing "vibrant articulations with the music."

What was this stuff she was talking about, I wondered? Later on, I went to her rink in Torrance, California, for some more work. This time Don came along. The session did not go well, and midway through a lesson, I kicked the boards in frustration because I wasn't getting it. Don saw that and he and Ricky came up with a solution. From then on, they stood on the ice together; Ricky would tell him what she wanted me to do and then Don would relay the instructions to me in terms I felt comfortable with. That enabled me to relax and apply Ricky's lessons. The Ricky-Don message system was how we created one of my all-time favorite show programs, "New York, New York," which we actually put together in one afternoon.

On one of my visits to Torrance, Don and I worked with Ricky and then went into a coffee shop next door to talk over my program. "I'm a little intimidated by Ricky," I said. "She's this larger-than-life character. I don't know, Don."

"It's going to be all right. I know she's a little different from what you're used to, but she has a lot to offer. You'll see."

Don was right. Although I initially resisted doing ballet and off-ice dance work, Ricky taught me the necessity for applying those skills and gave me a true understanding of movement, particularly hand, head and upper-body gestures that enabled me to communicate better with an audience. I may not have always agreed with her philosophy, but we shared a common goal that superseded any differences—connecting to the crowd.

After winning the Eastern Sectionals in 1981, I knew she had to be doing something right because I got a slew of compliments about my improved choreography. David won his sectional in the midwest, setting up a showdown at nationals in San Diego. Don and I got rooms at the Hyatt instead of the official competitors' hotel. Part of Don's strategy was to seclude me from the other skaters and coaches so I wouldn't get caught up in all the fuss between David and me. "Let other people talk about it," Don reasoned. "We don't have to get into it." It was nice to be away from the crowd. The Hyatt was close to the ocean, and I began each morning with a poolside breakfast on the hotel patio. The only problem was that I usually never got to finish my eggs and toast because the seagulls kept flying off with my food.

I met David in 1968 at my first ever competition in Bowling Green. I was nine and he was ten, and we spent the entire week hanging out together. I invited him over to my house and we watched TV and played ball with the neighborhood kids. David was an excellent all-around athlete, much better than I. He was a fan of the Cubs, Bulls and Bears, and he always wore the team sweatshirts to practice. Later when he was invited to skate in "Ice Horizons," we spent all our time vying for the affections of this beautiful older girl, Melissa Militano, who would go on to win the national pairs championship with her brother, Mark. Of course, we both acted like goofballs—wrestling and horsing around with each other to get her attention.

As a skater, he was a phenom. In 1971, at age thirteen, he was already the junior national champion, the youngest ever, and I was still in intermediate, two levels below him. I wouldn't win juniors for another five years. Keeping up on David's career was no problem because he was profiled in *Skating* magazine from time to time. I was in awe of him. Two years after winning juniors, David placed third in seniors at the '73 nationals, something I did not accomplish until I was nineteen. Then, in 1976, he was second at nationals, sixth at the Innsbruck Olympics and fifth at the world championships. His star was clearly on the rise.

A year later, Charlie Tickner asserted himself at the 1977 nationals, skating through the roof while David did not have one of his better performances. David won figures, his strength, but finished third in both the short and long behind Charlie and Scott Cramer. David did beat Charlie at worlds that year, finishing fourth. Charlie won nationals again in 1978, and followed that by winning his only world title in Ottawa, where David had a shot at a medal but finished sixth after a disappointing long program.

Charlie was untouchable after that. David was knocking on the door all the time, but he either had a little misfortune or faced somebody turning in the performance of his life. A lot of people figured him to be out of the sport by then, but 1981 offered a chance at redemption. David was taking his tenth shot at a senior national title. This time Charlie Tickner was finally out of the picture. He had retired and joined the "Ice Capades."

Don and I agreed that David was at the very least the sentimental favorite in San Diego, if not the odds-on favorite. Not only was he coming off two fourth-place finishes at the 1980 Olympics and world championships, but in my five years of competing against him, I had beaten him only twice, at the "Norton Skate" and at "Skate Canada." There was an added twist to the unfolding drama: he was being trained by my old coaches, Evy and Mary Scotvold, so I knew he would be in great shape and in peak form.

Our rivalry was much different from the one I had with Scott Cramer. While David was a competitive guy, he was a good man with a big heart. If I had wanted to, I could have taken advantage of him by being more aggressive during practices. I could have done my triple Lutz close to him, talked a little trash or gotten in his way while he was doing a run-through, but that wasn't my style. David was the type of person who would take a step back before he'd stick out his chin. Sometimes I felt Scott used to get inside his head as he tried to get inside mine. I had a more subtle approach. I never wanted anyone to see me miss a jump, ever. If I was warming up or doing a run-through, it had to be perfect. I didn't have to get in anyone's face. When I skated great in practice, everyone else would see it and start thinking he had to skate perfectly. That added pressure might cause him to get distracted and get his mind off what he was supposed to do.

In San Diego, the key for me would be figures and short program. Most of the time, David beat me at both. I expected David to show up in great shape and be hitting his triple flip consistently. His triple Lutz was iffy, which was where I had the advantage, particularly in the short program, because I could do it in combination with a double loop. A clean short for me would be enough to override losing to him in figures, and then it would come down to the long, where I was beating him on a regular basis.

Of course, nothing ever seems to go according to plan. In an upset, I won figures and David finished second. My short program was set to two pieces of music, *Samson and Delilah* and a Czech folk dance, and it just so happened I did the best short program of my career. I landed my triple Lutz–double loop combination, and the entire program felt effortless. David didn't have his best skate and finished third in the short, behind Robert Waggenhoffer. I was feeling confident. A top-two finish would be enough to win the title, regardless of how David skated.

I was glad Don had set us up at the Hyatt. I felt the need for a lot of space, a lot of time alone. That made it hard on my father, who was in town to watch me skate. He was joined by our good friend from Bowling Green, Sam Cooper. Sam always roomed with Ernie, which was good because Dad needed the company.

I enjoyed having my father come to competitions. He wasn't absorbed in the sport like most skating parents. He didn't care which jumps I hit or missed in practice, nor did he constantly wonder what my competitors were up to. Having Ernie there was usually a positive distraction for me because he didn't know a thing about skating. But he did have a tendency to follow me around at competitions and always wanted to meet me for breakfast at 7 A.M. sharp. So I'd be sleeping and get this a-up call at 6:30 A.M. to meet him down in the restaurant. Dad was an early riser and I wasn't. "Dad," I'd say. "You're making a big mistake." He'd chuckle and say, "See you downstairs in a few minutes." It sometimes seemed my father was trying to make up for all the time we had missed out on over the years.

Unfortunately, nationals was not the place to do it. On competition days, I would go into a trance and have a hard time paying attention to anything. I preferred to be alone a lot of the time, holing up in my hotel room listening to heavy metal music. At competitions, skaters can often become planets, and their family, friends and coaches the moons orbiting around them. Whenever I started feeling like the center of the universe, and felt that I was getting pulled in all sorts of directions, I feared I was going to turn in a horrible performance. That was when I needed some space. It was difficult for me to explain this to my father without hurting his feelings, so I asked Helen to look after him.

With victory so close, I wanted to give all my energy to my practice sessions and the long, so I decided to cut myself off from just about everybody except Don. When I wasn't skating, I sequestered myself in my hotel room listening to the J. Geils Band or Aerosmith.

I didn't see my father at all the day before the long program. The next morning, he came by my practice and I noticed he was looking drawn and haggard, as though he had been up all night. I had missed him at breakfast, so when the session ended, I went over to him to talk. He seemed to be avoiding my gaze.

"I'm feeling pretty good today," I told him. "I did a clean run-through and haven't missed a jump in practice."

"Scott, I want you to know I love you. I love you no matter what happens tonight," he said. I gave him a hug, yet something seemed wrong.

"Are you okay?" I asked.

"Sure, I'm just a little tired," he replied. "See you later." He turned around and walked away, taking slow and deliberate steps. Something didn't seem right, but I took him at his word.

The national championship in the year after an Olympics is sometimes viewed as a down year in skating. Most of the top skaters from the season before have retired. A few skaters might be hanging in one more year to get a shot at a title, but the younger kids look upon it as a prime opportunity to move up in the rankings. In skating, we talk about "waiting your turn," which means that sometimes an older skater has a little advantage over a younger skater who's knocking on the door. I was in the latter category the previous season, and now I felt my time had come. The only skater who could wrestle it away from me was David.

The night of the long program was one of those rare occasions when everyone skated to their maximum ability. David, Robert and I—it was as if all three of us were shot out of cannons from the rafters, flew to our spots on the ice, ripped off our capes and proceeded to skate the program of our lives. Bam, bam, bam—one right after the other.

David began the night knowing he had to win the long to have any chance at the title. His choice of music was inspiring, the theme from *Rocky*. Even pacing back and forth backstage, I could hear those trumpets in the opening stanza and feel the tide of emotion sweeping through the crowd. Just like the Sylvester Stallone character in the film, David was taking one last shot at a championship. He went out and landed six triple jumps and got a standing ovation. Don told me later—after the competition was over—that it was the best he had ever seen David skate.

I suppose somebody had to play Apollo Creed to David's Rocky, and the job fell to me. I didn't have a red, white and blue costume to wear; I skated in a tight-fitting blue stretch outfit—pants and a leotard top—with gemstones sewn on the front of the shirt. (I didn't like it but it was the style of the day.) For my five-minute-long program, Don had selected four pieces of music that would play on my power and speed: "Mutiny on the Bounty," Prokofiev's "Cinderella," Rick Wakeman's "Seahorses," and

"Spartacus." When they announced my name, I skated out and was warmly greeted by the crowd, and I was desperate to win them over. My opening move was a combination—a triple Lutz, then a triple toe with a step in between. I hit it and the crowd surged behind me. The momentum kept building after I hit my triple Salchow and another triple toe loop. The only error I made was doubling a planned triple flip. When it was over, I had the second standing ovation of the night and earned two 6.0s in the artistic score. Don and I went backstage knowing we were comfortably ahead of David.

Robert Waggenhoffer skated after me and hit everything in his program. He finished third and the title was mine. After all these years of working, I was finally the U.S. national champion. As I waited backstage, people came up and gave me hugs and handshakes. Don was just beside himself with joy. An ABC producer came up and tapped me on the arm. They wanted me immediately to go and do an interview with Dick Button.

When Dick asked me about my performance, I felt bashful. "I was okay," I said, trying to play it down. Then I realized I shouldn't be too shy. "Two sixes," I added. "It's the best week I've ever had."

That was about to change. As soon as I was finished with Dick, I went looking for my father. I had been difficult all week and I felt bad about avoiding him. Except he was nowhere to be found. It was strange; I felt like a kid lost in a mall, wandering from person to person, asking if they'd seen my dad. Sure I had asked Helen to keep him busy, but this was getting ridiculous, I thought. This was the biggest night of my life and he wasn't around to share it with me.

Then it was time for the medal ceremony. I stood atop the podium and tried to contain my emotions. I thought of my mom and swelled with pride, having come so far in two years since the letdown in Cincinnati. After receiving our medals, we were ushered from the ice backstage for a brief press conference, and when it was over I went searching for my dad again. That was when I spotted the team doctor, Dr. Franklin Nelson, and Dr. Hugh Graham, both Olympic judges, huddled together in a corner. "Where's my dad?" I asked. They gently pulled me aside. "Your father has had a minor stroke and he's in the hospital," Dr. Nelson explained. "Don't worry; he's fine."

I couldn't believe it. What should have been one of the greatest nights of our lives—something we'd share as father and son forever—suddenly unraveled. I'd had enough of hospitals and watching the people I love get sick and die. What was going on? Sam found me and he rushed me over to the hospital, apologizing the whole way for keeping me in the dark.

But Ernie had insisted on silence, so that I wouldn't be distracted. I couldn't believe his selflessness and his wisdom. I totally understood why I wasn't told. What would I have done differently had I known? Skated with a heavy heart? That didn't make any sense whatsoever.

On the ride to the hospital, Sam explained what had happened. Two days earlier, my father received a wake-up call in his hotel room, and when he went to reach for the phone, he couldn't move his left arm. When he got up and looked in the mirror, his face was drooping. He refused to go to the hospital and spent the day as determined to avoid me as I had been to avoid him. His symptoms improved, and after seeing me off at practice that morning he finally sought some treatment.

Now I was feeling really horrible for avoiding him. Getting in competition mode makes you do things you might regret later, and this was one of those times. Maybe I'd caused the stroke by making him nervous and unhappy, I thought. "He's all right," Sam said. "But the doctors want to medicate him, and he won't take anything until he speaks with you. I don't think he knows what happened tonight."

"I feel terrible about avoiding him all week," I said.

"Don't feel guilty, Scott," Sam said. "Your dad's gonna be okay. If anything, he could use some cheering up."

When we arrived, Sam parked the car and I rushed through the lobby, past the nurses' station, and went directly to Ernie's room. Sam was doing his best to keep up, barking out directions as I ran ahead. I burst into Dad's room, where he was resting in bed.

"How did you do in the long?" he asked.

He looked fine, and since Sam said he was okay, I decided to have a little fun with him.

"Well, I had to skate after David," I replied.

"Yeah, yeah, what happened?"

"David skated perfect. Really, really well. Then I went out and I didn't do my triple flip; I doubled it."

I could tell his heart sank. "Waggenhoffer went right after me and he skated clean."

By now my father was expecting the worst. "How did you do?" he asked.

"Never mind that, Dad. People are saying it was probably the best men's final ever because all three of us skated great programs."

"And you ended where?"

"Well, I got two perfect 6.0 scores for artistic impression," I said. Dad perked up a little when he heard that. "And I won nationals!"

My father let out a sigh of relief. "Oh, thank God," he said, putting his hand to his chest. Then he reached over and pressed the nurses' call button. "Can I have my medication now?"

The next day, Kitty and I were driving to the rink for the exhibition practices, and she suddenly burst into tears.

"What's the matter?" I asked.

"I don't know," she replied, sobbing.

But I did. She and Peter had just won their first national title and she was physically and emotionally exhausted, which was something I could relate to at the moment. That morning I had lost my temper with Don and Ricky, who had insisted that in the exhibition I skate to a new show program Ricky had set for me, to the music from Ain't Misbehavin'. I put up some resistance because I didn't feel I had rehearsed it enough, but Ricky and Don won. I skated to the number and as it turned out, the crowd loved it.

When nationals were over, I stayed on in San Diego with my father, who was resting and undergoing more tests. The good news was that the doctors concluded that the stroke was due to high blood pressure. Once that receded, he would be okay. Thank goodness the damage wasn't permanent. However, he would not be able to travel to the world championships next month in Hartford, Connecticut. Doctor's orders.

After Ernie's release from the hospital, he went home to Bowling Green and I returned to Denver to train. Two days before leaving for worlds, during a long program run-through, I caught the heel of my blade in the ice while attempting a triple Salchow. Instead of taking off vertically, my body went horizontal and I smashed down hard on my tailbone. I lay there for a few minutes, unable to move my legs. Finally I managed to get on my feet. I was in agony that didn't stop despite all the ice and heat I tried. I was incapable of sitting down, let alone jumping. I dreaded the flight to Hartford, and when the time came to go, it was as agonizing as I imagined it would be, so I stood most of the way.

On my first practice at Hartford, I played it safe and didn't try any difficult jumps. Kitty was there and she gave me lots of encouragement. We spent a lot of time together in Hartford, going to each other's practices and having lunch and dinner together. We had both skated here at the 1977 nationals, and returning brought back a lot of memories for me, since this was the last arena my mother saw me compete in before she died.

On the second day, I managed to hit some triples, despite the soreness. Good thing I was in great shape, or I wouldn't have made it through the week. My thoughts soon returned to how to beat David.

He had an advantage at this competition, since international judges were more familiar with him, and because of his solid figures. Don and I thought he might put some distance between us in that event, and that was exactly what happened. David got off to a good start, placing second in figures to my fourth. Since figures accounted for 30 percent of each score, the pressure was on for me to win the short, worth 20 percent, and the long, which counted for 50 percent. I had to put aside my tailbone troubles and attack. Despite the soreness, I managed to land my triple Lutz–double loop combination in the short and won the event. David was third. But his combined score had him in first, and I was in third. Basically, whoever won the long won the title.

Once again, David was great, making only one error, a missed landing on a triple flip. When I took the ice, I tried to get in my zone—ignoring the crowd for a moment as I focused on the ice ahead of me. My opening triple Lutz was right on the money. The toe loop afterward was the same. When I hit my last triple Salchow, I felt I had the title. In the last few seconds of my program, I tripped and fell during a simple footwork sequence and got back on my feet in a millisecond. Don't advertise your mistakes, I was thinking. As it turned out, it made no difference at all. I won the long and my first world title. Don said he was certain I would have gotten some 6.0s had I stayed on my feet.

David was third in the long and second overall. I was ecstatic about winning but certainly felt sorry for David. He'd had a great year, his best ever. I knew I wouldn't have skated as well as I did without him pushing me. During the medal ceremony, David climbed up on the podium and gave me a big congratulatory handshake. We had just been through the most intense two months of any American male competitors since the late 1950s, when David Jenkins and Tim Brown went head-to-head for national and world titles. David had been skating as a senior man since 1972, twice as long as I had. He was usually stronger than I in school figures but my freestyle skating was superior to his, and that was the difference.

I'm proud of my national and world titles, but if I could give one away, it would be to David. I've always loved him like a brother, and there were no hard feelings between us. We'll always share a special bond from 1981. Not since Jenkins and Brown in 1958 had two American men gone one-two at the world championships, and no pair has done it since.

Later in the year, David and I performed in an ice show in Sun Valley, Idaho. We had a great time working together and took the same flight back to Denver, where David had recently taken a job with the United States Olympic Committee. We got to wondering about why our friendship had recently cooled when we obviously got along so well. We finally realized the answer—our mischievous buddy Peter Carruthers. David had dated Kitty briefly back in 1978, and Kitty and I were still involved. It seemed Peter didn't want either one of us dating his younger sister. In his overzealous attempts to protect Kitty, he had been gleaning information from her on both of us and reporting back to us what the other had said, fostering misunderstandings. David and I decided it was time for some friendly payback. On the plane we concocted a plan: compose a letter to Peter from a nonexistent USOC official accusing him of padding his skating expenses. The punishment: his eligibility had been suspended. Back in Colorado, David typed it up on official letterhead, which he had easy access to in his new job, and sent it out. A few days later, Peter received the letter and flipped out. Kitty, who was in on the gag, didn't let him suffer too long. He was so upset that she quickly confessed the letter was a forgery from David and me. Too bad; we were ready to let Peter stew for a week or so.

In the spring, I was invited to New York to take part in the Wide World of Sports Twentieth Anniversary dinner. The banquet was held at the Waldorf-Astoria hotel and hosted by Jim McKay, the legendary sports broadcaster. I sat at a table with Kitty and Peter, and Elaine Zayak, the ladies' national champion. There were celebrities and sports heroes at every table: Sugar Ray Leonard, Muhammad Ali, Olympic champion speed skaters and skiers. . . . I wanted to start asking people for autographs.

I was never comfortable at these events. I felt like a dweeb because of my lack of social etiquette, and sometimes I made a fool of myself. A couple of months earlier at worlds I had made such a blunder. It's customary for the winners in each category to give a thank-you speech to all the international officials at a reception. When it was my turn to step up to the microphone, I hadn't prepared anything to say. I looked around the room and felt intimidated. So I just leaned forward and blurted, "Thank you," and then awkwardly backed away from the microphone. Then it was Christopher Dean's turn. He had just won the dance world title with partner Jayne Torvill. He reached into his pocket and pulled out a piece of paper. The son of a gun had prepared his speech ahead of time! He was so eloquent, and I just wanted to bury my head in a soup bowl. I had never felt more humiliated in my life.

Surrounded by friends, I felt all right at the ABC dinner. Jim McKay was onstage addressing the crowd when he looked down at our table. I was picking at my dinner when it occurred to me that Jim was talking about me.

"Look, kid," he said from the stage, "dating is between you and Susan. I can't do anything about that."

At first, I didn't understand what he was talking about, and then it came to me: prior to the national championships, ABC had come to Bowling Green and interviewed me for one of those "up close and personal" profiles. I had made a joke about wanting to be taller so I could land a date with my fantasy woman, Susan Anton, a blond bombshell who was almost six feet tall and everybody's favorite pinup girl. I didn't think the remark would make it on the air, but it did.

The next thing I knew, a spotlight swung over to a corner and there was Susan, dressed all in black and being her usual alluring self. She started singing, "You Must Have Been a Beautiful Baby Because Baby Look at You Now," and walking in my direction, slithering between the tables like a cat. My hair was now standing on end. Then she took me by the hand and guided me up onstage. "He's so cute," she purred to the crowd. She kept on singing and blowing in my ear. I was blushing and Kitty was sitting at the table, her hands over her face, laughing hysterically. I was amazed the network had gone to such trouble to bring us together, but as embarrassed as I was, I had no complaints. Susan looked me in the eye and said, "I know good things come in small packages because I date a man who's five-foot-two-and-a-half." Man, I nearly melted when I heard that. Of course, she was referring to her boyfriend, actor Dudley Moore. I guess I had to wait my turn in this department, too.

Chapter Nine

The Dark Side of the Moon

My first year defending a national and world title was a personal disaster. I was twenty-two years old and had spent the past decade training with some of the best skaters of my generation. My idol, Gordie McKellen. Then Charlie Tickner, winner of four U.S. titles in a row. I trained with Terry Kubicka, the 1976 American champion, and Robin Cousins, Olympic gold medalist. I'd had the privilege of seeing these great skaters up close and had put them on a pedestal. I'd always hoped to join them someday.

But I wasn't comfortable with my new status. I didn't believe I belonged on the same level as these champions I had worshiped all my life. Despite working hard since age nine, I was convinced that the sport must be taking a serious dive if I was the world champion. That attitude would be my undoing for the entire year. Winning, it seemed, screwed me up.

My summer in Denver, when I should have ascended to Gordie McKellen–like status at the CIA, was a downer. I was king of the rink, yet spent weeks moping around like a disgruntled serf. My workouts were halfhearted, and then I started coming in late for sessions. It was fear: fear that I couldn't live up to the high expectations, fear that I had peaked way too soon and now had no chance of surviving the competition gauntlet until the 1984 Olympics. There was plenty of time for some young kid to come up and take it all away. How could I go full tilt every day knowing that could happen? So I didn't. The last two Olympic champions hadn't even won a world title prior to winning the gold medal. How in the world could anyone hang on for four years with so many good skaters out there?

I had been pushing myself for two years; maybe I was also burned out. I had a national title, a world title and had made an Olympic team. Most skaters would take one of those things and walk away happy. In fact, most people around me assumed I would quit after 1981. I never considered it. But sometimes I wondered if I would have been better off had David beaten me in the past year. That would have made me hungry for the 1982 season.

Instead, I just broke down like an overheated pickup truck. On nice summer days, I played hooky and didn't go in to work out or get my lesson with Don. People thought I had an attitude problem, yet the truth was I was psyching myself out. If I couldn't do a perfect run-through, why skate at all? World champions don't miss. They skate clean, always. That was what I convinced myself of.

Laziness wasn't the problem. The worry that I wouldn't get through my long program without making a mistake was. Once I started missing jumps, I'd never hit them again. That was the kind of stuff that was actually going through my head.

Don was beside himself all year. He didn't know what to do. We'd be working on that dreaded double flip–triple toe combination—the one that ate me alive in 1979—and I'd be missing them left and right. It drove me crazy because all the people clawing after me—Brian Boitano, Robert Waggenhoffer and Mark Cockerell could do the combination easily.

"I don't know why I can't do this. I just can't," I said.

"Yes, you can," he argued. "Now go out and do it again."

"Nah, I don't want it," I whined. "It's hard. To try to repeat the last year, and the year before, I don't know if I can do that again. I don't know if I have it in me."

It took some work, but I made a major adjustment in my triple toe so I could improve my consistency. I retooled the jump. In a combination, a skater must take off for the second jump using the first jump's landing foot. Because I rotated my triple toe in the air with my feet side by side, it was difficult after landing the flip to get the proper hip snap at takeoff to turn three times in the air. In June, Don taught me how to rotate the triple toe loop with my feet crossed, which made it possible for me to do the combination. In fact, I landed it on the first day using Don's technique, but the combination gave me trouble all season long.

There was no hiding my lack of confidence. Like a good coach, Don tried to give me pep talks, and let me know it wasn't the end of the world. He kept a smile on his face during the crisis as though everything would turn out just fine. I'm sure he was praying I'd snap out of it. Sometimes we had harsh words. On days when I couldn't hit a thing, rage took over my body and Don would cut the session short and tell me to go home. I repeatedly threatened to quit.

Some days I did feel like hanging them up. I had pulled it together well enough to win the "National Sports Festival" in Syracuse and "Skate America" in Lake Placid, but I wasn't in great shape and I was doubling the toe loop on the back end of the combination. I could get away with that early in the season, but the hatchet would fall at nationals or worlds.

Don put on a happy face as long as I was winning. He understood that the demon side of me didn't stem from arrogance or ego. The culprit was insecurity. He just focused on getting me ready as best as he could.

My long program that year combined five pieces of music mixed into a four-minute-and-thirty-six-second program. The long had been five minutes every year prior to this, but had been cut by thirty seconds for the '82 season. The decision was well received by everyone, particularly those of us training in altitude. Don used most of the music from the 1981 program—the powerful opening from *Mutiny on the Bounty*, followed by Prokofiev's *Cinderella* and a slow section to Rick Wakeman's "Sea Horses." But he and Ricky added Delibes's *Sylvia*, where I try to convey some humor on the ice by poking fun at ballet. My signature ending—an up-tempo brass rendition of Tchaikovsky's *Swan Lake*—stayed the same.

As the new year approached, Don was getting a little worried, since I still hadn't done a clean run-through in practice all year. As my frustration built, I became a maniac and started yelling at other skaters who dared get in my way during a run-through. That wasn't me. It was demons. That's the only way I can describe it. Demons.

On December 29, the veil that covered my skating all year finally lifted. I did a clean program in practice and Don breathed a sigh of relief. "Great job," he said after I finished.

"It's about time," I replied. "Better late than never." The eastern sectionals were just a week away.

That year, Easterns were staged in Morristown, New Jersey, at the William G. Mennen Arena. It's pretty rare to see a defending national champion, let alone a world champion, competing at a sectionals event. Medalists from the previous year are granted byes to nationals the following season. But I didn't like going to nationals cold, and I found Easterns a great way to get tuned up and shake out any nerves.

Since my main competitors—Santee and Waggenhoffer—were competing at the Midwestern and Pacific Coast Sectionals, my goal at easterns was not only to win, but to win big, so I could send them a message that I was still in command. That meant hitting the combination in the short program.

The required figures were an inside rocker, paragraph double three and a back change loop. As I traced each figure, strains of J. Geils Band's *Freeze Frame* album raced through my head, especially the song "Insane, Insane, Again." I always hitched my mind to a rock tune when I practiced and competed at figures. There's a mutual flow between rhythm and tracing. At the "Norton Skate" in 1979, my first international victory, I had gotten psyched up to a David Naughton disco tune called "Makin' It." Heavy metal and disco may not seem very conducive to performing school figures, but it worked for me. At easterns I won all three figures handily.

Morristown was close enough to Philadelphia that Barb Camp drove up to watch Easterns. She actually came to a lot of my competitions and kept up with me after I moved to Denver. I was glad she was there for Don on the morning he found a growth on his arm. He drove all the way to Philadelphia to see a doctor, and it was identified as melanoma. That scared the hell out of me. Fortunately it was not the variety that had killed my mother, and they were able to control the spread.

The short was held on a Thursday during that first week in January. I was consumed with that combination jump and barricaded myself in my hotel room most of the day. It was just me and my boom box blasting AC/DC's "Back in Black." Though my event didn't start until 8 P.M., I arrived three hours early to get in one last practice session.

I spent the session working on my combination jump. It was something I hadn't done in competition all year, and time was running out. Earlier in the season at Syracuse and Lake Placid, I landed the double flip fine but doubled the triple toe loop. I couldn't let that happen here.

Don wasn't feeling too great after his visit to the doctor. As he stood by the boards, he looked grumpy and ashen. Before I compete, I sometimes panic and complain I can't jump anymore. Don was usually reassuring, but not today. When I started in about my problems with the combination, he didn't want to hear it. He cut me off and barked, "I don't care if you don't understand how to do it; just do it." I was a little taken aback and just skated away.

I was the first skater up in the order. I skated out to my spot and the crowd gave me a nice hand. "From the Philadelphia Skating Club and Humane Society, Scott Hamilton," the loudspeaker announced. I took my pose at center ice and waited for the start of my short program music, "Turn Me Loose" and "All that Jazz." There were seven required elements in my two-minute short program, none more important than the combination jump twenty seconds in, which I hit cleanly. I won the short. Two nights later, I won the long, despite doubling a planned triple Salchow.

My final performance lacked some spark, but I accomplished what I had set out to do—hit the tricky jump combination. Nationals were three weeks away, and there was plenty of time to smooth over the rough spots.

Indianapolis was like the Arctic circle when I arrived on January 24. It snowed all night and continued for the remainder of the week. Still, the city laid out the welcome mat. For the duration of nationals, they re named the downtown street by the official hotel "Avenue of Champions." Peggy Fleming came to town to perform in an outdoor exhibition. Even the arena where they were staging figures was packed each day with huge crowds. Skating was enjoying a resurgence in popularity, largely due to the overall strength of the U.S. team. In the men's, David, Brian, Robert and I were vying for spots on the podium; Elaine was dominating the ladies, but Rosalynn Sumners was poised to make a huge move in the rankings; in both dance and pairs, we had teams among the top five in the world; Judy Blumberg and Michael Seibert, and Kitty and Peter.

The first couple of days in Indianapolis were frustrating. Through the luck of the draw, I was assigned end ice during figures practice, a major problem because the Zamboni crosses over end ice more often than the rest of the surface. By watering the same patch over and over, the machine creates pits and valleys that flood with water, making the execution of school figures problematic. That put me in a lousy mood.

There were plenty of other things to fret about. David, Robert and Brian were looking awfully good. Brian had a triple Axel he was going to do in combination with a double toe loop. It was a good thing for me that I was the defending national and world champion. All I really had to do to win was stay on my feet and avoid blowing up. David and Robert needed to clearly outskate me to pull off an upset. Brian had the jumps to contend with, but his figures and artistic presentation needed more seasoning. Time and experience would take care of that.

Besides, Brian was just a "puppy." *Time* magazine had described me as an "exuberant puppy" when I made the Olympic team in 1980. So I began calling young seniors like Brian, Paul Wylie and Jimmy Santee (David's younger brother) "puppies." And a puppy, I kidded them in the dressing room before practice one day, had to do twice as much in a program to win than a dog because the dogs were there first. Around the rink, Paul started calling me "Scooby-Doo" and I nicknamed him "Scrappy," Scooby's sidekick who wanted to take on all comers. Just to make sure nobody forgot their place, I had a bunch of T-shirts made up after the Cycle brand dog food. Paul, Jimmy and Brian got Cycle One T-shirts, while David and I got Cycle Threes.

Our first day of freestyle practice was uneventful, except for the Ricky and Don sideshow. They always had a lot of fun teasing me. As I warmed up for practice this time, they burst into laughter every time I skated by. It turned out Don was describing in detail to Ricky all my on-ice habits and mannerisms—before I did them. He knew just when I was going to crack my knuckles, skate in small circles and stroke figure eights. I started getting annoyed. Here we were at nationals and Don was goofing around. I was already upset with him for missing a figures practice earlier in the week. So I fired him—for the hundredth time. John Nicks, who coached Tai and Randy, could never figure out how I got away with it. Mr. Nicks demanded the utmost respect from his students. But my firing Don on a regular basis was a running gag of ours. It kept us loose in tense situations. Don, of course, was back on the job later in the day.

During the figures event, the skating officials assigned me a terrible piece of ice with paint oozing through the surface. It wasn't deliberate; it was just that by the time I skated, the only clear patch of ice left happened to be where the paint was coming up. Because you are balancing yourself on one blade and skating very slowly, paint can bring you to a grinding halt, which was what almost happened to me. I got through the inside rocker, a three-circle figure, just fine. On my second figure, disaster struck. To execute a paragraph double three, you are allowed only one push to complete two full circles. By the end of that second circle on the front paragraph, you're crawling back to the center (the starting point). When my edge caught the wet paint, I darn near came to a stop. I had already registered a complaint about the ice conditions, but the referee, Claire Ferguson, had said it was the only decent patch left. I went back to Claire, the future president of the USFSA, showed her the problem with the ice, and asked for a reskate.

"Claire, there's paint on the ice and I can't do a thing about paint. My blades can't go through paint."

I got the reskate, but some of the other skaters publicly griped about the decision. It was another example of the defending national and world champion getting a break.

David was one of the best in the world at school figures, but I had beaten him at figures last year in San Diego, and I did it again. David was second, Robert Waggenhoffer was fifth and Brian was sixth heading into the short program.

On the day of the short, another supporter showed up to my practice, Jo Jo Starbuck, the champion pairs skater. Jo Jo and partner Ken Shelly were U.S national pair champions from 1970 through 1972. But that's not what made her great. She was one of the most beloved people in the sport. Everyone melted around her. She was like Glinda, the good witch of the north, who would watch me from a distance, sense when I was feeling most vulnerable, and then float over to guide me through my journey with sage advice and nurturing.

I had met her in December at a professional competition Don was judging. We exchanged phone numbers and spent many nights talking on the phone. I was feeling so self-destructive at that time in my life. Jo Jo was always there with unconditional support, and I loved her for it. She came to Indianapolis for a professional obligation, but she took me aside on competition day, filled me with positive reinforcement and worked her magic.

Things were not going David's way. Not only did he finish second in figures, he pulled a groin muscle doing a flying camel in practice the day before the short program. He said he was only 75 percent fit, which showed on Friday night in Market Square Arena. He left out the triple toe loop portion of his jump combination and finished fourth.

I wasn't any better. In warm-up, I obsessed about that evil double flip–triple toe, just as I had in sectionals earlier in the month. Carlo and Christa Fassi were sitting nearby, and I joked with them that I was going to miss my combination. Twenty seconds into my program, my fear evaporated—I nailed the combination. A moment later, I attempted my double Axel, a two-and-a-half-revolution jump off a forward edge. It was an easy jump for me, despite the fact that you have to elevate going forward while facing all this ice out in front of you.

I knew something was wrong when I heard the crowd gasp. My butt felt cold and wet. I was down. Not since "Skate Canada" in October 1977 had I fallen on my double Axel. Dick Button, calling the event from the ABC booth, was frantic. I finished my program with a smile—never advertise your mistakes. But I came off the ice furious.

My technical marks ranged from 5.2 to 5.4, registering the mandatory three-tenths to five-tenths deduction for a missed double jump. That mistake and Robert's clean skate left me in second for the short but still in first place overall. David was in second overall, Robert third, and Brian Boitano was kicking at the door in fourth. Dick Button asked in an on-camera interview what had gone wrong and I didn't feel like talking much. "Oh, dopey me," I said, trying to laugh it off. It was a dumb mistake and I was humiliated. I had probably hit that jump 150,000 times in practice without a problem. I made a guarantee to Dick: "I do the jump at the same place in the long program. I'll hit it next time."

On my way to the dressing room, I bumped into Evy Scotvold. Evy, Mary and I had had conversations since that awkward moment at the 1976 nationals when I switched to Carlo. It broke my heart to leave them, and I told them later that it was a shame we couldn't have stayed together. It was just an unfortunate set of circumstances that broke us up. When I saw Evy, he had that familiar judgmental look on his face.

"What's your problem?" Evy asked.

"I don't know," I replied. "I'm in shape but I can't skate!"

Evy shook his head and patted me on the shoulder. "I want you to go back to your hotel room and take a long look in the mirror at your own worst enemy."

That remark made me crack up. Back at the hotel that night, some skaters were joking that since I'd gotten permission to reskate the second figure earlier in the week, I would be requesting a reskate of the short. I'm certain David and Robert felt that I was vulnerable. I was wondering what the competitors and judges would be thinking in Europe after they learned I got second in the short. What was my old nemesis Sonia Bianchetti going to do with this piece of bad news?

Friday night turned to Saturday very quickly. I woke up thinking I had to redeem myself. Then I opened the paper and read a story that the judges had ignored my fall and "held me up" in second place. The article suggested there was nothing I could do to lose! I didn't know which was worse.

At practice that day, I watched Robert and Brian train and was certain they were going to skate clean. David's injury left him a question mark. I wasn't in a social mood that day and had had only six hours' sleep the night before, so after lunch I hid out in my room listening to music and watching TV until it was time to leave for the rink.

On the night of the long program, I must have appeared nervous because Don went searching for sports psychologist Bruce Ogilvie. When he came back with Mr. Ogilvie, Don said with a perfectly straight face, "I happened to bump into Bruce." I laughed and asked Dr. Ogilvie where Don had found him. Don made a graceful exit and Dr. Ogilvie and I talked for about fifteen minutes about what I wanted to accomplish tonight and what I needed to do to skate a great program. Finally I was able to relax a little.

That night, Mark Cockerell, in fourth after the short, made an attempt at immortality. He planned a quad jump, and if he hit it he would become the first skater ever to land one in competition. But he took a hard fall, and it would be another six years before Kurt Browning landed the first quad at the 1988 world championships.

A Santee would play a major role in the event—only it wasn't David; it was his younger brother Jimmy. He and David were complete opposites. While David would be out in the corridor jumping rope before practice, you could always find Jimmy in the dressing room, nursing a cup of coffee and holding court with his sense of humor. Skating in the group before us, Jimmy accidentally dug his toe into the ice while attempting a triple Lutz and left a particularly sizable hole in the Lutz corner of the rink—the one I use to make the jump. Jimmy's reputation for Lutz craters preceded him, and I had been kidding him all week—"Don't mess around in my corner of the rink."

"Hey," he'd joke back. "Why would I want to mess around in my corner? I have to jump there."

Everyone who skated after Jimmy had to watch for it, including his older brother. On his warm-up, I yelled at him in jest, "Warm it up in your corner!" But lo and behold, he made a huge, gaping hole. When I went out to warm up, I could hear fans in that part of the arena shouting, "Watch out for the hole," every time I got close to it.

Brian was the first skater out of the box. And he was unbelievable. His performance that night heralded the brilliant career to come. Brian had been awesome the year before in San Diego, and the only thing that had kept him off the podium was a lack of experience. His sixth-place finish in compulsories here gave him a chance to make a move. It wasn't just the number of triples Brian hit that left us all shaking our heads in wonder; it was the variety: Salchow, toe loop, flip, Lutz and Axel. That night he was also gunning to become the first American to hit a triple Axel–double toe loop combination. I didn't want to watch his program and went backstage far from the ice. When I heard the place in his music where he was attempting the Axel–toe, I covered my ears to avoid the din of the crowd. I knew he'd successfully landed the combination because I could feel the hum of sixteen thousand delirious fans.

I was up next. Brian had skated great and I wanted to match his momentum. I ignored the Santee crater—how many more things could go wrong this week after reskating a figure and blowing my short program? As I went into my Lutz, I heard the crowd gasp. I had narrowly missed the hole. With the crowd going nuts, I landed five triples and four double Axels, and won a standing ovation. After I finished, I skated over to the corner to see just how close I had come to hitting the hole Jimmy made. I missed it by an inch. No wonder people in the stands were yelling at me to watch out. Dick Button grabbed me as I came off the ice and I breathlessly exclaimed that it was the best I had ever skated. My numbers for both technical and artistic came up big—a total of four 5.8s and fourteen 5.9s.

David skated after me, in obvious pain from the groin injury. He had already fallen hard in the warm-up, and we were all wondering if he could retain his spot on the world team, which he had owned for six years. David skated to *Rocky* once again, but the magic he'd had in San Diego wasn't there. He doubled the planned triple Lutz that had been giving him fits, though he did hit five triple jumps and a bunch of double Axels. His marks were 5.5s and 5.6s.

Robert, a terrific freestyle skater, then came out and skated a beautiful program, hitting seven triples. In the end, I placed first, Robert second, and David third. David had really struggled, and the judges had given him some generous "lifetime achievement" marks at Brian's expense. Brian got third in the long but fourth in the standings, and was denied a place on the world team, even though he completed his triple Axel–double toe combination, a first for U.S. men. All things being equal, Brian belonged on the podium. He was awesome.

Brian, understandably, didn't take it well. At the skaters' party, there were tears and people kept telling him he had been ripped off. Later he went on a long walk with Rosalynn Sumners, the seventeen-year-old from Washington State who won her first national title that week. I think talking to her helped Brian see he had a lot to gain from Indianapolis. Though he didn't get the marks he deserved this time, that probably wasn't going to happen again. I could well remember skating great in the '79 nationals and getting shut out of the world team. But in the long run it balances out: for every time you feel penalized, there's going to be a time you get held up with better marks than a performance deserves. On that night, David got his "lifetime achievement marks." And I don't mean that derogatorily. You earn those marks, and David had more than paid his dues. When judges are forming the world team, they tend to make allowances for the betterment of the team and are willing to cut someone a little slack if they believe they will represent the country well and contend for a medal. Don't forget, David was the reigning world silver medalist who had a good reputation with international judges, and I think everyone in the building knew this was his last shot. He deserved one more chance. Skating is not the only sport where they make allowances like this. Don't Cy Young Award winners get larger strike zones? Aren't the best basketball players granted one extra step before they're called for traveling? Don't the referees sometimes look away when superstar hockey players commit penalties?

I tell young skaters that if they just keep pushing and plugging, they're going to succeed. If you're marked down in the short, don't get discouraged and blow the long. Because guess what—you've just validated those previous marks, and those judges don't owe you anything anymore. Do two clean performances as Brian did and they owe you. That experience made Brian the hungriest skater on the planet. So if you keep getting better, the marks will come.

As my rivalry with David was coming to a close—this was his last year of competition— there were plenty of skaters waiting in line to knock me off. The next skater to emerge in my sights was Norbert Schramm of West Germany. Norbert was a twenty-two-year-old German Army corporal and a talented painter, with a bowl-top haircut. A huge star in his home country, he finished seventh at worlds in 1981 and then won Europeans in 1982. He was suddenly hot, and the Germans were giving him a big push. One of his most powerful allies was Sonia Bianchetti.

At that time, Schramm lacked the discipline and polish of a champion. He could do the jumps, but his training habits were suspect. In order to prepare with no distractions and get used to the time-zone change, Don and I spent two weeks in Oberstdorf, the national training center for the West German team, preparing for the world championships in Copenhagen. Norbert was there too, at least part of the time.

On my first day at practice I did a clean run-through of my long program and worked hard on figures. I felt pretty good and appreciated the change in scenery because practicing in Denver was getting a little stale. I could just tell Norbert felt he was going to challenge me that year. But he hurt his hip in practice and he stopped skating. The next day I heard he was well enough to go skiing and cruise around in his car, acting like a playboy. Skiing with worlds just a couple of weeks away? Not a good idea. Skipping practice? Even worse.

Another problem for him was his coach, Erich Zeller. They weren't seeing eye to eye and got into big arguments. No doubt I was a major distraction for him. I didn't fool around. I was doing clean run-throughs all week and it was affecting his preparation.

Norbert's forte was bizarre, avant-garde programs, with techno-pop music filled with electronic blips and factory noises. He likened himself to an artist—striking odd poses on the ice and playing to the crowd. He liked to talk about putting his "feelings in the music," and during his performances he flapped his arms and made weird motions with his hands in front of his face. He did a scratch spin with his upper arms pointing out horizontally and his forearms bent vertically, stuff I would never do. But it made him fun to watch, for me as much as his many fans.

After watching Norbert's act for a couple of weeks, I left Oberstdorf more concerned about Brian Pockar, Fumio Igarashi, Canada's Brian Orser, Russia's Igor Bobrin and Frenchman Jean-Christophe Simonde.

What I didn't recognize was that the European judges were warming to Norbert's peculiar style.

After arriving in Copenhagen, the German press went to work on me. I tried to mind my own business, but they were writing that I didn't deserve to be champion and Norbert should replace me because he had better taste in cars and art. He was pegged as more worldly and creative; I was the meat-and-potatoes technician. So it was the artist versus the athlete. One night at a reception, the reporters kept asking me if I was going to quit after this competition.

"I'm in it through the Olympics," I said defiantly. Then they wanted me to pose for a picture with Norbert, who of course took his sweet time before coming over to say hello.

"Norbert, come here and get in the picture," the photographer said.

Norbert was standing next to me and we waited for the flash. After snapping a couple of frames the photographer looked at Norbert and said, "Pick up Scott and hold him in your arms."

"No, I won't do that," I said, and I walked away. I'd had it with the German press.

The setting for the competition was the Brondby Hallen ice rink. I began the week placing second in figures behind French champion Jean-Christophe Simonde, who was the best in the world at compulsory figures. David was third. Norbert had started out in eleventh after the first figure but it was all uphill after that. He made up ground in the next two figures and climbed to sixth.

When Jean-Christophe missed his combination, and I skated a clean short, I moved into first overall. Norbert skated well and sat in third place entering the long. On March 11, long program day, Norbert skated before me and turned in a bombshell of a performance. In his fire red costume, he came out and landed every jump, and the audience loved all his weird moves and positions. Even his shaky landings added to the effect. The crowd loved him. Bouquets of flowers rained on the ice when he finished. As I skated around in circles waiting for them to call my name, I was thinking, just get in the top three and the championship is mine.

I more than succeeded. Substituting a nice triple toe walley—a slight variation on a toe loop—for my shaky triple flip, I hit six triples in all and finished first. But when I got off the ice, I told Don I had stunk. Even though I won five of seven judges from Norbert, who finished second in the free and second overall, I felt my performance was flat. I skated clean but lacked my usual energy and speed.

So Norbert got a place on the podium by being modern, outrageous and playing to the crowd. He hit his jumps and skated out of his mind.

And he taught me something: don't be afraid to be different. A week earlier, I had no respect for him. But now I was impressed by his panache. It was clear the ISU and European judges were grooming him to be the next world champion. I could see it

After competing, I stood in an aisle to watch the ladies' final. Elaine was about to skate, and all my attention was on the ice. She was a close friend and had won nationals a year ago with me in San Diego. Rosalynn Sumners had beaten her this year at Indianapolis, and now Elaine was mired back in seventh place after the short. But all week the buzz was that she was going to attempt something no woman had ever done before—six triples in her long program, just as many as the men. Most of the other women at that time were doing maybe two triple jumps, maximum.

The stories about Elaine were unbelievable. We'd heard rumors she could land double Axels in flimsy rental skates and was even hitting triple Axels in practice. She was ahead of her time in this respect. At worlds, her coach, Peter Burrows, realized that if the rest of the field placed a certain way, and Elaine won the long program, she could win the title. Elaine lived up to her billing and landed four triple toe loops and two triple Salchows, winning the world championship. She was just sixteen years old. Later that year, the ISU implemented a new rule that prohibited skaters from repeating the same triple jump more than twice. It was forever dubbed the "Zayak rule" and was passed only in response to what Elaine accomplished that night in Copenhagen.

After she skated, I went to the mezzanine and ran into Helen McLoraine. I had been avoiding her lately and she was not happy about it. Don told me she was getting frustrated with my attitude at competitions. Once, when she felt slighted, she went back to her hotel room and threw her purse in disgust. Who could blame her? She was doing something for me that in my mind I could never repay. My skating expenses were $11,000 a year, and Helen contributed a total of $96,000 in all toward my skating career. I was reacting to my feeling of obligation like an immature kid trying to exert some independence and autonomy from all the grown-ups around him. I owed Helen a huge debt of gratitude, but I was incapable of expressing it. Sometimes, though, my behavior was misinterpreted, like what happened this time in Copenhagen.

Helen and I started talking, and suddenly I was surrounded by a swarm of people wanting autographs. They kept stepping between us and we gradually got separated. I signed as many as I could, and when I looked over at Helen, she was talking to someone else. As soon as there was a break, I gracefully made my escape and went downstairs to congratulate

Elaine, forgetting to say good-bye to Helen. I found out later from Don that she felt slighted that I had disappeared on her. I was so upset for hurting her feelings even though I hadn't intended to. I apologized to her later. Still, it was clear I needed to show more sensitivity to what was happening around me. I resolved that Helen and I needed to spend more time together, and that was what we did.

That night I met up with Peter Carruthers, who had placed third at worlds with Kitty. Kitty and I were still dating off and on, but we were in a cooling-off period. Our relationship was winding down, and by the summer, we would cease to be an official couple. It was hard to figure. One moment we couldn't get along, and the next we couldn't live without each other. No matter who else we dated or how long we were apart, we always remained friends. I always wondered if things would have been different if skating hadn't gotten in the way. We bonded in 1980 chasing the Olympic dream and had an incredible time in Lake Placid, competing without pressure and enjoying the party atmosphere, which included a special Olympic Valentine's Day. A year later, we were both national champions and all our skating dreams were coming true. I had moved away and we tried to keep up a long-distance relationship. Then we'd take a breather, but when we met up again at competitions, the soap opera would heat up again. We'd have conversations long into the night, even if we were competing the next day. I remember at easterns in Morristown we talked all night and I had a long program to skate later the same day. I managed to skate pretty well, too. Romantic tension was at times a welcome distraction because it kept my mind off of competing, but there was much more to our relationship. Kitty got close to me as no one ever had. She has seen me at my happiest and at my most melancholy. She was there for me during my lowest of lows—such as when I was dropped from the world team at the Cincinnati nationals, and later, when I was devastated by Frank McLoraine's death. She also has shared in my biggest moments in competition, such as winning nationals and worlds in 1981.

But as we got to be better skaters, work took up more and more of our time. Kitty always felt that success ruined our relationship, and she might be right about that. We got pulled in too many directions and had gotten too competitive with one another. Still, I spent most of 1981 longing for those blissful days in Philadelphia, training all week and spending the weekends with Kitty. I missed her, and the withdrawal pains were hard to overcome. Through all my ups and downs, I wasn't an easy guy to figure out, yet Kitty was always there for me. What more could you ask for?

By the end of the competition in Copenhagen, Kitty and I were going our separate ways again. I was hanging out a lot with Peter, and he was telling me that the European press was now hounding them to quit "while on top." Yeah, right. I think they wanted all the Americans out of there so they could win all the medals next year in Helsinki. It was infuriating. Though I had won, the victory was bittersweet. I was preoccupied by Norbert's performance and the crowd's ecstatic reaction to his skating. It left me feeling depressed, even though I felt I was the better skater. At Oberstdorf he had looked terrible; then he came to Copenhagen, finished second, and made me feel like I was chasing him.

I needed some cheering up, so Peter and I hit the town, which left me in bad shape for the exhibition of champions on Sunday. The queen of Denmark was there, sitting front row center, and I skated atrociously to "New York, New York," wiping out on a double Axel and popping a triple Lutz. Dick Button tried to cover for me, telling viewers, "His mistakes are like water off the back of a duck," but I left the ice humiliated. "That was my first queen," I finessed on camera, trying to explain why I messed up. "I was nervous."

Maybe this self-loathing thing of mine had gone too far. Don was fuming over the exhibition and he let me have it. I had no business coming in so unprepared, he said. To make matters worse, Norbert stole the show again, in a way I can appreciate now. After he skated, he glided over to the queen and started flirting with her. He was shameless and people were shocked. But I loved it and the fans loved it; his popularity in Europe exploded.

On the plane flight home from Denmark, I reflected on my peculiar year. I was winning, and I was unhappy. I had heaped so much garbage on myself the past season, much of it my own doing. Yet in competition I had survived. I went to easterns and survived that somehow. I went to nationals and survived that. All that negative stuff I put on myself was me being a jerk. Copenhagen proved to be a big turning point for me. I finally felt worthy of my title and realized I didn't want the Norbert Schramms of the world taking it away.

Earlier in the season, I had told Dick Button that skating wasn't fun anymore; it was becoming a job. Now my mind-set began to change: Somebody has to be champ and it might as well be me. After all, it's only a competition. Once I put it all in perspective, the misery went away.

That spring, Don and I vowed that the 1983 season would be different. We made plans to beef up the technical difficulty, and with Ricky's help put together a fresh new set of programs. I didn't want to appear stale. I loaded up my schedule with two internationals, easterns, nationals and worlds. I was going to beat back the Schramms and the Orsers and rededicate myself as I had for the 1980 season. Life had to get better. It could only get better.

Chapter Ten

The Makeover

Right after winning worlds in Copenhagen, I went out on the ISU tour with the other world medalists. For me, it was business and pleasure. As the world champion, it was my chance to establish a presence in Europe. As a twenty-three-year-old male on the loose, it was a chance to have a great time. I remember our performance in Leningrad before 25,000 fans because it was one of the largest crowds ever to see a skating event. In the audience was a little boy named Viktor Petrenko who would grow up to one day win Olympic gold in Albertville, France. We performed in Luxembourg, London, Germany and Switzerland.

The tour was almost pure pleasure. The practices were loose and free of competition pressure, though we all still tried to outdo one another. At night we went to bars and clubs, and visited all kinds of foreign restaurants. I had some wonderful friends, including my roommate Brian Pockar.

We were both practical jokers and did everything we could to annoy each other. Brian's favorite joke was to get up early in the morning, fill the room with shower steam while I was asleep, and then blow cigarette smoke in my face. That was his idea of a wake-up call. My idea of unpacking was tossing Brian's clothes out of second-story windows. Not very mature stuff, but it sure kept us entertained.

It was harder connecting with the Eastern Bloc athletes because of the cultural, political and language barriers. Most of the Russians and skaters from Eastern European countries kept to themselves and spoke in their native tongues. But once in a while there were breakthroughs. During our first show in Oslo, Norway, East German Katarina Witt, then the world silver medalist, was skating to *Romeo and Juliet*. She was just eighteen and it was her first time touring. We were watching her perform in a sleeveless dress and noticed her armpits were unshaven. Well, some of the veteran skaters, like Kitty and Canadian pairs skater Barbara Underhill, took Katarina aside and gave her some pointers. Katarina shaved but thought their concern was kind of funny. Body hair is just not that big a deal to Eastern Europeans.

No one was spared during that first performance. Barbara was almost seriously injured when she and her partner, Paul Martini, tried a dangerous bounce spin—in which Paul rotated his body holding Barbara out in a horizontal position by her feet and waving her body up and down as the centrifugal force kept her from crashing onto the ice. Well, after a couple of turns, Paul's hands slipped and all he had hold of were Barb's fishnet stockings. She went down hard, right on her chest. Fortunately she wasn't hurt.

Then it was Brian Orser's turn to foul up. He attempted a triple Lutz, lost his bearings in the air and landed in a split. All the guys watching doubled over and groaned. Brian got up, brushed the ice off of his costume and started howling along with us.

The jokes could sometimes go overboard, and looking back on it, I did stuff I'm pretty ashamed of. On the tour's second stop in Helsinki, we arrived the night before a matinee exhibition and a group of us hit the bar—Peter, Brian Pockar, Tassilo Thierbach, an East German pairs skater, and a fourth skater who shall remain nameless. We spotted a pretty blond girl sitting alone in the corner and Peter started sending her drinks, saying they were from the anonymous skater sitting at our table (we'll call him Tony). This girl kept picking up her glass and winking at Tony, and he kept moving closer and closer to her until he was sitting next to her. What Tony didn't know was that this woman was a lady of the evening and the rest of us had pooled our money so she would flirt with him. He took the bait. I don't know what happened that night, but Tony came to practice the next day looking pretty wan. I didn't bother to watch, but I heard he did not have one of his better performances in the exhibition.

After doing the ISU and Tommy's tour together, Kitty and I began seeing other people. The distance, we decided, was too much to overcome. Back in Denver, Don, Ricky and I got right to work. We scrapped my old programs and Ricky set new routines. She chose new music—"Ben Hur" and *Flight of the Bumblebee* for the short and a new jazzier sound for the long with "Sing, Sing, Sing," "Snowfall" and "Blue Danube," followed by my tried-and-true ending, *Swan Lake*.

We also decided to up the ante technically to turn it into the hardest long program I'd ever performed. For instance, instead of turning forward for the triple toe, after the opening triple Lutz, I continued skating backward, which made the takeoff for the triple toe almost impossible. We also added a double Axel–triple toe combination.

At this point I started dating Lea Ann Miller, who skated pairs with Billy Fauver. Lea Ann and I had gone out in 1978–79, when I was taking from Carlo in Denver, only she was training at the Broadmoor. I had such a bad reputation Billy used to try to keep us apart, so Lea Ann and I used to see each other in secret. We had split up when I moved to Philadelphia, but the relationship rekindled in the fall because she and Billy were traveling back and forth between Wilmington and Colorado Springs to train and we started seeing each other again. Lea Ann was a wonderful skater and a beautiful woman. She is also a talented choreographer. She invited me to spend Christmas with her family in St. Louis, Missouri. Since Easterns were fast approaching, I couldn't afford to take off for more than a day or two at most. So I took Lea Ann up on her offer instead of going home to Bowling Green. She made me feel welcome, and I got to know her dad, Larry, who had become a good friend of my father's, sitting together during competitions and eating with one another at mealtime.

I came from a traditional Christmas dinner background—turkey or ham for the main course, mashed potatoes, stuffing, cranberry sauce and squash. The Millers did it a little differently. We had lobster, then bundled up to go to midnight Mass at a Presbyterian church. Not being a churchgoer, nor a suit-and-tie kind of guy, I asked Lea Ann if I could wear my Hawaiian shirt. No problem, she said, and that was what I did.

In early January I won Easterns and set my sights squarely on the Pittsburgh nationals. I felt secure about defending my title—both David Santee and Robert Waggenhoffer had retired—leaving nineteen-year-old Brian Boitano as my primary challenger, and a dangerous one. He was such a strong free skater I couldn't afford any mistakes. One major miss and the championship might be his. I felt the judges owed him that.

I didn't want to leave any room for doubt. I wanted to dominate early and began by winning all three school figures. On Friday night, the Civic Arena was packed with fifteen thousand fans for the short program. I was paranoid about bombing because I had not had a disaster in competition in more than two years. It was like waiting for a time bomb to go off. However, I skated a clean short and won, though Mark Cockerell and Brian also hit their triple Lutz–double toe combinations.

On the night of the men's finals, the Civic Arena was sold out and scalpers were getting double the eleven-dollar face value of the tickets. Eleven dollars? Can you imagine? I skated well again, completing five triples, including my double Axel–triple toe combination. Then I did a comic rendition of the waltz in a style borrowed from an old number made famous by Jackson Haines, one of America's founding fathers of fig- ure skating. Don's thinking was if this part of the program amused him, it would entertain the audience. It was a stretch to try comedy in a routine, and a risk because we didn't know how the judges or the crowd would react to the segment. Nobody else was doing it. As I was mimicking the dance, I could hear people laughing, which was exactly what we wanted. The judges enjoyed it too: I received all 5.9s for artistic and nothing lower than a 5.8 for technical.

Thank goodness I'd done my part to make the judges' decision an easy one, because when Brian took the ice a few minutes later, he proved again why he was the best jumper I had ever seen. He hit six triples in all—including a Lutz, loop, Axel and a triple flip–double toe combina- tion. He finished second, as I had hoped he would. In fact, I was hoping he'd come in second in more ways than one. I had won figures, the short and the long. It was just the kind of decisive victory I needed going into worlds.

A month later, when Don and I flew to Finland for worlds, Brian was on the same flight, and I sat with him and tried to give him a few point- ers. "Practices can be intimidating at your first worlds," I warned. "Don't let anyone intimidate you."

He was polite and just nodded. But Brian wasn't even concerned about another skater trying to unnerve him. He was so anxious just to get out there and skate after missing out on making the world team the previous year in Indianapolis, it never occurred to him that some of the veteran skaters might try to bother him.

Years later we were touring in different productions and crossed paths in a Kansas City hotel used by both tours. A bunch of us were hanging out, and I confessed to Brian that back in the early 1980s, I worried he might catch me. "And when you didn't make worlds in 1982, I got even more scared because I knew you'd come back next year even better," I said.

Brian couldn't believe his ears. "I was in awe of you. Half the time I was competing against you, I wasn't even sure you knew who I was."

As much as I had worried about him, Brian said he never believed he had any hope of beating me. He was resigned to placing second or third until I was out of skating.

The day after I checked into my hotel in Finland, a package arrived in the mail from Japan. I unwrapped two new costumes, but these weren't just your standard two-piece bejeweled-variety outfits. They were fashioned after one-piece speed-skating suits—lightweight and body hugging, save for the flared pants. One costume was royal blue with a yellow stripe down one sleeve and the opposite leg. I'd wear that for the short. For the long, it was silver stripes down both arms on a black body. There wasn't a sequin in sight.

These were radically different costumes from what the other men were wearing in Helsinki. We'd made the decision to try a new look the previous summer in Lake Placid while attending the North American training camp. One afternoon, Don was browsing in the Sun Dog ski shop when his eye caught some one-piece ski suits manufactured by Descent, a Japanese ski company.

He knew I was sick and tired of wearing beaded outfits. Nobody outside the skating community seemed to appreciate the difficulty of doing a triple jump or the stamina required to get through a four-and-a-half-minute program. Instead, all we heard were jokes about our costumes. Even sportscasters who should know better would ask, How can you consider yourself an athlete when you wear sequins?

Don returned and told me about the outfits at Sun Dog. We had already been talking about the unitard we saw sprinter Evelyn Ashford wear at a track meet, so I went back to the store and took a look for myself. I liked them. When Don and I went to the NHK competition a few months later, we met with a Descent sportswear designer to talk over design concepts, look at fabrics and take pictures and measurements. When the finished product arrived in Helsinki, I took one look and thought, "Throw a cape on my back and I'd look like 'The Greatest American Hero,'" a popular TV show at the time. But I was thrilled with them, as was Don. He felt the new apparel reflected my style of skating—athletic, with an emphasis on body line and strength. I considered myself to be closer to a gymnast than a ballet dancer, and these costumes reflected my strengths without interfering with the performance.

Men's costumes had gotten way too flamboyant. It was almost as if some of the guys were competing to see who could wear the most ridiculous-looking outfit. For a couple of years, I had worn this electric blue long program costume with matching boot covers to go with the sequins and glitter. All the guys were wearing boot covers with boldly colored costumes sprinkled with gemstones, but I wasn't comfortable with it. I didn't want to be known for my "balletic style," but for being an athlete, the best all-around skater in the world. No way did I want my potential Olympic moment to be marred by a costume that I would be embarrassed to look at ten years down the road. I didn't want to look back and think, "How could I have presented myself that way?" (I still wince when I see pictures of that bright blue outfit with sequins.) When I wore the new costumes that week, Don and I got a big thank-you from the ISU because even they thought some of the outfits the other skaters wore were over the top.

I was also motivated by something else. I was convinced an athletic appearance would make men's skating more accessible to the average television viewer. It might also get cynics to start taking figure skating seriously as a sport.

At the time, skating was being marketed solely toward an artistic audience, a very subjective group with varying tastes. Ignored was that a vast portion of our fans loved athleticism, and that was the direction I felt men's skating should be going. I watched Kurt Thomas bring gymnastics to American masses and I wanted to do the same for skating.

Not everyone was in agreement with me. Dick Button, the voice of figure skating, felt I was worrying too much about image rather than what I did on the ice. He said the quality of my skating was what counted, not the costume. But did Dick Button ever wear beads in competition? No. In his day, the late 1940s and early 1950s, men wore black Eisenhower jackets and bow ties—very traditional. I just wanted a modern outfit without the beads, and something in sync with my skating style. So when I tried the new outfits on in my hotel room, I instantly felt better about myself.

Once practice got under way, costumes became the least of my worries.

Under those ominous gray and snowy skies in Helsinki, there was something brewing between the European federations and the international judges. I believe they were plotting my overthrow. Earlier in the year, Paul Wylie, who was taking from Carlo Fassi at the time, said Carlo had predicted I would never win another world title after 1982. That was a challenge—fighting words that kept me motivated throughout the year. But maybe there was something to his prophecy, because something sinister was afoot here.

I started out with a second-place finish in figures. No surprise there. Jean-Christophe Simonde practically owned that phase of the competition for three years running. My closest rivals, Norbert Schramm and Brian Orser, were fourth and eighth respectively. But Don was getting feedback from the U.S. officials that the entire panel, save for U.S. judge Hugh C. Graham, wanted either Norbert or Brian to make a strong move on me. So I went into the short determined to skate clean, and I did. I hit my triple Lutz–double toe combination and completed all the other elements. Yet I didn't get the marks I wanted. And I continued to stew as I watched the other skaters. Losing the short program now—one year before the Olympics—could affect my credibility as world champion. I wanted this worlds more than any other for that very reason. I was feeling vulnerable. I had spent the past year working hard to defend my title— new music, increased technical difficulty, even the new outfits. Now I felt forces were plotting to take it all away.

My instincts were right on. When all the short program marks were in, four judges had Brian first, four judges put Norbert first, and Dr. Graham placed me first. I had eight seconds. Since you need a majority of marks to earn the placement, Brian and Norbert were each one judge short of winning the event. I had the highest majority with eight seconds and one first, giving me first in the short. It was a bizarre outcome considering that I earned only one first-place score, but not unprecedented. Charlie Tickner had done the same five years earlier in Ottawa when he won the '78 worlds. That's the way it goes. By trying so hard to elevate their favorites, those eight judges canceled each other out. Brian wound up in second, Norbert third. Overall, Brian was sitting in sixth and Norbert in third.

At this point, I was going to be hard to catch. And those judges were being watched; it was obvious what happened in the short.

On the night of the final, Norbert skated just before me, and as he came off the ice after a decent program, he looked in my eyes and dared me to skate better. "Okay, now you have to skate your best," he said, challenging me to outdo him.

And I got angry. Really angry, although I kept a perfectly straight face. He was trying to psych me out, but I was not going to let him know he was getting under my skin. I came right back at him and casually said, "No problem." I went out onto the ice wearing my heart on my striped sleeve. After the earlier judging controversy, I already had a chip on my shoulder the size of a building. Now I was furious. Instead of going out there praying I wouldn't miss my opening Lutz, I instinctively knew it was going to happen. I hit six triples and nearly a seventh when I barely touched down with my free leg on a landing. The championship was mine.

I left Helsinki as three-time world champion. Norbert took the silver and Orser got the bronze. Boitano hit his triple Axel and came in seventh. For two years, the Olympics seemed so far off that they were nearly out of my reach. Now they were less than a year away, and I was still in control.

It's funny. You go into every competition thinking this might be the one where the forces conspire against you and you lose. And even when you do come out on top, the margin between winning and losing seems so slim. Yet when I stepped back and looked at what I had accomplished in two calendar years, it was daunting. I was the first American men's champion to win three world titles since David Jenkins from 1957–59, the first man to win three consecutive world championships since Ondrej Nepela from 1971–73. The Olympic gold medal, for the moment, was mine to lose.

After worlds, I hit the road again on the ISU tour. Though I loved touring around Europe, the disorganization took some getting used to. Sometimes practice ice would be canceled at the last minute, and shows didn't always start on time. Things aren't always done on the schedule and pace we were used to in America. But the good times outweighed any of the shortcomings. On a stop in Switzerland, we had a day off after a performance in Porrentruy, and I went out partying with a group of skaters: Barbara Underhill, Brian Orser, Jozef Sabovcik of Czechoslovakia and Tassilo Thierbach of East Germany. We played a drinking game called quarters, at which I had a reputation—well deserved—for being quite good. It's a very popular game on college campuses, with a million crazy rules, including one that the words *drink* and *beer* cannot be used during the game. The object is to bounce a quarter off a table into the "beverage" mug, thereby earning the privilege of handpicking a victim (pointing only with your elbow) to chug the liquid and catch the quarter between his or her teeth as the last few drops of brew are sliding down the glass. I was on fire that night—sinking seven quarters in a row. Each time I raised my elbow toward Brian, who diligently inhaled six glasses of spirits and snagged the quarters. But then he had the nerve to try to beg off when I selected him for the seventh time. I wouldn't hear of it. "Be a man," I told him. "Consume that beverage! Now, mister, now!"

"I can't," he replied. Then, like an obedient ISU tour rookie, he consumed the beverage. When he was finished, his face went blank. He looked in his glass and it was completely empty. Then he started to gag, "Aaah, aaah." I was laughing so hard, I felt like I was going to wet my pants. I ran to the bathroom and Brian came running in behind me, thinking he might be able to regurgitate the quarter. He hacked and coughed, even tried slapping the back of his neck, as though the quarter were stuck in his throat. No chance. The sucker was gone, off on its fateful journey through his digestive tract. Poor Brian was so flustered, I tried to make him feel better in my own inimitable way. While he was relieving himself in the urinal, I cracked, "Look, two dimes and a nickel." Brian somehow retrieved the quarter later and kept it as a keepsake. To this day he threatens to slip that very piece of silver in my glass the next time we play quarters. I can just hear him saying, "Guess what you have between your teeth?"

By the end of the ISU minitour, I got to be good friends with Brian and Jozef. On our last night together, we were hanging out in a pub in Garmisch, in what was then West Germany, and started talking about the Sarajevo Olympics, just a year away.

"Wouldn't it be great," I said, "if it were the three of us on the podium next year? It doesn't matter which medals, just that us three would be getting them?"

We raised our mugs and offered a silent toast—to the winners of the 1984 Olympic men's figure skating event.

After I got off tour in May, I went home to Bowling Green to skate in the "Ice Horizons" show. I flew into O'Hare and was picked up by my Denver buddy Brent Landis, who had moved to Chicago to attend law school. Then we drove on to Bowling Green.

Because of media obligations and performing in the show, home-comings were getting a bit hectic, but I made the best of them. Most of the time I didn't get to see as much of my dad as I would have liked. His health was noticeably declining. In another month he would be traveling to the Cleveland Clinic for open-heart surgery, and later in the year he returned for surgery on a herniated disk in his back.

Brent and I pulled into Bowling Green at about 3 A.M., but despite the hour, I asked him to swing by Memorial Gardens cemetery. He pulled up by the front gates and parked. I got out of the car alone and walked to my mother's grave site. It was dark and chilly, but I sat down and spent fifteen minutes catching her up on the competitions and tours from the past season. She could probably tell I was feeling more secure with my standing in the skating community. For the first time in two years, I felt that the world title belonged to me and no one else could take it away until I was ready to give it up.

Of course, there was plenty of competition waiting to knock me off. Orser and Boitano were coming on strong, and they would be dominating the men's division in a couple of years. But nothing was going to get in my way, not with the Olympics just a year away. "Mom," I said, "I have come a long way these past couple of years. I've gone from being an insufferable Mr. Hyde for most of 1981 to a confident Dr. Jekyll for the past twelve months. I like being Dr. Jekyll a whole lot better. And so does everyone around me."

When I returned to Denver to resume training, I decided that everything I did, every choice I made, over the next nine months would be geared toward winning the Olympics. I fantasized about it daily, visualizing myself standing atop the podium, the national anthem playing, hearing my name announced as "Olympic champion." A gold medal is yours for life after you win it. That was the gist of what Janet Lynn had told me back in Wagon Wheel in 1972. The title is all yours and no one can take it away

I had witnessed many skaters make horrible career mistakes to take themselves out of the running for a world or Olympic medal. I wasn't going to let that happen to me. I was not going to step on Olympic ice wondering whether I should have trained harder.

The plan was to treat every practice like a competition, drilling my body over and over so I could perform without even thinking. I wanted complete muscle memory, to have every step in my short and long program memorized, right down to the number of crossovers I did before I attempted my Lutz or toe loop.

It was an obvious idea, just tough to execute. Part of the process included letting myself get nervous before every run-through in practice. The more anxiety I felt, the more pressure I put on myself to skate clean. That made me competition-tough and reduced the chances of something unexpected happening.

Life now revolved completely around skating. Lea Ann and I broke up because the time constraints and the geographical distance got to be too much for both of us. My days were maxed out. I got up early and was in the rink by 7 A.M. to work on compulsory figures and short program. I'd come home in the early afternoon to eat lunch, watch *General Hospital* and have a short nap. I was back at the rink at 4 P.M. to work on my long program for a couple of hours. Then it was back home for dinner and a night of sleep.

Living in Brent's home was a treat. Dr. and Mrs. Landis screened my calls, and Mrs. Landis cooked for me and did my laundry. Their basement was my sanctuary. I decorated my walls with signed pictures of Susan Anton, photos of pair champs Tai and Randy, and a photo of me being introduced to Jimmy Carter in the White House after the 1980 Olympics. I also kept a list of proverbs and adages passed on to me over the years. Some of my favorites were "If you fool around with a thing for very long, you will screw it up," and "Everything that comes before the word 'but' is a lie."

My coach, Don, had a few laws to live by himself: "There are no excuses, only reasons." Another favorite: "The absence of pain is death." Brian Pockar gave me one of my favorite laws: "In competition, you'll skate 20 percent better or 20 percent worse than in practice." More often than not, that's true. It seemed all of these sayings applied to skating.

One of my strategies was to learn from other skaters' successes and failures. From Charlie Tickner, I learned the consequences of playing it conservative at big competitions. He skated with a level of caution at the 1979 world championships that undermined his ability to give his best performance. And yet he's the only skater I've ever seen whose performance at a national championships earned a standing ovation from a panel of judges, which happened in 1977. He demonstrated that hard work and perseverance can win the day.

John Curry taught me something about tenacity. When I arrived in Denver back in 1976, he told me he completed twenty-six consecutive perfect run-throughs of his long program before the Olympics. That was a goal I set for myself this year.

From Dorothy Hamill I learned about peaking at the right time for an event, which she always seemed to do. Tai and Randy, who had to withdraw from the 1980 Olympics due to Randy's injury, showed how important it is to be selective about what you do on the ice before a big event. Gordie McKellen gave me the gift of how to put your heart and soul into a performance and how to take command of an audience. And from Janet Lynn I learned to smile throughout a program.

Skaters weren't my only influences. Bruce Springsteen, Neil Diamond and Billy Joel—they share themselves onstage and allow the audience to enjoy the moment with them. I'll never forget seeing Neil Diamond perform; when he finished a song, he paused and smiled at the crowd, and we all smiled back. He projected his joy for singing. Without ever knowing it, he taught me a valuable lesson on how to project my love of skating.

And it can't always be about skating all the time. I like to enjoy life, and even during intense training periods I wasn't a complete hermit, though Brent seemed to think I was pretty boring to be around much of the time. I'm sure I was, compared to the old days when I trained with Carlo.

One night in the summer of '83, Brent was home from law school and I broke up my routine for a rare night on the town. We went to a dance club called Confetti, and this tall, gorgeous woman came over and sat on my lap. She had big red hair and knee-high boots. Brent gave me that look—"She's a babe—ask her out." I was too shy. But we talked for a while, until finally she said, "I have to go to work."

Brent chimed in, "Hey, Scott, you can take her to work."

"Sure," I said. We hopped in my new car, a Mazda RX-7 my father had helped lease for me, drove a short way down the street, and I dropped her off at her job. When I returned to Confetti, I suggested to Brent that we call it a night. I was tired and had to be on the ice early. We drove out of the parking lot and passed by a striptease joint called Shotgun Willy's. Suddenly I got my second wind.

"How about just one more drink?" I said to Brent.

"Nah, I don't want to go in there."

"C'mon, just one."

Strip bars don't do much for me, either, but we made an exception that night. We went inside and got a table. Then out from behind a curtain strutted a very familiar-looking woman. Poor Brent was slack-jawed. "Oh, my God!" Brent yelled. "That's the girl from Confetti."

Nights out on the town with Brent were rare that summer. Skating was foremost on my mind. When the USFSA asked Don and me which international competitions we wanted to do leading up to the '84 season, which would be capped off at the Olympics in Sarajevo, there was only one at the top of my list—Golden Spin in Zagreb, Yugoslavia, scheduled for November. At first I was just anxious to compete there so I could make a stop in Sarajevo to see the ice-skating arena for the Winter Games. Then Don got a call from a U.S. skating official. They didn't want me competing at Zagreb because I would be going up against Norbert Schramm on European soil. They feared he had a shot at beating me, and I did not need a loss to him leading up to the games. Their concern was that a defeat could make me appear vulnerable and might influence how the European judges marked me at the Olympics.

That only made me want it more.

It was true that if Norbert was to have any chance at the Olympics, he had to beat me somewhere first, but I wasn't about to duck him. As a competitor, I wanted him to know that he could never beat me. If he felt his losses to me at worlds were rip-offs, my goal had to be to set him straight. He needed to know there was no shame finishing second to me and that first place was not a consideration. The best way to convince him was to do exactly what the USFSA was telling me not to do: confront him in Europe. So I said to Don, "Tell the USFSA that I want Zagreb and I want Norbert's blood."

And I got it. I beat him soundly. My only mistake the entire week was doubling a planned triple flip in the long program. Norbert didn't seem to be prepared and had a rough time. He finished third, but he was still in early-season form—lots of shaky jumps and unsteady landings.

Don and I left Zagreb on November 21 and took a train to Sarajevo to inspect the Olympic ice facility, the Zetra. I didn't want to show up in February and get all wide-eyed and intimidated by the arena. I wanted to get the lay of the land and have it implanted in my mind as I prepared for the '84 season. At the last minute, Norbert decided he wanted to tag along. Don and I had planned this months before and had even reserved ice time in a rink in the area. Norbert even wanted to jump in on that. Don told his people to forget it. We didn't want any distractions.

Rosalynn Sumners was also with us, and she was having a rough week. Roz was the defending world champion and she had just been beaten in Zagreb by the Yugoslav champ, Sanda Dubravcic, who had finished thirteenth at worlds. Poor Roz cried the entire train trip to Sarajevo. When we arrived, she got sick and stayed in her room, eating continuously. She was so pale and puffy, we were kidding her all week, calling her "Casper the miserable puffball." Roz can look back and laugh about the experience now. She is one of the best-conditioned skaters I know. But that week was a forgettable one for her.

We celebrated Thanksgiving at the Hotel Bosnia and explored the different ethnic quarters in the city. The food was amazing, and the people were friendly and outgoing. While I enjoyed parts of the city, I noticed the air was smoggy. Outdoors, it came from cars and industry. Indoors, it came from all the cigarettes. (At the Olympics, the television crews would nickname the city "Planet Smoke.") I met some skiers and they warned me about something called "Yugo throat." Because the air is so dirty, outsiders tend to pick up a hacker's cough after spending a few days there. So when I left, I made a mental note to bring along an ionizer from home when I returned for the games. I was leaving nothing to chance.

When I got my first look at the Zetra skating venue, it was smaller than I anticipated. It seated less than six thousand, and it was a mess. There were slabs of cement and piles of lumber everywhere, so it was not the best time to be sizing up the place. I was struck by how far away from the hockey boards the seating was situated. The judges and the kiss-and-cry area also seemed farther from the surface than they should have been. I supposed it would all come together in time.

As I surveyed the rink, I closed my eyes for a second and tried to picture the arena filled with people and the Olympic symbols on display. I imagined myself skating around the ice, my long program music playing in the background. And if I listened real closely, above the din of the construction noise, I could hear the national anthem playing, and if I looked real hard through the clouds of dust and debris, I could envision an American flag being raised to the rafters. Yes, I thought to myself. That would be one heck of a view inside the Zetra a few months from now.

Chapter Eleven

The Last Amateur

It was a simple plan on the face of it. Finish in the top two in figures, and in the top three in the short and long programs, and I win an Olympic gold medal. The prize goes to the best all-around skater, so my strategy was to be well-rounded in all the disciplines. There was strength in having no weaknesses.

I had been training for this competition for four years, ever since I stepped into the world skating picture at the Lake Placid winter games. But I had been thinking about the Olympics for much longer than that.

As a boy, I knew the Olympics were special from the reaction of my parents on the night Peggy Fleming won an Olympic gold medal at Grenoble, France. We gathered around the television in the old Brownwood house to watch her skate her long program. There was no short program then, just compulsory figures and one freestyle event. My mother was mesmerized by Peggy's grace and beauty, which was lost on me at the time. I had been skating for only a month and was still learning the basics. Just getting around the rink without falling was a major accomplishment. What most impressed me about Peggy was that she was the only U.S. athlete to take home a gold medal from those games. And she was a skater, no less.

I kept on practicing and improving, encouraged by my mother and father, who made sure I got to the rink to skate. In those days I didn't think about the Olympics; they seemed unattainable, so why bother to fantasize? It wasn't until I won juniors in 1976 and realized I had an outside chance of making the 1980 team that I started thinking about them seriously. Then the Olympics became for me what they are for every competitive skater: the ultimate event.

That remains true today. But much about the games and their meaning to skating has changed. The skaters who competed in Sarajevo were the last amateurs. With each Olympics after 1984, the rules were gradually relaxed, allowing amateur skaters more commercial opportunities. The way the bylaws stand today, money doesn't separate amateurs and professionals anymore. Now the only difference between them is Olympic eligibility. A top amateur today can earn seven figures performing on tour and competing in events sanctioned by the International Skating Union, retaining their Olympic eligibility and banking their money at the same time.

The winter games themselves reflect these changes in status. They're bigger and more commercial, with sponsors dominating the television airtime as much as the athletes. Unlike when I competed, money influences television coverage now, and there is a danger in that.

When I was announcing at the 1992 Olympics for CBS, producer Rick Gentile called together the broadcasters, producers and directors and showed us a hilarious film clip called the "Bud Light Olympiad." Every sport, every event and every aspect of the games had a sponsor. Before turning on the video, he said, "Let's hope it doesn't come to this." The room got dark and a relay race was projected onto the screen. The voice-over began, "It's the Jaguar Great Britain relay team vying for the Federal Express gold medal against the Welcome to Jamaica team. And it's coming down to a photo finish, sponsored by Nikon." It sounds silly and ominous at the same time. I'm convinced that if the Olympics emphasis is commerce, sports fans will find something else to do.

And yet the Olympics are more important than ever to the skaters as individual athletes. There are so many televised competitions now that the national and world championships have lost their luster. In my era, the best amateur skaters met once a year at the world championships. Today, they also meet at the Grand Prix final, which is held months before worlds, and possibly at a few other events. You can also see the top amateurs today competing against professionals, something that was outlawed in my time. I don't think the average television viewer can tell these competitions apart, but *everyone* knows the Olympics.

Funny thing about the Olympics—the rules are the same and the judging identical to every other skating competition, but that's about all there is in common. You can win five world titles and they don't add up to one Olympic gold medal. It's because a typical era in skating runs in four-year cycles, and the gold medalist becomes emblematic of the period and whatever the style and technical trend is in vogue at the time. It is the best stage to shine on, and to the victor goes a special place in skating history.

My Olympic experiences served as bookends to my career, at least on a world-class level. Lake Placid marked my entrance in 1980, and the Sarajevo games would be my exit from the amateur skating scene. After winning the 1981 world title, most skating people assumed I would quit. There is much a thing as peaking early, and I wondered if I had done just that. How could I hang on for another three years? But I had no intention of quitting so soon. For one, where would I go from there? The touring shows at the time were geared to promoting female champions, so it would have been silly for me to hang it up. So I marked my calendar—and the Sarajevo Olympics became the most important date on it.

When I arrived in Salt Lake City the first week of January for my last national championships, I was ready to deliver the performance of a lifetime—a clean sweep of all the disciplines to send a strong message to the Orsers and Schramms lying in wait that I was the one to beat next month in Sarajevo. The first test was Wednesday morning at the Bountiful Recreation Center, the site of the compulsory figures event. I swept all the three figures on all nine judges' cards, usually by several tenths of a point higher than the second-place finisher.

There was one small distraction. Don showed up late to the figures event, and I got so upset I fired him on the spot and kept on firing him for the rest of the day. Once again, John Nicks couldn't believe his ears, but it was all in good fun.

Over time, my association with Don had changed from a typical master-pupil relationship to that of a business partnership. Back in Philadelphia in 1979, I needed a strong personality to whip me into shape. As each year passed, Don backed off more and more. He allowed me to take responsibility for my training and didn't need to prod me to work hard. He believed I was perfectly able to reach down and pull off a capable performance when the time came to produce. He knew the score. In ice skating, a singles competitor is out there alone, and he must have the mental strength to perform without depending on anybody. Once I was able to master that, he let me go, yet he was always there for me when I needed help.

By the next morning, I had rehired Don and he was back on the job guiding me through the short program. This season I was skating to *Samson and Delilah* and a Czech folk dance, the identical music I had used in 1981. I went out and swept every judge, hitting my combination—a double loop–triple toe. Brian Boitano and Mark Cockerell hit triple Lutz–double loop combinations and placed second and third respectively. This season, the double loop was the mandatory jump, and you were permitted to perform any triple jump in combination with it to complete the required element. I chose the loop–toe loop combination because it was more consistent than my Lutz–loop, and my plan was not to take any unnecessary risks. It might cost me first place in the short program later on in Sarajevo, but if everything went according to plan, it wouldn't matter.

The long program was set for Friday, and I had five triples planned—Lutz, flip, toe loop, toe walley and Salchow. My number opened to George Duke's "Guardian of the Light." As I stood still on the ice, the opening seconds were filled with crackling laser sounds. Then for the next ninety seconds, it was pure action—triple Lutz, triple flip (had to fight to save the landing), some intricate and fast footwork into a triple toe walley. Then I made a transition into a slow dramatic portion to some haunting Asian jazz music by the band Hiroshima. The section lasted a minute and fifteen seconds and included a triple toe loop, double toe loop combination and two double Axels. Then came the humor section, which ended with a triple Salchow, revving up the engines for the last push to get through the last quarter of the program—double Axel, double Lutz, delayed Axel, and Russian split jumps, concluding with a scratch spin meant to transform me into a blur.

Bob Ottum, a writer for *Sports Illustrated*, dubbed the program the "Triple wow theory of audience and judge grabbing." Don and I wanted people on the edge of their seats, then out of their seats, then back on the edge, and then out of them again.

My program followed a blueprint that exploited my strengths—speed, footwork, a big opening triple Lutz and an athletic resolution. I left the music selections to Don, who went for maximum impact at the beginning and ending of the program, with something slow, even humorous, for the middle segments.

While I was an amateur, I always opened my long with my toughest jump first, the triple Lutz. Don liked it that way because he felt putting the most difficult element in the program at the beginning gave it maximum impact. I preferred it because I quickly got it out of the way. So much for grand strategy. But it worked, because I never missed the jump in the long. We always saved my triple Salchow for near the end. It was consistent, and after I hit that final triple, I could skate fast and carefree to music that exemplified that freedom—*Swan Lake*—with some Russian splits and double jumps for fun.

We kept this formula for four years. Sometimes we'd mix in some new music, add a new element or some clever choreography, and of course there were the new costumes. But while there may have been a new wrinkle, we never changed the basics of the program, just the dressing. Every year at Christmas, you walk by the same department stores and notice the new window displays. But it's still Christmas and it's still the same store. Only the decorations are different. That was our approach.

It worked to perfection in Salt Lake. After my long, the crowd gave me a standing ovation and the judges awarded me four perfect 6.0 scores for style. It was a dream nationals, my best ever. I won every aspect of the competition by every judge—it was the exact push I was looking for heading into the Olympics. I wanted everyone to know I was ready, in shape and unbeatable.

I flew back to Denver with Don and we spent the next month hunkered down at the CIA, fine-tuning my programs and getting as much rest as possible before leaving for Europe. I tried to keep my distractions to a minimum, but Bob Ottum, the *Sports Illustrated* writer, did spend a couple of days with us for a profile he was writing about me. One morning after he watched me practice I took him to lunch in Georgetown, a city in the mountains forty-five minutes west of Denver. It was a gorgeous day—cold but sunny—and I was feeling pretty good. Bob was sitting in the passenger seat, explaining that he was planning on writing that I was a veritable lock for an Olympic gold medal.

"Scott, you haven't lost a competition in more than three years," he said. "In all that time, you've never lost the long program. I can't see you getting beat."

I kept my eyes on the road and didn't say much of anything. But now I was getting a little uncomfortable. Did I really want a major magazine describing me as a shoo-in for the Olympic title? Bob was practically dusting off a pedestal for me and all I could think of was that I hadn't won anything yet. We came to a stoplight and we both spotted this little blond-haired, freckle-faced boy standing on the side of the road. He sneered at us, raised both arms and flipped us off with an ear-to-ear grin. Talk about getting some perspective. "You know," I said to Bob, "that's the nice thing about being a celebrity. You get greeted so warmly wherever you go."

We both cracked up and I relaxed a little more. When we arrived at the restaurant, the Happy Cooker, we ordered some food and Bob began asking some questions about my programs and choreography. When the waitress returned with my soup, she gave me this funny look and then began playing keep away with my lunch.

"I know you're someone," she said, pulling back my soup from my place setting. I looked at her stone-faced while she ran through the possibilities. After a minute, she yelled, "Skater!" but it was still some time before she guessed who I was and I finally got something to eat. After she left the table, I couldn't resist the opportunity to poke fun at myself again.

"That's another nice thing about being famous," I told Bob. "You always get served promptly in restaurants."

As our departure day for Sarajevo drew closer, my training intensified. In a typical day, I spent most of the morning on figures and then at 12:45 P.M., began run-throughs of my short program. After a break for lunch and a nap, I returned to the rink at 7 P.M. to work on my long program. By saving the long for the end, I built stamina. In all, I was on the ice a total of six hours a day.

One afternoon I came home from practice and found a letter lying on my bed. It was from David Jenkins, the 1960 Olympic champion and the last American man to win a gold medal. Amazingly, he grew up in Akron, located in the eastern part of Ohio. We also felt a kinship because we were both men of less than average height with receding hairlines. David's brother, Hayes, had been the Olympic champion in 1956, so David had the added pressure of succeeding a sibling when he made his bid in Squaw Valley. What an achievement for a single family.

Growing up in Ohio wasn't all we had in common. David had also trained in Colorado, at the Broadmoor arena with the famous Austrian coach Edi Scholdan, a member of the World Figure Skating Hall of Fame. Not only did he attend medical school while actively competing, but as an athlete he was way ahead of his time. His routines included more than one triple jump, which would not become the standard for another fifteen years, and he was the first skater anywhere to land a triple Axel at an exhibition.

David told me in his letter to stay positive and focused on my goal. He also stressed to keep an eye on the competition, but not to the point of getting distracted. "Just look over your shoulder long enough to know what the people behind you are doing, but stay looking ahead," he wrote.

It was good advice. A week after receiving David's letter, I was on a plane to Europe with Don. Our final destination was Yugoslavia, but we didn't fly there directly. We stopped in Paris for a few days to get acclimated to the time-zone change and to check out one of my competitors, the French champion Jean-Christophe Simonde. The first thing I did when I got to the hotel was take a nap. But then, after a bite to eat, we went to practice at a nearby rink.

"Don, do you want the short or long?" I asked.

"Long," he replied.

Although jet-lagged, I did a clean long program, virtually right off the plane. From the day I left Denver for the Olympics, I didn't miss a jump in a single run-through. I wouldn't realize just how important that was until competition week in Sarajevo.

On this day I was less concerned with my performance than with my rivals. While I stood resting against the boards, Don was giving me a couple of pointers but I wasn't paying any attention. I was watching Jean-Christophe warm up some jumps across the rink. He was considered the best compulsory figures skater on the planet, and I had never won figures at the world championships. Don and I had stopped over in Paris to see how my figures stacked up with his. If mine were comparable, I'd done my job.

I noticed Jean-Christophe was struggling with his free skating, but after he saw me skate, his intensity picked up a notch. Over the next couple of days, the triples he was missing when I first arrived, were landing cleanly. As Don and I were leaving for Yugoslavia, his coach came up and shook our hands profusely.

"Thank you so much for coming by," he said in a thick French accent. He explained that I was just the catalyst Jean needed to step up his training. And here I had felt guilty for coming over to spy on his figures. But it was worth it. When I left, I knew I was going to hold my own.

A few days before the start of the games, Don and I flew to Zagreb and then took a smaller twin-engine plane to Sarajevo. A charter bus met us at the airport and took us through the city, which seemed much cleaner and prettier than it had looked during our trip in November. We drove past ancient mosques and stone clock towers that lined both banks of the Miljacka River. In the distance, I could make out gondolas ferrying passengers up and down the snow-covered Trebevic Hill. I remember passing by the National Library, which resembled an old castle. This structure and many others, including the ice arena where I competed, were destroyed eight years later in the Bosnian war. But on this day, watching the children chase dogs in the streets and families shop for groceries in the open-air markets, there was much joy and anticipation in the air. The city contained such a variety of architectural styles—Latin, Roman and Ottoman—and the people reflected their surroundings. I was amazed by the ethnic diversity and how well everyone seemed to get along. The strife that was to come years later was such a stark contrast to the Sarajevo I knew.

I checked into the Olympic village and went to my room, which was actually a new apartment with four bedrooms, a common living room and bathrooms. I plugged in the ionizer I had brought from home and took a bus over to the practice rink to meet up with Don, who was staying in an apartment at the media village with some other coaches. As I was stretching out by the ice, I noticed a small group of judges and reporters watching from the other side of the arena. Judges almost always come to practices to size up the skaters and get an idea of what to expect in a program. Some critics of the system feel judges should stay away from workouts and not let what they see during a week of practices influence them on competition night, but I feel practices are part of the event. By watching several workouts, you can tell who is prepared and in shape and who is not. Strong practices, however, don't compensate for a bad performance. Whatever you've shown during the week, you still have to perform under competition pressure. I always tried to do flawless practices because not only did they influence judges, they put my rivals on notice that I was ready to compete.

On that first day in Sarajevo, I didn't hold back. I did clean runthroughs of my short and long programs. I felt ready to go. In fact, I wished the competition could have started that night. That was how strong I felt. But I would have to rein myself in. I wasn't competing for another week, and the last thing I wanted to do was peak early.

Because the food in the village was pretty bad, Don and I went into the old part of town and had a pizza dinner at a Turkish bistro. We stood in line with Bulgarian bobsledders, Austrian skiers and Russian speed skaters, and after an hour managed to get a table. With all the athletes eating in the room, there was electricity in the air I hadn't felt since Lake Placid in 1980. There was also a ton of smoke, since the locals took a liking to black cigarettes. The secondhand smoke turned my throat into sandpaper, so Don and I made a point of getting to the restaurants early, eating fast, and getting the heck out before it got crowded.

Over the next couple of days, my father, Sam Cooper and Mrs. McLoraine flew into town. They watched the opening ceremonies at Kosovo Stadium, and while I didn't carry the flag as I had in Lake Placid, I was sky-high with adrenaline as the crowd of 35,000 cheered wildly. As we circled the infield, I was surprised by all the American flags I saw in the stands.

My father, Sam and Mrs. Mac joined Don and me on our evening forays into the city for dinner. Otherwise I kept my socializing to a minimum. I was so determined not to get sick, I spent a lot of downtime in my room, breathing in the ionized air and listening to rock music. Every time I tried to take a walk or go visit a friend, there always seemed to be a reporter waiting outside my apartment, wanting to ask a few questions. I could understand they had a job to do, but how many times could I comment about being favored to win the gold medal? Four years ago I'd had the run of the Lake Placid village. I could go to practices and take in other events in relative anonymity. Not so in 1984. Everything had changed now that I was expected to win.

From the first day of the games, all the top male skaters were in town and practicing. There was a little gamesmanship going on between me and one other competitor, who was getting too close to me while I was doing my triple Lutz. The Lutz is a perfect jump to bother someone on. Because you're skating backward, you can see another skater bearing down on you as you go into your jump. This guy decided to enter into his Lutz jump on the same path I took. When I lifted off the ice, he was probably no more than twenty feet away and closing quickly. If I fell down, he would skate right into me. I didn't, but as I skated away I shot him a look and later in the session, I landed a couple of triples in his face as he was conferring with his coach. There weren't any problems after that.

My good friend Brian Orser was not in my practice group. But one morning he came out to watch my practice. I did a clean run-through of my long program, and when I finished, I glanced over to see his reaction. He was standing with his coach, Doug Leigh, and looking at me the way I had looked at Norbert a year ago in Helsinki. The expression on Brian's face said, "Is that all you got?" I knew I was in trouble. At that moment, I realized that he was going to beat me in the long program. And that was even before I heard from Don that his triple Axel was on, a jump I didn't have in my repertoire.

Brian wasn't the only challenger. Jozef Sabovcik was also looking good, and Norbert, as always, had to be dealt with. My German rival had just left his coach, Erich Zeller, right in the middle of the European championships and now was taking from Carlo Fassi, just as Scott Cramer and David Santee had before him. But Brian posed the greatest threat because of his free skating ability. His emergence was a slight distraction for me and Don. Over the past few years, I had always won the long program at the world championships, and now it looked like it might not happen here in Sarajevo.

After practice that afternoon, Don and I went to get something to eat and I told him my concerns about the long. There was no need to panic, he said, as long as I stuck to our plan of dominating the entire competition as a whole. "Top two in figures and top three in both freestyles," he kept on reminding me. "Your greatest strength is your lack of any weakness. This competition is yours to lose."

Winning each event would be fantastic but not essential. I already knew the short program was probably my weakest event because my jump combination—the double loop–triple toe—could be marked lower than the triple Lutz–double loop other skaters had. But I could still expect to be in the top three if I skated well, which was just fine.

The key was placing high in all the events, but Don and I both knew figures took on added importance, because it was the one area where I was vastly superior to Brian. If I managed to win first, something I had never done at the world level, I was home free, barring a disaster in the later rounds, of course. Not only could I eliminate Brian from gold medal contention, I could knock off Jean-Christophe as well, since I was the stronger free skater. After scouting his figures in France, I felt in my heart I was capable of doing it; now I just had to show it.

Don and I had worked together for four years eliminating my weaknesses one by one—compulsory figures, spins, presentation and the flip—and doing everything to maximize my appeal to an international panel of judges, who put a heavy emphasis on solid, all-around skating ability. Because of the exposure and the media attention, the judging at the Olympics was more intense than a typical world championships. A mistake by the panel would be magnified by ten. But this was the same group of decision makers who had been watching me grow and mature as a skater for the past four years. I had won three world titles, and that's the kind of pedigree you want going into an Olympic games.

That week, *Sports Illustrated* came out with its cover story billing me "Mr. Gold Medal." I was as sure a bet as Secretariat in the Belmont. Yeah, right. Didn't they ever hear of not counting your chickens? Part of me could do without the hype—there was still a competition to skate and it might light a fire under one of my competitors. On the other hand, why not tell the world I was unbeatable? It could just as well get my rivals nervous and reaffirm my status with some judges. There was no harm in that at all.

The pairs short program was held on the first day of the games, and after dinner I went to the Zetra to cheer on the American teams: Peter and Kitty; Billy Fauver and Lea Ann Miller; and Burt Lancon and Jill Watson. The arena only seated several thousand people, but it was noisy, like a packed high school gym. Kitty and Peter skated beautifully; they always seemed to pull off a clean performance when it counted most. They were tied for second after the short. The biggest shocker of the night came when Canadians Paul Martini and Barb Underhill, gold medal favorites, blew up and crashed. A month from then, this team would win a world title, and yet one bad outing at the Olympics had put them out of medal contention.

The next day at practice, Don was very subdued. I think he was trying too hard to treat this competition like any other and not make any waves that would disrupt my concentration. He hardly said a word all morning. I did another clean run-through, and his response was, "All right, good job. You look strong."

That night my sinuses started bothering me and I had trouble sleeping. All the next day, the problem persisted. After dinner, I went back to my room to watch the finals of the pairs competition on television. Since I wasn't feeling well and was competing in figures the next day, I passed on going to the arena. Once again, Kitty and Peter were awesome, hitting every element. They'd been fourth in Helsinki the year before, but in Sarajevo they won the silver medal, the first American pairs team to win silver since Karol and Peter Kennedy in 1952. No American team has ever won gold.

I didn't sleep much that night. I was thinking how Kitty and Peter had achieved something I wanted very badly for myself—the performance of a lifetime on an Olympic stage. While they were probably out in the city celebrating somewhere with their family, my mind was playing flashbacks of my times with Kitty: our first meeting in Boston; our trips to the Jersey shore; Lake Placid. Even though we hadn't dated in almost two years, part of me hoped we could get back together, and part of me realized it was wishful thinking.

During the night, I started coughing and woke up a couple of times to get a glass of water and some cough drops. I needed to hunker down and fight off this encroaching illness. After a light breakfast of oatmeal and toast the next morning, I took a bus over to the Zetra for the figures event. Don was there early. "No need to fire you today," I told him outside the dressing room.

"Go get changed," he said with a chuckle.

A figures competition in no way resembles the kinetic atmosphere of the freestyle events, in which the skaters can play to the audience and draw them into the performance.

Figures events are conducted in virtual silence before sparse crowds. Since rapid movement is not of primary importance, competitors dress for warmth and the costumes are understated and conservative. If the freestyle is like going to a party, figures are the skating equivalent of going to church. When it is your turn to skate, you are concerned only with the judges, who stand silently and watch, looking in their boots and overcoats like dark clouds on the horizon. Your coach remains off to the side, behind the boards which serve as a barrier. It can feel like you're alone on a raft in the middle of the ocean.

When I began my first figure in Sarajevo, a left forward inside rocker, there were nine judges and several officials standing around my patch, about ten to fifteen feet away. A couple of other competitors were off to the side doing figures on warmup patches, but I was the only skater being marked. Each figure I performed that morning took about three minutes to complete. It was about precision, control, rhythm and contained aggression. Unless I was assertive, I'd have no chance of beating Jean-Christophe.

When I pushed off to begin my first tracing, my head was filled with the Kool and the Gang song "Get Down on It." When I practiced and competed, that was the only thing I heard. It was perfect music, the ideal rhythm and beat, for getting down on my figure. The music didn't leave my head until I was through. After finishing, I glided over to the boards and conferred with Don. At this point, you have to trust the judges implicitly. I felt good as they hovered over my tracing and marked their score sheets, and my instincts were correct. On the first figure, I defeated Jean-Christophe by the slimmest of margins, five judges to four, and won the figure overall.

On the second figure, a right forward paragraph double three, I won six judges to Jean-Christophe's three. And on the final figure, a left back change loop, I swept the panel. Man, I was psyched, and Jean-Christophe was just beside himself. Brian Orser was all the way back in seventh place. Brian Boitano was eighth and Norbert was ninth. I looked around and the Zetra was maybe a quarter full, the seats occupied by the most placid crowd you'll ever find at a skating event. There was only a nominal media presence and just a couple of ABC cameras to record my victory, and yet, I realized as I left the arena that day, I might have just won the gold medal right then and there. Barring a blowup in the short and long programs, I was fulfilling Don's prophecy. The competition was now mine to lose.

One cannot underestimate the importance of figures and the years it takes to master them. Frankly, growing up I loathed them; I felt they were boring to do. By my last year in amateur skating, I loved practicing them. There's a certain thrill you get after skating a clean freestyle program, but when you're done there's nothing left behind to see. When you do a great figure there is something tangible to admire. You can see your work traced onto the ice and appreciate it like a painting on a canvas. You can chart your improvement day by day. Over time I discovered a great satisfaction in the challenge of using the edge of my blade to create perfect circles eighteen feet in diameter.

There is also no doubt that figures contribute mightily to fine edge control, balance and footwork in free skating. I found that as I got better at figures, it took less effort to get through a long program. Those skills are so important that the governing bodies have introduced a new series of tests called "moves in the field" so skaters can develop the dexterity they once gained from figures. But it's no substitute, in my opinion.

As you can guess, I was upset at the elimination of figures in 1990, and not just because they were the primary reason I won an Olympic gold medal. They were important for all the competitors. It took years of painstaking practice to master the craft, and if you didn't, you were often out of the medal hunt. Now the sport is increasingly dominated by teenage champions, like Oksana Baiul, Tara Lipinski and Michelle Kwan, all of whom were world champions before their sixteenth birthdays.

Dropping figures changed the way the sport is judged. Now all it comes down to is who performs the best free skating. That's more exciting and easier for fans to understand, but that is not what skating was all about. It wasn't a track meet about who could skate the fastest or jump the highest. Skating required a degree of concentration, maturity and focus that separated it from other sports, and that was what compulsory figures brought to the table. They may not have been as dramatic as triple jumps, but they were every bit as important.

What I see out there today are a lot of pure jumpers, many of whom haven't learned to skate. And while this new generation of skaters should certainly feel proud of their technical achievements, it's sad that they'll never develop their edge skills in a more grounded and patient way, nor feel the personal satisfaction of creating the perfect figure.

Another reason I hated to see them go was because the decision seemed predicated on appeasing television and catering to the weaker athletes. Gee, you can't do figures? Well, let's eliminate them, why don't we? There was a lot of jealousy of American skaters because we had the facilities, the coaches and the ice time for good figures training, unlike countries where the sport was still developing. Banning them also completely blurred the lines between amateur and professional skating, and it made it much easier for the two levels to merge. But we can't go back in time and reintroduce figures to the mix. It's done and you have to respect what's in place now.

After winning stage one in Sarajevo, I returned to the village and spent the rest of the day in my room, listening to music and writing in my journal. My sinuses remained clogged and my condition was rapidly developing into a head cold. But there was little time to get cured. The short program was taking place the next day.

When I woke up the next morning, I was sneezing and congested. At practice that morning I did a clean run-through of my short. I appeared strong, showing no ill effects. The benefits of training hard all year were now coming into play, since I could anticipate relying on conditioning and muscle memory to get me through the next couple of days. It enabled my body to do the work without thinking my way through it. Don had been developing this characteristic in my head for years: train as if there is no tomorrow and then rein yourself in for the performance and let fate carry you, almost as if you don't care (I said almost!). Don called this "refined indifference." A sports psychologist might call this mental approach "paradoxical intention."

Sometimes, though, even the best mental preparation can't factor in unusual distractions. When I arrived at the Zetra on short program night, the atmosphere was as thick and heavy as the smoke-filled air in a Sarajevo restaurant. Listless and pale, I looked even whiter in my modified silver speed skating suit with blue stripes flaring down the sleeves. My body was going in slow motion as I stretched and did some calisthenics in a corridor under the grandstands, already getting edgy from the noisy crowd. When it was time for my warm-up, I stepped out on the ice and heard people calling out my name and saw banners and American flags waving in every part of the arena. I raced around the rink to get loose and began my warm-up routine—Axels, then double Axels, then triple jumps. The crowd sounded so close, as if they were right on top of the ice. There was a small group of very vocal and very rowdy Americans sitting about halfway up the arena. They were chanting my name, and my adrenaline shot up. This wasn't helping, I thought. I started missing jumps and then I hit the boards during my footwork sequence. Arrrgh! I looked up into the crowd and calmly motioned my arms, signaling them to quiet down. I was distracted and freaking out, and no amount of cheering was going to settle my nerves.

With about a minute left in the warm-up, I finally composed myself and hit a triple jump. This was not the time to lose my poise, I thought. Not before the do-or-die short program. You never want to miss in the short at a world-level competition—ever. There's an old saying in skating—you won't win the title in the short, but you sure can lose it. In this event, a single fall can be twice as damaging as a spill in the long program because the judges are required to make mandatory deductions. And I was dying out there.

I was fortunate I was not the first skater up. God only knows what would have happened. I had about five minutes to wait, so Don and I went back to the locker room to cool off. Only I didn't calm down. I found a mirror and stood in front of it and called myself every name in the book. What was I doing letting the crowd throw me off? The walls were reverberating with four-letter expletives. Don stood off to the side quietly. After a few minutes of sounding off, I got so tired I just sat down on a bench and ran through my program in my mind. Later on, Sam Cooper let me have it for calming the crowd during the warm-up.

"Why were you telling people to quiet down? They're only there to support you," he said.

"You're right," I answered. "I just lost it. I couldn't handle the enthusiasm because my adrenaline was way too high."

About a minute before I was to take the ice, Don and I made our way back to rinkside. I did some stretches as the skater before me finished up. I turned to Don.

"I'm good for four falls tonight," I said seriously.

"No, you're not," he said. "You're the best."

As the announcer introduced me to the crowd, I took my position at center ice. The crowd was still whooping and hollering, but now my mind was focused on the task. As the music started, my legs felt heavy and my breathing a little labored. When I hit my double loop–triple toe combination, I immediately felt better and stepped up my pace. I made my only mistake midway through the program. Going into a required camel change–camel spin, not one of my strongest elements, I was balancing on my left skate and spinning counterclockwise with my right leg extended. When I went to change legs, my right toe pick caught the ice. It slowed down my spin dramatically and I was unable to complete the required number of rotations. I knew it would result in a deduction.

The short was close. Brian Orser hit a triple Lutz–double loop combination and his spins were solid. He won the event in a broken tie with his stronger technical marks. I finished second and couldn't complain. I had a second place to go with my first in figures and was staying within the game plan. Most important, I had survived the do-or-die short. After two events, I was in first place with a commanding lead. At the press conference later, I played down my illness and blamed my cautious effort on my attitude. I didn't want to start making excuses when the real reason I got upset had to do with my reaction to the crowd. "I was caught up in everything," I said. "But I'm happy."

That night we went to dinner with my father, Sam and Mrs. McLoraine, and there was a definite feeling of optimism at our table. Don had done the math and he figured out it would take a fifth-place finish or worse in the long for me to lose the gold medal. My rivals had marks all over the board. Brian Orser was still close enough that I couldn't forget about him, but I was in control. I hadn't finished fifth or lower in a long program since the 1979 nationals. There was almost no chance that would happen.

We had a day off before long program night. Don and I considered bagging practice to break up my routine a little. Workouts had been going almost too well, but we decided not to change things. In retrospect, I probably should have taken the day off. After practice I felt even sicker, and when I woke up the next morning I had an ear infection to go along with my congested sinuses. The right side of my head was totally clogged, and I noticed at practice it was affecting my balance and jumping. Every jump seemed twice as hard and nothing came automatically anymore. I was slow and deliberate, thinking through my jumps instead of relying on muscle memory. I imagine if both sides of my sinuses had been equally congested, I probably would have been okay. But with just the right side affected—I could neither breathe out of my right nostril nor hear out of my right ear—my balance was thrown.

I stayed in my room for the rest of the day and headed for the Zetra late in the afternoon. I had a good draw—I was skating after Brian Orser, which meant that even if Brian skated well, the judges would have to leave some room at the top in case I skated well. Of the medal contenders, Brian was the first skater out. He had been awesome all week in practice, and his performance now was near flawless. While Don watched him, I stayed backstage, concentrating on what I had to do. He landed a lot of triples—Lutz, Axel, toe loop and a triple Salchow combination. He received all 5.8s and 5.9s from the judges. Boitano was next and he skated great too, with one minor blemish on his landing of the triple Axel. He finished fifth.

My turn. While Boitano was waiting for his marks to come up, I skated in little circles by Don and cracked my knuckles. I was ill and my head was full of junk, but I tried not to think about that. I had done twenty-three consecutive, perfect long program run-throughs prior to the Olympics, nine of those this week. That was what I tried to concentrate on.

Just before I was introduced, I skated over to Don and we exchanged a few words, words we had been repeating to one another before every big event the past four years.

"I'm scared," I said.

"Not half as scared as I am," Don replied.

As I waited for the announcer to call out my name, my right hand instinctively reached over to the band on my left wrist, and I rubbed my palm against the woven cotton. Then it was time. I took a deep breath and glided to center ice. Although winning the competition was in my reach, what I was thinking was that what I did in the next four-and-a-half minutes would become my signature performance forever. Millions of people around the world were watching and waiting. And what I was about to do on the ice would be remembered for a long time. I wanted to skate great. I raised my arms and got into starting position.

"Don't choke," a voice in my head warned. So much for the power of positive thinking.

The music began and I started to relax a little. A few seconds later I was gliding backward about to execute my triple Lutz. Lift, rotate, bang! "Wow, that was effortless," I thought. The flip was next. During my approach, the adrenaline rush that carried me through the first minute of the program was wearing off. I started thinking about the takeoff, and when I reached back with my toe pick, I felt my body turn a second too soon. I knew instantly I couldn't get in two rotations, let alone three. I went up and made a single, and it felt like I was hanging motionless in the air. I couldn't wait to get it over with. "Ahh," I groaned. "There was the mistake I expected might happen." I came back and landed my triple toe walley. It felt good and I let out a smile. I was still feeling embarrassed about the botched flip, but it wasn't the end of the world. After landing a triple toe loop combination, I had one more triple ahead of me, the Salchow. I was now entering the last minute of my program and had been on the ice more than three minutes, except it felt like twenty. When I'm feeling great I fly through this program, but today it was taking so long, I thought. I had to keep pushing. I didn't want to miss any more jumps. As I left the ice on my Salchow, I felt my body turn sideways, not into the vertical position I desired. The result was a double. "Okay," I thought. "I couldn't possibly skate any worse than that."

When it was finally over, I waved to the appreciative crowd. They didn't see me at my best today, but they saw the best I had in me. Hard work, I realized, is never wasted. Because if I had not trained vigilantly all year, the illness, combined with the pressure, could have done me in over the course of this long week. That didn't happen. It may not have been pretty, but I survived.

I skated over to Don and my choreographer, Ricky Harris, who were waiting together by the barrier. All I could do was mumble an apology to Don. "Sorry," I said. "It's tough out there. I had no balance."

Don smiled and gave me a pat on the back. He didn't say it at the time, but he was thinking about my perfect performance in Salt Lake City and how nice it would have been to have traded in that long program for this one. "I wish we could turn the clock back a week," I said, gasping for air as we sat down in the kiss-and-cry area. "I think that's when I peaked."

A little girl in a blue dress skated over and gave me an armful of flowers she had gathered up from the ice. I gave her a kiss on the cheek. Then my marks came up on the board—from 5.6 to 5.9 in the technical, and 5.7 to

5.9 in the artistic. About what I expected, though I must admit, there were some lifetime-achievement scores mixed in there. That left me second behind Brian for the long, but I was still in first overall. We did it. We won the gold. Dick Button approached me in the kiss-and-cry area to do an interview for ABC. He knew I had wanted to skate better and tried consoling me. "You elected to leave out a couple of triple jumps," he said kindly. But that wasn't true at all. There was no point fooling anyone. "I made mistakes," I corrected him.

I went backstage for a few minutes to gather myself. For a while I actually felt awful. I hadn't lost a long program to anyone in three years. And to this day I regret not skating better at the Olympics. But I had accomplished the ultimate goal—winning an Olympic gold medal. That was something to be proud of. I needed to cheer up. I had won the gold, for Pete's sake! People were coming up and congratulating me and I had this dour look on my face.

I saw Brian and shook his hand. He was psyched winning the silver, coming all the way up from seventh place after figures. Jozef, skating after me, took the bronze. As I waited for the medal presentation, I took some solace in knowing I still managed to win a couple of first-place ordinals. One of them came from a French judge, Monique Georgelin, who put me ahead of Brian because she liked the content and balance in my program. Sure it was a lifetime-achievement mark—but those types of marks aren't gifts; skaters earn them. I had spent three years touring in Europe and promoting events over there, and many of the judges had appreciated it. Don and I had even made a special trip to France the previous fall to perform in an exhibition, and maybe I was being rewarded for making the effort. At the same time, the judge from Canada didn't mark me first in any discipline, even figures. That was because she was pushing Brian. A little national bias might be expected, but . . .

Don tapped me on the shoulder. It was time for the medal ceremony. The stands were still packed. Officials were rolling out a red carpet for the awards presenters and setting up the podium. Brian, Jozef and I stood off to the side and watched the flags being installed on the cable lifts. I started to feel chills. In a moment, something was about to happen that I had been waiting for all my life. I was going to be introduced as Olympic champion. When they called out my name, I think I smiled for the first time all night. I took my place at the top of the podium. Brian and Jozef followed. I thought back to that night in Garmisch a year earlier when all three of us had been sitting around fantasizing what it would be like to share the podium in Sarajevo. Now here we were. I leaned over to Brian and Jozef.

"Remember Garmisch? Remember Garmisch?" I repeated, laughing.

It had been a long week, an even longer four years, and my emotions came pouring out when the first few notes of the national anthem echoed across the arena. As I watched the American flag rise to the rafters, my worries about skating poorly were overcome by this absolute feeling of triumph. I felt pride winning a gold medal for my country, and I felt lucky that so many people I cared about—my father, Mrs. Mac and Sam—were present to share the moment with me. And I felt for those who weren't there, like my mom, Dr. Klepner and Mr. Mac. Tears welled up in my eyes, and I remember mouthing the words, "This is for you, Mom." The medal was definitely hers as much as mine. She kept the faith when I was a sick little boy and doctors were telling her I had only a year to live. Then she and my father made it possible for me to keep on skating when reason seemed to dictate I should quit to save the family from going into bankruptcy. This victory was all the sweeter because I knew what it was like to lose. I had finished ninth the last time my mother saw me skate, and that was still a thorn in my side, even after all these years. Mom, I thought, I think I finally made up for that one.

So many other things were going through my head—conflicting emotions I hadn't expected. I was thrilled I had won but a little sad that it was all coming to an end. I was now goalless; the moment the music stopped, it would be like stepping off a cliff into a great void. There's a lot to be said for having a fantasy that pushes you to strive and achieve. But once you have it, once it's firmly in your hand, you have to start over again. Kind of tough to do when you haven't figured out what you're going to do with the rest of your life. So mixed in with all the pride I was feeling was some apprehension.

When Brian, Jozef and I stepped down from the medal stand, we took a victory lap around the Zetra. The banners and flags were waving again and people were calling out my name—only now I didn't seem to mind all the hoopla. I spotted a fan in the front row holding a conduit pipe with an American flag attached to it. He waved the flag and tried to hand it to me but I passed by him too quickly. Just as we were about to get off the ice, I said to Brian, "Would you mind going around one more time? I figure this will be the last time that you'll be looking at my back in an awards ceremony. So let's go one more time around."

This time I grabbed the flag and held it aloft as we made another circle around the rink. While I had always felt that a world championship was an individual achievement, there was something special about winning an Olympic medal for your country. It's not just yours; it's something to be shared with everybody. So carrying the flag seemed like an appropriate way to say thank you for the public support. But I also felt personal satisfaction, despite making a couple of mistakes. I had trained hard and skated well all season long, especially my performance in Salt Lake City. I may have a regret or two about my long program performance in Sarajevo, but I had no regrets about the effort and the sacrifices that made this moment a reality.

As I skated around the Zetra, I remembered the time my mother took me walking through my old Bowling Green neighborhood shortly after I passed my first figure test. She had sent away for a small patch with the United States Figure Skating Association emblem embroidered on the front and planned to sew it on my patch jacket. She knocked on each door, and proudly boasted to the neighbors that I had passed my first test "with flying colors."

"Someday Scotty is going to the Olympics," she said over and over. At the time I felt a little embarrassed, but I was also flattered by my mother's confidence in me. Just a year earlier I had been a sick little boy, and now I was having some success at an athletic pursuit, something I'm sure my mom thought she would never see in her lifetime. That was plenty enough reason to celebrate then.

Now, with millions watching, I had passed my biggest and most important test of all.

Chapter Twelve

Show Biz

There was a moment after winning the gold medal in Sarajevo when time seemed to stand still. I was backstage at the Zetra, a few minutes before the medal ceremony, accepting congratulatory handshakes and hugs. There was a TV camera in my face and skating officials, television crews and competitors milling around. It was a strange sensation, almost dreamlike. Other medalists will know what I mean: something big has happened to you, but you just don't know how big or what it all means. People are around, yet you're alone in a state of euphoria. That's when Doug Wilson, the ABC sports director, came over and shook my hand.

"Your life has changed forever," he said.

"Aw, c'mon," I said modestly. I figured Doug was just being polite.

"No," Doug replied, shaking his head. "You'll see." His tone was very serious now. "When you get home your life will be completely different. Where were you three weeks ago and where are you today? Three weeks ago doesn't exist anymore. Your life is brand-new."

I didn't believe him at first, and actually forgot about it until much later. It's real hard to pay attention to anything that's said to you the first ten minutes after winning any competition because that's the best part of the whole week. After days of draining practices and three pressure-packed events, everything you have worked for is finally realized and smashes into you like a giant snowball. At the Olympics it was more like getting hit by an avalanche. It would be some time before Doug's words would register.

Nothing seemed out of the ordinary for the remainder of the week, except my conversation with President Ronald Reagan.

"The president has been trying to get hold of you all day," a USOC public relations man said. "Come with me."

We went to the communications office in the Olympic village and they got President Reagan on the line immediately. I didn't believe it, not until I actually heard his voice. He sounded just like he did on television. After he congratulated me, I was completely tongue-tied and froze for a second. All I could think of doing was thanking him and then we hung up. I felt like such a fool being at a loss for words.

I stayed in Sarajevo and had a celebration party at the Holiday Inn with Don, my father, Sam, Helen, Ricky and other skating friends. I later watched Katarina Witt edge Rosalynn Sumners for the gold medal in the ladies' event. Jayne Torvill and Christopher Dean made history when their free dance to *Bolero* won them a string of perfect 6.0 artistic marks from all nine judges. Kitty and I spent some time together during the rest of the games. We were both on a natural high and enjoyed taking in some events and hanging out in the village. Although I had a worlds to compete in, Kitty and Peter were all through with amateur skating. They decided that winning a silver medal was the best way to go out, and I couldn't argue with that.

On the final day of the games, I marched in closing ceremonies and then flew home with Don in first class. It was a great ride back to the United States. I slept part of the way and posed for pictures with passengers and flight attendants. People kept asking to see my medal and I kept showing it. I had never seen a gold medal myself until I won one, so I could feel a little bit of that awe.

But what I remember gaining most from the experience was that the process was much greater than the result. And I still feel that way. I don't mean to downplay an Olympic gold medal, but it would be meaningless without the years of preparation, setbacks, comebacks and successes. The camaraderie, the rivalries, the discipline, and the people who gave me so much—from Rita Lowery to Pierre Brunet, from Mary Scotvold to Carlo, to Don and Ricky, and so many others—all of that was more satisfying over time than any medal. What I accomplished working toward that end had more meaning than the end itself. Since there will be a thousand national champions, a thousand world champions and hundreds of Olympic champions, what you have that will always be yours is the process. That was the personal experience Janet Lynn was referring to when I met her on my first practice in Wagon Wheel back in 1972. That experience and what you gain from it is yours forever.

When we landed in Chicago, Don and I went our separate ways. I was spending the night in Chicago with some of my pals. He went to make his connection to Denver and I ventured to baggage claim. I thanked him and told him I'd be seeing him in a couple of days. He gave me one of those looks—Have a good time but don't forget, we still have a world championships coming up.

It took some time reaching my bags. Walking through the airport, people were nodding at me and saying hello. A couple with young children stopped and asked for my autograph. When I got to baggage claim, I spotted Brent across the room, waved at him and started moving in his direction. Then I heard a young voice call out my name. Then another and another. I had run smack into two hundred Chicago kids on their way to Washington, D.C., for a school field trip. They crowded around me and I spent the next hour signing autographs. This had never happened to me before outside of an ice rink. I had been signing autographs at competitions for four years, ever since making the '80 Olympic team. However, in public I could usually go about my business without being recognized.

Just a few weeks earlier I had walked through this very same airport while making my connection to Paris. I was running around looking for the time and began asking strangers for help. People walked right past me without saying a word. I literally could not get the time of day. I was so embarrassed I started to laugh. I might as well have been trying to sell religious materials. Now as I signed the last piece of paper, I remembered Doug's prescient words in Sarajevo. Now I'm beginning to see what he was talking about, I thought.

Later, Brent and I went to the Park Hyatt hotel to hook up with Mahlon Bradley, who had finished up at Harvard and was in medical school at Northwestern. We were going to go out and have a night on the town. Brent and I walked into this swanky lounge and sat down at a fancy oak bar. There was classical music playing and all the men were wearing ties and jackets and the waiters were in white. Brent and I were dressed very casually—jeans, golf shirts and tennis shoes. "What's this, some kind of law library?" Brent said. We were surrounded by all these businesspeople dressed to the hilt, and we were getting dirty looks. Though I was feeling a little uncomfortable, I wasn't going to let it bother me. I had been on the straight and narrow for six months, and was ready to let loose and have a good time.

Out of the corner of my eye I saw the maître d' approaching. Uh-oh, I thought, are we getting tossed out for violating the dress code?

"Excuse me, gentlemen," the maître d' said. "We would like to buy you a drink."

That got everybody's attention. The eavesdropping suits expecting us to get the heave-ho were scratching their heads now, wondering what the heck was going on. I thanked him and said, "A couple of beers would be fine. I'll have a Coors. Brent, what do you want?"

The maître d' interrupted. "No, no, no," he said. Then, like a scene from a vintage 1940s movie, he clapped his hands and a waiter appeared. "A bottle of Dom Pérignon, gentlemen. Compliments of the house."

The table of suits couldn't believe what they were seeing. And I couldn't believe what I was hearing. That was when I realized I had been recognized. "That's great," I said to the maître d'. "But can we still have a couple of beers anyway?"

The next day it was time to return to Denver, where the city fathers were giving me a victory parade. It's not something I would have asked for myself, but the community wanted to thank me for representing Denver in a positive way. It wasn't necessary, but a Learjet was sent to Chicago to ferry me back to Denver for the parade. It belonged to Bill Daniels, a pioneer of cable television and a fellow man of "average" height. I didn't know Bill at the time; his only impression of me was what he had seen on television and read about me in *Sports Illustrated*. After I had skated in Sarajevo, I was very candid with Dick Button about my disappointing long program performance, and Bill liked my honesty. And since we were both short in stature, he figured I was his kind of guy. Later, I learned the man's generosity knows no boundaries. He once tried to donate his house to the city to be used as a mayor's residence, but they turned him down because the home was too big.

On the morning of February 23, I was met at the Denver airport by dignitaries and friends, including members of the ladies' coffee club from the Colorado Ice Arena. They gave me a special present—a giant doughnut larger than a birthday cake. I think the gift may have had something to do with me helping myself to about three years' worth of coffee and doughnuts from the refreshment table they always set up for their club skating sessions. Then I hopped aboard an antique fire truck with cheerleaders from the old Denver Gold of the United States Football League and led the parade through the downtown Sixteenth Street Mall to Denver's Larimer Square, which was filled with five thousand people. As I looked out over the shopping plaza, I was incredibly taken by the moment and all the trouble people had gone through to put together this celebration. Mayor Federico Peña gave me the key to the city and for the day renamed Larimer Street, Scott Hamilton Street. Dottie Lamm, Colorado's first lady, was there representing her husband, Governor Dick Lamm. A congratulatory telegram from President Ronald Reagan was read to the crowd. One of the gifts I received was a two-hundred-pound gold-colored fire hydrant from the Denver Water Department. Now what was the use of having a fire hydrant? Well, I had mentioned somewhere that I wanted to buy a condo and, being the worldly and tasteful bachelor that I was, decorate it with public works paraphernalia. So on parade day I got my fire hydrant. Not to be outdone, Mountain Bell came through with an antique phone booth two weeks later. By the end of the day, not only did I have my future condo completely decorated to look like every street corner in town, I was completely overwhelmed. "This," I told the crowd, "has been the best day of my life."

A couple of weeks later, I got to meet President Reagan with the rest of the U.S. Olympic team. On my second White House visit, I was much more discreet and left my camera at home. I was still nervous because I had been elected by the athletes to present the president with a team jacket. Fresh in my memory was our conversation from a couple of weeks earlier. This time I had a little speech prepared. "Mr. President," I said as I handed over the jacket, "I'm sorry for being so short with you on the phone when you called me in Sarajevo, but as you can see, I have been short most of my life."

I looked up at the president and waited for his reaction. He began to laugh and I let out a sigh of relief. This man, whom I respected and admired so much, was laughing at one of my self-deprecating jokes. Nicely done, I thought.

With all the distractions, training for worlds was more difficult than it had ever been before. One additional distraction came from Coca-Cola, which had offered me a television commercial. The money on the table made it tempting, but doing the ad would have ended my amateur status and made me ineligible for worlds. I could have skipped the competition, but I didn't want my Olympic performance to be my last as an amateur. Maybe if I had skated better in Sarajevo I would have passed on worlds; then again, maybe not. I also came to the conclusion that TV commercials come and go, money comes and goes, but world titles are forever. Who would remember me in a Coke ad twenty years from now? Besides, with the government planning to take a big chunk of my earnings in taxes, it didn't make any sense to me. My lifestyle certainly hadn't changed to where I needed the income. Money didn't mean a thing to me at the time.

So in late March, Don and I flew to Ottawa, Canada, the scene of my first worlds six years earlier. The second time around, it was nostalgic and anticlimactic. There was neither the media scrutiny nor the hoopla surrounding an Olympic games. Don was low-key, almost somber. It was our last competition together, but nowhere near as intense as the other battles we had endured together in Helsinki, Copenhagen and Hartford. The "defeat clouds," as Don called them, that always seemed to gather early in competition week, and then abruptly vanish, didn't appear on the horizon this time. Letdowns are natural in an Olympic year, so we took it in stride.

On the ice, it was almost a repeat of Sarajevo. I was first after figures and Brian Orser was seventh. I won a measure of revenge by taking the short program from Brian, but he turned around and won the long free again. I left Canada as four-time world champion. Brian was second and Alexander Fadeev of Russia was third, and they would be battling for the title next year. My reign was over.

Though there was little fanfare at the time, I had just won my seventeenth amateur competition in a row. I'm not sure anyone else was actually keeping track, but this is the career achievement I'm most proud of. I had been undefeated since the fall of 1980, when I finished second in Saint Ivel.

The thought of sticking around for another four years, or even another season, didn't make any sense. Orser, Fadeev and Boitano were coming on strong and would probably kick my behind. It was time to get out.

I decided my final performance as an amateur would take place on the very rink where I had learned to skate sixteen years ago. The "International Stars on Ice" show in Bowling Green that year was incredible. Kitty, Peter, Rosalynn and Brian Boitano all performed. After the show we went over to Dave's bar and closed it down. During the Olympics Dave had held a press conference in the parking lot of his bar. He hung up a huge banner—"Hamilton Captures Gold"—and eighty of his friends gathered around to toast me with Kamikazes. A TV news helicopter caught the whole occasion on tape, including a shot of poor Dave trying gallantly to give a live interview while half in the bag. We ended the night at a roller-skating rink owned by Dave's relatives. He opened up the place and we all skated around like a bunch of maniacs until the sun came up.

I officially gave up my amateur status in Denver by performing in a nonsanctioned benefit show to raise money for cancer research and the Denver symphony. It was important to me to lose my eligibility by breaking the rules, rather than by accepting money. After that night, I was officially professional, and psyched to be moving on.

During another show at the Broadmoor that summer, I got into a conversation with Lois Nesselhauf, an officer with the Broadmoor skating club, about the old days when I was being coached by Carlo back at the CIA.

"One of the things that kept me going all these years," I said, "was

Carlo's decision to choose Scott Cramer over me. I wanted to show him he picked the wrong Scott."

Lois smiled. "I think you showed him."

I felt no malice for Carlo. Even though he took on all my biggest rivals—Scott, David and Norbert—in an attempt to knock me off, I managed to come in first at the finish line, and that was enough to bury any feelings of bitterness. In fact, in the years to come, Carlo and I became very good friends. He judged a number of professional events I competed in, and we formed a bond and had fun in a way that wasn't possible years earlier. We were alike in a lot of ways—both outgoing and gregarious. Our old teacher-pupil relationship eventually evolved into mutual respect and friendship.

"You want to know something?" Lois said on that night at the Broadmoor. "Carlo says the biggest mistake he ever made in his coaching career was letting you go."

I don't mean to gloat, but hearing those words made me want to jump up and give Lois a high five. What Carlo did had been driving me for a long time. Now, it was time to move on.

That spring, the time had come to finally select an agent, a decision I had been putting off for months, actually years. I had been getting a lot of pressure since winning my first world title in 1981. But in my day an agent wasn't necessary until you were all finished with amateur skating. I couldn't accept commercial endorsements, and appearance fees for doing Tommy's tour and other exhibitions were set by the USFSA. Still, these guys knew how to dazzle—remember the mouse in *Dumbo*? They were masters at the art of the pitch, and while I wasn't interested in what they had to offer, I was impressed by their tactics. One executive took me to lunch, popped a big stogie in his mouth, and told me he knew Lorne Michaels and could get me a guest-host spot on *Saturday Night Live*. He also mentioned that he could fix me up with supermodels. Other agents promised to deliver book deals and movie projects based on my life, along with the moon, the stars and the sun.

I talked to sports agents like David Fishof, who has represented NFL quarterbacks Vince Ferragamo and Phil Simms, and recently put the Monkees back on tour. I was also approached by Hollywood agents like George Taylor and skating agents like Michael Rosenberg, who worked with Dorothy Hamill for a while.

The wheeling and dealing really picked up steam in the months leading up to the Olympics. The dollar figures being bandied about got so distracting, I asked Don to screen all the inquiries and report to me later after things calmed down. "I'm just a dumb jock; you figure it out," I said facetiously. Actually, I just wanted to concentrate on my skating, and then worry about business. While it was nice to talk about the future, something these guys were especially good at, that's all it was—talk. I was an old-school kind of person who believed there was no future unless I performed in the present. I just didn't need the headache, not in an Olympic year.

I put off all my decisions until after the Ottawa worlds. In April I met with Bob Kain of IMG. He was the agent who would represent me if I signed with them. It became clear he was everything I was looking for in a personal agent, someone who would be able to devote a lot of time and attention to me, as Don had been able to as a coach. With Don, I wasn't "one of many," and that accounted for much of our success. And I wanted a business relationship like that too. Bob was so easy and down to earth, I instantly signed with him.

A few days later we made the formal announcement in Atlantic City that I was retiring from amateur skating. The rest of the week was a whirlwind. Bob was with me when I threw out the first pitch for the New York Yankees' home opener; then we took George Steinbrenner's limousine to catch a play-off game at Nassau Coliseum between the New York Rangers and New York Islanders. Kenny Morrow, my friend from Bowling Green who played for the U.S. Olympic hockey teams in 1980, scored the winning goal in overtime for the Islanders. Bob also took me to tennis star Vitas Gerulaitis's fund-raising dinner, where we watched an exhibition tennis match between Bjorn Borg and John McEnroe at the Sheraton Hotel. I sat at center court and posed for pictures with Cheryl Tiegs and Andy Warhol. There was a party afterward, and Vitas spent the night trying to fix me up with some beautiful women. It was heady stuff, far more than I ever expected would happen. I enjoyed every moment and kept thinking of Doug Wilson's prophetic words back in Sarajevo. My life was changing drastically.

Still, there were things I wanted right away that would take many years to accomplish. I hoped to be the first male skating star to have his own television special, but Bob was pessimistic. Wrong sex, wrong country, he said. If I were female, it would be possible. If I had been born in Canada, it would get done up there in a minute. Being a male skating star in America limited your opportunities. After all was said and done, after all the carrots had been dangled and pulled away, it was clear that the bulk of my income would be derived from the same place champions in the past had made their money: skating in an ice show.

Bob went to work negotiating a contract with "Ice Capades." Don had already laid the groundwork, and Bob closed the deal with "Ice Capades" president Dick Palmer, making me the highest paid male skater in the history of the show.

I was on Tommy's tour and staying in New York City when Bob called with news of the contract. "It's done," he said. "Go on out and have a great time." That night I celebrated by going to dinner with Kitty and Peter and my good friend Dennis St. John, the drummer for Neil Diamond. Then Dennis and I went to a private party at a club called the Limelight. We weren't invited, but since I knew all the bouncers and the doormen, they waved us right in. Dennis and I were standing at the bar when I saw this beautiful woman in a black-and-white dress across the room. I was no pickup artist, but I was so taken by her that I uncharacteristically took the plunge. I walked over and said, "I'm sorry, I just have to meet you. My name is Scott."

Her name was Beverly Bean. She was 21, blond and about my height. We talked for a while. I asked for her phone number and she gave me her card. She was a college student who modeled sportswear and taught diving while holding down a straight-A average. She was smart, gorgeous, and athletic, and we hit it off.

We spent a lot of time together that year. She joined me for part of Tommy's tour and also accompanied me to Boston for a fund-raiser I was skating in on behalf of Children's Hospital, where I had been treated for my childhood illness. Over the summer she came to Denver for two visits. I took her to all my favorite restaurants and Pinehurst Country Club, where I played some golf and Beverly sunbathed by the pool. We got very close very fast.

My agreement with "Ice Capades" gave me financial security I had never imagined. It enabled me to purchase a $180,000 two-bedroom condo in a downtown Denver high-rise that I'd had my eye on for months. I also bought a used Mercedes convertible 380 SL for myself and a Ford Crown Victoria for my dad. My lawyer and accountant urged me to buy a large house to build equity and take advantage of mortgage interest deductions, but I decided against it. I wasn't going to spend much time there and didn't want to worry about the upkeep.

But with my father it was different. Ernie was retiring soon from Bowling Green State University, and I wanted to do something special for him. So one weekend when I was visiting him, we went out to the garden to pick some vegetables.

"I want to buy you a house in Florida," I said.

"Thanks, but I can't accept that," he replied.

"Take it," I said to him. "You supported me all these years, and you and

Mom worked extra hard so I could skate. You suffered, you gave and you sacrificed. It would make me feel a whole lot better if you accepted this from me."

He picked out a two-bedroom house on a lake in Lake Placid, Florida, a tiny community with no traffic, no headaches and year-round fishing. That was all he wanted, a quiet place with no hassles. He bought himself a speedboat, but I finally convinced him to replace that with a more manageable pontoon boat that he could get in and out of safely. Frankly, I was worried he might kill himself in a motorboat.

I didn't sign my contract with "Capades" until summertime—after a wild fishing trip in Mazatlán, Mexico. Bill Plage and I hooked up with coaches Ron Ludington and John Nicks and we went barhopping on a couple of nights. My running gag for the week was yanking out an anti-theft device while the car was moving, killing the engine. Then when I put it back in, the car would backfire really loudly. One night, on the way home from a nightclub, we piled a dozen people into the back of Bill's Jeep, John and I riding on the back hanging on to the roll bar as we cruised through town. Now John was also an executive with "Ice Capades," so when he returned to Los Angeles, he gave Dick Palmer a full report on my escapades in Mexico.

When I showed up at Dick's office to ink the deal, I was a little bleary-eyed and tired from the recent vacation.

"You probably won't live long enough to even open with 'Ice Capades,'" he quipped.

My party-boy reputation was haunting me again. "Mr. Palmer," I said with complete conviction, "I will never miss a show and I will never miss a press obligation."

"Okay," he said. "We'll see."

Rehearsals for "Capades" began in August in San Antonio, Texas. The company ran three tours simultaneously—east, west and continental—and each had a kiddie act—Smurfs or Snorks. I put together two numbers, a solo to "Take the 'A' Train," and a tongue-in-cheek comedy number to "Nobody Does It Better" and "You Only Hurt the One You Love."

I started out with the West Company, opening the tour at the Summit in Houston. Dad and Helen were on hand to watch me during my premiere night. I learned quickly that the audiences were much different from the crowds at worlds and nationals. During my performances, I often heard kids talking and laughing, and I mastered the art of the quick bow so I could get off the ice to make way for the Smurfs. It was a lesson in humility. I had dreamed of being a show skater, and I was gradually learning for myself it wasn't what it was cracked up to be.

Part of the problem was that "Ice Capades" didn't know what to do with me. They were very successful at promoting female stars, such as Dorothy Hamill. There was a consensus that principal women skaters sold more tickets than their male counterparts. Since a male skater could never be as popular as a woman, why bother promoting him?

Critics also didn't like my numbers—they were not what they were expecting. So for the second half of the tour, I skated to "Chariots of Fire" and "New York, New York," the show program Ricky Harris had choreographed for me. I would always dedicate that number to the children in the audience.

Despite the difficulties, I had a great time with the cast and crew. There was a hierarchy in Capades. At the top were guest stars like me and principal skaters. The next rung consisted of line skaters with seniority and the HAPs (half-assed principals)—skaters who were understudies and had a short number or step-out but also did some line work. The rookie "line" skaters had it the toughest. Not that I had any control over it, but they received the worst spots in the dressing rooms and as many as five skaters would share a hotel room because their pay was so low. We had nicknames for everybody. For instance, anyone on tour who lived out of a Winnebago was in good fun referred to as "trailer trash." Actually, it was a nice way to live on the road, and if I had made a career with Ice Capades, it would have been my lifestyle of choice.

While I had my own private dressing room, I preferred to hang out with the other principal men because I hated being by myself. When I was performing in West Company, comedian skater Gigi Percelli used to hold some pretty intense card games backstage. Just to show how small the skating world is, Gigi was married to a woman named Leslie, who played a character in the show named Jane Blond, a takeoff on James Bond 007. Leslie's first husband was Kevin Bupp, the show skater I idolized from my Bowling Green days. Gigi and his son, Joey, also were instrumental in helping me acquire a back flip in my second season on tour. I also got some coaching on the maneuver from Greg Weiss, a gymnastics coach whose son Michael is the current U.S. men's national figure skating champion.

One night during one of Gigi's poker games, pairs skater Chris Harrison was immersed in his hand when he looked up and noticed another cast member walking by, someone who went on right before him. Chris was puzzled—the performer was already in full costume.

"What are you doing dressed so early?" Chris asked.

"What do you mean? I just got off the ice," the skater replied.

Chris froze for a second and then threw down his cards. He was due on the ice in less than a minute and he wasn't even in costume. I ran ahead to warn his partner, Lisa Carey, who was furious because Chris had a bad habit of arriving just as they were supposed to go on. "Chris is going to be a little late," I told a livid Lisa.

Back in the dressing room, Chris tore off his warm-ups and went running toward the arena, pants half-on, skates unlaced. As his music began to play, we helped him get dressed the rest of the way while Lisa skated solo. Their number was half over when Chris finally made it out on the ice. And when they got off, the performance director was waiting for them. Chris was slapped with a big fine.

In the Continental Company, the guys formed a club called the Principal Men's Gaming Society. Our dressing room was filled with games and toys—darts, remote-control cars, miniature hockey and electric road race sets. The group included Brad Dowd, Bob Mescalic, Tommy Miller, Tom Dixon, and Richard Dalley. Richard was an ice dancer paired with Carol Fox. Fox and Dalley, as they were known, were terrific performers who were a little accident prone—enough so that I rarely missed their numbers. Poor Richard was having a really tough time with his back, which accounted for some of the mishaps. On one Saturday when we had three shows scheduled, he took muscle relaxers to relieve the spasms. It didn't help. During one number, Richard fell not once, but three times as his legs kept getting tangled in Carol's dress with each attempt to get up. On the third fall, Carol was so fed up and embarrassed, she just skated away.

Keeping Richard waiting was a specialty of Carol's. She always seemed to be taking the curlers out of her hair just as their names were being announced to the crowd. During one show in Hershey, Pennsylvania, she galloped up at the last second, flipped off her guards and skated onto the ice. Richard was so flustered he stepped onto the surface without taking off his plastic guards, fell down, and slid about thirty feet on a surface covered with a half inch of water because we were in the middle of a heat wave. We had a special honor for the ugliest fall of the week—the Booboo Piggy, a plush hog made up to look like the winner. That week, we were decorating it for Tom Dixon, but after Richard's fall I ran back to the dressing room and said, "Stop working on the piggy; we have ourselves a new winner."

Another time, stunt jumper Steve Taylor won the piggy with the most memorable crash. His job was to skate full speed toward a Plymouth minivan, leap onto a trampoline, and propel himself over the vehicle. This time, his skates slipped off the trampoline and his feet went out from under him. He hit the side of the van, chest first, hung on with his arms and gradually slid onto the ice. He lay there for a minute with some bruised ribs, but fortunately he was all right. When he received his Boo-hoo Piggy, the word *Plymouth* had been stamped backward on the stuffed animal's chest.

Skating for "Capades" could drain the lifeblood out of you. Once I caught the flu during the Pittsburgh-Philadelphia run of shows and I didn't take a day off, which was probably not the smartest thing to do. A bad virus had the potential to lay up one third of the cast, which actually happened the year before I arrived. The traveling and work load made for a grueling pace. And sometimes, we partied just as hard as we skated.

One of my best friends on tour was Greg Letourneau, the show's assistant manager and sound supervisor. He was big, around six feet, two inches tall, so we were like Mutt and Jeff. Once in a while I could persuade him to sneak away to join me for an afternoon round of golf. After most shows we'd get together with some of the guys and go out. We liked low-key places, crew hangouts like the old Penn Bar outside Madison Square Garden, and cast hangouts such as Grandma's Saloon in Duluth, Minnesota. We'd meet girls, of course, but our nights on the town were more about good food and laughs. Now and then we might stay out too late, which was fine for me because I got to sleep in. Poor Greg used to pay for it because he would have to be at work early the next morning.

During the Denver stop in my first year, I threw a big party for the cast and crew. Since I'm not content to just stay in one place, I rented a big double-decker bus, loaded it up with soft drinks, beer and wine, and took the entire company out on the town. The road trip began promptly at 7 P.M. and traveled from pizza joint to jazz club and from bar to bar.

When we played Toledo, I invited some of my "trailer trash" friends to hook up their RVs at my father's house twenty miles away in Bowling Green. Ernie always looked forward to our visits because he could recruit the extra manpower for some of the heavier chores around the house, like the time we installed a heavy-duty bird feeder by his vegetable garden.

I wasn't friends with everybody that first year. One of the difficult adjustments I had was dealing with many of the gay men on the tour. Frankly I was sick of people constantly assuming I was gay because I was a figure skater. This fear of being labeled definitely played a role in my decision to radically alter my costumes in my last year of amateur skating.

Some people still think I'm gay. My friends get asked this question about me all the time. I was recently in Los Angeles and met an actress from a popular television series. Midway through our conversation, the subject of sexual orientation came up.

"You mean you're not gay?" she asked.

I said, "No, I'm not."

"Oh, my God, I thought you were gay."

I had to ask her the $64,000 question. What was it about me that made her so certain I was gay? Was it the way I was acting or my mannerisms?

"No, no," she said. "You're just funny and sensitive."

Even though she didn't say it, I have to believe that being a figure skater had something to do with it. I didn't bring it up.

"Thanks for the compliment," I replied diplomatically. "But I'm straight."

I grew up in a very conservative town where being gay was not acceptable. I'd be remiss to say that environment didn't shape my thinking. When I joined "Capades," I had a monster chip on my shoulder. "Homophobic" was an accurate description of my feelings toward gay men. I used to joke about the lifestyle, partly because I had spent the previous sixteen years fending off the cruel humor directed at me. "Fairy," "sissy," "faggot," I had heard them all. I liked girls as much as the so-called macho guys giving me a hard time, but that didn't matter. I was a figure skater, so I had to be gay.

In my first year on tour, I was on the defensive and didn't associate with any of the openly gay skaters. I lightened up considerably in my second season and became accepting of gay lifestyles. Gay men and women are entitled to live how they want, and their lifestyle should be embraced, not shunned or judged. My mother was a very open-minded person and accepted people for who they were. She would not have had any patience with my fear and intolerance.

There was another reason for my attitude change. I learned some of my closest friends in skating were gay, people I had trained with, partied with and roomed with on tours. What was I going to do then? Forget everything I liked and admired about them? Never speak to them again?

Former Canadian champion Brian Pockar and I were great friends. In 1982, I invited him to Bowling Green to be a guest in the "International Stars on Ice" cancer benefit. It was a great show that year, which included Kitty and Peter, and U.S. dance champions Michael Seibert and Judy Blumberg.

Every night we went out to some of the local hot spots, and Brian, being an attractive guy, was getting approached by women everywhere we went. Girls were falling all over him. One gorgeous college girl approached him in a bar and said flirtatiously, "Do you like wax melted on your body?"

While I'm standing there hyperventilating with envy, Brian is ignoring her. "I do, I do," I volunteered. But she wasn't interested in me. Clearly Brian wasn't smitten with her. It was a couple of years before I understood why. On that night, I just shook my head in disbelief. "Brian, what are you doing?" I asked incredulously. He just shrugged it off. "Oh, I'm just not into it," he said.

The funny thing was, Brian was a pro at teasing women, and his favorite target was Judy Blumberg. All week long in Bowling Green Brian fended off college coeds and hit on Judy hard, though I could never really tell if he was serious or kidding. One night while hanging out with Kitty in her hotel room, I heard Brian knocking on Judy's door, which was just down the hall.

"Judy, let me in," Brian said. I could tell by the tone of his voice he'd had a little to drink.

"No, Brian. You're drunk. Go away."

"Judy. Judy. Let me in."

"No."

"Judy. Let me in. I want you, Judy. I want you."

"Brian, go away."

"Okay, but if you don't let me in right now I'm rejecting you."

Kitty and I were howling. Then a few minutes later, Brian was back at the door, harassing Judy again.

Another great friend was Rob McCall, the Canadian ice dancer I had gotten to know on the Tom Collins tour in 1984. Now, if you can make me laugh, you're a friend for life, and Rob was one of those people. He never made a secret of his sexual orientation, and I must admit I did feel awkward around him early in our friendship. But Rob was a great guy—generous, smart and creative in addition to being hilarious—and those were the qualities that mattered to me. Sometimes, though, my humor was in bad taste. During a pro competition in Paris in the fall of 1985, Paul Martini and I were kidding around and started making some off-color jokes in Rob's presence. Rob let us know we had crossed the line. I learned something from that. I had to take a hard look at myself and decide what kind of person I was going to be. Why was I acting homophobic if I had good friends who were gay?

An Olympic gold medal is no barometer of who you are as a human being, and in the mid-1980s, I still had some growing up to do. I finally concluded that what people want to do in the privacy of their own homes should remain in the privacy of their own homes, period.

Years later, ESPN Sports host Roy Firestone asked me about it an interview. "I know that you're proud of your manhood and your masculinity," he began. "How do you feel about the fact that figure skating has a feminine image and that most people think that all figure skaters are homosexual?"

I explained that there are possible environmental circumstances that could account for why the public at large thinks that way. For one, most competitive male skaters grow up at an ice rink and 80 percent of the people training around them are female. Those girls become your friends; they're the people you spend most of your time with. Their language becomes your language. Their mannerisms and behavior, your mannerisms and behavior. The result could be that you speak and act more "effeminately" even if you're straight.

Another reason for the stereotype is that skaters don't move like your ordinary football or basketball player. The sport has elements of ballet and dance along with athleticism and speed, and some people don't believe straight guys can move gracefully. They've probably never heard of Elvis Presley or Mikhail Baryshnikov.

Whether someone wants to be open about their sexuality is a personal decision. Some male skaters have kept their lifestyles "in the closet," particularly in the United States, where it's less acceptable compared to countries like Canada and England. A competitor or show skater who is gay might justifiably fear coming out because he could alienate some of his fans, lessening his appeal. On the other hand, there's Rudy Galindo, an openly gay skater who has had a lot of success and is very popular.

On the ice, skaters bare their souls and share their lives. For some it might mean expressing the sorrow they feel when they lose a friend or loved one. For others it might be the expression of joy when they fall in love or have a child. I believe it's the diversity in skating that makes it such a great art form. If your sexuality is an important part of your makeup and you want to show it on the ice, then go for it. Do what makes you happy. Some people will like it, and some won't.

At the end of my first season in "Capades," my relationship with Beverly began to fall apart. I had a lot of issues to deal with. I was brand-new to professional skating and preoccupied with establishing myself on tour with "Capades." I was also struggling to come to grips with my newfound celebrity. I may have appeared secure on the ice, but off it I was mentally and emotionally all over the map. I often wondered why Beverly was attracted to someone like me. At this time in my life, I had few social skills and felt clumsy and awkward around nonskaters. You might think a gold medal would give me security away from the ice, but it didn't, at least not around someone like Beverly.

As Beverly and I became more intimate over the winter, I withdrew, and by the spring I had stopped calling. It wasn't anything she said or did. I just couldn't deal with an intense commitment. Months later on my next visit to New York, I finally contacted her and we had one very uncomfortable dinner. I could tell I had really hurt her. Insensitive and stupid was the best description of my immature behavior. She deserved a lot more than I could offer at the time.

By 1985, I had put a lot of wear and tear on my Olympic costume. Between shows and competitions, I had probably worn it more than two hundred times. It finally gave out in an ice show I was doing in Tacoma, Washington. Just as I was being introduced to the crowd, the zipper that ran down the front of the costume went "poof." It was dark when the zipper went, and when the spotlight came on I was standing at center ice, the zipper undone all the way down below my navel. My pale chest beamed like a lightbulb and my face, done up in theatrical makeup, was like a lamp shade. It was a hilarious sight, but not one of my proudest moments. When I skated near the show's producer, Peanuts cartoonist Charles Schulz, a longtime fan and supporter of skating, he gave me one of those looks: "What the heck is going on?" So the next time I passed by his seat, I said, "Pretty sexy, eh?"

I finished up my first "Capades" season in Kansas City and the rest of the cast moved on to Austin, Texas, to wrap up the final week of the tour. For various reasons I did only two-thirds of the dates, and Austin was not on my itinerary. But I was not going to miss a closing-night party. I had to be there for the last bash of the year.

After the company left Missouri, I hatched a plan. I'd give them a head start, go to Austin, hide out, and then appear minutes before the close of the show. The only person I let in on the plot was my good pal Greg Letourneau, who needed to know so he could alert the orchestra on a moment's notice that I was skating the final number.

I flew to Austin with my costume and skates and took a cab to the hotel where the cast was staying. Since I was a couple of hours early, I helped the crew load up some steamer trunks on an eighteen-wheeler and then relaxed over a beer, which I drank on an empty stomach. I don't usually drink in the daytime, so that was not a good idea.

That night, I slipped into the arena during the second act and hid out in a hallway. I put on my costume and skates and waited until the final number was over. Then I gave Greg the signal.

"Scott's here," he said. "Play 'New York, New York.'"

As the first few notes of "New York, New York" filled the arena, Greg signaled Paul Heath, a principal skater with "Capades," to introduce me to the crowd.

I glided out under a spotlight and the house went nuts. The audience wasn't expecting to see me tonight and neither was the cast. Everyone peeked through the curtain, psyched for an awesome performance.

I realized quickly I was in no condition to skate. The beer, the labor, the travel, the lack of sleep from the night before, kind of took my legs out from under me. Made for a challenging performance, to say the least. I did manage to hit a triple toe loop and got a standing ovation. Talk about an anticlimactic performance. I came off the ice shaking my head, but all I could do was laugh with embarrassment. Oh, well, at least the wrap party made the trip worthwhile.

Chapter Thirteen

Skating for the Money

When my first year in "Ice Capades" was over, I flew to Sun City, South Africa, for another pro competition. I won again, but that wasn't what made the trip memorable. It was the golf.

I had played sparingly since my first lesson with Frank McLoraine in 1976, and still wasn't much of a golfer. That didn't stop me from hacking up Sun City's beautiful resort course, which was overrun with warthogs and baboons. One afternoon, I was playing with John Evert, brother of tennis star Chris Evert, and we ran out of balls. A long way from the clubhouse, we had no choice: one of us had to wade into the pond and retrieve as many lost balls as we could find. Emboldened by a couple of beers, I stripped down to my underwear and made the plunge. I found a dozen balls and, fortunately, no alligators or mamba snakes.

I actually didn't play any golf until the skating event was over. The deal here was two nights of competition and then five days of vacation—that's the pro world for you. Many an afternoon was spent on the links or lounging by the pool, which was a popular spot for the guys. The piña coladas they were serving had nothing to do with it. Poolside was swarming with topless show girls, swimming and sunbathing in thongs by day, entertaining hotel guests in a dance revue by night.

On our last day in Sun City, all the skaters got together for a celebratory golf tournament. Of the guys—me, Norbert, Toller Cranston, Allen Schramm and David Santee—David was by far the best golfer of the bunch. David, always the organizer, split the group into two teams and actually tried to keep score, as if it was the Ryder Cup or something. He gave up after a couple of holes. Some of the women, like Elaine Zayak and Lisa Carey, had never played before, and it would take them fifteen shots to get from tee to green. If they got close, we let them throw it toward the flag to save on time. Carol Fox refused to deal with water hazards, so she took her putter and slapped the ball around ponds, over bridges and onto the greens. I think on one par-four hole she took a thirty-five.

Not all pro events were this laid-back, but there was more of a relaxed atmosphere than in our amateur days. When I turned pro there were two major events to compete in, the "World Professional Championships," called the "world pros," and the "World Challenge of Champions." In the world pros there were two events—a technical and an artistic, each worth 50 percent. In the challenge of champions, you were judged in one event and then performed an exhibition. Both competitions were created and produced by Dick Button.

Given that I was skating ten to twelve shows a week for Ice Capades, the world pros were tough to prepare for. It was almost impossible to train when I was doing 6 A.M. press calls and skating in a show the same night. On Saturdays I was often doing three shows in a day. Still, Dick's events were the only game in town, and I missed competing. So in late 1984 I entered my first world pro, going up against Charlie Tickner, Toller Cranston and Norbert Schramm.

The world pros were set up much differently from amateur competitions. Instead of using judges certified by the ISU and USFSA, Dick invited international coaches to score the skaters. The technical portion emphasized jumps, spins and footwork, and the artistic number stressed choreography, style and presentation. There were no figures.

While the skaters took the competition seriously, the stakes weren't nearly as high compared to a nationals or worlds, and there was also more camaraderie among the competitors. But Dick's events drew big crowds of more than fifteen thousand, and the seats were filled with knowledgeable skating fans. You didn't want to appear uninterested or unprepared to an audience like that. I was ready to go with my triple Lutz and chose two exhibition numbers to compete with: for the technical, I skated to Gary Glitter's "Rock n' Roll Part II," and for the artistic, I performed to "Amazing Grace."

In 1984, the format was two competitions in one—a team event pitting recent Olympians like me and Norbert versus the pro veterans, which included Charlie and Toller. But they also ranked our scores individually. I skated both numbers very well and won. I left Landover thinking I was going to have a great pro career.

In my second year of pro competition, I got an education in the politics of professional judging. In 1985, Robin Cousins, the gold medalist from the 1980 Olympics, entered the world pros. While his primary strengths weren't necessarily his jumps, there were few skaters who were his artistic equal. I knew I needed two flawless performances to beat him.

We competed twice that winter and I came in with a surprise. I performed my Olympic long program for the technical number, completing four triple jumps, three double Axels and my new weapon, a back flip. I decided to learn it for two reasons. For one, it got an amazing reaction from the crowd, even better than doing a triple jump. For another, Robin had one. I didn't want him to one-up me.

Well, the back flip didn't make a difference. Robin came out, hit one triple toe loop and beat me in the technical. A triple Lutz, Salchow and toe loop involve considerable risk compared to a single triple toe, and yet my jumps were overlooked. Robin then won the artistic event with a brilliant performance to "Satan Takes a Holiday," and finished first overall.

I was crushed. Not because I lost. It had been five years since my last defeat; hey, it was bound to happen sooner or later. What upset me was the judging. It seemed completely arbitrary. Dick had a way of debriefing the judges to affect the scoring. "I think a beautiful open Axel and a gorgeous camel spin are as important as the triple Lutz," he'd say. It didn't take a Ph.D. to figure out the message he was sending: "Robin has a beautiful open Axel and camel spin. I think that counts as much as Scott's triple Lutz." Dick has a right to his opinion and I know skating is a matter of taste; I just didn't feel he should be influencing what other people think.

Later in 1985, Robin and I met again in Paris at the "World Challenge of Champions." I chose to skate to "Amazing Grace," and landed a clean triple Lutz, triple toe, double Axel, and back flip. I was definitely on. I got the crowd going, and when I took my bow, I thought there was no way in the world that Robin could beat me.

He didn't skate clean and he didn't have the same energy as he had in Landover. I thought I had him. Yet he was generously scored and won again.

I was astounded by the outcome and Robin was embarrassed. While he definitely won in Landover, this was no contest. Robin even apologized to me! I was really annoyed with Dick. Though I have a lot of respect for him and recognize that his success in skating is unparalleled—seven U.S. titles, five world championships and two Olympic gold medals speak for that—I sensed he didn't want me to succeed in competitive pro skating.

I rejoined the "Ice Capades" tour, and during a stop in Manhattan I set up a breakfast meeting with him to express my concerns.

"The system of judging is way too subjective," I argued. "How can a skater prepare if the judging is so loose?"

And Dick's response was, "Oh, I don't want to have anything to do with the judging system. I've been trying to get rid of the responsibility for the judging procedures for a long time."

"Just tell me the rules," I said. "Tell me what I need to do to win your competition and I'll build my programs to do just that."

But he insisted he was not pushing any style of skating, or lobbying for a particular outcome. I left the meeting completely dissatisfied. Ideally, I felt judges at pro events should be given some basic guidelines and left alone. My philosophy was to let the competition be a competition—no one should enforce a judging system that pushes professional skating in a certain direction. Professional skaters perform the skills they do best, and it's the diversity of performances that make skating an art form. Robin was going to be Robin; I was going to be me. I didn't think we all had to skate one certain way.

So I decided the best solution was to stop complaining and take matters into my own hands. I could make some changes in my routines and rededicate myself to hard work. I was determined to control my own fate.

Robin's success against me was the push I needed to stop resting on my laurels. I was relying too heavily on my jumps and lacked the artistic polish of some of the veteran skaters. Despite my criticism of the judging, I had tremendous respect for Robin. He was a terrific all-around skater who could take advantage of his great height (six feet) and his long limbs; for example, while doing his camel spin, he could reach back with his right arm and wrap his hand around his left thigh, which requires a lot of flexibility. Robin was a seasoned pro and it showed. I had some catching up to do.

I decided to shake up my routines and went looking for a new choreographer. There was a lot of buzz in skating about the director of a proscenium show called "Concert on Ice" at Harrah's Hotel in Lake Tahoe. She was a young and gifted choreographer named Sarah Kawahara, a former principal for "Ice Capades" who at the time was working closely with Peggy Fleming. Sarah, who used to skate for Canada, was an extraordinary artistic performer, but she also had a strong personality, something I felt I needed to bring my skating up to the next level. I finally got a chance to meet her in Los Angeles at a barbecue I was giving at a house I was renting for the summer. I was immediately struck by her innovative ideas about moving your body to music. She really played a skating body like a musical instrument. When I asked her if she'd consider working with me, her reply was blunt: "It's time you became a professional skater." I thought to myself: "This is the kind of person I need to push me."

Ever since, we've been testing the boundaries of ice skating. Sarah did much more than just incorporate modern dance and jazz principles into my skating. She helped me produce numbers that would leave people thinking, "Wow, I've never seen it done *that* way before." That was the kind of direction I needed to start enjoying myself on the ice again, something that had eluded me the past couple of years.

Our new look included a technical program she choreographed called "Flight," a saxophone number by David Sanborn. It was one of my most demanding numbers ever, end to end footwork and jumps, including a triple Lutz followed by three double Axels in a row. The emphasis was on speed and footwork up and down the ice, with very few crossovers. It was not your traditional amateur program, and it went over very well with the judges at the 1986 world pros.

For the artistic section, I skated to "Battle Hymn of the Republic," a moving Ricky Harris program that I dedicated to the U.S. skaters who had died in a plane crash on their way to 1961 worlds. I needed to skate a perfect program to win, and gave my wristband a familiar rub before going on the ice.

I got the perfect score for "Battle Hymn"—10s across the board from the judges. I needed every one of them. This time around, I was able to beat Robin by one-tenth of a point—100 to 99.9.

I finished second in the 1987 world professional championships in Landover, without much preparation due to a recently healed broken foot. Still, I felt I was getting the hang of it. It just takes a while to find your niche. Once I did, I got in a groove and started to relax and let my personality come out on the ice.

Brian Pockar once told me there were three phases in skating. Phase one was winning. Phase two was making as much money as possible. And phase three was being the best you could be. That was my experience exactly. Winning was the total priority for me as an amateur. Making money was my priority during my first few years as a pro. I accepted every job that came my way because I was in great shape and could handle the workload. As time passed, money became secondary, and phase three kicked in.

Of course, there are those rare skaters who seem to have a firm grasp of all three phases the day they turn pro. That describes Brian Boitano, who retired from amateur skating after the 1988 World Championships.

Not that he needed any help, but once again the judging changed in Landover when Brian began competing. All of a sudden, Dick's competitions became a showcase for technical skills, in particular triple jumps. Just when I was ready to capitalize on my artistic talent, it was counting for less than Brian's incredibly consistent triples. He'd won a gold medal performing two triple Axels in his long program, and there was no letup when he arrived in Landover for his first pro meet later that year. He had mastery over a jump I had no desire to learn all over again, not at that stage of my career. Part of the problem was my takeoff on the double Axel. I don't jump off a skid. I elevate off a clean edge, which makes doing the triple Axel much harder.

So my strategy became this: whatever ground I gave up to Brian in the technical number, I'd have to surpass him by a greater amount in the artistic portion. Well, I could never do that. Even when I'd receive a perfect score of 50 in the artistic, it was never enough to make up for the ground I had lost in the technical event. There were a few times over the years when Brian made mistakes and I could have pulled ahead with a clean skate, but on those occasions I made costly errors myself. It would take me six years to beat him. As a consolation, I believe I have the honor of finishing second at Landover more than any other skater in history.

There was no shame in finishing second to Brian. Between 1988 and 1992, Brian could match the top amateurs jump for jump. Many felt he could have been competitive with Kurt Browning, who was the dominant amateur during that four year period. I was satisfied anytime I managed to beat Brian in the artistic number. There were such things as moral victories when you competed against Brian, who was at the peak of his career.

In the summer of 1986, just as I was getting comfortable as a performer and a pro competitor, my show skating career came to an abrupt end. Metromedia was selling "Ice Capades," and the new owners, represented by Tom Scallen, were making noise about my contract. This disgusted me. For two seasons I had been contracted to play twenty cities in twenty weeks, and usually did more dates by filling in for other skaters, doing everything management asked. Now they were unceremoniously offering me one week of work at 20 percent of my weekly salary. Call it what you want, but they were firing me.

Bob Kain countered their meager offer by saying that if "Capades" didn't want me, IMG might start their own winter ice show with me as the headliner.

During the negotiation, Bob and Tom had an exchange that was forever after dubbed the "bathtub debate."

"You know, Bob," Scallen began, "I was sitting in my bathtub the other day and I was thinking to myself, 'What a conflict of interest a management company would have promoting their own shows and putting their own clients in those shows.' That's what I was thinking in the tub the other day."

Bob had the perfect comeback. "You know, believe it or not, Tom, I was sitting in the bathtub the other day too. And I was thinking how unbelievably unfair it is that these skaters are basically slave labor who have to work for far less than they're worth because there are no other alternatives out there for them."

The bottom line was, "Ice Capades" didn't want me back. Tom made it clear that they felt male stars couldn't sell tickets. I thought that was a peculiar thing to say, ticket sales were strong wherever I skated.

That summer Bob invited me down to Florida to watch the Lipton tennis tournament in Boca Raton. I stayed with Bob at his parents' home in Delray Beach. One afternoon he suggested we have a meeting on the beach, so we grabbed a couple of folding chairs and headed for the sand. That was when Bob gave me the bad news. "Scott, 'Ice Capades' won't be renewing your contract."

"Two years in 'Capades'." I grimaced. "Not much of a career." It was a huge blow. I had worked so hard to improve my skating. And just as I had promised Dick Palmer, I never missed a press call or a show, even when I was sick or nursing a knee injury (we just choreographed around it so I could skate).

"Ice Capades" Company Manager Don Watson and I used to have a running bet. Would I be able to land the 10:30 A.M. Thursday matinee triple Lutz? I won most of them, I'm proud to say. Even Dick had to admit to me in our last conversation that I had proved him wrong. He thought I'd be a real load to carry, yet he conceded I never once let them down.

It was true. The one time I actually came close to missing an interview, I ran to the TV station to make it on time. It was in Seattle in my first year and Lisa Carey, the publicist for "Capades" who also skated in the show, told me to be in the hotel lobby first thing in the morning for a TV interview. Lisa always accompanied me on media calls, but she was staying with friends in another part of town, so we agreed I would go alone. A driver was supposed to pick me up and take me to the station, but nobody showed. I knew what time they needed me in the studio, so the desk manager gave me directions and I hit the road—on foot. I left the Travelodge, ran past the car wash with the pink elephant, and a few blocks later I was at the station, breathless and on time. Lisa turned on her TV and saw me sitting there gasping for air. "I just ran here," I explained to the interviewer. Poor Lisa was beside herself. The one time she wasn't there something went wrong.

But my work ethic didn't matter to the new ownership. No amount of hustle or determination was going to change their minds. They didn't even want to meet with me. I was panicked by the bad news. What was I going to do now?

I thought of a conversation I had had with Colorado Governor Dick

Lamm back in 1984 after my gold medal victory parade. He invited me to his office to meet with him and I figured it would be one of those photo opportunities politicians always take advantage of when a celebrity visits. But that wasn't it at all. We met privately, just me and him. No fanfare. One of the things we discussed was "hometown hero syndrome." With time, he said, interest in what I had accomplished would pass, and not to depend on being in the public eye forever. Life is constantly changing, he said, and I should be ready for that. Now I see exactly what he meant. My career was at a crossroads and my next move would be crucial. Bob was way ahead of me in this department. His warning to "Ice Capades" that IMG would start its own production was not an idle threat. He wanted to follow through with it.

"I'm for it," I told him in Florida. "I can help." Working for "Capades" gave me some insight into how a large tour is produced, and I wouldn't forget those lessons. There were plenty of days I'd be pushing through a number, landing a triple Lutz, only to overhear a bunch of Cub Scouts and Brownies talking and laughing through my performance. The children cared more about the kiddie acts than watching me skate. Though champion skaters may draw their own audience, that's not the sole reason why families come to these shows. They come for pleasure and entertainment. But I always believed there was an untapped market for a skating production to entertain more diverse audiences: the hardcore skating fans and the general show-going public.

By staying in a show like "Capades" too long, I ran the risk of having my enthusiasm for skating sucked dry. After a while the jumps start to go, then the pride. You stop improving and start giving performances that ring of, "Look at what I was, not what I am." I didn't want that. I was in my prime and wanted to develop a large audience and a long career.

So on that sunny day in Florida, Bob and I laid the groundwork for a touring ice show directed by topflight choreographers and starring elite skaters performing sophisticated numbers. The emphasis would be on skating, athleticism and contemporary entertainment. No kiddie acts, gimmicks or show girls. We both felt skating had untapped potential.

Elizabeth Glaser once said, "There is no map for life; unfair things happen. The challenge is what you do with these things." Losing "Capades" became an opportunity to launch my own show, albeit a small one with only a handful of dates. Other skaters had tried it before and failed. Others, like Torvill and Dean's world tour, showed there was a strong market for something new and different. I was going to take my shot.

Chapter Fourteen

A Billion Nickels and Dimes

In October 1986, we gave birth to "Stars on Ice." It wasn't called that in our first year, though. The original title was "Scott Hamilton's America Tour." IMG thought I had some marquee value and it would sell some tickets. The inaugural cast included Brian Pockar, Toller Cranston, Rosalynn Sumners, Michael Seibert and Judy Blumberg, 1980 Olympic team member Sandy Lenz and the pairs team of Chris Harrison and Lisa Carey.

Rehearsals took place in Denver at the South Suburban Ice Arena. The location had nothing to do with nostalgia. We were operating on a tight budget and South Suburban gave us cheap ice. To save on overhead, all the skaters were put up in the homes of local skating families.

The group was full of characters. If there was a single person on tour who personified what "Stars" meant to all of us, it was Rosalynn. She had a frustrating experience in Sarajevo—popping a double Axel in her long program and barely losing the gold to Katarina Witt, who would later become one of her closest friends. When Roz turned pro in 1984, she joined "Disney on Ice" as a headliner and spent two miserable seasons on the road, playing second fiddle to Donald Duck, who was celebrating his fiftieth year as a Disney character. In one number, she even decorated the top of Donald's cake while the chorus sang "Happy Birthday." Roz was a great champion, and it was not the way she wanted to be remembered. She parted ways with Disney the same year I left "Ice Capades."

The creation of "Stars" was the best thing that ever happened in her skating career. Even during our first rehearsals, I could tell she would thrive in a small company that emphasized skating, not kiddie entertainment. She just kept on improving as a performer and became a mainstay on the tour until her retirement after the 1999 season. Yet there would be an adjustment period for her. Since we were initially a budget operation, the hotels IMG picked out for us didn't always suit Roz's tastes. After a couple of years, Roz started upgrading herself to the best hotels in town when the ones IMG had picked out didn't rate. In some instances I did the same thing so I could enjoy room service and a nice view.

Easily the most eccentric skater in the cast was Toller. One day we pulled up to the house where he was staying in Denver and we found him lying on the front lawn dressed in his trademark black pants and sweater, meditating under a huge pile of red, orange and yellow leaves. "Just taking in the moment," he said by way of explanation as he hopped in the car. That's Toller for you.

When I was toiling at Wagon Wheel trying to get a double Axel, Toller was a big star in Canada, and, along with Gordie McKellen, one of my idols. He was one of the most outrageous performers I'd ever seen. He was so bizarre on the ice, moving his body around as if it was in another dimension—you didn't know where or what he was going to do next. He successfully combined avant-garde skating with athleticism and was one of the top showmen of his era. While he won an Olympic bronze medal in 1976 and won freestyle titles at three world championships, his contribution to skating went far beyond those numbers.

As time passed, Toller became very sensitive about his place in the sport. Once we were in Paris skating in an exhibition and Toller discovered he was second on the bill, not the place for a headliner. He threw a fit, so I volunteered my spot later in the program. Great skaters like Toller deserve the respect of their protégés. I deferred to him because he had the whole package: entertainer, athlete and artist.

In the early 1990s, he went through some hard times with drugs and personal difficulties. But his humor and imagination never abandoned him. He always had brilliant one-liners and they came in an instant. In one show when Toller didn't have one of his better days on the ice, he skated off and was met by one of the production people, who'd missed his performance. The crew member innocently asked how he had skated.

"Well," Toller said in his aristocratic Canadian accent, "let me pull the pistol out of my mouth and I'll tell you."

During those first few days in Denver, we didn't win any contests for our organization. And sometimes we cut corners in practice. One group number in the works was performed to "On the Town," from the famous Frank Sinatra–Gene Kelly musical. In this number, Chris and Lisa performed a death spiral, in which the man pivots while holding the outstretched hand of his partner, who is spinning around in a horizontal position parallel to the ice. I came up with a crazy idea: to slide underneath Lisa during the move. There was barely enough room, but I felt I could pull it off.

"Shouldn't we practice it?" Lisa suggested.

"Nah, I can do it without rehearsing," I said reassuringly. I would give it a try later on in the tour.

After a week of work in Denver, the cast flew to New England for the opening leg of the tour, a whirlwind five shows in five nights in five different states. From October 21 to October 25, we took early morning flights from college town to college town, leaving us pretty wiped out from lack of sleep.

The debut performance was in a hockey arena on the campus of the University of Maine in Orono. I'll never forget the venue because there was a ferocious-looking stuffed bear greeting you in the lobby of the building. Before going on, I peeked around a curtain and saw that about 2,500 rowdy fans had packed the place. They were clapping their hands, chanting for us to come out on the ice. "Maybe we're on to something here," I thought.

While I was feeling optimistic, Bob Kain and other IMG honchos were holding their breath. The school's electricians were convinced they could supply four hundred amps of power for our lighting system from a one-hundred-amp wire connected to an outdoor pole. They figured the weather was so cold the electricity could pass through their cable without overloading the wire. So they rigged up a cable to the panel and ran it through a four-inch-wide hole in the wall of the arena and then connected it to our lighting system. No problem—until the big finale.

After I closed the show with "Battle Hymn of the Republic," the cast returned to the ice for the final bow. As we waved to the crowd, the houselights came up, maxing out the power. The electricity passed through the outdoor cable just fine, but when it reached the part of the wire going through the hole in the wall, it began to melt the cable. In that one small insulated section, the air around the cable was too warm, causing the system to overload. Kapow! There was a huge explosion, and we all looked up toward the rafters as sparks and flames lit up the ceiling. It was like an indoor fireworks show, only the blast had caused the cable to blow apart. "Cool," I thought. It looked so good it took a second for us to realize this wasn't part of the show.

Then I got really scared. Out in the audience, it looked like people were getting burned by the cinders floating down from the wiring. In fact, there was only one injury: a man working in the building tried to grab a spotlight wire, received a shock, and was treated at the hospital. We hurried off the ice and the building was immediately evacuated by the fire department. We were without sound and light, and there was a concern that fumes from the burned-out cable might be toxic. The next thing you know, news camera crews were on the scene as the Orono fire department investigated the accident. As we got on the bus to drive to our hotel, I could only imagine how Tom Scallen would react when this got back to him.

We traveled the next morning to Burlington, home to the University of Vermont. When we showed up, there was nobody around to let us in the building, which was typical. Our four-man crew was exhausted from breaking down the sets, loading up the semitruck and driving straight through to Burlington.

We were running so late Bob Kain suggested we perform under house-lights. Nothing doing, I told him. No lights, no show. It would have been ridiculous to skate under houselights because all the numbers and costumes were set with spotlights in mind. Bob commenced a search for volunteers, and headed to campus armed with a roll of twenty-dollar bills, free tickets and a promise of free beer after the show. He rounded up a makeshift crew from fraternity row and with help from our guys, they got the lighting system up and running in two hours.

Adding insult to injury, the building wouldn't let us change in the locker rooms for fear we'd steal the school's hockey equipment, so we all had to change in a single bathroom. Bob hung a curtain down the middle of the room so the girls and guys could dress in privacy. Of course, that curtain dropped lower and lower with each passing moment, so by the second half of the show, it might as well have been a coed dressing room.

The third show at the University of New Hampshire in Durham was uneventful, and we headed on to Morristown, New Jersey, where we skated at the Mennen Arena, the site of 1982 Easterns. The crew was so tired they were running on fumes. I actually helped them unload the truck and then got ready to skate.

It was a big night. We had advance word that Dick Button and Torvill and Dean were going to be in the audience, which made us all pretty nervous. We had another good turnout and the show went off without a hitch.

On the bus drive to Philadelphia, we were in high spirits. We had recovered from the Maine misfortune, and despite all the logistical problems, ticket sales had been terrific. That was about to change. At showtime the arena at the University of Pennsylvania was only one-third full—a box-office bust. Every nickel and dime we had made in the previous four shows went up in smoke, just as our lighting system had in

Orono. Barb Camp bought something like four hundred tickets herself and tried to sell them, but not even that could save us.

Wouldn't you know, Philadelphia is now one of the biggest stops on the "Stars on Ice" tour, but back in 1986, it nearly killed us. The first leg of the tour barely broke even.

Things got better on the second and third legs in early 1987. The crew finally got some local help at each stop, and after a show one night, the two new tour buses pulled up to the venue. We thought we were in seventh heaven. The first bus was forty-five feet in length, complete with a thirty-five-inch TV, beds, couches, and a fully stocked refrigerator. The driver told us it had previously been leased by Eddie Murphy. The second charter bus looked okay, but it was like comparing Motel 6 to the Four Seasons.

"The other one is for the crew," somebody said, so I climbed on the deluxe bus, sat down on a couch and exclaimed, "Man, this is living."

Just as the entire cast was ready to kick back and enjoy the ride, one of my good friends from the crew, Reggie Rush, climbed on the bus, looked around, and laughed. "You guys belong on the Partridge Family bus; this one's for us." It seemed IMG didn't rent the crew a bus after all; the crew went out and leased one for themselves while the skaters were stuck in the jalopy leased by IMG. Apparently Reggie and his people felt they could get a cheaper and better bus than IMG, and that was exactly what they did. The crew felt bad for us, so as we were piling off, they announced that some of us could stay. "Just the girls," Reggie said. In a moment, half the cast immediately went in reverse. What good samaritans, I thought as I settled in for a long and bumpy ride to the next town.

On our third and final leg of the tour in the spring of 1987, one of my more memorable shows was at the War Memorial Auditorium in Syracuse, New York. When I first attempted my risky trick of sliding under Chris and Lisa's death spiral, my body made it, but the little finger on my right hand didn't. Lisa ran over it with her blade. I couldn't leave without stopping the number, so I skated on, dripping blood all over the ice and trying not to get it on my white sailor costume. During a break in the number, I skated over to Bob, who was sitting next to Yuki Saegusa, another IMG agent, and Gary Swain, the tour manager. "Someone get me a Band-Aid, quick!" I said. Bob, Yuki and Gary all looked at each other to decide whose job it was to get the Band-Aid. Meanwhile, my finger was dripping blood like a leaky faucet. Yuki went to get a bandage and I wrapped up the gash to stop the bleeding. When the number was over, the lights came up and there was blood all over the ice, causing one fan to faint. The nurse at the arena almost passed out, too. After the show I had to go to the hospital and needed ten stitches to close the wound.

That first season was a money loser, but we did well enough for IMG to roll the dice one more year, this time with an expanded thirty-city tour. By the end of the first season, we had increased the cast, adding the pairs team of Lea Ann Miller and Billy Fauver, and Barbara Underhill and Paul Martini, the 1984 world pairs champions. Our grosses in the second year were only $40,000 a night, leaving us far in the red.

I tried not to get discouraged. IMG promised to keep backing the tour because it was something they really wanted to succeed. It was a long-term prospect. I kept my fingers crossed because my desire for show skating was as strong as ever. My role model was Richard Dwyer, one of the great showmen of all time. He was the legendary performer with "Ice Follies" and "Ice Capades" who made a career of skating in a top hat and tails to Tony Bennett songs, giving out bouquets of roses to ladies in the audience and winning everyone over with his charm. What I admired most about him was that he had a long and successful career and a following all his own, which was exactly what I desired. This tour could give me that, so I hoped and prayed IMG would stick with the tour and not get dismayed by the losses.

That second season, IMG renamed the show "Stars on Ice" and added Dorothy Hamill to the cast. The new banner was a smart move. Bob felt if you associated a show with a single person, or a couple of performers, the production could die when that star went away. Dorothy was a great addition, a beloved champion with a beautiful artistic style. She is one of the most popular skaters ever, and everything should have been perfect.

It wasn't.

One of the problems was that I never hit it off with her fiancé, Ken Forsythe, a California orthopedist. The very first time we met, we were in New York doing publicity for the show and he came over and introduced himself while I was putting on my skates. "I hear you're a doctor," I said, to make pleasant chitchat. "I'm looking into changing my diet so I can bring up my energy level and live a healthier lifestyle. Is there anyone or anything you can recommend?"

Ken suggested I avoid nutritionists. "If they call themselves a nutritionist, they're usually a quack."

"Oh," I said, "you mean like their medical diploma is written in Spanish, or something like that?"

Ken didn't laugh at my attempt at humor. Instead, he just gave me a real funny look and mumbled, "Something like that."

I came to learn that Ken earned his medical degree from Guadalajara University in Mexico. Oops.

Later on in the tour, we butted heads over my foot injury. I was limping through shows because I had fractured the metatarsal shaft on my right foot. I had injured it during a workout when my left blade accidentally cut through the top of my right skate. When I mentioned it to Ken, he shook his head and scoffed. "There's no way, no way at all it's fractured."

"Why would you think that?" I replied.

"Because you couldn't put weight on it if it was fractured. It would hurt too much."

"I know," I said. "That's why I have to leave the tour. I did three shows on a fractured foot, and during the fourth show I couldn't put any weight on it. I'm going home because it won't heal until I get off my feet."

But Ken didn't want to hear it. He had his own diagnosis. "You're lying," he sneered. "There's no way in the world it's fractured."

I didn't like being called a liar. I said something back that I'd rather not repeat.

Besides my problems with Ken, there was more trouble brewing between Dorothy and me. Since "Stars on Ice" was my baby, I was putting a considerable amount of time and energy into the production. I helped choose the music and the costumes and advised on any show issues. Yet IMG wouldn't give me a production credit because it might have offended Dorothy. Clearly IMG was doing everything it could to build a relationship with her, and sometimes I felt it was at my expense.

On tour, Dorothy and I rarely spoke, and we went our separate ways after each show. She went out with her friends and I went out with mine. Not only did we hang with different crowds, we chose to skate in our own production numbers, with our friends supporting us. Each night, it was a competition between my number, "A Man of Many Colours," and Dorothy's, "Ice," a spoof on a jewel heist. Dorothy's cast included Michael Seibert, Judy Blumberg, Barbara Underhill and Paul Martini. My group was Lea Ann, Bill, Toller, Rosalynn and Brian Pockar.

"Colours" had music written exclusively for us by my good friend Rick Neilsen, lead guitarist for Cheap Trick. It was inspired by a book Don Laws had recommended to me, Jerzy Kosinski's *The Painted Bird*. A character in the novel tells a fable about a bird that is painted a different color from its flock, and subsequently shunned and killed by the other birds. In my interpretation, a traveler arrives in a world of black and white and teaches the people there that they each have their own special color within, a color that could be loved and respected if they allowed it.

We acted out this theme with visual effects, starting out the number by filling the ice surface with smoke as the cast performed wearing only black and white. In the ending, we shrouded the rink in a multicolored haze as I went around to each skater and released a zipper or a string to change the look of their costumes. Bill, for instance, had a reversible jacket that changed from black to purple. When I pulled a cord on Lea Ann's costume, puffy yellow sleeves appeared on her arms. A zipper down the side of Brian's pants released blue panels. Roz, who played Princess Helena, had her dress transformed into red, and Toller, with a rainbow-colored cape appearing on his back, had the most dramatic costume change of all.

In "Ice," Dorothy portrayed a jewel thief, and her cast wore trench coats and skated to crowd-pleasing songs like "Secret Agent Man" and "Diamonds Are Forever." It was real tongue-in-cheek and perfect for Dorothy, who knew more about rocks than anyone, yet had no problem poking a little fun at herself. It was a great number and got tremendous crowd response.

In one respect I felt bad for Dorothy, because I believed she was getting bad advice from Ken. It seemed to me that Ken often pretended he knew all about business and skating when he didn't. Bob Kain tried more than once to reason with him.

"Ken," Bob told him one day, "if you want to be financially secure, get a job as a doctor and stay out of Dorothy's business."

Ken didn't listen.

My lack of respect for him was apparent and didn't sit well with Dorothy. If you didn't accept Ken, she wasn't going to accept you. This was the man she loved, and they came as a unit.

There is no happy ending to this story. Dorothy and IMG eventually parted ways and it was ugly. They ended up in litigation. Dorothy moved on to another agency, and later she and Ken got financial backing and purchased "Ice Capades." Unfortunately the company was ailing when they took over, and they couldn't turn it around financially. They sold off their interest and Dorothy later filed for bankruptcy. She also divorced Ken.

I didn't like being on bad terms with anyone, especially Dorothy. She's an icon in the sport, innovative, creative and enormously popular. Our relationship is at a stalemate, and it's such a waste because I can't think of one thing about Dorothy I don't like. No one knows what the future holds, but I hope maybe we can repair the damage and become friends someday.

Chapter Fifteen

The Two Brians and Debi

As the 1988 Olympics approached, amateur figure skating was undergoing some drastic changes. Factions in the ISU continued to whittle away at compulsory figures. My old friend from Italy, Sonia Bianchetti, had wanted them out of the picture for years, arguing that the public neither liked nor understood them. I can't dispute that, though I believed figures gave individual skaters skills they could obtain nowhere else. The public would benefit indirectly by watching a polished skater with strong edges, balance and footwork. Figures remained a vital part of the sport through the 1990 worlds at Halifax, and then they were gone. The sport is still grappling with the impact, not all of it good.

My old coach Carlo Fassi predicted that once figures were abolished, the sport would be dominated by fourteen- and fifteen-year-old girls. Maybe he was on to something there—the last two Olympic gold medalists, Oksana Baiul and Tara Lipinski, were sixteen and fifteen respectively—but the most recent world champion, Maria Butyrskaya, is the oldest ever at twenty-six. His other prediction was that Asian women, because of their small body type, would have a distinct advantage over North Americans and Europeans. We'll have to wait and see on that one.

It's no secret that younger girls have always benefitted from having lightweight bodies and narrow hips, allowing them to rotate faster in the air on triple jumps. School figures were always the great equalizer that gave veterans a better shot at a title. Once their jumps started to go, the older skaters could concentrate on artistry and figures and make up for any shortcomings in their jumps. Lose your jumps today and you're done.

I think changing bodies are the reason for the high turnover among women. Men get stronger as they grow older, but the onset of puberty usually adversely affects a girl's jumping ability.

Between 1984 and 1988, the athletic gap between men and women continued to widen. The triple Axel became a mandatory jump for men, and quads were on the horizon. The top men were doing two triple Axels in the long program and triples from all six different takeoffs—Axel, Lutz, flip, loop, Salchow and toe loop. Two skaters in particular stood apart from the others—Brian Orser and Brian Boitano.

I first saw Brian Boitano skate at the 1977 nationals when he was a little thirteen-year-old with a monster triple toe and triple Salchow. A year later in Portland, he came back about a foot taller. It didn't bother his jumps, which were only getting better. He got a triple Lutz the same year I got mine, except I had more than five years on him. In 1978, he was the junior champion at nationals and clearly destined for greatness, if he could put all the other stuff together. I would have bet that since he was still growing and learning all these new jumps, consistency would be a problem. But in all the years I watched him skate, I hardly ever saw him miss. Skaters like him come along once in a generation. Even in 1978, I knew I had to stay as far ahead of him as possible so he wouldn't pass me by.

Brian was always at least 50 percent stronger than he had to be. As he matured, he developed a powerful upper body, which enabled him to rotate with tremendous speed. His lower-body strength allowed him to save just about any landing. His triple toe was like a double toe for anyone else. His triple Salchow was like a single Axel for mere mortals. When he got his triple Axel, he hit it with 80 to 90 percent consistency, his Lutz probably close to 100 percent. Amazing.

That consistency was what made him such a dangerous competitor. By avoiding mistakes, he put extra pressure on the other skaters. Some guys could double a triple jump and still get the mark, but not with Brian in the game. If you didn't skate your best, you didn't win. And as much as I would have liked to have beaten him a few times after we both turned professional, his greatness gave us all a measure of credibility.

From early in his career, I was impressed by his integrity and discipline. When I say integrity, I mean a skater who is dedicated to training and getting the most out of his talent. Brian had it. In 1982, he arrived at nationals with a triple Axel–double toe loop combination and became the first American to ever hit it. He still didn't make the world team but he came back even stronger the next year.

There was a funny side to Brian, too. When he made the world team in 1983 and went out on Tommy's tour, I gave him a nickname, Odie the

The triple toe used to be one of the
most exciting elements in skating;
now the guys are doing quads.
(Heinz Kluetmeier/*Sports Illustrated*)

Torvill and Dean we're not, but whether
it's the Make-A-Wish Foundation, the
Special Olympics or the March of
Dimes, it's a thrill to raise money and
promote charities for children.
(Laura Keesling)

In 1985, I was *American Skating World* magazine's choice as professional skater of the year. (Christie Jenkins)

Interviewing a victorious Katarina Witt after she won the 1987 world championship. I was still finding my way as a skating analyst. (Christie Jenkins)

My father and I sharing some good times on an Alaskan vacation in 1989. (Personal collection)

Through skating I've made good friends from all around the world. Here I am with my pals, Brain Orser, Peter Carruthers and the late Sergei Grinkov. (Personal collection)

Sergei and I taking a break during a "Stars on Ice" rehearsal in 1995, just before he passed away. (Chris Lenney/*Lake Placid News*)

One of the few times lately the whole family has been together was when Nana Helen died. From left to right, my cousin Dick, myself, my cousin Dave, Sue, and Steve. (Marjorie Ives)

On the job at the 1992 Olympics with two of my favorite people in the world, Verne Lundquist and Tracy Wilson. (Personal collection)

Celebrating my biggest professional win ever, the 1994 Gold Championship, where I defeated both Brain Boitano and Viktor Petrenko. (Gerry Thomas)

Upside down with Brian Orser in Lillehammer in 1994. (Karen Plage)

In the 1994 world professional championships, I did a parody of an early 1970s Olympic short program, complete with retro costume—jump suit and tie. The music was a combination of Gershwin and one of my all-time favorite pieces to skate to: Sabre Dance. (Laura Keesling)

Dining out in 1995 with (from left) Karen, Katarina Witt, Oliver Schmidtlein, and Kristi Yamaguchi. (Personal collection)

Keeping warm at the Lake Placid airport in 1995 with Sergei and Ekaterina Gordeeva. (Personal collection)

In one of my all-time
favorite numbers, "Hair,"
I begin as a hippie, flip
out, and transform
into a square.
(Heinz Kluetmeier)

Talk about getting cut down to size! Karen and I taking a seat at the Delano Hotel in Miami's South Beach.
(Aja Danova-Steindler)

Happy to be horizontal while on the "Stars on Ice" plane.
(Rosalynn Sumners)

Brian Orser and I getting down to a rap number in the 1992 Canadian "Stars on Ice."
(Emma Abraham)

As Wayne Fontane Jr., my parody of a lounge lizard, I skated to the song "I Love Me." Man, in those days, I had the young ladies swarming around me. I hope they loved me as much as I did. (Emma Abraham)

Bill Plage (Karen's dad), the master outdoorsman, and Bob Kain, the cofounder of "Stars on Ice," relaxing while shooting a little pool at my home in Denver. (Rosalynn Sumners)

Paul Wylie and I opened the 1993 "Stars" show chatting with the crowd. You know what, Paul? I still think I'm taller. (Emma Abraham)

I love playing the host. Partying at my Denver home in 1995 with Katarina, Paul, Kristi, David Baden, Roz and Karen. (Rosalynn Sumners)

With my choreographer, Sarah Kawahara, on the set of my first network television special, "Scott Hamilton's Upside Down." It aired the week before I was diagnosed with cancer. I owe Sarah my entire professional skating career. She's a genius. (Ari Zakarian)

I kept a low profile at the Cleveland Clinic while undergoing chemotherapy in 1997. My friends—(L-R) David Baden and Lara and Doug Ladret—cheered me up by showing up at the hospital room in skullcaps just days after I shaved my head. (Personal collection)

Part of my cancer treatment included occasional doses of golf at Sherwood Country Club near Los Angeles. (Personal collection)

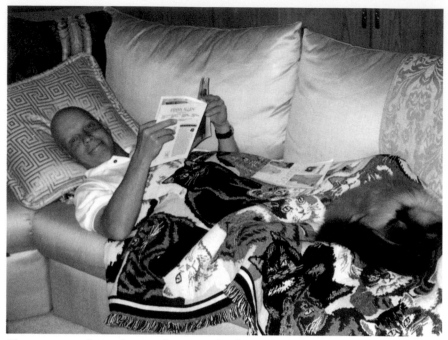

If you want to know how to how to relax between rounds of chemo, you can learn a lot from a cat, especially Ashley. (Personal collection)

Having survived cancer myself, I want to support cancer research as much as possible. Here I am in 1997 receiving the Lombardi Symbol of Courage Award from Sam Donaldson at Georgetown University's Lombardi Cancer Center Gala benefit. (J. R. Black/Washington D.C.)

I loved doing this dance number with Jayne Torvill in the finale of the 1997 tour. (Emma Abraham)

Is it the clothes, or the shoes, that make the man? Performing to "One Week" by Barenaked Ladies in 1999. (J. Barry Mittan)

Clowning around with Tara Lipinski in the 1999 "Stars on Ice." (Emma Abraham)

On the ice—where I feel most at home. (Kimberly Butler)

Roadie, after a Garfield cartoon character. Brian loved helping out other skaters with the props in their show programs. If you needed someone to remove a scarf from the ice or put out two chairs, Brian was your man. He liked doing gimmick numbers himself; my favorite was his imitation of a robot. He wore this outrageous costume with an electric power pack on his chest decorated with miniature flashing lights. I can still hear him backstage, running back and forth asking, "Has anyone got any extra batteries?" It was hysterical.

As much as he liked using gimmicks early in his career, Brian's forte has been performing numbers that tug at the heart, to music that plays up his power and dramatic style. As a pro, he won repeatedly by sticking to what he did best. He was a phenomenal athlete-technician and his classic programs, to *Phantom of the Opera*'s "Music of the Night," and Pavarotti's "Nessun Dorma," showcased his strength.

Some skating parents are very overprotective and interfere in their child's skating. Brian's parents, Donna and Lou, were unconditionally supportive, but they never intruded. They were content to sit in the stands, smiling and applauding for all the skaters, not just their son, who was usually more talented than the rest.

Brian Boitano's main rival after I retired was Brian Orser. In 1984, he was designated the heir apparent to the world title. He'd finished second to me both at the Olympics and worlds, winning both freestyle long programs and setting himself up as the guy to beat in 1985.

It didn't work out that way. Alexandr Fadeev, who had placed third at the '84 worlds, peaked at just the right time for the 1985 season. At the Tokyo worlds, he won figures, short and long program in convincing fashion and upset Orser. Boitano made a strong move as well and finished third.

At that time, I was pulling for Orser to win a world title. We were close in age, and I had so much respect for his skating. When I covered worlds for CBS in the mid-1980s, Brian and I always got together for a bite to eat. I became close friends with his parents, Butch and Joanne, who were very sociable and loved to entertain. At competitions, they would throw parties in their hotel suite, and Butch used to kid around a lot with my dad. They got to be great friends. I used to bump into his mom at doping control and we struck up a nice friendship while waiting for Brian to get finished with drug testing. We'd sit around cracking jokes and telling stories. She admired me for wearing a wristband in my mother's memory, and I was grateful to her years later when she would check in on my sick father while I was away covering the 1994 Olympics for CBS. That's the kind of person she was. I always felt Mrs. Orser was cut from the same cloth as my mom.

Her son was a better skater than Boitano in the first couple of years of their rivalry. Orser had the triple Axel, the experience, the artistic maturity and credibility with the judges. He had placed at every worlds since 1983. But in 1986, Boitano skated better and won his first world title. Suddenly they were even. Orser had now placed second three years in a row at worlds to three separate skaters and it was starting to weigh on him heavily as the 1987 season approached.

The world championships that year were held in Cincinnati, Ohio. I was covering it for CBS, but the heck with journalistic objectivity; I was pulling for Orser to win. Always playing the bridesmaid had to be aggravating. It reminded me of what David Santee went through years earlier when he couldn't crack through at the U.S. nationals. David was on the podium with four different national champions—me, Charlie Tickner, Terry Kubicka and Gordie McKellen—but never managed to win it himself. Brian won the Canadian championships year in, year out; it was just tough getting the big one.

But the 1987 Cincinnati worlds was his event. He beat Boitano and finally reached the top of the podium. After he skated, I knew he had won and I left the CBS booth to congratulate him as he came off the ice.

"You were awesome," I shouted.

Ironically, the loss Boitano suffered in Cincinnati worked in his favor. Had he won in '87, I'm uncertain whether he would have gone to choreographer Sandra Bezic for his '88 long program. Up till then, Brian was a pure athlete; Sandra gave him a program that would enable him to compete artistically with Orser. A former Canadian pairs champion who is now considered among the top choreographers in history, she gave Boitano the total package. It turned out to be a very important strategic move. Possibly his whole preparation for the Olympics would have been different had he beaten Orser in Cincinnati.

I watched the men's event in the 1988 Olympics with great curiosity. I couldn't attend, because I was performing in Lake Tahoe. ABC was good enough to pump in a live feed to the hotel so I could view the men's event as it was airing on the East Coast. Then I went on camera to comment.

I was feeling ambivalent about how a new Olympic champion would affect my career, particularly if Boitano won. Before the competition, I remember driving up to Harrah's in a snowstorm with my good friend and publicist Michael Sterling, and feeling depressed and vulnerable about my future. Would there be enough room for two American Olympic gold medalists? Michael reassured me that whatever Brian accomplished, it wouldn't deny me a career because we both have something unique to offer. "Brian is unto himself as you are unto yourself," Michael said in his inimitable way.

Still, I had my doubts.

On the night of the long program, the two Brians, as they were commonly referred to at the time, skated brilliantly and the judges basically tied them, but Boitano won the tiebreaker in the long program—which that year was the technical mark—and that proved to be the difference.

Orser had turned out of his triple flip, his only mistake but a costly one on a night that Boitano skated a perfect program. He did two triple Axels, one in combination, and another triple–triple combination jump. It was the finest performance of Boitano's life, and at the time the best Olympic performance by any man in history. That was what Orser finished second to. Nothing to be ashamed of there.

I'm sure he's had his share of second-guessing and sleepless nights wondering what might have been. Being as competitive as he was, that was a given. But he is also a grounded individual with phenomenal family support. I think he has made his peace with what happened in Calgary, He was a world champion and made it twice to the Olympic podium, a huge accomplishment.

Over time, I realized Michael's observation was true. Both Brian Boitano and I had something unique to offer the skating world. Sure I had to move over and make some room for him. He dominated the pro events for quite some time and also teamed up with Katarina Witt and promoter Bill Graham to start a rival tour to "Stars on Ice." I was no longer the top American male in the business.

But somebody had to take a backseat when I came in, and now it was my turn. When I joined "Capades" and toured with the same company as Charlie Tickner, they cut his numbers from two to one per show, so I could do an extra performance. I felt bad about that.

I decided that the whole key to longevity in this business was not to worry about what other people were doing. My goals were to stay tuned to the market and to what I was producing on the ice. Once I started to concentrate on that, I found my value rising every year.

Success, in large part, came down to how you sold yourself. If you were only valuable as the reigning Olympic champ, then you were subject to whatever happened in the industry, guaranteed to be replaced in four years by a new model. The trick was to transcend the title, promoting yourself as a unique entity. I wanted people to buy me as an individual, not just because I owned an Olympic gold medal. While I was no longer the reigning Olympic champion, I did have something special to offer to skating fans. I was always game to try something new, like creating a new program that would surprise some people. Staying fresh, combined with old fashioned hard work, were the key ingredients to staying ahead of the pack.

The Olympics also brought new talent to the "Stars" tour. After the Calgary games, we signed Brian Orser and the Canadian dance team of Tracy Wilson and Rob McCall. American champion Debi Thomas, an Olympic bronze medalist, also joined the cast.

New faces always meant new energy, and that was what this group delivered. Dorothy Hamill never did another full tour, but guest starred with us. She was pregnant and she showed a lot of grit trying to skate when she was feeling ill. There were times she came running off the ice after a performance looking for the nearest bathroom. She was also getting sick prior to skating her number. The following year, in 1989, she did a few more guest appearances and brought along her new baby, Alexandra.

In 1989, I finally got my producer's title, and one of the more unpleasant aspects to the job was mediating the occasional disputes. I didn't covet this role; I sort of inherited it, since I was the veteran of the group. Most of the problems were minor, until Debi Thomas's second season with the company. Debi had a good first year with the tour. But her loyalties were divided between college and skating, and the wear and tear of trying to balance both started to show.

She had a successful amateur career, winning two national championships, a world title and an Olympic bronze medal. In Calgary, she was in first after the short program, and her nemesis, Katarina Witt, didn't skate her best in the long, leaving room for Debi to mount one last charge. But Debi missed several jumps and was unable to capitalize.

At that time, Katarina was putting 100 percent of her energy into skating. Debi was trying to juggle attending Stanford University full-time and training for the Olympics, not to mention the added responsibility that came with being recognized as the first ladies' world champion in history who was African-American.

On tour, Debi was extremely unhappy. I always felt that the pressure of being the first African-American to win a national and world title was too much of a burden for her to shoulder. The expectations placed on her may have been unreasonable. She was a unique symbol of hope, a role model, and seemed to have the world at her fingertips. Yet deep down, I think all she wanted to do was skate, go to school and live her life in privacy. I don't think she was cut out for the public eye, or at least for what some people had in mind for her.

Defending a national title is stressful enough without the added strain of being a paragon of your race. Debi was a terrific athlete with a wonderful sense of humor, but I sensed a sadness inside. And it all came to a head during her second year on tour.

Since Debi was trying to hold down a full academic load at Stanford, she skated with us only on weekends. So the skaters had to learn all the group numbers with Debi skating and without her skating, doubling our workload. Making matters worse, Debi's heart wasn't in it. Her dream was to become a doctor, and skating became a means to pay the tuition bills. It was essentially a hobby to her, yet for the rest of us the tour was our life.

Debi became alienated from the cast and tempers flared. Brian Orser in particular went at it with her. During one tour stop in Canada, Debi said she didn't feel like rehearsing. These were the early days of the "Stars on Ice" Canadian tour, and Brian was doing everything he could to make it a success. When he found out Debi refused to practice, he stormed off the ice and confronted her in the ladies' dressing room. They had it out and the shouting could be heard back out on the ice. In very blunt language, Brian told her to put on her skates and get on the ice. This was a crucial period in the tour's existence and the dissension was killing us. What was more, when she wasn't around, there was a noticeable increase in morale among the skaters, and this didn't go unnoticed.

The tension that hung in the air wouldn't dissipate. When we met in Aspen for rehearsals for the fourth tour, the cast staged a rebellion. Debi arrived in town with a group of friends, stayed in a separate hotel and ignored the rest of us. When rehearsals began, she was showing up forty-five minutes late and holding up the production. Everyone ran out of patience with her indifferent attitude. I was now a producer in addition to being a performer, so I was nominated to have a talk with Debi.

Now, I liked Debi and kind of felt sorry for her. She was unhappy, and no one deserved to be that unhappy. I just wanted people to be happy, especially on the tour. It killed me when someone wasn't having a good time.

I also hated confrontations. Rather than deal with unpleasantness, it was easier for me to run in the opposite direction. Not this time. Everybody was urging me to do something.

I met with Debi at rinkside to find out what was going on. The other skaters were a short distance away rehearsing, but I could tell all eyes were on us. "Look," I explained, "this can't go on anymore. This is our livelihood and we depend on you to work and show up on time. You have as much responsibility to us as you do to yourself. People will be coming to watch you skate and they deserve your best."

Debi was silent for a moment; then she seemed to make a decision. "I hate it," she confessed. "I just hate it."

"But you committed to this," I said firmly. "You have to try to find some way to love it. Fool yourself. Do whatever it takes. You're in the last year of your skating career, so find a way to apply yourself for one more season."

I suggested she take the rest of the day off. Go out, have a cup of coffee, ten drinks, a good cry, whatever she needed to do to clear her mind. Suddenly Debi burst into tears. And all these feelings started pouring out about the pressure she was under from family, friends, the cast and worrying about her future. It seemed like she never had an opportunity to vent. Most of her friends were outsiders who had no interest in her skating career. My heart was breaking watching her bawl. More than anything else, I wanted Debi to be happy. The rest of the cast would survive. So I said, "Look, as much as we're upset with you now, we all want what's best for you. We want to work with you and we need your help. So if you can find a way to do this, stay on with us. If you can't, for your own sake you should leave."

There, I had said it. Debi composed herself and said she needed some time to think. After she went back to the dressing room, I turned around and joined everyone on the ice. A couple of the cast members skated up to me and said, "So, did you give her the business?"

"Nah, I just talked to her," I told them. "I didn't give her a hard time."

"You didn't let her have it?"

Some of the skaters were a little upset that I hadn't read Debi the riot act. We were all feeling unusually stressed and tired from training in altitude and learning a million new steps. I didn't feel like playing the bad cop. But you know what? Debi turned herself around. Later that same day, she returned to the rink and told me she was ready to work. And from that point on, she was the center of the universe on that tour. Debi transformed into a different person, laughing and telling jokes. She started going out with us after shows and the old humor was back. Because she was torn between a career in medicine and show skating, she never had the luxury of savoring her time on the ice like the rest of us.

And boy, did she ever perform. One night in Toledo she injured her ankle and she had to be carried from the ice. Later it ballooned into a black-and-blue lump. I assumed she would be down for at least a week. But she taped it up and two nights later was doing triple toe loops. Her skating was awesome and she was excited about being on the ice again.

We were all seeing a side of her we had never seen before, and it was truly inspiring. That season she was our morale officer—the complete opposite of what she had been before. And when the tour was over and we said our good-byes, there wasn't a dry eye among us. Debi wouldn't return the following year, but I knew that because her last season was successful, she would savor that part of her skating career. That was something she could keep with her for the rest of her life.

Chapter Sixteen

Behind the Mike

When I broadcast my first world championships for CBS in 1985, I viewed television commentary as a potential fallback job after a few years of pro skating. At that time, the life expectancy of a male show skater wasn't much longer than that of the mate of a black widow spider. And since my career with "Ice Capades" had crashed and burned, I was wise to think ahead. If not for "Stars on Ice," my show skating career would have short-circuited after two years. With sports broadcasting, I could stay connected to the sport long after I stopped performing.

It didn't work out that way. Fortunately, my show skating career has gone on much longer than I anticipated. So I juggled both pursuits, sometimes paying a high price—burnout. I was always trying so hard to prepare for the "aftermath," only there was never an "after." In fact, the farther away I got from winning my Olympic gold medal, the busier I got.

By late 1991, I had covered thirteen figure skating events for CBS: five world championships and five European championships. That's a lot of work by skating standards, but I was still a novice in the sports commentary world. Looming on the horizon was my biggest assignment yet: the 1992 Winter Olympics in Albertville, France. Bad news: I still wasn't ready for prime time.

During my first couple of years in broadcast, I was teamed with John Tesh, the former *Entertainment Tonight* host turned best-selling composer. Now, John is six feet, five inches tall and I'm five-foot-three and one-half inch. At the start of each show, the host and the analyst stand together and introduce the event to viewers, otherwise known as an "on-camera." Except with John, I was the only one who was standing. John took a seat beside me.

I was a mess on-camera in those days. Thank goodness for people like producer David Michaels, who guided me through a number of difficult broadcasts. On some nights I felt like a pilot trying to land a plane in the fog with no instruments and no runway lights. David was my trustworthy air-traffic controller in these dicey situations, but he couldn't keep me from developing bad habits, like overusing phrases and clichés, especially my all-time classics, an exuberant, "He nailed it!" and a subdued, "Nicely done." Verne Lundquist's favorite was the expression I used when someone bombed—"But what he did, he did very well."

John and I covered the world championships in 1985 and Europeans and worlds in 1986, and while we clicked away from the set, we never melded into a good broadcast team. I was just too inexperienced.

I was bombarded with criticism. I was too "shrill," too "wordy," too "nice to the competitors," and "not critical enough" and came off as a "homer" for the U.S. skaters. It was all true. When I got excited, I blurted out words as fast as I skated and tended to cheer everyone on. That's who I am, and I had trouble reining in my enthusiasm.

Many football and basketball announcers hone their voices by watching old tapes of previous world championships and pretending to call them, but I was an advocate of learning by doing. A CBS executive, Ted Shaker, once tried to give me pointers on what I needed to improve. I got defensive and said, "The number of events you've assigned me doesn't equal one-half of a football season. You give a football analyst a season to prove himself before you start criticizing him. I've been with you for many years, but I've done only about eight or nine events."

Still, I knew I needed some coaching. I spent time working on breathing, toning down my voice and organizing my thoughts before I spoke. Even with all the training, mechanics are only part of the job. You need a good rapport with your cohost for a successful broadcast, and that was a problem when CBS matched me with Tim Ryan in 1987. For me, doing an on-camera stand-up was about as relaxing as sharpening my skates with my teeth. If I could do commentary for the rest of my life without ever having to do another "on-camera," I'd be a happy man. Tim knew I was uncomfortable and tried to help out, yet sometimes it backfired. Before going on the air, Tim liked to do his homework. He would ask me to debrief him on the upcoming events and what to look out for. But he had a tendency to borrow my insights, leaving me little to say.

For instance, let's say during the 1987 world championships, Tim would want background on the ladies' finals, in which Debi Thomas, Katarina Witt and dark horse Caryn Kadavy were nearly tied entering the long program. So I would explain to Tim, "After figures and the short program, what we basically have is a three-way race for the championship. But for Katarina to win, she needs some help to pull up over Debi and that help, ironically, could come from an American, Caryn Kadavy, who could bump Debi out of first place if she finishes ahead of Debi in the long."

A few minutes later, it would be time to go to work. So Tim would begin his on-camera like this: "Hello, everybody. Welcome to the world figure skating championships in Cincinnati, Ohio. I'm Tim Ryan, and tonight it's the ladies' event. This is what it comes down to: We have a near tie among the top three skaters. Ironically, an American, Caryn Kadavy, could factor in the medals today if she finishes between Katarina Witt and Debi Thomas in the long program, but she will have to finish ahead of fellow teammate Thomas for Katarina to win. With me, as always, is expert Scott Hamilton. Scott, what can we look forward to tonight?" Now it was my turn to speak and I would have absolutely nothing to say, except "Let's watch them skate, shall we?" Insightful, eh? But when you had only one take to say your piece, there was not a whole lot of time to prepare new material once the old material was gone. I don't think Tim was doing anything besides trying to be the rock of the broadcast to make things easier for me. But often I was left speechless. Eventually I learned how to ration the information I gave him. He could do his job without sandbagging me, and it worked out fine.

After Tim, CBS brought in Verne Lundquist in 1989, the host I've been working alongside for the past decade. Verne is a terrific pro. He had covered football, basketball and golf, and helped my confidence by giving me a chance to speak. When I got too technical, Verne would furrow his brow or ask me a question so I could translate what I had said into English. Verne and I used body language so we wouldn't talk over each other, interrupt, or say something at the wrong moment. For example, if I wanted to speak during a performance, I put my hand on Verne's arm until I felt there was an appropriate break in the program, then speak. You never wanted to be talking during a triple Axel attempt, for instance. And when he wanted to ask me a question, he reached over and put his hand on my arm so I wouldn't speak. That way we wouldn't gab through the routine or talk at the same time.

Our first assignment together was the world junior figure skating championships in Colorado Springs. It wasn't a difficult job—just one on-camera and voice-overs. Five weeks later, we teamed up for the European Championships in Leningrad. But before Verne and I worked our first extended assignment together, I was competing in a pro event in Moscow.

It was a memorable time in world history. The Berlin Wall was down and the Soviet Union was opening up and liberalizing its economy. Dick Button had arranged for his "Nutrasweet World Challenge of Champions" competition to be put on in Moscow, the first pro skating event ever staged in the Soviet Union. There was so much change going on, yet one thing remained the name: it was the middle of winter in Moscow and it was freezing.

During practice that week, I felt good. Earlier in the season I had finished second to Brian Boitano at Landover and won $20,000. I was skating well, hitting my jumps and looking to be competitive. On competition night, nothing felt unusual. I found a vacant dressing room and paced in my electric blue jumpsuit, trying to get mentally prepared. Then I put on my top, a blue sweater, and went out to mingle with the other skaters. Patrolling the backstage area in Moscow's Palace of Sport were imposing Red Guards dressed in traditional green Red Army uniforms with the red lapels. I kept making faces at them to get them to laugh. It didn't work.

Earlier in the week, I was interviewed by my old friend David Santee, who was calling the event for ABC. I was skating to Sanborn's "Flight" and I remember explaining my program to David. "It's wall-to-wall three minutes of skating," I told him. "That's my strength. The hope is that I stay vertical and get through the program."

Those were fateful last words. On the night of the event, I skated second. There's no break in my number, so I started out in fourth gear and planned on doing my Lutz about fifteen seconds into the program. David was telling an ABC *Wide World of Sports* audience how for the past few years, I had been one of the busiest pros in the business. "But Scott has managed to keep his technique very high."

He had barely gotten those words out of his mouth when I launched into my triple Lutz, with about the worst technique you ever saw. I missed my takeoff completely and rotated horizontally in the air like a missile out of fuel, completing just two-and-a-half revolutions. When I hit the ice, I had to break my fall with my left arm to keep my head from hitting the surface.

"That had to hurt," announcer Roger Twibell lamented on the air.

"He had no feel for that whatsoever," David added.

My next jump was the double Axel, a relatively easy element—unless you tilt backward in the air, as I did this night. When I came down I was completely off balance, and I tumbled over on my back. "My goodness, again?" Roger said, baffled by what he was seeing.

This time I couldn't break my fall. My neck snapped backward and the back of my head caromed off the ice. As I rolled over onto my stomach, I heard the crowd groan. I just lay there for a second, looking down and trying to gather my thoughts.

Though I probably should have called it quits right there, I slowly got back on my feet and began stroking across the ice until my head cleared and I could figure out where I was in my program. I heard some applause and some rhythmic clapping. It had been my experience that Russian audiences don't react to every move or jump, and hold back their applause until the end of the program, so this was unusual. "The crowd is behind me," I thought.

Somehow my survival instincts kicked in. I should have eased up on my next jump, the triple Salchow, but I went for it and landed on my knees.

"He's got one more triple in his program," David said.

"Is it worth doing?" Roger asked.

"Knowing Scott, he'll try to make it happen."

David was right about that, and I hit the triple toe and finished up with my back flip. I was fourth out of four skaters, but got a huge hand from the audience. Though my head hurt, the good news was that I was still in one piece.

I sat down in kiss-and-cry and just started laughing at my performance. David came over to interview me and asked what happened on the Lutz. I shrugged my shoulders. "I didn't find my center. I lost all form of balance. I was skating real well up until that point, wasn't I?"

David chuckled at my joke. "What did you think going into the triple toe loop?" he asked.

I couldn't help but laugh at his question. I answered right away. "I thought, 'I've got to land one of these jumps. I'm really not that bad.' The crowd was thinking, 'Poor guy, what else could go wrong?' You know, Dave, I never skated that bad in my life. Last year's world pro was the first time I missed my triple Lutz; this year was the second time."

A big smile broke across my face. "I don't think I'm coming back, Dave. This is it, good-bye."

There was a twinkle in my eye when I said that. But it was no fun mopping up the ice like a runaway Zamboni.

Since this competition was set up with the exhibitions taking place immediately following the scored event, I had to skate right after my debacle. And as the fourth-place finisher, I had to go first. Backstage, I tried to get hold of myself. I was really upset and on the verge of kicking in a few doors, but you wouldn't have known it by looking at me. My self-deprecating humor is a wonderful defense mechanism. It beats having a nervous breakdown. When it was time to go on, I walked to the ice (I was in no hurry!) and could hear the crowd buzzing. I imagined what they must have been thinking, "What's he going to do for an encore?"

My answer to that would have been, "Just try to stay on my feet, folks." Before stepping on the ice, I ran my blade across the ice like a beginner would to see how slippery the surface was. The arena filled with laughter and I immediately relaxed. I did a clean performance to "In the Mood," and wondered just who had possessed my body thirty minutes earlier.

I left Moscow down in the dumps, and was not in a cheerful mood when I got to Leningrad for Europeans. After checking in to my hotel, I went over to the old Lenin Sporting Complex to meet with Verne.

Verne had spent most of his career covering football and he didn't know much about figure skating, or just how tight-knit the skating community was. It took us about a half hour to get from the backstage area to the broadcast booth, as I stopped to sign autographs and speak with officials, coaches and judges, people I had known since my amateur days. Russian fans approached me, too. Verne was puzzled. It was just dawning on him how popular skating was around the world.

Verne and I were checking our notes when Toller Cranston, who was working the event for Canadian television, came running over to us. Toller was just as wild and unpredictable on TV as he was in person. Once while observing Katarina Witt perform in a seductive costume, he described her as the "whore of Babylon."

Tonight it didn't sound like he was joking when he told us, "The tanks are rolling in Moscow," and ran off with a panicked look on his face. Oh, man, I thought, a civil war is about to start. Verne and I got up from our chairs and ran to a CBS trailer looking desperately for a CNN feed. When we got there and told the tech guys what was going on, they looked at us like we were out of our minds. "Toller," I said to myself, laughing. "What a practical joker."

On the flight home from Leningrad, I was preoccupied by my lousy performance in Moscow. I felt ashamed and embarrassed, and seriously considered whether I should quit competing. I had had a great week of practices and then blew up. How could that have happened?

My plane landed in New York and I got a connection to Pittsburgh, where I was scheduled to do some press interviews for an upcoming "Stars on Ice" show. On my way to the baggage claim, I bumped into a friend, Lynn Swann, a network sports announcer and a former wide receiver for the Pittsburgh Steelers. I had met him at the 1981 nationals when he was learning the television trade with ABC. I commiserated with him about what happened in Moscow and he left me with some thoughtful words. "If you do anything long enough, everything will happen to you," he said.

It was a little easier living with myself after hearing that. I was bound to blow up sooner or later. I decided to keep on competing.

Verne and I worked together for two years, and in 1991 CBS added a third member to our team, Tracy Wilson. Like me, Tracy comes from a small town, in her case Port Moody, a city of ten thousand outside Vancouver, British Columbia. Her father, Dave, once told me he would know he did his job well if Tracy could have the finest of wine and rarest of roast beef with the queen and a burger and beer with the boys. And that's Tracy. She puts on no airs and she's comfortable in every situation.

In the mid-1980s, Tracy and her dance partner, Rob McCall, were the Canadian dance champions, and big stars in a country where figure skating is the number two sport behind hockey. I was sitting next to her when she was recognized for the first time in the United States. We were skating in the Tom Collins 1984 Olympic tour and I was having the time of my life that spring after winning the gold medal. I was in great shape, partied every night, and never missed a triple Lutz in three weeks of exhibitions. After the show in St. Louis, we went out to a place called Pop's, a roadhouse saloon just over the border in Illinois. Norbert Schramm, who had a wild crush on Tracy, tagged along with us. He spent the entire night making goo-goo eyes and stroking her leg. Poor Tracy had no interest in Norbert, and she was getting very uncomfortable with his advances.

Then a woman walked up to our table. Tracy, thinking she was going to ask for my autograph, didn't pay much attention at first. But the woman had come to see her. "You're the one who did the 'Stray Cat Strut'," she said, mentioning the number she and Rob skated to on tour. The smile on Tracy's face could have melted a glacier. Later she went looking for the woman to give her a Tom Collins tour pin. I also think she needed a break from Norbert, because she was gone for quite a while.

Tracy and Rob won a bronze medal at the 1988 Calgary games and then joined the "Stars" cast. They were a great fit. Rob and I were in a card-playing foursome with Brian Orser and Billy Fauver. Our marathon games of Kaiser, Hearts and Euchre passed the time quickly on the long bus rides between cities. Rob's sense of humor made the trips even shorter. There are some people who through sheer force of personality can inspire joy and happiness in everyone around them, and Rob had that gift.

Brian and I laughed at all of Rob's jokes, but Bill was more selective. He was quiet and serious. Back in the late 1970s when I was dating Bill's partner, Lea Ann, he was so protective of her that we had to see each other in secret. That was how intense Bill got. Rob was one of the few people who could make him relax and smile.

Not many people knew it, but Rob was not only a great ice dancer, he was also a respectable free skater who could turn a nice triple toe loop. He also showed incredible talent as a choreographer. One of Elaine Zayak's all-time favorite show programs was a sexy and flirtatious number Rob choreographed for her. When I saw Elaine do the program, I told Rob he had done a terrific job.

"Thanks for the compliment," he replied with a wink. "But you should see me do it."

Tracy was a perfect counterpart to Rob. Sassy and daring herself, she could relate to anybody. When we opened the 1989–90 "Stars on Ice" tour in Butte, Montana, we celebrated the occasion at the Pair-a-Dice Lounge, a neighborhood joint with a pool table on the floor and hunting trophies on the walls. We arrived at the tail end of a wedding reception, and took over the pool table. Brian and Rob played some eight ball and Tracy took a seat at the corner of the bar. It was the night before the start of hunting season, so the crowd was in high spirits. A couple of us were a little shy around the locals, but not Tracy. The Pair-a-Dice reminded her of Port Moody. So when this surly guy in a baseball cap rudely bumped into her at the bar, Tracy casually said, "Excuse me." The guy didn't even apologize. Undaunted, Tracy asked, "What's your name?" "I'm Randy," he grunted.

Now in Canada, *randy* is the common equivalent of *horny*. Only this man didn't know he was talking to a Canadian.

"Oh," Tracy said, loud enough for all of us to hear. "That's a surprise."

This cowboy didn't know how badly he had been burned. He just looked at her funny, turned around and walked away. Tracy decided she was going to make it her mission to get his cap, which he had no intention of giving up. "You like it, don't you," he said gesturing to his cap.

"Yes," Tracy replied.

"You can't have it," he said. But she charmed him, and by the end of the night, he was introducing her to all his friends and their wives. And wouldn't you know it—she left with his cap on. That's her special gift—she can befriend anybody.

Tracy, along with the rest of the cast, would face a crisis in the spring of 1990. At the tail end of the tour, Rob came down with a cold that escalated into pneumonia. In one show, he got off the ice, started coughing and couldn't stop. Initially, we all thought it was just a flu bug going around, but he couldn't seem to kick it. That was when doctors diagnosed him with pneumonia. We were all very scared for him.

The tour ended in April, and Rob and Tracy were committed to go out with the Witt–Boitano show, just two weeks later. They made a plan to meet up in Toronto and then fly east to join Brian and Katarina in Portland, Maine.

On their travel day, Tracy arrived at the airport, took one look at Rob and nearly burst into tears. Rob, who had never missed a show, had lost twenty pounds in the space of fourteen days. Tracy spent all of about two minutes with him, biting her lip to keep the tears back. Finally she excused herself and ran to the ladies' room to compose herself.

Soon after they arrived in Portland, Rob's pneumonia recurred and he was rushed to the hospital. It was there that doctors diagnosed his illness: he had contracted full-blown AIDS. As Tracy suspected, there would be no more skating for the time being. Even though he never stated openly what he had, we just knew he was sick, and it was generally understood he had AIDS. He had good reason to keep it a secret. Previous U.S. laws, for example, banned HIV-positive noncitizens from crossing the border unless they revealed their medical status and were issued a temporary visitor's waiver. Rob still wanted to work with "Stars," so he kept his illness a secret.

In early summer, Brian Orser and I took Rob to the Pediatric AIDS picnic in Los Angeles, a major fund-raiser put on by the late Elizabeth Glaser. Rob had become diabetic and now was on even more medication—insulin, steroids, and other things he was taking to keep up his strength. But at the picnic he was in good spirits, laughing and cracking jokes. Amazingly, he kept up his self-deprecating humor. "I've always been a huge fan of Mary Tyler Moore and I loved her legs," he told me at the picnic. "That is, until I looked down and had them myself."

In the fall he came to rehearsals, but was in no shape to skate, so he assisted with choreography duties. Accompanying him, as always, was his pet dachshund, Beauregard, his faithful companion who never hesitated to chew up a hotel room. Poor Beauregard. Later that year in Toronto, when Rob was home resting, a friend accidentally let Beauregard outside and everyone gave chase. When they found him he had been run over by a car. Rob was devastated.

One day a bunch of people were visiting, and someone unfamiliar with Beauregard's fate asked Rob how his dog was doing. Everyone tensed up, except Toller. "Let me explain," Toller said, holding up his hands to indicate he knew how to deal with this crisis. "Beauregard," he said, pausing for maximum effect, "is as flat as a pancake." Mr. Subtlety shocked the room at first, but when Rob started to laugh, everyone else joined in.

Brian Orser was Rob's best friend, and Rob's illness preoccupied him all that season. During breaks Brian frequently left the show to fly to Toronto and visit with him. He took care of Rob for days on end, cooking his food and doing his laundry. Brian was having a hard time keeping up his energy on tour. And Rob wasn't getting any better.

Having AIDS meant more than having a fatal illness. It was a disease with a social stigma, something people feared and misunderstood. When Rob was sick, the media blared that AIDS was devastating the figure skating community. There were many skaters getting ill; there was no disputing that. I just felt journalists were pigeonholing the disease. "There it was—in skating. There it was—in Hollywood. There it was—in ballet. There it was—in the gay community."

In other words, it was everywhere, except in your own backyard, of course. I felt there was a concerted effort to isolate the disease with a certain group of people so everyone else could distance themselves from it. It was over there, not over here. That sort of thing.

Well, guess what? There's a percentage of society that is straight and a percentage of the population that is gay. AIDS affects people from all walks of life, not just gay men, and gay sex is not the only form of transmission. Some people also get AIDS from infected needles, some from heterosexual sex or bad blood transfusions, which was what happened to the late Elizabeth Glaser. Many infants contracted it at birth from their sick mothers. People need to understand all the risks.

Yet in the early 1990s, the media led a witch hunt, and that kind of reporting was a major disservice because it misled people into thinking they couldn't get AIDS. The reports also painted the skating community with a broad stroke, which was unfair.

In 1991, Rob McCall died of AIDS at the age of thirty-three. A year after his death, a tribute and fund-raiser was held in his memory in Toronto, which attracted skaters from all over the world and helped raise $500,000 for AIDS research at Toronto Hospital.

In 1992 I lost another friend to the disease—Brian Pockar, who fought the illness for three years. Brian discovered he was HIV positive in 1989 after catching the flu, but he kept his illness very private. He never talked to me about it, and I suspect the last thing Brian wanted was for people to feel sorry for him. He let his friends know in subtle ways that he was leaving us. For instance, he sent me pictures from the time we roomed together during the 1982 ISU European tour. "I thought you might like to have these," he wrote me in a note.

Brian kept right on skating until mid-1991, when his body finally gave out. He eventually returned home to his family in Calgary. When he got off the plane, he told his mom, "This is the last stop on the tour." Brian died three months later. He was just thirty-two. Once again my life was surrounded by death, and I was feeling despondent for quite some time.

With Rob's passing, Tracy's dance career was over. It's nearly impossible to lose a partner you've skated with your whole career and then achieve the same kind of professional success with another partner. I instinctively knew she was a natural for television and lobbied CBS hard to give her a chance. Not only was she articulate and personable, she had a megawatt smile. I had seen her work for the CBC at the world championships, and she had also done a pro competition for the USA Network. She was a wonderful interviewer, and I noticed skaters naturally opened up to her warmth and sincerity. With the Olympics approaching, I felt she could add considerable insight to our dance coverage and do interviews with the athletes.

CBS wasn't too enthusiastic about giving Tracy a shot. She was hardly a household name in the United States, and they wanted someone with more name recognition. I persuaded them to give her a tryout, and Tracy did the rest.

As I suspected she would, Tracy fit right in with our broadcast team. She also worked for a television network in Canada, and her assignments have included interviewing former President George Bush and the Canadian prime minister. She truly could have a burger with the boys and roast beef with the queen. Her father certainly got what he wished for.

As the 1992 Olympics approached, I was feeling a little apprehensive. Verne and I had developed a great rapport. The only thing we were lacking was a suitable amount of on-air time together. I was still more tense on camera than I was in person, and a little more experience would have been beneficial.

My other big worry was following Dick Button, "the voice of figure skating," who had been covering the Olympics for three decades. I felt that if I was going to follow a legend, I needed to do my homework. I wrote out notes—page after page—on all the contenders. By the time the first event began, I was completely scripted. And boy, it came across that way, too. I was so bent on saying something from my prepared notes, I wasn't reacting with any spontaneity to what was happening on the ice. My words sounded contrived, probably because I was overprepared. And my sentiments lay with the skaters.

When Americans Jenni Meno and Scott Wendland scored in the low 5s in the pairs event, instead of explaining why they were so far down, I said, "They presented themselves beautifully, and what they did, they did very well." Ouch, there was that phrase again. Then when a good friend, pairs skater Christine Hough of Canada, fell on a jump, I rushed to her defense, saying how she and her partner, Doug Ladret, were wonderful skaters with promising pro careers. I was too concerned about the welfare of the performers, at the expense of providing honest information to the audience.

I got hammered by the critics. I was a favorite target of Rudy Martzke, the sports TV critic for *USA Today*. They were right; I was pathetic, though the comments were pretty harsh. One critic wrote, "Give Hamilton a ski pass and put Boitano in the booth." Martzke wrote in his column, "Where's ABC's Dick Button when we need him?"

I'll tell you where: back home sitting in front of a television evaluating my performance with a *New York Times* critic. Dick was gracious in his observations, but the tone of the review was unfavorable. That piece of journalism made its way to the CBS bulletin board in Albertville.

I was angry because I wasn't getting constructive criticism, just blanket knocks on my work. Still, I had to pay attention—*USA Today* and the *New York Times* were powerful newspapers. Networks paid attention to what they wrote. Eventually the network made a move, too. They brought Tracy into the booth to help out.

Finally, I figured out what I needed to do. My choice was either to melt under the pressure or change my style. I chose the latter. For one, I decided I was no longer going to work in Dick Button's shadow. I was overly preoccupied with filling Dick's shoes and I needed to be myself. Dick is incomparable, but I felt I could create my own niche using humor and candor. The best thing I could do under the circumstances was toss away the script and react from the heart. You can't respond to a spontaneous event with week-old material.

Since that day I've never taken another note into the booth with me except for the program element sheets. That's all. I still do my homework at every event I cover. I know many of the competitors personally, plus I watch them all week in practice and observe their strengths and weaknesses leading up to competition day. I know what's coming in their programs and at what point they're supposed to do particular elements. But I don't choreograph my commentary anymore.

As soon as I just started being myself, Martzke began writing nice things about my work. In fact, in one of the columns he wrote as the games were winding down, he gave me a silver medal for the job I did after a rough start. Tracy got a "gold" and rave reviews, and I was thrilled for her.

It may not have been a vote of confidence, but a skit on *Saturday Night Live* certainly boosted my ego. Even when they poke fun at you, being parodied on *SNL* is a sign that you have arrived. Verne and I didn't know about it until the day after it happened, when Verne spoke with his parents in Omaha, Nebraska. CBS got hold of a tape and they shipped it to Albertville so we could watch. The late Phil Hartman played Verne and Dana Carvey played me. Dana kept using one of my pet clichés, "Nicely done," which was pretty funny because I was making a concerted effort not to use it anymore. I had gotten wind that the crew was betting on the number of times I would repeat the phrase during the games. The top prediction was 213 times, and that guy was running around telling everyone he had the pot won. The actual count came in under twenty-five. At the wrap party, I stood up and thanked everybody and then directed my attention to the technical crew: "And you jerks didn't think I would find out about the bet."

As time went by and I got more experience in the booth, I improved, but never at the expense of hurting a skater. I don't harshly criticize unless there's a good reason, and as a result I've managed to keep the trust of competitors. I'm not paid to judge; I'm paid to observe. If somebody's out of shape, I'll know it and report it. If someone throws in a jump at the end of a program, misses it and blows a chance at a medal, I'll tell the audience it was a mistake. But I won't call anyone stupid or say they choked. Unlike in many Olympic sports, most skaters are there to represent their country and aren't competing for commercial reasons. These days, the toughest part for me is keeping track of all the new eligible skaters.

A new group of stars emerged from the '92 games, including Paul Wylie, who arrived in Albertville on the heels of a controversy. There's a funny story about Paul that began at the national championships a month before the Albertville games. Chris Bowman won, Paul finished second and Mark Mitchell took third. Since Todd Eldredge, the '91 national champ and world bronze medalist, had a bad back and couldn't compete, the USFSA voted him a place on the team. The other two spots went to Chris and Paul.

Mark's camp made no secret of their disgust with the result that placed him third, knocking him off the team. Mark also had a few people in his corner who felt he had outskated Paul that night. It wasn't Paul's fault the judges liked him better, but when he arrived at the press conference after the medal ceremony, he was met by a hostile group of reporters, who smelled a controversy and wanted blood.

One cynical journalist asked, "What are you doing here? Don't you think it's about time you gave it up so someone else could have a chance?"

Paul certainly was an old-timer. He was twenty-seven, this was his eleventh year in seniors and he was trying to make his second Olympic team. At age fifteen, he was a national juniors pairs champion with partner Dana Graham. A year later in San Diego, where I won my first nationals, Paul was the 1981 junior men's champion. After his tenth place in the 1988 Olympics, the consensus was that he'd hang it up. He was a smart guy who didn't need skating, so why was he hanging around for so long? He should finish his studies at Harvard, where he was a student, and move on, everyone said. Everyone except Paul. He felt there was unfinished business. So he stuck it out another four years, never winning the national title he coveted so much, never placing at worlds, but never quitting either.

Now that he had made the 1992 Olympic team, there were grumblings that he was taking the spot of a younger skater who deserved a shot. Most critics pointed to his lackluster showings at the world championships— eleventh in '91 and tenth in '90—as to why the judges should have left him off the team. No one expected him to contend in Albertville, possibly not even Paul himself. His career had been plagued by untimely falls and subpar performances, including his long program performance at this very nationals. Paul was so convinced he wouldn't finish high enough to medal that he changed into street clothes after his performance and psychologically prepared to move on to the next phase in his life. But he slipped in there after his primary competitors made mistakes, too.

His problem was never talent—he was loaded with it—and he has been a crowd favorite since his first senior nationals back in 1982 in Indianapolis. It's just that he had a habit of folding when it mattered the most. At major events, like nationals and worlds, he would commit the cardinal sin of blowing up in the short program and then not be able to climb out of the hole he dug himself. Even great skaters can get buried at international competitions if they freeze during the short. Evy Scotvold once said Paul's biggest obstacle may have been his brain; he was too busy thinking out there. He wasn't giving muscle memory a chance.

Evy's relationship with Paul got pretty stormy in Albertville, just as it had with me when I trained under him at Wagon Wheel. I heard that one day during practice Paul got upset after Evy forgot to watch him do a jump, and Evy lashed out: "Look, you owe me. I don't owe you. I've put everything I had into you for the last seven years, and you can't stay on your goddamn feet." Sometimes nothing wakes you up like a cold slap in the face. Evy, being the coach that he is, obviously knew Paul needed something like that.

He didn't let Evy get to him. In fact, he picked it up a notch during practice. Evy's tirade must have worked. That week in France, the fickle skating gods were watching over Paul. Every now and then things just happen for no particular reason, but at the end of the day, it all seems to make sense. Paul was about to have one of those weeks in Albertville.

Nothing was going right for his competitors in France. Todd reinjured his back traveling over from the United States, fell on a double Axel in the short and sat in ninth place, far out of contention. Bowman touched the ice with his hand on a triple Axel combination and finished seventh. Kurt Browning, the three-time world champion and favorite, fell on his triple Axel and finished fourth. Paul was next, and for once he didn't let this opportunity slip by. He skated clean in the biggest short program of his life and finished third behind Viktor Petrenko of Russia and Peter Barna of Czechoslovakia. With the leaders floundering, Paul found himself with a chance to medal at the Olympics.

He had an excellent draw for the long program—after both Petrenko and Browning. In this scenario, the judges wouldn't have to conserve any marks for the favored skaters. Browning, who was limited from a back injury, skated poorly and finished sixth overall. Petrenko was next. He hit his triple Axel–triple toe combination and another nice triple combination, but he, too, lapsed near the end of his program, falling on a triple Axel and popping two other jumps. He still got high marks, but there was room for Paul on the podium if he could skate another great program. Paul started out strong, hitting two planned triple Axels—one more than Petrenko. Skating to the theme from the movie Henry V, he left the audience spellbound with his spins and Russian splits and received the night's only standing ovation. He definitely won the crowd. There was some sentiment that Paul should have won it all—he hit four clean triple jumps, though none in combination. His mistakes were a two-footed landing on the triple Salchow and doubling a planned triple Lutz at the end of his program. Had he done the Lutz, I don't think a judge on the panel could have denied him. The difference was Viktor's triple Axel–triple toe combination in both the short and the long programs, which raised the bar for the next generation of male skaters. The judges rewarded him for that, overlooking his errors.

Earning second was an awesome achievement for Paul, who had exceeded everyone's expectations. At the press conference in Albertville, he was facing many of the same group of reporters who had dissed him at nationals. "So," he began with a wry grin. "What are we all doing here?" The place broke up.

I was psyched for Paul, who's like a brother to me. Although he's very conservative, he can hang out with any crowd. Some of his best friends are skiers sporting earrings and tattoos. Yet he's very much the intellectual and a terrific debater, though he always manages to come out on the short end of *our* arguments.

After the Olympics, Paul was accepted to Harvard Law. He likely anticipated that the 1992 Olympics would be the last moment of his skating career. Winning a silver medal changed all that. He joined "Stars on Ice" and continued getting deferments from Harvard. In 1998, he'd decided he had enough of skating. One more year of grinding it out on tour and he might not enjoy it anymore. He also had a change of heart about his future and applied to business school. He was accepted to Harvard again and we celebrated with a cast dinner in Madison, Wisconsin.

I know one thing for sure: he can look back on his life with few regrets. I think his faith got him through those periods when others were doubting him. Whether it was amateur skating, graduating from Harvard with honors, or "Stars on Ice," he completed everything he started. Nobody can ever say he didn't go the distance.

There was another star to emerge from Albertville, my close friend Kristi Yamaguchi. We just call her "Yama" for short.

We've all heard about how she grew up toting around a doll made in the likeness of Dorothy Hamill, the last American woman to win Olympic gold before Kristi. I actually met her for the first time at the 1981 nationals in San Diego. I was sitting in the stands watching the competition when this adorable little girl came up to me and offered me a single flower. I didn't know it then, but she was a nine-year-old juvenile-level skater who had traveled down from San Francisco to watch nationals with her mom and a group of skating friends. I saw her again in 1988 when I did an exhibition in Oakland, where Yama trained with her coach, Christy Ness. By this time, Kristi was a junior world champion in singles and a junior world-level pairs skater with partner Rudy Galindo.

But my fondest memory was the first time I made her laugh. It was at the 1990 world championships in Halifax, Nova Scotia. Kristi had finished second at nationals in singles and had won the U.S. pairs title that year with Rudy, but Halifax was a frustrating competition. While finishing a respectable fifth in pairs early in the week, she ended up fourth in singles. It had been a long couple of months and she was exhausted. During the exhibition skate the last day, she and Rudy were just about to go on the ice to perform when Kristi erupted into tears. She looked up at me in the CBS booth and all I could think of doing was waving a box of tissues at her. I ran downstairs and started handing them to her one by one, enough for a year's worth of tears. "Are you okay?" I asked. Kristi nodded, then broke into this big smile and glided out onto the ice laughing.

A lot changed for Kristi after that competition. Her pairs coach, Jim

Hulick, died, and Kristi decided to drop pairs skating to focus on singles. It was a wise move. In 1991, she won her first world title, and the following season captured the big three—nationals, Olympics and worlds.

Kristi didn't think she was going to win the gold in Albertville, despite being the defending world champion. She arrived in France squarely in the shadow of Midori Ito, the Japanese champion who had a huge triple Axel, better than most men's. Even Kristi's U.S. rival, Tonya Harding, another skater with the triple Axel, was getting more hype. Kristi figured her turn would come at the next Olympics; after all, with the change in schedule, the games were only two years off. Not wanting to come away from Albertville empty-handed, Kristi attended the opening ceremonies and circulated in the Olympic village, soaking up the entire Olympic experience. She did escape the scene for three days of training in nearby Megève, where her coach said she hit peak form. Meanwhile, the triple Axels and triple combinations that Midori was landing so effortlessly when she first arrived in France began abandoning her as competition time grew closer.

If there ever was a time when the media influenced the outcome of a championship, this was it, I'm sad to report. Japan hadn't won a gold medal in the Winter Games in two decades, and the country had all its hopes resting on Midori. The Japanese media were relentless in the pursuit of Midori, and the former world champion began unraveling under the weight of all the pressure. Tonya Harding, meanwhile, sabotaged her own chances by showing up only three days before the short program, telling everyone she was immune to the jet lag that came with the nine-hour time difference between France and her hometown of Portland, Oregon. The truth, her coach Dody Teachman explained later, was that Tonya lacked the necessary confidence to compete at this level and was looking for excuses when she failed.

Tonya was sixth after the short program. Midori, needing only a finish in the top three to seriously contend for the gold medal, made a strategic choice to save the triple Axel for the long and substituted the simpler triple Lutz for her required combination jump. Unnerved by the media onslaught, she fell anyway and the result was fourth place. Kristi skated beautifully and placed first in the short, followed by her roommate Nancy Kerrigan. Kristi was now in control. By finishing fourth, Midori could not win if Kristi placed second or better in the four-minute long program.

Kristi's long was a Spanish number to "Malagueña," choreographed by Sandra Bezic, one of the architects of Brian Boitano's 1988 Olympic gold medal. She hit her opening triple Lutz–triple toe combination and immediately captivated the crowd with her artistry. Some people think you need to jump big to be successful. Not Kristi. While she was in awe of the size of Midori's and Tonya's jumps, she skated within herself. Her niche was floating across the ice with incomparable grace and beauty and then turning a flawless triple jump with perfect control.

Midway through Kristi's long program in Albertville, she stunned the audience of nine thousand by nearly falling on her triple loop and turning the triple Salchow, a nemesis her entire career, into a double. Still, she finished strong, and the overall performance was wonderful. She received marks of 5.7 and 5.8 for the technical half, and eight 5.9s and one 5.8 for the artistic score. There were no error-free performances among the top women that night. Midori fell on another triple Axel but then inserted a second one in the program. I saw it coming and alerted the audience. When she hit it, her smile lit up the building and she took home a silver. The old Midori was back. Nancy got the bronze.

As it turned out, there was no need for Kristi to stick around in amateur skating for another two years. She had her gold medal and was ready to move on to professional skating. "Stars on Ice" was blessed to get her. As a skater, she just continued improving, both artistically and technically. She still goes out each night on tour and does all her triples, no small feat after being out of amateur skating seven years. I was fortunate, too. Not only did the tour gain a great skater, but I made a close friend. Actually, Kristi is more than a pal; she has become a loyal confidante with whom I can share everything. And I'm a lucky man to know her as few people do.

Chapter Seventeen

Split Personality

I reached a crossroads in 1992. Professionally, I decided to leave IMG after Bob was promoted to senior executive vice president and could no longer handle my day-to-day affairs. I also reinstated as an amateur skater. In the previous two years, I hadn't performed up to my expectations at the world pros and other competitions. So I set an ambitious goal: to regain every jump I had during my Olympic year in 1984.

My living situation was also undergoing change. I sold my condo in downtown Denver and bought a large home in the suburb of Englewood, not far from Cherry Hills Country Club. I wasn't making the move alone. Karen Plage, whom I had been living with since 1990, was with me.

I had met Karen back in 1981, when she was very young. Her mother Lynn was the public relations person for the skating club at the Colorado Ice Arena, and Don Laws taught Karen's younger sister, Maureen. My first encounter with Lynn had come two months after winning my first world title. It was May and I hadn't skated in a couple of weeks. I had just returned from the USFSA governing council meetings in New Orleans and was pretty tired from a recent series of ice shows. And I was coming down with a cold. I needed to spend a day just unwinding by the lake at Brent's house. Instead, I was back in an ice rink. Let's just say I wasn't in a gregarious mood.

The CIA was presenting "Showtime on Ice," its annual club show, and Lynn had set up a full morning of publicity to promote the event. Lynn asked me to do some interviews, which was no problem. I arrived at the rink without my gear.

"Where are your skates?" Lynn asked.

"Back at the house," I replied.

"We have TV stations coming. I need you to skate to promote the show."

"No way," I said curtly. "I need to take it easy today."

But Lynn would not take no for an answer.

"You have to skate," she said. "Go get your skates for these people."

I wavered and tried to talk her out of it. "Really, please, Lynn, I know this is a publicity thing, but I've just come off tour, all these club shows where I had to jump through a thousand hoops. Please, just let me do the interviews and no ice stuff. Let Paul [Wylie] do the skating. He's the junior champion."

I started coughing for effect, but Lynn wouldn't budge. She insisted on my skating. "Nope," she said. "I'm driving you over to your house, you're picking up your skates, and performing for these reporters."

Lynn drove me to Brent's house and I got my skates, forgetting my blades were as dull as a butter knife because I had recently messed them up by walking on concrete. When I returned to the CIA, some local television stations had their cameras all set up at rinkside. A few spins and some Russian splits should do the trick, I figured. I began stroking around the rink, and when I took my first corner, my dull blade couldn't dig into the ice and I wiped out badly, sliding right into some barrier lights. Glass shattered everywhere and I tore a hole in my pants. What a fiasco. When I got off the ice, I was bleeding from a minor cut on my leg. Poor Lynn tried to help me but I walked away from her, sat down in a corner, folded my arms and did my best imitation of Mount Saint Helens before the eruption. Lynn wisely kept her distance. Then this man whom I had seen around the rink before sat down beside me.

"Are you all right?" he asked sympathetically.

"Yeah," I said through gritted teeth. "I'm just really kind of mad right now and I'm trying not to inflict myself on anybody."

"Why are you skating if you didn't want to?" he asked.

"Because that witch over there made me, even after I told her I was sick and hadn't skated in a while. She was relentless. She just wouldn't let me out of it."

The guy shook his head. "That was pretty lousy of her," he said. "You have every right to be angry."

That made me feel better. A little empathy can go a long way during a temper tantrum. That is, until I found out this man happened to be Lynn's husband, Bill Plage. I felt so humiliated. There I was letting his wife have it and he patiently sat through my tirade. After cooling down, I apologized to him profusely, but he told me not to worry about it.

Bill and I became fast friends. With Brent moving to Chicago to attend law school, it was nice having a buddy to pal around with. Before long I was a frequent guest at their home. They had a beautiful house and Bill loved to entertain, hosting barbecues and dart games. Other times I'd go over to watch boxing and football. After a while I felt so comfortable I even started bringing over my girlfriends.

When I told Bill I wanted to play more golf, he took me out to his country club in Denver. We went to Broncos games and I visited them at their vacation place in Vail. After Brent went away to Chicago to attend law school, I got even closer with the Plages and was treated as a member of the family.

I didn't know it at the time, but Bill and Lynn's daughter, Karen, had a crush on me all those years. After Karen graduated from high school, she started intimating that we should go out. I was a lot older than she, and I thought, "Naw, better not go there," though the attraction was mutual. I was uncertain how Lynn and Bill would feel about it.

We did socialize in groups, like going to football games and barbecues. Karen would sometimes bring a boyfriend and I would sometimes bring a girlfriend. Yet she continued dropping subtle hints that she was interested in more than a friendship. "Nope, nope, nope, no," I kept telling her. "Your dad is one of my best friends—and he has a collection of guns!"

Though I felt I was too close to Bill to date Karen, my feelings were undeniable: I enjoyed spending time with her. She was smart and way beyond her years, physically and mentally. At five-foot-nine, she's much taller than I, but that didn't bother either of us. We clicked where it counts the most—in the heart.

A turning point in how I perceived Karen occurred one summer while I was vacationing with the Plage family at their Vail condo. It's beautiful up there, surrounded by the mountains and fresh air. I spent mornings playing racquetball with Bill, and afternoons swimming or just hanging out by the pool. I remember Bill and I were sitting in the Jacuzzi talking when Karen emerged from the pool in a one-piece bathing suit. She was still too young for me but I must have done a double take. "Whoa," I thought. "She's gorgeous."

The next thing I know, Bill is chiming in: "Karen's growing up, eh?" Nothing gets past him, I thought. I looked away and felt embarrassed for ogling his daughter. "I really hadn't noticed," I said, rather unconvincingly. He saw right through that line and we both started to laugh.

For the next couple of years Karen and I continued to flirt, but that was as far as it went, until we met up one night at a Jack Mack and the Heart Attack concert in Denver. I had gotten to know the guys in the band very well and always went to see them when they were in town. I loved their sound—old '60s R and B. I first saw them perform in the summer of 1984 at the Los Angeles Olympics, and they later provided music for programs I did in Ice Capades and "Stars on Ice."

I went to the concert with a date, and Karen came along with her mother. She looked like a million bucks and distracted me all night. By this time she was modeling locally and really knew how to put herself together. During the show she leaned over and quietly told me she was jealous of my date.

"Yeah, right," I said sarcastically.

"No, I'm really serious," she said.

I looked in her eyes and knew she wasn't kidding. Uh-oh, I thought. I knew I wasn't strong enough to hold out forever. A couple of times after that, she would drive into Denver with her friend Lucy and I'd take them out to Denver's night spots. The more time we spent together, the more I realized how incredible she was. She was funny, easygoing and an excellent listener.

But I didn't get up the nerve to ask her out until I found out she was dating a man who was even older than I was. She was obviously trying to prove a point, and it worked. Man, I hated this guy. He was a photographer Karen had met on a modeling shoot. My nickname for him was Slick. Now I was the jealous one.

When Karen was a college junior, I suggested we go out for dinner. Just the two of us. We went to the Sushi Den in Denver, and that was where we had our first dinner alone. We talked all evening about our feelings for each other. And we both agreed we were ready to pursue a relationship. Karen then dropped the photographer.

Because of my relationship with Bill and Lynn, it wasn't an easy choice to date Karen. I didn't even discuss it with them. I decided that if we were going to take that next step, I had to pursue a relationship with Karen with sincere intentions and total commitment. Up to this point I had really botched every relationship I had been in, and the Plages got to see some of these fiascos up close. They knew I had a track record of dating someone for a while and then bolting when things got serious. It was that fear of getting too close that had me hog-tied, and those inhibitions resurfaced time and time again. I traced part of my anxiety to losing my mother and Mr. McLoraine. Perhaps I feared commitment so I wouldn't get hurt again when someone close to me left. That's not a healthy way to live your life, but it seemed to be the pattern I had fallen into. With Karen, I wanted to make it work no matter what.

From the start, the biggest adjustment Karen had to make was accommodating herself to my touring schedule. I was constantly in and out of town doing pro competitions, covering skating events for CBS and performing with "Stars on Ice," which was expanding to new cities every year. After Karen finished college, she moved into my condo, but she spent much of her time there alone. Sometimes Karen joined me on tour, particularly in the larger cities, like New York, Los Angeles and San Francisco. But those were tough dates because there were always many show-related commitments that took time away from Karen. She also came along with me to Paris and Munich, when I was competing there in pro competitions, which worked out much better.

Paris was one of our first trips together. It was the summer of 1988. Brian Boitano and Katarina Witt had just turned pro and this was their first event. The promoters were billing the competition as the "Gods of Ice," but all the competitors knew better. What it really should have been called was, "Come watch Brian and Katarina win their first pro competition." For the rest of us, it was like the Washington Generals going up against the Harlem Globetrotters. We all knew going in that this was a showcase for Brian and Katarina, but when I skated my first number clean, hitting three triples and my back flip, I at least expected some decent marks. The judges put me in fourth. I was upset and poor Karen was furious. "What are they doing?" she fumed backstage after the marks came up. I was resigned to finish at the bottom of the heap and in my second routine I went out and skated like it. Never mind that I've always preached that you should never justify bad marks for your first program by skating lousy the next time out; I was down in the dumps, and that's exactly what I did.

When it was over, Karen and I decided we were not going to let what happened spoil the rest of our trip. We had four more days in Paris and we were going to cheer up and enjoy ourselves. Remember that scene in *Pretty Woman* where Richard Gere spoils Julia Roberts with new clothes and jewelry? That was me and Karen. My way of protesting was that I was going to spend every last dime of that fourth-place prize money on her and not bring one penny back home. We had the greatest time—four nights in a hotel on the Champs d'Elysée, dinners out at five-star restaurants every night, and Karen got some great outfits. There's nothing like a good old-fashioned shopping spree to cheer you up.

When I was out on tour, Karen and I spent time together in larger cities relaxing and sight-seeing. Loneliest for me were the one-day stops in small towns where the solitude was overwhelming. Karen and I spent a lot of hours on the phone and the rest of the time, I devoured Tom

Clancy novels, listened to music in my room, watched TV and conserved my energy for the shows.

For both of us, my returning home was always a big adjustment. Road life creates a rhythm all its own: hotels, buses, airplanes, fast food, shows, interviews, packing, unpacking. I was meeting hundreds of people, and after the tour was all over, I'd come home to Denver and Karen. I should have looked upon the time off as a chance to relax, yet I found it a challenge resettling into a routine with one person and getting back on Karen's wavelength.

She was really good about leaving me alone for the first week or two back home, when I was still wired into travel mode. I wake up in the morning thinking I had to catch a bus somewhere or do a press call, and there would be nothing. So on those first few days, I wandered around, a little shell-shocked from the tour, yet still spinning my wheels pretty hard. But Karen was patient and usually good about putting up with me.

When we first started living together, my small condo shrank even further after Karen moved in with her things. I had always dreamed of owning a home, so in October of 1992 we moved to a house in Englewood, a leafy suburb of Denver. It had lots of space: five bedrooms, a pool and a four-car garage. Even without the wedding ceremony, I felt we were husband and wife building a life in suburbia.

Though buying the house seemed like a good idea at the time, it started driving a wedge between Karen and me. Soon after we moved in, I had to go back out on the road. Decorating and landscaping the place was a massive undertaking, and Karen had to do it all without me. It was a two-person job and I wasn't around to chip in. I basically handed her the keys and said, "Here you go—take care of this and I'll see you in a few months." Karen did a great job. She chose themes for each room, picked out paint, furniture, fabrics and shrubs. When I came back I was floored by the job she had done. But we both felt a little frustrated because I had not been around to share in the fun and the burdens that come with owning a new home.

Some of our best times in Englewood were during the holidays. That was when Karen, the queen of Christmas, transformed the house into a winter wonderland. We'd pick out a twelve-foot tree and set it up in the living room. Karen liked to decorate it in a traditional style—white lights, intricate ornaments and our special topper made of Waterford crystal. Underneath the tree would be a pile of presents that Karen always wrapped with the greatest of care. When you walked through our front door, you could smell the pine and the garlands, and every room in the house was filled with Christmas knickknacks and displays. For Karen, the planning and shopping began right after my August birthday, and then she'd want to leave the tree up until March.

While we had to work out issues with my travel schedule, Karen always remained loyal and committed to me. I expected to skate only a few years after the 1984 Olympics, and Karen was hoping my career would eventually taper off. And after the 1992 Olympics it did, though not for very long. But I was enjoying my career in skating. With each opportunity I felt obliged to take on more work and responsibility. I'm a driven, ambitious person and constantly on the move. Not only did I want to succeed for myself, I felt the more I took on, the better it would be for the next generation of skaters, especially the men. As a male in a sport dominated by females, I was hell-bent on putting us on equal ground. I figured my credibility was tied to increasing my popularity. Thus I accepted a heavy workload and travel schedule. Someone needed to tear down some walls and barriers to make it easier for the next guy, and I figured it might as well be me. Fortunately I have been able to do that with "Stars on Ice" and my work with CBS.

Late in 1992, I decided to reinstate as an amateur and became eligible to compete in events sanctioned by the ISU and the USFSA. Though technically I would now be eligible for the 1993 nationals and worlds, that wasn't my reason for returning. I wanted to compete in a new series of pro-am competitions the governing bodies were putting together as they prepared to let pros compete in the 1994 Olympics.

Brian Boitano had been agitating for several years to lift the barriers between amateur and professional skating, just as had already been done for virtually every other Olympic sport. Now it was becoming a reality. I definitely felt the sport should be open to everyone.

My motives for reinstating were different from Brian's—who had his eye squarely on the 1994 Olympics, as did Torvill and Dean, Katarina Witt and the Russian pairs team of Ekaterina Gordeeva and Sergei Grinkov.

While I didn't rule it out right away, I was less interested in competing at the world and Olympic level than I was in skating in the pro-ams against the guys who were eligible for those events. For me it was a personal challenge. I had had a couple of down years competing in pro events, and my jumps were inconsistent. I was losing my edge.

I went back to the drawing board in the summer of 1992 and called on a new coach, Kathy Casey, to whip me into shape and help me get my jumps up to speed. I also spent a little more than a week in the summer of '92 on Cape Cod working with Evy, and then returned to Denver to train with Kathy, who helped me get back my triple flip. I got into the best shape of my life that year, even better than I had in 1984.

In early 1993, I competed in two USFSA-sanctioned pro-ams. There was an amusing piece of irony to the experience. I was thirty-four years old with almost nine years of pro skating under my belt, yet I was competing as an amateur. Paul Wylie, who had spent an eternity skating as an amateur, entered these contests as the designated professional.

I finished third in my first event, even though I outjumped both competitors who finished ahead of me—Paul and Mark Mitchell. I landed four different triples; they landed three. I obviously got dropped because the judges didn't like my program, a new number set to a Jack Mack and the Heart Attack rendition of the classic rock song, "A Whiter Shade of Pale." I blended some famous political speeches from the 1960s into the music, and the package didn't go over well with the judges. Still, I nailed a triple Lutz, flip, toe, Salchow, back flip, and a double π.

In my next pro-am in April, I went up against Brian Boitano, and I almost beat him. I made one mistake, which is usually one too many versus Brian. My crime was doubling a planned triple toe loop in the artistic program. If I had hit it, I might have won because we were very close in the technical program. After it was over, I was wondering if I would ever be able to beat him.

Even though I didn't win those two events, I felt the season was a success because I more than held my own against the younger skaters. I could not say the same about my decision in 1992 to leave Bob Kain and IMG. When Bob was promoted, he could no longer represent me. It was a huge blow, and I decided to leave IMG and handle my own affairs. While his rise in the company was great for him, I didn't want to be lumped in with the rest of IMG's clients. My status with "Stars on Ice" remained the same, and my relationship with the cast was unaffected, except that I was out on my own.

After cutting ties with IMG, I was pitched by other agents—from Michael Burg, the event promoter who went on to represent Tara Lipinski; to Jerry Solomon, who would take on Nancy Kerrigan as a client. (They eventually married.) They were good people, but I didn't want to rush any decision. In the meantime, I managed my own career and let my attorney at the time field calls and look over any contracts I had negotiated on my own.

It wasn't long before I was regretting my decision to leave IMG. For one, it became a lot to manage, more than I anticipated. I had also hurt Bob and had damaged our friendship, which weighed on me heavily.

Signing with a new agency had its drawbacks: I'd be starting over again from scratch and training them on what my priorities were. Did that make sense after all the energy Bob and I had put into "Stars on Ice"? IMG had invested millions in the skating division and they wanted to pour even more money into the tour. I wanted to be an influential part of the program, so as time went on, I rethought my decision.

At the end of the year, I sat down with Bob and told him I wanted to return if IMG could find the right situation for me. I hated what had become of our friendship. I admitted that leaving was a mistake and apologized.

A lot had changed since I left. "Stars" had signed Kristi Yamaguchi and, with my help, Paul Wylie. (Even though IMG no longer managed me, I recommended the agency to Paul, who was very interested in touring with "Stars.") IMG also bought out Bill Graham Presents' interest in the Boitano–Witt tour, tying up its tour dates, bringing on its founder, Stan Feig, as a "Stars on Ice" consultant and hiring the tour's superb director, Sandra Bezic. Brian and Katarina were reinstating to compete in the '94 Olympics, shutting down their tour for a season. IMG had decided that there wasn't enough room in the marketplace for "Stars on Ice" and Boitano–Witt, so they made a business decision to buy them out.

Brian got very upset about this, but IMG went to him right away and offered him a place in "Stars." They wanted him in the show badly, and I very much wanted to tour with him. We have been friends for years, and touring with him would have been a blast. Brian decided to sign another deal with Tom Collins and "Champions on Ice." Perhaps it was an emotional decision for him, since a tour he had started was now more or less going into my hands. I know Brian's producer, Stan Feig, wanted to stay in the skating business, and with their tour taking a year off, he was facing a long hiatus. And what might happen to Brian and Katarina's marquee value if they both lost in Lillehammer? Maybe Stan felt it was too big of a risk. In any event, we're glad he came aboard; he gave "Stars" production values it never had before.

The merger, combined with the signing of Kristi and Paul, was a quantum leap for the production. And since then the show has just gone through the roof. The budget quintupled and the grosses went up. So did the profits. From that point on, revenues for the show began growing at the rate of 15 to 30 percent a year.

One day at the end of the 1993 tour, it hit me how far "Stars" had come in seven years. We had gone from booking shows in tiny college arenas to major venues in large cities; from living with skating families to staying in five-star hotels. One of the hardest things about show skating is just finding the best forum to show your talent, and that was what "Stars" was providing me and the rest of the cast: an incredible opportunity to do the work we love.

I'm a firm believer in living with your choices, the good and the bad, and learning something from them. I certainly have had my share of poor career decisions, like leaving IMG. But I have made a few good ones, one of which was starting "Stars on Ice."

Chapter Eighteen

Saying Good-bye Again

In the fall of 1993, I asked my dad to take a vacation with me. He was sixty-five years old and his health was on the decline. So we made a plan for the summer of '94—a visit to Hawaii—just as soon as I wrapped up working the Lillehammer Olympics for CBS, and touring with "Stars." Ernie loved the islands, but we had never spent any time together on my favorite island, Maui.

I was feeling a sense of urgency to make up for lost time. Back in June, I was at home in Denver and making plans for the summer, including a visit to Boston to see my relatives, especially my maternal grandmother, Nana Helen. I hadn't seen her in a while and felt guilty for being out of touch. On June 24, I called my cousin to let him know I was coming to town. His wife answered the phone.

"Hi. It's Scott. How's everything?" I asked.

"Well, this morning Nana passed away," she said quietly.

I was stunned, caught completely off guard. I knew Nana had been ill. I just didn't know how seriously. I sat down for a moment to take it all in. Like my mom, Nana was a big skating booster in the family, and had followed my entire career. She'd had it so hard back in 1977 when my mom and grandaddy passed away three months apart, but she weathered the losses with courage and stayed close to the family. Her devotion to me was unequivocal; I could always count on her for love and unconditional support. Man, I was going to miss her.

I flew to Boston for Nana's funeral, and it was the first time the whole family had been together in years. It was great seeing everyone, but I felt I should have tried harder to stay more in touch. It's not like I wasn't thinking about them. It's just that we all had our own lives to lead, and people can grow apart when they're not living in the same area. Still, I had regrets and vowed to do something about it.

What I could do was make the effort to see the people I cared most about. Time spent with my father had been sparing. In the summers of 1991 and 1992, we had had a great time together in Toledo at a pro-am golf tournament put on by actor Jamie Farr. Ernie flew up to hang with me and see some of his old friends from Bowling Green. My father wasn't walking well, so I'd get him his own golf cart and he'd follow my foursome around, or I'd ride with him, sharing a few laughs and talking about the people and the course.

Our best getaway together was in 1989, when we spent a week fishing in Yakutat, Alaska, north of Glacier Bay. There the days were twenty-two hours long, and nighttime wasn't any darker than twilight. It was incredibly relaxing under smog-free skies, far away from telephones, airports and obligations. When I was little, my father and I used to fish in Lake Erie for white bass and perch, but the catch was nothing like the fish we trolled for in Alaska, where the rivers and lakes were teeming with salmon.

We were joined by Karen's dad, Bill Plage, a master outdoorsman who loved to hunt and fish. He was the perfect host for an Alaskan adventure. My friend Andrew Kastner, the guitarist for Jack Mack and the Heart Attack, and his brother Stanley, also came along.

Save for Bill, it was like the cast of *Seinfeld* doing Outward Bound. I planned to rely heavily on Bill's judgment. One afternoon before the trip, I asked him if we'd see any bald eagles in Alaska.

He looked at me with a perfectly straight face. "Maybe," he said. "Only if we keep our eyes open."

Well, duh, eagles in Alaska are as common as pigeons in Central Park. They were everywhere. Bill needled me the entire trip about that one. One day we were walking along a pristine river and saw an eagle gliding toward the water, talons and wings outstretched. With incredible power, speed and grace, it snatched a fish from the water, dropped it on the shore, and pounced on the fish with its talons until it stopped moving. The eagle then devoured its meal right on the riverside.

We fished in the morning and at dusk. The scenery was awesome—mountains and forests that went on for miles, rivers and lakes that were crystal clear. The wildlife was amazing. Once while walking to Harlequin Lake, the path strewn with evidence of grizzly bears—the kind of evidence you step over and around—I got to thinking, What if we stumbled on a bear and had to make a break for it? My father had a bad heart and sore feet from diabetes, and I was petrified he might get attacked.

Actually, my father and I were bigger dangers to each other than any bear. One morning we put on our waders and went out in two boats to catch salmon. After a couple of hours of fishing, Bill found a good spot for us to stop our boats.

Andrew and Stanley got out of their boat first. Bill got out of our boat and went to the fishing hole. I stepped out next, and then turned around to lend my father a hand. As I was helping my dad ashore, he threw one leg over the side of the boat, and wouldn't you know it, the boat drifted back farther into the water. Dad's legs spread apart so wide he looked like a wishbone ready to snap. Just before the moment of truth, he quickly sat down on the edge of the boat to keep from falling. I dragged the boat ashore and tried again, to no avail. My father couldn't get out and I was no help whatsoever. Andrew, Stanley and Bill were laughing uncontrollably. The comic relief went on for about five minutes, until I couldn't contain myself anymore. And my dad, laughing harder than I had ever seen him before, still couldn't get out. "Dad," I begged, "stop laughing or you'll never make it out of the boat." But it was useless; he was beyond reach, just like the rest of us. Finally Bill came back and helped me get Ernie out of the boat.

During our five days together, I couldn't believe how much my father had aged. It hit me one afternoon while halibut fishing off the Alaskan coast. Nobody was catching a thing. Then all of a sudden Ernie's line started to go. Bill had warned us that reeling in a halibut was like pulling a Volkswagen off the bottom of the ocean. The fish is flat and wide, and, weighing in at thirty-five pounds, it could put up unbelievable resistance. I could see my father was having trouble wrestling with the fish. "Dad, gimme your rod," I said excitedly, and he handed it over. I gave him my pole, and seconds later, he had another one on that line. As I brought Dad's fish into the boat, Bill hooked it with a gaff and brought it in. I grabbed Dad's pole to help with the second fish. When I looked up, everyone was staring at us. Dad was the only one catching any fish! He had the touch, because he caught them all that day, but he wasn't strong enough to reel them in.

At night—or day, I should say, since the sun was always up—we'd all go out for a beer. My father had a taste for Seven and Sevens, and a couple of nightcaps would relax him. We were staying in a small town and all it had was a municipal airport, a post office, a general store, a cannery and two bars. At least they had their priorities in order.

These were pretty down-to-earth drinking establishments that drew a tough crowd. On our first night out, Bill gave Andrew and Stanley a serious warning. "You guys have a weapon, a gun or anything?" he asked.

"No," they said. "Do you have a knife at least? Because if things get out of hand later on, if you at least have a knife, nobody will bother you. If you don't have a knife, I can't guarantee you that you're going to come out of here alive."

Andrew and Stanley turned pale. My father and I, savvy to Bill's games, bit our tongues. "Don't worry," Bill said to the brothers. "I have a knife and I'll wear it on the outside of my belt and make sure everyone sees it. No one will bother us." Poor Andrew and Stanley spent the rest of the night docilely nursing their drinks and being careful not to look cross-eyed at anyone.

That was the best trip my dad and I ever took. We both wanted to return, but I got the jitters thinking about walking along the trail to Harlequin Lake and knowing that if a bear charged us my father wouldn't stand a chance of getting away—and that there was no emergency medical care in easy reach. But the Maui trip was ironclad. Too much time had passed, and I was worried my father soon might not be able to travel anymore.

That fall, however, his heart condition took a turn for the worse, and I began to worry that he wasn't going to survive the winter. It was so bad the doctors wanted to perform a bypass, but they were afraid he wouldn't survive the surgery.

Late in the year, he went to Columbus to visit my brother, Steve, and his wife, Valerie, who was a nurse. Ernie and Steve had grown very close after Steve left the Coast Guard in 1991, and they spent a lot of time together. Dad went to Valerie's hospital for additional tests, and then he had a sudden heart attack and almost died in Columbus. He spent a few weeks recovering in the hospital and at my brother's house. When he was well enough, my sister Sue, who had moved back to Bowling Green, drove him back to Florida.

He insisted on going home, perhaps because he knew his time was running short and he wanted to be in familiar surroundings. He had lived in Lake Placid for four years and he loved it there. When he was a child, his family escaped the New England winters each year with Florida vacations, so it brought back special memories. And since his friends Bob and Deloris Parrish lived across the street, he didn't feel alone.

While his decision to convalesce at home seemed all right at the time, we soon learned that he wasn't taking care of himself. Bob went to check on him one day and found my father lying helpless in bed. He was pale and thin and hadn't left his room in days, not even to eat or take his medicine. They rushed him to a local hospital but he was in such critical condition he was transferred to a hospital in Orlando. If Bob hadn't found Dad that day, he surely would have died.

My father made a remarkable recovery from that setback, and I spent my days off from the tour at his bedside. During one visit, Dad's mother, Olga Hamilton, passed away. Ernie was too ill to travel, so we held a memorial service in the hospital chapel. Her death was a setback my father couldn't bear. Losing his mother was as grievous to him as the death of our old family doctor, Andrew Klepner, had been to my mother back in 1977.

As the week went on, I sensed my father was giving up. I told him to hang on, and kept reminding him of the Maui trip. Talking about the future seemed to lift his spirits. I promised I'd be back to see him right after covering the Lillehammer Olympics. But as I left the hospital to rejoin the tour, I was very afraid I'd never see him again.

It was as crazy a time in skating as it was in my personal life. The Tonya Harding scandal had taken over the sport and the national headlines. On January 6, Nancy Kerrigan was hit on the leg by an attacker as she was leaving the ice after a practice session at the 1994 nationals in Detroit. Nancy withdrew from the competition and Tonya went on to win her second national title, or so it seemed. Investigators learned that the assailant, Shane Stant, was working with two accomplices, one of whom turned out to be Jeff Gillooly, Tonya Harding's ex-husband. Within days, Gillooly and his cronies were arrested. Tonya, who had recently reconciled with Gillooly, was implicated in the assault by him. (She later pleaded guilty to hindering prosecution.) But Tonya kept her spot on the Olympic team, suing the USFSA to make sure they didn't drop her.

After I arrived in Norway, I called my father, who was still in the hospital in Orlando. He seemed to be in better spirits, which made it easier to concentrate on my work. There was a lot of news to cover. Besides the Tonya–Nancy saga, each skating event was featuring former Olympic champions who had reinstated to compete in the 1994 games. They all had their own reasons for returning. Gordeeva and Grinkov, who won gold competing for the Soviet Union in 1988, were still competing for Russia, but they viewed this Olympics as an opportunity to skate for themselves and celebrate the experience as husband and wife. They skated brilliantly and were awarded the gold, a medal Ekaterina says they won for each other.

Next up were the men, which included former Olympic champion Brian Boitano in the mix. He had been very vocal about pros deserving a chance to compete in the Olympics, and when the time came to ante up, he had to put himself on the line. Whether or not he was having second thoughts, it was almost as though his decision to come back was made for him. Brian had a strong week of practice and I felt he could pull off an-

other win. But he missed his triple Axel combination in the short program and dropped out of contention. All the top contenders had disappointing short programs, including Kurt Browning and Viktor Petrenko.

I felt terrible for Brian. Two years earlier in Albertville, he and Brian
Orser were sitting in the stands watching the men's competition and you
couldn't help but notice how disappointed they were in the quality of the
skating. They were both still in their prime, especially Boitano, who was
arguably the best skater in the world at the time. But reinstatement for
Brian came two years too late. When he took the ice in Lillehammer, he
was six years removed from his Olympic title, and a leg injury had interfered with his training all season.

After missing his triple Axel in the short, he made a mistake on the
same jump in the long. Two missed triple Axels? It was something I had
never seen him do in all my years of competing against him and watching
him perform. His sixth-place finish didn't tarnish his career. Brian has a
loyal fan base and tremendous respect among skating people. It's not as if
everyone stopped watching Brian to go out and see Alexei Urmanov, the
guy who did win. Alexei is a great skater, but American fans prefer their
American champions, so the stardom and goodwill Brian had built up
over the years didn't wash away with one rough outing, though I'm sure
Brian wished the outcome had been different.

So did I. I disagreed with the judges' decision to award Alexei the gold.
I think they went with the safe choice—Alexei's classical style instead of
Elvis Stojko's pure athleticism. While Alexei was a powerful skater, I ob-
jected to his packaging—boot covers, tights and flashy tops with puffy
sleeves. It made him appear soft. In my opinion, Elvis' repertoire of triple
Axels, quads and triple combinations deserved the title, but the judges
didn't want to go there yet.

Over the next few days, Tracy and Verne called the dance event while
I spent a lot of time watching the ladies' practices. I was furious at all the
attention Tonya was getting and felt her presence damaged the credibility of figure skating. Tracy, Verne and I were determined to keep our focus
on the skating even though the world press was turning the Olympics
into just another sensational tabloid event. This was a competition, first
and foremost, and I didn't want this becoming the Tonya Harding games,
nor did I want CBS becoming the Tonya network. But CBS was all over
the story, and Connie Chung and her news crew were following Tonya all
over the city. They weren't alone. Tonya and Nancy were on the same
practices, and on their first day of skating together, Verne and I counted
four hundred members of the press jammed into a space with room for at
most two hundred. I really felt for the other skaters on Tonya's practice.

There were competitors out there with fifteen years of dedication and work riding on this single Olympic event, and they had to endure a three-ring circus.

After their first practice, I went back to the CBS trailer in disbelief. Tonya was in no shape to contend for a medal. What a waste of an Olympic team spot, I thought. I had skated with her in an exhibition a couple of months earlier and saw all I needed to see. Tonya blew in and skated two numbers, and her second routine lasted a little more than a minute, which spoke volumes about her attitude. It just seemed so lazy and halfhearted, and even then I wondered how she could ever be competitive in Lillehammer with that attitude. She could talk all she wanted about her asthma and injuries, but a ninety-second performance—it may have been only seventy-five seconds—is a rip-off to paying customers.

In the dance event, I watched my good friends Torvill and Dean place third behind two Russian teams. They skated very well, winning the audience as always. All this time, I had been keeping in touch with my dad. Two days before the ladies' short program, I checked up on him again and the news wasn't good. His voice was garbled and he seemed disoriented, and I feared he was on the verge of another setback. I went to bed that night thinking the worst. Dad always seemed to bounce back, but I was worried he might not hold up.

On Wednesday, February 23, the day of the ladies' short program, I went to the morning practices and was wowed. All the top contenders looked like they were on. I had never seen Nancy skate better than she was performing now. Oksana was skating wonderfully, too. Her short program, The Swan, was one of the most amazing numbers I had ever seen, and I was looking forward to seeing it on Olympic ice. Later that day I called my father again. Though he was hooked up to a kidney dialysis machine, he was feeling better and stronger than he had in days. He sounded better, too. He was one resilient son of a gun.

That night at Northern Lights Hall, Nancy was brilliant. Her comeback was nothing short of amazing. She won the short program—33 percent of the total—and she was in a position to control her destiny. Because of the scoring system, all one of the top three skaters needed to do was win the long program and the gold medal was hers. Though there was still Surya Bonaly of France and Oksana Baiul to contend with, Nancy had it in her. Don't be fooled by the pretty veneer; she was one of the toughest people I'd ever met.

Our friendship began in the summer of 1992, when I went to Cape Cod for a few days to work with Evy and Mary Scotvold, who were coaching Nancy at the time. She was dating a friend, Michael Collins, son of Tom Collins, and she was Paul Wylie's housemate. One day during a round of golf, I noticed how Nancy attacked the ball and never let up. Having two older brothers probably had something to do with that. She was used to hanging around guys and she joined right in with the chatter. She was fun and easygoing.

After the attack in Detroit, we were all concerned about her leg and wanted to help out any way we could. So when her agent and future husband, Jerry Solomon, called and said he was putting together a televised fund-raiser celebrating Nancy's return to the ice, I was happy to participate. They wanted all the top skaters and were billing the event as a benefit for the charity that had supported Nancy's mother, Brenda, who is legally blind. I accepted an appearance fee that CBS paid so I wouldn't be cutting into the charity's amount. My fee was bargain basement—a fraction of what I normally charge—and I was pleased to be part of the show.

Since I worked for CBS, which was televising the exhibition, I heard about the costs of the show and had some serious questions about how the production was being run and how much of the revenue was going to charity. Despite my misgivings, I flew to Boston to skate in support of Nancy.

When I arrived at the ice arena at Northeastern University, I sought Nancy out to let her know my concerns were nothing personal and there were no hard feelings.

"Nancy," I said, "this has nothing to do with you and me as friends." But she was very cold and shut me down.

I kept trying. "I don't want this to affect our friendship," I said.

"Okay, whatever," she replied, but from that day on our relationship was never the same.

Neither was Nancy. The person I knew from previous summers didn't exist anymore, and I felt for her. By the time she reached Lillehammer, a wall had been raised around her, and the steely but good-natured competitor I had known in the past had disappeared. She seemed bitter and had a chip on her shoulder, which I could understand because she had been through a lot since the attack.

While I tried to cut her a lot of slack, I was hurt when she wouldn't accept any discussion of my concerns about her charity event or my attempts to smooth things over between us. That didn't stop me from working with her. After the Olympics, I performed in her Disney TV special in Lake Placid, New York. I busted my hump for her, arriving in Lake Placid on my only day off from the "Stars on Ice" tour, and then put in a fifteen-hour day with the other skaters.

At the Olympics, Nancy and I didn't talk and I left her alone. I try not to get into any competitor's face when I work an event because it can be a distraction, and I make it a habit not to approach skaters to ask for interviews. I leave that to the producers.

While Nancy was practicing well, I felt she was having a difficult Olympics. The overwhelming media blitz from the previous month not only interfered with her training and her preparation for the games, but also stole away her joy for skating. All summer and fall she had trained hard and enjoyed every minute. But after the assault, she was hounded by the press, which turned her rehab and her training into a complete downer. There seemed to be a cloud hanging over her head. When you think about it, maybe she was justified in being angry. If someone had whacked my knee during my Olympic year in an attempt to keep me from competing, I'd feel bitter too.

On Friday, February 25, an hour before the ladies' long program, I got a call from my publicist, Michael Sterling: my father had suffered another heart attack. His condition was critical, and the doctors were asking for family to come down there right away. Steve and Sue dropped everything and made the trip to Florida. Michael told me he had already checked with the airlines and it was impossible to get a plane out of Lillehammer until the following day. I had prayed all week for Dad to hang on until I got home and now my worst fears had been realized. With the ladies' long program about to start and no way to get out of town, I was resigned to calling the event. I felt helpless.

That night, the ladies' final was played before the eighth-largest television audience of all time (the short program was fourth on the all-time list, with 127 million viewers). Yet as I watched the ladies compete, my mind was thousands of miles away. I wanted to be on an airplane to Orlando, not in a broadcast booth wearing a tux and a headset. People have asked what was running through my mind during those minutes where I was commentating before 119 million television viewers while my father was at death's door. The answer is, "Guilt."

I was berating myself for not being available to my father. I was feeling remorseful for being a terrible son, for spending too much time working and not enough quality time with my family. You have only so many days with your parents, and I was not there for him when he got sick.

Not only did I regret the lack of time I spent with my father, but I had been selfish. I should have made more trips to Florida on my own instead of always asking my father to drive to see me when I was skating in Orlando, Tampa or Miami. Sometimes he'd stay with us for the entire Florida tour, traveling with us on the cast bus. He was such a good sport, and the other skaters loved him.

I wish we had connected more over the years, like the quality time we spent together in Alaska. He was able to mend his relationship with my brother, Steve, and they became close in a way we never did. My father and I were on such different planets. I was an entertainer and he was an academic. He was devoted to me and we loved each other despite our differences, yet it was hard to find common ground to bond. If only we'd had more time together, perhaps we could have filled the void in our relationship.

Maui, I thought, might be our last chance to spend some time together. As I sat in the CBS booth and watched the last two groups of the ladies' event, I tried to send my father good vibes. Hang on, Dad, I thought. Just hang on. We're going to Hawaii.

Tonya Harding was skating in the second-to-last warm-up group, and in tenth place after the short. She should have just gone out on the ice, done her thing and gotten off. But that's not Tonya's way. When it was time for her to go on, she was nowhere near the ice. She was backstage with her coaches, replacing a broken lace on one of her boots. There was an even bigger problem. Tonya and her coaches neglected to bring a spare pair of laces to fit her boot, so they were replacing the broken lace with one that was much smaller than what she normally wore. Unbelievable.

As Verne and I watched what was transpiring over a monitor, I recalled for the audience that Tonya had experienced similar snafus at a couple of other events in recent years—including the 1993 "Skate America" in October, when her blade had broken, and at the 1993 nationals, when her costume fell apart, forcing her to stop in the middle of her program and start over. In my head I was thinking, This act is getting old; problems that skaters experienced maybe once in a lifetime were happening to her over and over. But out loud, I felt it was appropriate to give her the benefit of the doubt. "This is every skater's recurring nightmare," I said.

Just seconds away from being disqualified, Tonya hurried onto the ice. "It's not going to hold me," she blurted out as she passed by a CBS camera. I looked over at Verne and said, "She's still worried about the lace—she should be worried about her performance unless her equipment isn't ready."

Apparently it wasn't, After popping a triple Lutz, she quit skating and erupted into tears. She went over to the judges' panel, flopped her right skate up on the boards in front of the referee and explained her problem. I really thought they might disqualify her. I don't know what Tonya said, but the referee gave her the additional time to fix her boot—and allowed her to skate last in the group. Good for Tonya—but very bad for the next skater up, Josée Chouinard of Canada.

Tonya went backstage and started relacing her skates once more. Then I heard the loudspeaker announce Josee's name and I shook my head. "I'm sure Josée is not prepared. This could throw her way off," I told the audience. "She has got to compose herself and psych herself up."

The problem, I explained, was that a skater expects to prepare while the previous skater is performing. Now Josée's routine was interrupted. It had to be distracting to her, and indeed, she did not skate well. She was in great shape, yet she wound up turning in a mediocre performance. That was really cruel to Josée, and it's something I won't easily forgive Tonya for.

"I'm sure she was severely affected by Tonya Harding," I said over the air that night. And while the referee's ruling benefitted Tonya, "It just seems unfair to the rest of the skaters."

When Tonya finally did skate she took advantage of her second chance, missing only one jump. She was exhausted at the end of her program, but she managed to finish and wound up eighth overall. Though we didn't know it, it was the last time she would ever compete in a sanctioned amateur event.

In the final group, three skaters had a chance of winning if they finished first in the long program—Nancy, Oksana Baiul and Surya Bonaly—who held down first, second and third, respectively. Oksana had two-footed her triple Lutz in the short, but her high artistic marks kept her in the hunt. Since the long program counted for 67 percent of the total score, there could easily be a shake-up in the top three.

Earlier in the day, Oksana had left the practice ice in tears. She had been involved in a collision the day before and had injured her right leg, shoulder and back, and couldn't finish her run-through. Later, doctors had administered a legal dose of painkiller so she could skate the long program. Meanwhile, Nancy had what I considered her worst practice of the week.

During the warm-up, I could tell the painkillers had done wonders for Oksana. Nancy also looked strong. There was a strong pro-American contingent in the crowd, which would surely help Nancy if they didn't get too excited. Then someone tossed a stuffed animal in Nancy's path, almost hitting her. "It's getting dangerous out there," Verne cracked.

Lu Chen of China skated first and skated well. (She would end up with the bronze medal.) Nancy was next and opened up her program with a triple flip, but she doubled it. "Knowing Nancy," I said, "she'll fight for every triple from now on." And she did, hitting her triple toe–triple toe combination and a nice triple loop. Then three minutes into the program, she landed a triple Lutz, her hardest jump. It was an incredible performance, especially considering what she had gone through the prior month. Save for her error on the triple flip, she hit everything in her program and won a standing ovation. You could just tell Evy and Mary had gotten her into the best shape of her life and the year of hard training had saved her after the injury from the attack in Detroit. As she came off the ice, there was bedlam all around her. Americans were yelling out her name and hurling teddy bears and flower bouquets on the ice, but Nancy was searching the stands looking for her mom and dad.

As Oksana warmed up, the rink was still being showered with tributes, and it took a while for the skate girls to clean up the ice. Oksana skated around in small circles, avoiding the gifts that littered the surface. She seemed completely focused. When Nancy's scores came up, there were 5.7s and 5.8s in the technical marks, perhaps a little low considering everything she did. Her artistic scores were solid 5.8s and 5.9s. There was still room for Oksana.

Oksana skated beautifully. She hit her triple Lutz but slightly two-footed her landing on the triple flip. I saw it from my position, but Oksana was 150 feet away from the scorer's table, and some judges might have missed the error. It was a key jump in the program because Nancy had doubled her flip. Oksana also landed a triple loop and Salchow and then made a second error in the last part of her program—doubling a planned triple toe loop. Had Oksana skated out the program, it's hard to say what would have happened, but in the last seconds, she threw in an extra triple toe loop, before ending with a double Axel–double toe combination. She obviously felt she needed that triple toe and the combination jump to beat Nancy. Given her injury the day before, I felt it was a gutsy performance.

The judges thought so, too. By the slimmest of margins, Oksana won the long, 5 judges to 4, and with it the gold medal.

Katarina Witt was the final skater of the games and performed to "Where Have All the Flowers Gone," a moving tribute to war-torn Sarajevo. "It was a time so wonderful for all of us who competed in Sarajevo," I said. My mind flashed back to the Zetra and the beauty of that historic city. I'd had some great times with my father there, and now he was in a hospital, clinging to life. My voice was cracking and I could barely get any more words out, so I stopped talking. Katarina had won two Olympic gold medals, and a lot of people wondered why she wanted to do it all over again. But her parents had not been able to witness her victories in Sarajevo and Calgary. They were in the audience tonight, watching their daughter perform for the first time on Olympic ice. I understood exactly why she did it over again. It was funny watching Katarina compete, because though she had nothing to prove to anyone, I could see all of her competitive juices flowing back and she started overreaching a little. Still, it was a touching performance.

When Katarina finished skating and we had signed off for the night, I left the booth and went to the CBS trailer to check on my father's condition. I called the hospital in Orlando and was connected to the nurses' station. I introduced myself and asked for an update.

There was a brief pause on the other end of the line. "I'm sorry," the nurse said. "He died a short while ago. I'm so sorry."

They tried to put me through to Steve, who managed to make it to the hospital in time to see my father before he passed away, but he had gone for a walk. Sue had tried her best, but arrived at the hospital too late. I hung up the phone and left the arena, not saying a word to a soul. I went outside and walked aimlessly around a parking lot. My network parka was useless against the cold and I began shivering, so I walked even faster. My mind raced back and forth between memories: backyard cookouts in Bowling Green; a special ice rink in Sarajevo; a seedy bar in Alaska; and, finally, a dreary hospital room in Orlando. Dad, Maui would have been terrific, maybe even better than Alaska, since we wouldn't have to worry about those darned grizzly bears. I can't make it up to you, but I'm sorry. I'm really sorry I couldn't be there with you these past couple of days.

Eventually, CBS producer David Winner found me and I told him what happened. He sat with me for a while and then we went back inside to do a couple of fixes on the tape of the ladies' event. It was being shown in the United States in several hours.

While I was outside in the snow, the producers at CBS sensed that a big story was brewing over the judging between Oksana and Nancy, and the scoring by Jan Hoffman in particular. Jan was the two-time world champion from the former East Germany, a great competitor who inadvertently played a huge role in my amateur career when I beat him at the "Norton Skate" in 1979, legitimizing my presence in the international skating scene. I was instantly a strong contender for the 1980 U.S. Olympic team. It was easily one of the biggest victories of my career, and without that triumph, Lord only knows what would have become of my skating future.

When I returned to the trailer to do some editing, the CBS broadcast center in Lillehammer was asking Verne to revoice the last thirty seconds. They wanted to play up the fact that Jan cast the deciding vote and that he was formerly an East German.

I rolled my eyes and looked to Verne and David. I knew what was going down. They wanted to imply that Jan, the judge from what was Communist East Germany, had a bias toward Oksana, who was from what was once Communist Ukraine.

I was beside myself and so was Verne. I knew Jan as an honorable man, a person with integrity. If he had a bias as a judge, it was toward the more artistic skater, not whether she was of communist origin, for goodness' sake. My feeling was borne out four years later, when he was one of three judges casting a first-place vote for Michelle Kwan in the long program at the Nagano Olympics. Compared to winner Tara Lipinski, Michelle was considered the more artistic skater, so Jan was certainly consistent in his preferences. That wasn't the issue here, though. The implication was politics, and CBS wasn't alone in playing up this angle, only I didn't want any part of it.

At first glance, it did appear the judging of the long program broke down along political lines—four western countries awarded Nancy first place, while three former Iron Curtain countries and China went with Oksana. The ninth judge, Jan, scored Nancy and Oksana in a tie, but since the tiebreaker was the artistic score, his vote went to Oksana because he had given her a style mark of 5.9 to Nancy's 5.8. So Oksana's margin of victory turned out to be one-tenth of a point.

I believe Oksana's victory had less to do with politics than with culture. The eastern judges have always had a traditional preference for classical music and balletic style, and the western judges have tended to favor popular music and dance movement. Nancy and Oksana's skating styles reflected those preferences.

"We can't do this to Jan," I said to David. "We can't paint him with a broad political brush. It's unfair."

But my opinion was moot. The broadcast bosses had decided to play up the political angle. Verne wound up doing the voice-over. After he explained the breakdown of the scoring country by country, he came to Jan: "That left it up to the German judge, Jan Hoffman, a former East German," Verne said.

Later that night, Verne and I were driving back to the hotel in the CBS van and I couldn't stop thinking about what we did to Jan. "I don't like it," I said. "We nailed a guy who judged the competition arguably right on the mark. He did absolutely nothing wrong."

Jan had given a one-tenth edge to Nancy in the technical, which was justified, and a one-tenth difference to Oksana in the artistic, which was also justified. A year later, CBS did go to Jan's hometown in Germany and we interviewed him and gave him an opportunity to explain his decision. Then we aired the piece in prime time during "Ice Wars." It was small consolation, but I felt better after that.

The 1994 ladies' event was a great competition, one of those rare events that could legitimately have gone either way. Some skating pundits feel Nancy got ripped off in the short and long program judging. Oksana, they say, two-footed a triple Lutz landing in the short and should not have been placed among the top three. But it was a minor deduction and most of her technical scores did reflect the mistake. Regardless, you could not dismiss the artistic level of her short program despite the flawed landing on the triple Lutz. *The Swan* was one of those rare performances that can be labeled a classic. You've got to reward that artistic quality. In the long, Oksana and Nancy both performed five triple jumps. They both completed toe loop, Salchow, loop and Lutz, and Oksana might have gotten full credit for a slightly two-footed triple flip. The difference could have been Nancy's triple toe combination, but in the eyes of five judges, Oksana's artistry was the margin of victory.

Any event with so many great performances is good for the sport. Both skaters were truly deserving of the title.

But they can give out only one gold medal, and I think the frustration many felt for Nancy, she felt for herself. Her disappointment showed at the most inopportune time: with the whole world watching, Nancy was overheard on the air saying Oksana need not worry about putting on any makeup for the medal ceremony because she was just going to cry again anyway. The broadcast center caught the remark and unilaterally decided to air it. Verne and I had no idea it was airing. It wasn't the worst thing ever said about a competitor, but the media declared open season on Nancy. Perhaps they were holding her to an unfair standard.

True, Nancy had lost patience with Oksana in the heat of the moment, but all in all, I thought she handled herself well. During the whole sordid Tonya Harding affair, she didn't say anything that was damning or condemning. She really rode above the fray, and I give her tremendous credit for that. It's tough enough to win a gold medal under normal circumstances. Imagine going through what Nancy experienced! I would not have wanted to trade places with her for anything.

Since there was absolutely nothing I could do for my father, I decided to stay in Lillehammer another day to cover the figure skating exhibitions. Karen was with me, and Verne, Tracy, David and Helen. I waited a day to tell Helen because I wanted to do it in person. After I gave her the news just before the start of exhibitions, she was devastated. I felt fortunate being surrounded by good friends. Everyone was there for me, listening when I needed to talk, giving me space when I preferred to be alone. Hard as it was, I continued to work, though my mind was somewhere else.

I asked my good friend from Bowling Green, Dave Meek, to help Sue with the funeral arrangements. Then I flew to Florida and did a couple of "Stars on Ice" dates. Ernie would have wanted me to keep working, and what else was I supposed to do? Sit around and feel sorry for myself? I felt better keeping busy. On my days off, I went to Lake Placid to arrange his estate and close down his house. It was depressing going through his things, but every now and then I'd come across something that would make me smile, like the pictures from our Alaska trip. Sue and Steve wanted some keepsakes, so I arranged to have everything shipped to Ohio. I collected some old family photos and took them with me.

When it was time for the funeral, I headed north, and was joined by Peter Carruthers and the Plage family, Bill, Lynn and Karen. Dad, like Mom, had been cremated, and we buried him alongside her in Memorial Gardens cemetery, just as he wanted. It was a small ceremony, mostly family and friends. Aunt Marjorie and Uncle Bill flew in from Boston. David Santee came in from Chicago, and Tom Collins also made the trip. I gave a brief eulogy at the church service but tried to keep to myself most of the day. I wasn't totally despondent; I felt a sense of peace knowing my mother and father were together again. In some ways, he had started dying the day she died, and he had certainly endured an extraordinary amount of sickness and pain in recent years. It was difficult to watch, and I felt better knowing he was no longer suffering.

I didn't stay around long after my father's funeral. Peter, Karen, Lynn and I drove two hours to Detroit and caught a flight to New York City. There was a "Stars on Ice" show to skate and I had no intention of missing it. How strange it must have appeared—performing in Madison Square Garden hours after laying my father to rest. I didn't skate because I felt an obligation to my employer; they would have given me all the time I needed to deal with my loss. I performed because that was what I needed to do. And it was what Dad would have wanted me to do.

From the airport we headed downtown, straight to the Garden. I stepped out on the sidewalk and stood still for a moment, soaking up the familiar sights. Across the street, the old Pennsylvania Hotel rose majestically into the sky. As the electric billboard above Penn Station heralded the "Stars on Ice" show that night, yellow cabs raced down Seventh Avenue, and the scent of roasted almonds and chestnuts filled the air. I felt a surge of energy that only New York seems to give me.

As I approached the Garden, I thought about something Karen has said over and over: that I am more comfortable sharing myself with an audience of sixteen thousand than I am when I'm in a room with one or two people. She's not alone. Many friends have told me the same thing. I can't analyze it, but they're right. And that's just the way it is.

That might explain the rush of adrenaline I felt as I ran through the doors of the building. Tonight I would fill myself with skating, the crowd and my friends. Backstage, everyone was great. There were warm hugs and lots of tears. After changing into my costume and warming up, I stepped on the Garden ice and skated in the opening of the show. And just before my first solo of the night, something came to the surface that I had known subconsciously for many years. It wasn't just that I had trouble separating skating from the rest of my life. Skating *was* my life. Performing in "Stars" was not just a terrific way to make a living, but the essence of my being: the cast is my family; the road, my home; the ice, my blood. It might not be that way forever, but it's who I am today.

Chapter Nineteen

Revival

Nothing would be the same about figure skating after Lillehammer. There was an explosion and promoters were flooding the sport with new events. At the start of 1994, I honestly thought my career would melt away with the spring thaw, which was only natural for a skater ten years removed from his Olympic prime. Producers and competition organizers would have another set of Olympic medalists to fill their events and programs. Some goals—like my own television special—seemed out of reach forever. But that spring after the tour, the phone started ringing and didn't stop.

The person the media claimed was responsible for the new boom in skating was nowhere in sight. Tonya Harding returned home from her eighth-place finish in Norway, pled guilty to hindering prosecution, and was sentenced to a combination of fines, community service and probation. The USFSA also banned her for life, meaning she could never again compete for the United States as an amateur skater or in any event sanctioned by the USFSA.

But was she entitled to a future as a professional? There were some who argued yes, but I feel she has no place in skating. I think there is a certain way to apologize for your actions, and a prepared statement written by a lawyer doesn't do it for me. She has never taken responsibility for what happened.

As far as her appearing in skating events, it's my position that if you are going to build up the sport and market it to a mass audience, it requires a quality foundation, not the carnival atmosphere she would have brought to the table. And that was all she had to offer, I'm sorry to say. I had no desire to work with her, and other skaters shared my sentiment.

I also decided I would not cooperate with any promoter who included her in an event. Look, I could announce tomorrow that I was going to jump off the Empire State Building nude, and it would certainly draw a crowd and television coverage. That was the appeal of Tonya Harding, and I wasn't going to be any part of it. There's a high road and a low road. And yes, you can make a lot of money taking the low road. But you only go around once, and I didn't want to look back on my career with any regrets about being involved in something that perpetuated the tabloid mentality of that story.

Don't misunderstand; I sincerely hope Tonya finds happiness in her life. I don't wish her ill, yet at the same time I don't believe she belongs anywhere near the skating world. That said, with recent ratings of skating events down from what they have been in other years, I wouldn't be surprised to see Tonya performing again somewhere soon.

The newest and freshest star to emerge from Lillehammer was Oksana Baiul. After winning the gold medal at Lillehammer, she was thrust into the limelight and the professional world, her leg never quite fully recovered from the injury in Norway. Still, she tried to fulfill a busy schedule of pro competitions and appearances.

Oksana went on to make a lot of money, but since winning the Olympic title in 1994, she has won only a single pro event, and her personal troubles dragged her down even further. She'd already had so many things to deal with in her life. As a baby, she was abandoned by her father; as a young girl, she was orphaned when her mom died. Then she was raised by her Ukrainian coach, Galina Zmievskaia, Viktor Petrenko's mother-in-law and coaching mentor, and Viktor and his wife took Oksana under their wing. While I believe most of the people around Oksana meant well, no one could prepare her for what her gold medal would entail. She was surrounded by an inexperienced group and had absolutely no experience herself. It's little wonder she was unprepared to cope.

I began hearing stories about Oksana's descent but didn't witness anything myself until we did an AIDS benefit in Toronto a couple of years after the Lillehammer Olympics. Midway through the rehearsal, we took a break and Oksana disappeared, leaving her skates right by the ice. When it was time to go back to work, everyone was looking for her. Apparently she had gotten bored and left the arena to go shopping. She came back with a bunch of Versace bags hanging from her arms. Word had it she dropped $30,000 in one afternoon. Was this an indication of self-destructive behavior? At the time it seemed like nobody thought anything of it. People closest to her were used to it.

Oksana was also undergoing physical changes. She grew a lot after the Olympics, and weight problems set in, exacerbating her injuries and ruining her jumps. Then in 1997, she got into a car accident while driving under the influence of alcohol. It didn't seem to alarm her as it did the rest of us.

Shortly after her car accident, we were both performing at an event in Charleston, South Carolina. I believed she had many problems and I wanted to help. She was hot, and promoters wanted her for every event, but sometimes you've got to say no. She was a special skater and heading toward disaster. I sat with her and urged her to select quality over quantity of events. I felt she was overbooked and not giving her bad knee the necessary time to heal.

Oksana's thinking was that she had to make the money right away. "That's not true," I said. "Dorothy Hamill could make as much money now, if she chose to, as she did twenty years ago. It's all about longevity. It has nothing to do with today." It didn't register. Perhaps coming from her situation—poverty, no parents or siblings—it was hard to look at the big picture. We sat together for a while as she cried. It was so sad. Inside, she has a good heart, just not the best foundation to make smart choices for herself.

By this time, Oksana had split from Galina and the Petrenko family, her only support. In many ways she was acting like a rebellious teenager, and her mother figure also happened to be her coach. It was the kind of thing that goes on in every family, including my own. You reach a certain age and you want to establish your independence. Oksana was an Olympic gold medalist and a millionaire at sixteen. To put it in perspective, when I was that age, I was still a fairly obscure skater trying to make it to nationals—as a junior. And as a person, I had no clue who I was and certainly wasn't emotionally prepared to be an Olympic champion.

Several months after our conversation, Oksana left the Tom Collins summer tour to enter alcohol rehab.

Oksana's experience was proof that it doesn't really matter what you accomplish at the Olympics. What matters is how you handle yourself in the aftermath. In the end, your choices are yours and yours alone. She cannot forget she is an Olympic gold medalist and the media and the public will watch every move she makes. And while an Olympic medal can pave the way for the rest of your career, it's not the end-all. What you achieve depends on several factors: who you choose to work with, how you structure your career, your preparation on the ice and your public image off it. You have to keep in shape and work on choreography and choosing music. There are also numerous off-ice opportunities, like being involved in charity functions.

After rehab, Oksana showed signs that she was coming around. During the 1999 pro season, she was skating better and looking happier and healthier than she has in years. Undeniably, Oksana has a special gift, and a presence on the ice that I love. But she needs to wake up and realize that what she accomplished in Norway five years ago is in the past, and the professional world is a brand-new game. And what you become in the critical transition period from amateur to professional can be your identity for the rest of your career.

Nancy Kerrigan chose a different life from Oksana after Lillehammer. She decided she didn't want to compete very often and geared her work schedule to touring in shows. She got married to Jerry Solomon, her agent, and gave birth to a baby boy, settling down in a home near her parents in Boston. Nancy and I didn't speak much until shortly after the Nagano Olympics, but it had less to do with any grudge than the fact that we just rarely crossed paths anymore. We were on different tours and leading separate lives. I finally bumped into her in early 1998 when "Stars" was playing in Worcester, Massachusetts. She was there to interview Paul Wylie for a sports cable TV talk program that she hosts. Before the show, I saw her in the hallway backstage and we had a really pleasant talk. She seemed very happy, telling me about her son Matthew and her plans to have another child. I came away from the conversation thinking that Nancy really has got her act together. Being an international celebrity was less important to her than being a mother and a wife, and you have to admire that. Make no mistake about it, she's a success in all departments. I'm glad there are no hard feelings between us.

As for me, the offers came pouring in after Lillehammer. I couldn't believe it. A year earlier I had felt all washed up, and now the landscape was completely different. Promoters were competing like crazy to line up the handful of high-profile skaters for televised competitions and specials. One opportunity that came my way was Dick Button's inaugural "Gold Championship," which pitted Olympic gold medalists, past and present, against one another. Only I guess the promoters felt I was ancient history, since I wasn't invited to compete until Alexei Urmanov dropped out of the event.

Yet there I was in November of 1994, in first place after the technical program and standing at center ice in Edmonton, Canada, with a rare opportunity before me: a chance to finally beat Brian Boitano in pro competition.

Getting a crack at beating Brian came along about as often as the Olympics—around once every four years since he retired in 1988—which shows you just how consistent Brian was during that span. I had never capitalized when Brian flubbed up in the past. I followed his errors with mistakes of my own, and would always leave the rink feeling a little emptier each time.

Now I had a chance at redemption, and a chance to win a competition to which I hadn't been invited in the first place. They wanted to fill the card with three skaters—Brian, Viktor Petrenko and Alexei, the newly crowned Olympic champion. They asked me only after Alexei pulled out. He had decided he didn't want to lose his eligibility by competing in one unsanctioned competition. So they called on me to fill out the card.

I arrived in Edmonton thinking I had no chance against Brian and Viktor, and I said so to everyone in sight. Announcing for NBC were Hannah Storm and Kurt Browning, and they said my prediction was just my way of trying to ease the pressure on myself. But it wasn't a ploy; I was just being realistic, because these guys had spent the previous year training for the Olympics and they had their legs under them. They both had triple Axel combinations in their technical programs—big artillery compared to me. As I expected, they came out and hit everything. Viktor nailed his triple Axel–triple toe combination, a triple Lutz and two triple Salchows. But his momentum was spoiled when he singled a triple loop and doubled a planned triple flip.

Brian was up next. At five-foot-eleven, he's very tall for a skater, and his size and speed are two of his best assets. His jumps look as though they are over the boards. Brian opened with his trademark triple Lutz, one arm stretched high like the Statue of Liberty. Then he hit his triple Axel–double toe combination, another triple toe, a triple flip–triple toe combination and a triple Salchow at the end of his program. Awesome, just awesome. Six for six on triples.

I was the last skater out but it took a while. There was an extra long commercial break, and when I first went out on the ice to start my program, my coach, Kathy Casey from Colorado, called me back. I had been training with Kathy since 1992, and she was crucial to my resurgence in competitive skating. Up in the booth, Hannah suggested to Kurt that the long wait might freeze me, but Kurt thought it could work to my advantage: the more time the audience had to cool down after Brian's solid performance, the more they could concentrate on what I was going to do. "All the attention is on Scott, and he likes it that way," Kurt said.

He was right. My job was to bring the crowd right on the ice with me, and I didn't want any interference from the specter of Brian's and Viktor's sterling performances. I wore classic black for my technical program and skated to big-band standards, opening with "I'm Getting Sentimental

Over You." My triple Lutz was high and clean, but I needed my next jump more than any other, the triple flip. When I hit that, I clenched my fists and got real busy to "In the Mood." After I hit my triple Salchow, the audience was clapping with the music, and I had them after the triple toe and two double Axels. I was feeling so confident during the program, I skated by Kathy and gave her a high five. I ended the program with a back flip, a Russian split and a fast scratch spin. When I got off the ice, the crowd was on its feet, going ballistic, and so were Kathy and I. It was one of those rare times skating against Brian when I sat down in the kiss-and-cry and couldn't wait for my marks to come up. The only downside was that Karen couldn't be there to share the moment. So when the TV camera zoomed in close for my reaction to the marks, I took the chance to give her a message: "Karen, I wish you were here—I really do. I'm having fun tonight."

My technical scores were solid, all 5.8s and 5.9s, but I had perfect 6.0s across the board from all seven judges for the style marks. I turned back to the camera because I had to acknowledge the person responsible for the perfect scores: my choreographer, Sarah Kawahara, who was watching from California. "Thanks, Sarah. That's all you," I said to her.

I needed every single 6.0. The final score in the technical was close— 59.3 for me to 59.2 for Brian. Finally I had beaten Brian in the "tech," as we like to refer to it. I heard later from the judges that they preferred the versatility I showed in my program. I did more spins, more footwork and more complex steps than Brian, and my jumps were just as clean, though he had more technical difficulty. Viktor was a distant third, so the competition was down to me and Brian.

For the artistic program, Brian and I couldn't have been skating to more contrasting music. Brian was performing to Pavarotti singing "Nessun Dorma" and I had picked "Walk This Way," the '70s Aerosmith tune. I wore a colorful costume to match the music, and Brian was outfitted in more subdued attire, befitting his dramatic program. Since jumps were not as crucial in the artistic number, my strategy was to take full advantage of my footwork, working the crowd by keeping the beat to Joe Perry's up-tempo guitar licks. Brian led off again, and as expected, he landed everything—triple Lutz, triple toe and a triple flip. Had he done a triple Axel, he might have been impossible to beat. But the crowd and judges loved it—Brian received four 6.0s in all for his artistic program marks.

Now it was my turn. As I glided out to center ice, the arena was pitch-black because this event was performed using theatrical lighting. But I could feel the anticipation in the crowd. I had skated to "Walk This Way" on tour with "Stars," so when the spotlight came on and the audience saw my costume, they knew what was coming and gave me the energy I needed to get through the program. One thing was for sure: the crowds in Edmonton wanted to be entertained, and that turned out to be an advantage for me. Within a few beats of the music, the audience was clapping, and a rush of adrenaline surged through me. I hit a double Axel, and as I was going into my triple Lutz, a thought crossed my mind: "Hit this jump and I could win this." I relaxed and decided that if it was meant to be, it was meant to be. I landed it. I looked into the crowd and gestured them to bring it on, inviting even more cheers. When I nailed my triple toe, the crowd went berserk and I knew the night was mine. "Just sell the rest of it," I reminded myself. "Work every face in the crowd." After my footwork sequence, I launched into a back flip. The fans went absolutely nuts. They were fantastic.

Then I sat down in kiss-and-cry. I didn't want the night to end, especially after a row of 6.0 scores lit up the board—four in the technical and five in the artistic. I felt chills. That was when I knew I had finally beaten Brian Boitano, the greatest competitor I've ever seen. It was what I had been waiting for all these years as a pro—beating Brian after he skated well—and it was the best I had skated in a decade. It was the tenth year since my perfect program at the Salt Lake City nationals and my gold medal win in Sarajevo, and I was savoring it just as much, if not more. In fact, Ottawa worlds in 1984 was the last time I had ever beaten Brian. This moment was the affirmation of my entire career.

Dick Button was very gracious to me in offering his congratulations, and Brian was classy in defeat. I saw that he was down so I walked up to him and said, "Don't be upset. This is the greatest night of my life. And it's only the greatest night of my life because we both skated really well and it never happens like this for me. Never. This happens for you all the time. So I hope you're as happy for me as I am."

Brian laughed and then shook my hand. Once he understood how much it meant to me to win, I think he appreciated that he was a big part of it. I've been in that situation before where I've skated well and somebody comes along and wins by a couple of tenths of a point. If they prevail and it doesn't mean a thing to them, that bugs me. But if they're excited about it, I can handle the loss a little bit easier.

I didn't sleep that night, didn't want to. I wanted the day to last forever. I came into the event feeling that I had no chance of doing a thing against Viktor and Brian, and I ended up on top. And man, it was awesome.

I went out for a celebratory dinner with Kristi Yamaguchi and a bunch of other people. It was late and there was only one open restaurant in town, so everyone—skaters, judges, coaches and officials—gravitated there. I was having a great time. On his way out the door, Toller Cranston stopped by our table and dropped a check on my plate. "It's the judges' tab," he said, laughing. It was a big bill, probably because they knew I'd pick it up.

And why not? The guaranteed prize for third place was $140,000, which was ridiculous enough. And I made $200,000. That's right. In my last Dick Button competition in 1991, the prize money was $40,000 for first, $20,000 for second, and $12,000 for third. Now first place paid 200K.

Viktor, Brian and I were joking earlier that if you come in third, you win a condo, and if you come in first you win a condo and a Porsche. It really was an absurd amount of cash. Sure my friends on the Professional Golfer's Association tour at the time might have made more than that winning any event, but they had to beat out more than 150 other golfers over a four-day tournament.

I didn't get too carried away with the money. I passed on buying the condo, but I couldn't resist buying a Porsche and a set of vanity license plates to go along with it: they read "EDMNTN."

Chapter Twenty

Sergei

My win at Edmonton came during one of the busiest years of my life. All season long, I was going nonstop from rehearsals to competitions to commentating gigs. But I flew from Canada to Lake Placid to rehearse for the 1995 "Stars on Ice" tour feeling at peace with my skating for the first time in a while. In the wake of the 1994 Olympics, the tour went on to have a terrific year, selling out almost everywhere we went. People just couldn't get enough of skating.

One of my favorite moments in the show that year was the finale, in which the cast performed to a medley of classic Rolling Stones tunes. There was a section in the number where the skaters paired off and slow danced under dim lights to a song called "I'm Out of Tears." My partner was Ekaterina Gordeeva, Katia to her friends. I always looked forward to our little dance. It was a chance to get caught up on what Katia and her husband Sergei were doing. I'd start off the conversation the same way every time, and it was no different in Amherst, Massachusetts, our last U.S. stop before heading to Canada.

"So how was your day?" I began. Before I could finish my sentence, we both broke out laughing over my predictability.

"Pretty good," Katia replied.

"I have a present for you after the show," I said.

"Oh, I don't have anything for you," she said bashfully. I could tell by the tone of her voice that she was a little embarrassed at receiving a gift from me and not having something to give in return.

"Well, your reaction to my present will be my present," I said.

Katia clearly didn't understand, so I rephrased my sentence. "If you like what I give you, that will be my gift."

"Oh, okay," she said.

We danced for another minute and then we parted company. She took Sergei by the hand and they glided to center ice to do their step-out. Near the end of the show, we went into the audience to shake hands before the final bow.

"Katia," I yelled across the ice. "It's time for your present." I skated over to the tunnel where we enter the ice and pulled aside the curtain. Standing there was little Daria, Katia and Sergei's two-year-old daughter. She was all dressed up in a finale costume—a purple sequined dress that wardrobe supervisor Alan Herro had sewn together, and a pair of tiny polished white skates. It was identical to what the older girls were wearing. Nobody could take their eyes off Daria. With her golden hair, her father's smile and her sparkling blue eyes, she was adorable. I picked her up and brought her onto the ice.

Katia's reaction was priceless. She was beaming and her eyes welled up with tears. Katia held out her arms and gestured for Daria to come to her. The crowd started to cheer and applaud, but Daria grew frightened by the noise and froze. She took a few tiny steps, stopped and reached for her mom. Then Sergei swooped in like Superman, scooping up his daughter with one arm and taking Katia's hand for the final bow. In my "closing of the tour" speech to the crowd, I had the thrill of introducing "the newest and youngest member of our cast, Daria Grinkova."

It was like the sappiest TV commercial—and just as surely brought a lump to everyone's throat. This beautiful family, the golden couple with their perfect angel, twirling beneath the lights. It's an image I will never forget: Sergei, Katia and Daria, smiling and holding each other in what was Sergei's last U.S. performance for "Stars on Ice."

The next fall, the cast assembled in Lake Placid to begin rehearsals for "Stars" tenth season. Who would have thought the tour would have survived a decade? From our humble beginnings, we had grown into a fifty-six-city tour, including dates in all the major markets. This year promised to be special.

I enjoyed returning to Lake Placid each fall, with its memories of childhood competitions, the summer training camps with Don and Kitty, my total of three "Norton Skate" titles, and of course the Olympics. Those experiences are still precious to me, but they would forever be overshadowed by what happened on November 20, 1995.

On that Monday morning, I had recently returned from the "Gold Championship," where I had given an uninspired performance and finished third. It was the complete opposite of the year before—from the performance of a lifetime to a total meltdown.

My mind just wasn't on the task. Before skating in the event, I holed up in my hotel room, listening to a song by Edwin McCain called "Alive." It's about a man who just lost his wife and father and how music and the good times in life kept him going, letting him know he was alive. But I didn't feel alive; I felt empty. The euphoria from last year's performance in Edmonton was long gone, replaced by ambivalence and exhaustion. I was overbooked and feeling massively depressed about my skating. And when it was time to perform, all the pressure I had been feeling converged on me at once.

I kept up a crazy schedule in part because I didn't feel I had a lot of time left in skating, at least as a competitor. It was hard keeping up my jumps, and I was starting to feel old. Back in late 1993 when Brian and Katarina were getting ready for the Olympics, I got the sense that there was nothing out there left for me, and that I was being put out to pasture like an old racehorse. I was grateful for the second chance, but as the year dragged on, all the work was taking a heavy toll.

Now I was looking at a season of eight pro competitions, eight commentating jobs, six TV specials and fifty-six dates with "Stars." All the while I was thinking how wonderful it would be if I could take my sore thirty-seven-year-old body and turn back the clock ten years. I was a wreck and the season had barely begun.

So when I saw Sergei at rehearsal that morning, I was in need of some cheering up. We had a ritual where I would say in Russian, "*Gadela moi bolshoi druck*" ("How are you, my big friend?"), and Sergei would respond in English, "I am fine. How are you?" Then I'd answer in Russian, "*Herosho*" ("I am good"). After Sergei and I did our usual exchange, Katia gave me a big hug. I think she sensed I was feeling a little down in the dumps. Then they gave me some good news. Daria was on her way to town with Katia's mother. I could tell Sergei was very excited about seeing her. We all were.

Little Daria, nicknamed Dasha, is this amazing gift from the heavens. When she was born on September 11, 1992, I designated myself her godfather. So whenever I saw all the Grinkovs together, I would call out, "My family!" When Daria comes on tour, we call it "Dasha Day" because she infuses the cast with energy. On the bus she's a social butterfly, bouncing from person to person, smiling and giving everybody their ten minutes in the spotlight of her smile before hopping onto somebody else's lap. Sometimes when I was talking to her father, Daria would run over to sit between us and distract us from the conversation. She's the closest thing to a surrogate daughter that I have, and watching her grow up has been a privilege.

After rehearsals got under way, I was feeling better. Sandra Bezic was teaching us some new steps, which got my mind off the "Gold Champion"-ship debacle. In Lake Placid, there are three full-size practice rinks in all. While I was working with the rest of the cast, Sergei and Katia were excused to go next door to another rink to work on their program with their choreographer, Marina Zueva. Suddenly there were screams and someone yelling, "Call 911." Some of the cast rushed into the other rink, where Sergei was lying still on the ice. His coach was by his side, administering CPR. Katia had gone for help and when she returned, everyone had surrounded Sergei, praying he would be all right.

Paramedics rushed him to the hospital. Sergei was strong and young, just twenty-eight years old. I couldn't comprehend what was happening. I looked up and prayed to God, "Don't do this. How unfair and horrible it would be if something happened to him." While Katia and Marina went to the hospital, the cast assembled in the lobby of our hotel to wait for news. After a half hour of waiting, people were hungry, so Kurt and I made a run to McDonald's to get everyone some food, but when we returned to the inn, the mood in the room was somber and quiet. Roz came up to me in tears and handed me her cell phone. Bob Kain was on the line. "Sergei's gone," he said, sobbing. I had left for all of twenty minutes, and when I came back our whole world had changed.

State of shock barely begins to describe my feelings. There were tears and sobs throughout the room. Some of us huddled together on couches and chairs while others went off into corners by themselves and carved out their own private space to deal with the tragedy.

For part of the afternoon, we debated whether we should go visit Katia or respect her privacy and leave her alone. Someone called the condo where she was staying, and Katia sent back word that it was all right to come visit. We piled into a couple of cars and drove over to her place. When we walked through the door, she was sitting with Marina, looking at old pictures of Sergei. We stayed for a while, sharing memories and comforting Katia. A lot of those memories included Daria. Though time with his daughter was brief, Sergei lives in Daria, from the way she smiles to the way she picked up many of his mannerisms. They were very funny interacting together. Once during a rehearsal, I walked into the restroom to find Sergei attempting to give Daria a diaper change. He had her standing up in the sink and was trying to wash her off. Daria was squirming and laughing and squealing, "Ooh-aah, ooh-aah, ooh-aah." Sergei, for all his power and strength, looked helpless. He was so embarrassed.

Another time on tour, Daria slipped into the guys' dressing room after a show and spied on us while we were showering. I turned around just in time to see this scruff of blond hair and one little blue eye peeking around the corner of a stall. The next thing I knew, Sergei's voice was bouncing off the tile and Daria disappeared like a ghost, probably making a beeline back to the comfort of the ladies' dressing room. Those are memories I'll keep forever.

Rehearsals were canceled and Katia arranged a private viewing in Saranac Lake, near Lake Placid. Then she took Sergei home to Moscow for the funeral service. Representing the cast, Paul and I flew to Russia to attend.

The company had some time off before the tour got under way after Christmas. I had two competitions to skate, and I felt inspired by Sergei's memory to skate well, and I did. Then I went home to Denver and shut down hard. It was as if something inside me snapped and sapped all my strength. Of all the deaths I had experienced in my short life, Sergei's hit me the hardest. I was somewhat prepared when my mom and dad died. They were both sick and in pain, and part of me felt relieved that they were resting in peace. Sergei's death came out of nowhere.

Where does one begin to heal when you lose a close friend like this? I tried to think of the positive memories. I remembered a person who totally understood my sense of humor, despite the language barrier. He used to translate my sight gags for Katia, who never seemed to understand them even though she spoke better English than Sergei.

Obviously my friendship with Sergei wasn't the sort where I could sit down and bare my soul. The language barrier prevented that. Still, I regarded him as one of my best friends, probably because we were both overgrown kids. I remember a few days before he died, we were on the ice during a serious rehearsal with Sandra, and I threw him a funny look just to make him crack up. We never let our language differences get in the way of laughing together.

It had been that way since Sergei and Katia first joined the company for the 1991–92 season. They were newly married, and had their Olympic gold medal from Calgary to go along with four world titles. Even with those accomplishments, they were broke, since amateur skaters wouldn't start making big money for another few years. So they were ready to turn pro.

Even then it was tough. Russian skaters don't get the same mileage from their Olympic and world medals as North Americans. They often don't command the same dollars as American skaters with similar or even fewer credentials, although that's starting to change. The top show promoters depend on American ticket buyers, who pay to see the home-grown talent. It's one of those hard lessons in life. You don't always get what you deserve.

Katia and Sergei, though, brought something special to the ice, and they became mainstays on the tour. They were a powerful yet graceful pairs team; when Sergei threw Katia in the split triple twist, she would fly so high she could practically touch the clouds, and then she would land softly in Sergei's arms. I've never seen another pairs team do the element better, and as dangerous as the maneuver was, they did it every night while touring with "Stars." As a couple, they also worked as a team. Katia did all the talking because she spoke better English. Sergei was usually hesitant trying something new unless he figured he could do it really well. But he was the emotional rock Katia leaned on. You could see that characteristic emerge as they worked together, just in how Katia listened to him and respected his ideas and opinions. Yet they were also competitive in practice as they tried to outdo each other, jump for jump, spin for spin.

I'm partial, but after watching Katia compete and perform for more than a decade, I'd say she is probably the greatest female pairs skater of all time. Even better than Irina Rodnina, who was the dominant woman pairs champion in the 1970s. Irina's records will probably never be broken—three gold medals and ten world titles with two partners—but she didn't have to perform at the technical level required of today's pairs skaters, who must have triple jumps, triple throws and triple twists in these extremely dangerous routines. Katia is a brilliant performer, artist and athlete. I can't think of another pairs skater who even comes close.

After two seasons, Katia and Sergei left "Stars" to prepare for Lillehammer. Financially they were doing well, and competitively they were still in their prime. They knew they could win the Olympics again, so why not take another shot? They were very young when they won their first gold medal in 1988, and when they returned to the winter games six years later, a little older and wiser, they could appreciate the experience much more.

After their victory in Lillehammer, they joined the Tom Collins spring and summer tour, and I went to see them skate in San Jose. After the show, Katia pulled me aside. "Can I talk to you?"

Katia and Sergei were in a dilemma. She explained they had job offers from both Tom Collins and "Stars on Ice."

"We don't know what to do," Katia said. "We don't know if we should go back with 'Stars' or stay with Tommy Collins."

As she spoke, I was dying to get on my knees and beg them to come back, but with Daria in the picture, it was a big decision. "You have to find out what suits you, Sergei and Daria as a family," I said. "I can't make that decision for you. We'd love to have you back, more than anything. But if you choose to stay with Tommy's tour, where you have more Russian friends, I'd understand."

Then I smiled. "Just let me know what you're doing so I can make my plans," I said. "I'll come over to Tommy's tour if it means being with you guys." Katia laughed. In the end, ironically, I think Daria was what made them rejoin "Stars." Since she was going to spend a lot of time with them on the road, a smaller cast—thirteen compared to about thirty—and less travel, suited them better.

After a successful '95 tour, our tenth anniversary season should have been cause for celebration, but Sergei's death cast a pall over my entire year. Not helping matters was a flu bug that flattened me during the month of December. I lost ten pounds, turned white as a ghost, and dragged myself through that first month on tour. I tried to put my best face forward, but I wonder if the audience saw through that. We all missed him terribly.

Katia, in the meantime, spent the winter in Moscow with family, resting and contemplating whether she wanted to skate again. We spoke often by phone, and it was comforting to know she was getting on all right. In our last conversation in Moscow, I had urged her to keep skating. "You fill yourself on the ice. That's your home," I said. "That's where you've been most comfortable; that's where you spend most of your time. You should not leave the ice. You should stay there and let it feed you."

Skating helped us all deal with the loss. In the opening number on tour that year, we had planned a step-out for Sergei and Katia, a ten-second interval in which they were to do a spin and a lift. We didn't take it out in their absence. We trained a spotlight on center ice and kept it there: it was our tribute. In fact, it was so subtle not many people in the crowd even noticed. But during those few seconds, all the skaters watched the ice where Katia and Sergei would have been.

Each show, I performed a number, "One for my Baby," which was originally intended as a thank-you to the audience for all the support they had shown me through the years. It remained that, but it also became my personal tribute to Sergei, thanking him for all he had given me with his friendship. In the middle of the number, I would raise an imaginary glass in his honor.

On February 27, the cast went to Hartford, Connecticut, and joined a dozen other world-class skaters in a tribute to Sergei and Katia. It was originally a "Stars on Ice" date, but we gave it to Katia. The show was called "A Celebration of Life." At first we weren't sure how she wanted to participate, but we were thrilled when Katia decided to skate.

The scene at the civic center was overwhelming. A packed audience, including hundreds of skating people from around the world, had come to express their love and support. The night before the show, she hosted a dinner party and told me there she was afraid to perform. The whole idea of this show being centered around her was overwhelming.

"You can do this," I encouraged her. "You're an amazing skater."

The next day, an incredible collection of friends and talent assembled at the Hartford Civic Center, but the night belonged to Katia. The first half of the show we mourned Sergei's death and celebrated his life. The second half was symbolic of life moving on. Skating to Mahler's *Symphony No. 5*, Katia was magnificent, probably the most powerful performance I've ever seen on the ice. I was so proud of her, and totally blown away by her skating.

In the finale of the show, Katia and I entered the ice together as I portrayed a father figure who gives Katia an on-ice blessing to forge on and skate independently. It was Marina's idea, and while I was moved by the concept and honored to be chosen, I felt somewhat unworthy of the role.

Later on in the season, when we got the news that Katia wanted to return to the cast as a solo artist for the Canadian leg of the "Stars" tour, I knew she was well on her way. Some of the ten cities we toured in Canada held special memories, like Calgary, where Katia and Sergei won their first Olympic gold medal, and Halifax, where they won their last world title. We were all a little uncertain of how she would react traveling and performing on her own, but we were pleasantly surprised. Of course, there were times Katia kept to herself, and we respected her privacy and gave her the space she needed. But I noticed that with each performance, Katia got stronger and more confident as a solo skater. "Stars" was blessed to have her, and it was wonderful watching her improve and grow into a whole new performer.

Back in November, I had made a solemn vow that I would be there for Katia and Daria if they ever needed anything. There were times I felt too protective of them, like I wanted to carry them both and never let Katia's feet touch the ground. My goal that spring was to keep Katia's spirits high, whether it was just sending her a caring note or helping her out with jumps during practice. I wanted to be a shoulder to lean on.

About halfway through the Canadian tour—it's hard to pinpoint exactly when—the roles reversed. I was the one who needed the shoulder, and fortunately, Katia understood and was there for me. Making myself available to her was as consoling to me as it was for her. Being her caretaker had been my way of coping with Sergei's death.

What I realize now is there are no pat answers on how to deal with loss. Even today, people ask me how long it took to get over his death, and I have always replied, "I'm not over it." The truth is, I don't know if I ever will be.

What makes Katia's story all the more remarkable was that the odds seemed so against her. She had a sheltered childhood, most of which was spent in an ice rink. She was groomed to be a pairs champion, and then fell in love with her first and only skating partner. Little things men and women take for granted, like dating, breaking up with a girlfriend or boyfriend, venturing out on your own, were completely foreign to her. She spent her whole life under the protective umbrella of her family, her coaches and Sergei.

Katia is very close with her family. In Russian culture, the grandmother takes care of the children while their mother works. Then when the child grows up and has a baby, the working mother takes on the role her mother had, and the cycle continues. While that's not the common practice in America, it's Russian tradition. So Katia's mother and father, Elena and Sasha, already had an important role in Daria's life while Katia and Sergei were on the road. And they have continued their involvement in Daria's upbringing.

Katia's tragedy, coupled with her ability to grow as a skater and a single mother, has made her into an icon. It's hard to say exactly when this happened, but during the 1997 tour, it was clear her life had changed and it would never be the same. She wrote a book, My Sergei, which became a best-seller and became the subject of cover stories in major women's magazines. Everyone deals with loss at one point or another, yet her special ability to share her story of loss and recovery inspired many. People were awed by how well she has survived. Because I'm still trying to reconcile my own personal losses, I have learned a lot from Katia every day. It's more than being strong in the face of a grievous tragedy. It's recognizing that life was not meant to be fair; it was meant to be a challenge. I would come to learn about this on many levels.

After Sergei died, I picked up a wonderful book by Harold Kushner entitled How Good Do I Have to Be. One of its themes I grasped onto was that life is wonderful because of death, and that without death, life would be meaningless. It explains that if you didn't die, you would never be motivated to accomplish anything. And that without death, certain hall-marks and crossroads in life would cease to exist because they, too, would be insignificant. It helped me a great deal, enabling me to cope and giv-ing me a better understanding of death and its purpose in nature.

Grief can be a powerful catalyst. Eighteen years ago, when my mother died, her memory inspired me to skate and train harder than ever before. Her death awakened my desire to become a champion and gave me a pur-pose. Ultimately, her passing changed the course of my life.

In a similar way, Sergei's death jolted me out of the professional groove I was in. I was tired and stressed out, but in demand in what is usually the twilight of a skater's career. His passing was a rude reminder that our time on this planet is terribly short, and it forced me to take a hard look at my own life, not something I was accustomed to doing.

As the 1996 tour got under way, I thought about the fact that I had spent twelve years on a treadmill. At the end of each season, I would al-ways vow to make some changes, slow things down, say "no" to my agent once in a while and spend more time with Karen. Yet the treadmill kept picking up speed and the incline got steeper. I ended up doing everyone's bidding. I finally figured out I derived a lot of security from that treadmill; it had become the only life I knew.

While grieving for Sergei, I started pondering my station in life. One of the things I admired most about him was that he accomplished so much in his short time on this planet; he lived life on his terms, making every moment count. He had professional success and a wonderful family. Now I was asking myself why I didn't have certain things, such as a child and some semblance of a home life. I needed to deal with some of those things.

My lifestyle was still a serious problem. It always took a long time for me to unwind after coming off the road. The travel, jet lag, hotels, per-forming, nights on the town, sleeping in until noon—I was addicted to the routine, making it tough to adjust to a more normal existence. And since I was gone eight months out of the year, nothing ever got resolved. I had developed unhealthy communication patterns, and since I was gone most of the winter, nothing ever got resolved.

A lot of my close friends were married and had families, and this was an issue for me, too. Peter Carruthers had a son and Kitty had adopted two children herself (she and her husband, Bret Conrad, have earned a gold medal in this department; today they have four wonderful children). Both Barb Underhill and Paul Martini were married and had cut back on skating to spend more time with their families.

A person my age, and with my love of kids, should have had a flock of them by now. There are children all over the country whom I consider surrogate nieces and nephews. But Karen and I were never on the same page on whether to start a family.

No question, my career had consumed me for the better part of a decade, even longer. I'm doing the exact same thing I was doing when I was nine years old. Of course, it's on a much larger scale now, but it's still skating. I've often wondered if my devotion to career and my inability to start a family can be traced to the fear I have of losing the people I love, to death. My mother, Frank McLoraine, my father, and now Sergei; they kept going away. I can't let go of that fear, for whatever reason. Perhaps the losses have affected me more than I thought. Sergei's passing brought these feelings flooding back to the surface.

For much of 1996, I was in emotional turmoil. Those issues didn't go away, but they were put on the back burner in 1997. My poor health had been a dominant part of my childhood, and once again, my health was about to become all-consuming, taking precedence over everything else in my life.

Chapter Twenty-One

It's Not Going to Beat Me

How quickly life can change. One day I'm skating strong, seeing old friends in Bowling Green, and counting down the days to the end of the 1997 "Stars on Ice" tour. The next I'm on a tour bus racing to the Cleveland Cancer Clinic to find out if I have a malignant tumor lodged in my abdomen.

The bus trip from Peoria to Cleveland took the whole night. After we arrived on the morning of March 17, my driver checked in to a hotel to get some rest, and I remained on the bus sleeping. I was awakened by a knock on the door. Groggy-eyed, I looked out the window and saw that it was Bob Kain. It's time to go to the hospital, I thought. I put on a bathrobe and invited Bob in.

"I don't know how to thank you," I said, feeling at a loss for words.

"Don't worry about that," Bob said. "How are you feeling?"

"Not my best," I said quietly.

Bob took a seat while I went to shower and change. We had a long day ahead of us. By this time I was in excruciating pain. It was as though the realization that there was something foreign inside of me doubled the anguish. I couldn't even stand up and walk without wincing.

We got in Bob's car and headed for the hospital. Once there, I briefly met with some doctors and began a series of workups, which were more thorough than what I experienced in Peoria. I underwent a full physical, a biopsy and another CAT scan. They also drew some blood.

The biopsy was the toughest part of the day. The procedure began in a dim exam room, where they did an ultrasound on my abdomen to find the center of the tumor. A nurse smeared some lubricant on my stomach, and then a doctor rubbed a small paddle over my belly to pick up where the tumor was located. The sound waves produced a black-and-white image on the screen displaying my internal organs and the tumor.

Before inserting the biopsy needle—about the size of a good-size knitting needle—the doctor injected me with Novocain. "What we use to kill the pain will hurt more than anything after that," surgeon Jeff Ponsky warned. He was right. I felt like a whale getting harpooned, and I cringed when the fluid filled my abdomen, but after a few seconds the pain dissipated and I felt nothing. Then they inserted the biopsy needle.

The whole time, I was thinking my mom must have gone through a similar procedure herself when she was diagnosed with breast cancer. Now I was getting some idea of what she had experienced.

The results of the biopsy and other tests wouldn't be ready for another day, so I went back to the hotel and waited for Karen, who was on her way in from Denver. That night we took it easy, had a light dinner and relaxed at the hotel.

I couldn't help dwelling on the irony of the timing of all of this. For thirteen years I had dreamed of having my own TV special and it finally came to life last fall. I had performed in eight Disney specials, and *Scott Hamilton: Upside Down* was my reward for all the hard work I put in. It was fulfilling, yet brutal—long, long hours, shooting in four different locations with never enough rehearsal time. There was one number, a Charlie Chaplin piece I did with Katia, that was shot over two straight nights, twelve hours at a stretch, at MGM Studios theme park in Orlando. We worked outdoors, taking over New York Street. Since the scene was nighttime, everything had to be done before the sun came up. We became skating vampires; if we didn't finish in time, we were dead.

Up at the Pickering College rink near Toronto, Kurt and I did a cool hockey number for the special. During meal breaks, the largely Canadian crew would break into a pickup hockey game, which Kurt sometimes joined in. I usually went back to the locker room to keep warm. It was so cold it felt as if we were filming outdoors. And yet even with all the headaches and problems, I'd do it again in a second. The producer, John Brunton, is an incredible creative mind, and Sarah Kawahara would go on to win an Emmy for her choreography work in *Upside Down*. Thirteen years was a long time to wait to realize a fantasy, but it was worth it.

The special aired in early March, just days before my visit to the Cleveland Clinic.

On the morning following my biopsy, I met with urologist Eric Klein and oncologist Ronald Bukowski. Bob and Karen came along. After we sat down, the doctors got right to the point. I had a large, malignant nonseminomatous germ-cell tumor in my abdomen.

"The source of the tumor is your right testicle," Dr. Klein explained. He said the tumor formed from a drainage of cancerous cells through my lymph, starting from my testicular region. In the ultrasound, they had found some scar tissue on my right testicle and told me they were 100 percent sure that was what caused the tumor even though I didn't have a prominent lump. In some men, the symptoms can cause enormous swelling in that region, but not in my case.

After the doctors gave their diagnosis, dead air filled the office. I looked around at all the somber faces and decided to break the ice.

"Oh, is that all?" I deadpanned. "I thought it was going to be something serious." I got some chuckles from Bob and Karen, who were very familiar with my sarcasm. But my doctors didn't react, not even a smirk.

"No," Dr. Bukowski said. "This is serious."

"Hey, I'm just kidding, guys," I replied.

Doctors Klein and Bukowski looked a little baffled. I guess other patients don't react with the same kind of levity. But at that moment, I knew I had a fight on my hands, and humor was going to be one of the weapons at my disposal. Making people laugh and having the ability to poke fun at myself and my troubles are attributes I hope never abandon me. It may stun people that I can be so cavalier about something so devastating, like a cancer diagnosis, but this is how I get by. I wasn't going to give up my sense of humor (or lack thereof, depending on your perspective) now when I needed it more than ever, even if the jokes were at my expense.

Dr. Bukowski presented the treatment plan—a combination of chemotherapy and surgery. In order to keep the cancer from spreading, they first proposed shrinking the tumor with chemotherapy. The plan was four cycles of chemo, each spread over five days with sixteen days off in between. Once the tumor was a manageable size, the doctors could go in and surgically remove it.

As he spoke, I felt a glimmer of relief. I had been waiting for the ball to drop, so to speak: that the tumor had moved to other parts of my body. Fortunately, said Dr. Bukowski, it had not spread to my lungs or my brain (which, come to think of it, would have explained a great deal!). My cancer was in stage two, which was good news because it had not advanced into my vital organs or bone. I felt very, very lucky. Still, it was a large tumor, and I knew from my mother's experience that some cancers did not rest. For a long time I was afraid to ask how big the tumor was. Finally, after my third chemo treatment, I learned it was twice the size of a grapefruit.

The best news from the first meeting was that Doctors Klein and Bukowski felt that my illness was curable and I had an excellent chance at full recovery. When I left the office, my mind was made up: I was going to beat this thing.

One benefit about training under excellent coaches for three decades: I knew that if I listened I could absorb what they had to offer. I established the same rapport with my doctors. When they told me how they were going to destroy the tumor, I didn't resist or question their judgment. Their word was enough, and that was the end of it for me. I put total faith in my oncologist, Dr. Bukowski, a very funny man once I got to know him. He would be in charge of my chemotherapy. Dr. Klein, who was very calm and businesslike, would perform the surgery to remove the tumor and my bad testicle. Because of my ignorance about medical matters, I was grateful for their expertise and their confidence.

My first chemo treatment was set for Friday. The goal of chemo was to shrink the tumor and get my blood count back to normal. At 8,800, the AFP, or the alphafetoprotein indicator—a blood marker for this cancer—was off the charts. The normal amount ranges from zero to twelve. I wasn't going to think about that now. The cast from "Stars" was coming to town Wednesday to meet me for lunch. There was plenty of time to worry about blood counts and chemo later on.

While I was resting at the hotel, Deb Nast and David Baden were standing on a tour bus in Dayton, announcing to the cast what many of the skaters had already heard through the grapevine: that I had cancer. Everyone kind of knew something was up because show director Sandra Bezic had flown into town unexpectedly to rechoreograph the group numbers.

The cast went to the arena for practice, and as the bus pulled into the parking lot, everyone noticed a sign hanging outside the entrance: "Welcome to the Nutter Center." That was the actual name of the venue, and it was just too perfect.

That night the Dayton crowd was told I wasn't skating due to an injury. It was the first show I had missed in years. The next morning the bus drove north to Cleveland instead of east to Rochester, the site of the next performance. It was their day off, but the cast wanted to see me. Making the detour to see me was an awesome gesture and meant more to me than they'll ever know.

We had lunch in a conference room at the hotel. Although this was serious business, I didn't want people crying and getting all depressed, so Kurt prepared a David Letterman–style top ten list—of what to do with my soon-to-be discarded body part. Well, the list was a little too racy and of an insider nature to go into here. Let's just say the cast got very creative, and every joke was at my expense. By the end of the lunch, the list had grown from a top ten to a top twenty.

After lunch, my publicist, Michael Sterling, issued a press release announcing that I had contracted testicular cancer. But Michael was more concerned as a friend. I told him not to worry. "What's the worst thing that could happen?" I said. "That the chemo would cause the last three hairs on my head to fall out?"

While I thought about keeping my illness private, in the end I decided the public deserved to know. I was going to be missing shows, and those ticket buyers and skating fans needed to know why I wasn't performing. The optimism expressed by the doctors gave me the confidence to be open about my illness. My cancer was treatable, and I had to let people know I wasn't going to allow the tumor to win.

Since my first chemo treatment wasn't scheduled for another two days, Karen and I had a couple of days to hang out in Cleveland. On Wednesday, we went to see *The Empire Strikes Back*, which had just been rereleased, and then picked up an Aerosmith CD at a record store. On Thursday I went to the sperm bank.

Yep, since there was a fifty-fifty chance of becoming infertile from the chemotherapy, I spent part of Thursday at the fertility center, banking what would ensure future generations of Hamiltons. The issue of fertility produced an awkward moment at my Tuesday meeting with the doctors. As they were discussing the side effects of chemotherapy on men's sperm, I felt embarrassed with all these people in the room. "Nothing personal, but can I discuss this one-on-one with the fertility doctor?" I interrupted. Everyone got the hint and left the room so we could talk this over alone.

As I passed the time before beginning treatment, the cast moved on to the next date in Rochester. When they entered the arena, they saw that the building had erected a five-by-three-and-a-half-foot Styrofoam get-well card in the lobby. More than 2,500 people signed it during the show. "We know you'll kick this," one fan wrote. It was a message I planned to heed.

I had a present for the audience myself—a tape-recorded message I had prepared on Wednesday and given to the cast to play back to the crowd in Rochester. Just before the show started, my voice could be heard throughout the arena. "I'm sorry I can't be with you tonight," I said. "But you have a tremendous cast ready to perform. So enjoy the show and see you next year."

That Thursday night is one I'll always remember. It was my last night of the way things used to be. The next day I was going to the front line. After I checked into the hospital, Karen and I were watching TV when my hospital phone started ringing. It was Kristi calling from Rochester. There was some familiar-sounding music in the background, and then I heard Kristi's voice, then Kurt's, then Paul's and Rosalynn's. Every cast member got on the phone. I looked at my watch and asked myself how could this be? They were supposed to be on the ice. Then I realized they *were* on the ice. "We want you to know you're here with us," Kristi said. An hour later, my phone rang again. It was Kristi again. "I'm talking to Scott Hamilton," she yelled. "Do you want to say hi?" Then I heard this booming roar: "Hellooo, Scott!"

Imagine that, I thought. I was getting a phone call from several thousand people in upstate New York.

Those on-ice "reach out and touch me" calls ceased after that first night. The company managers got a little upset and decided it was unprofessional to carry phones while performing. However, I did make one last call myself when the cast made its last stop on the U.S. tour in Portland, Maine, two weeks later. Dave Hoffis, the production manager for the show, had figured out a way to wire my telephone call into the house sound system, which not only allowed me to speak over the system, but also allowed me to hear what was going on. I kept quiet until the finale.

In my absence Paul had taken over the emcee chores. Each night it was his job to thank everyone for coming and to wish them well. He ended his speech with, "We'll see you next year." This time I interrupted him over the loudspeaker. "Paul," I said, my voice appearing from nowhere, "you don't say good-bye like that. I can't believe I turned over the microphone to you and this is how you replace me? You say it like this: 'WE WILL SEE YOU NEXT YEAR!'" I could hear the crowd laughing and applauding. I spoke for a few more moments, telling the audience how much I missed them. "I'll be back next year," I said. "That's a promise."

Friday and my first chemo treatment arrived quickly. I had conjured up all these horrible images of what chemotherapy was supposed to be like, but the reality was much different from my dark scenario. I had imagined lying in bed in a sterile hospital room surrounded by huge beeping machines as tubes pumped liquid through my body. I envisioned some form of dialysis procedure similar to what my father had been through. It was nothing like that at all. The staff at the clinic prepared me well: Laura Wood, who was in charge of experimental therapies; Ruth Studer, who served as a liaison with the departments at the hospital; and Diane Shiesley, who handled my CAT scans in radiology and imaging. I was put in a private area of the hospital for security reasons and had a nice, cozy room. The amenities included a TV, a VCR, wood-framed chairs and a plush couch. It reminded me of a nice hotel suite. On my first day I saw some of the other patients and deduced that I was the youngest by a considerable margin.

I anticipated one thing accurately—there were plenty of chemicals, all enclosed in heavy-duty plastic bags, which hung from an IV tree by my bed. I sat on the bed and Nurse Mary Brinkman introduced herself and told me she was going to insert an IV needle in each arm, the second one serving as a backup in case the first shut down.

When Mary was getting ready to apply the chemicals, she slipped on a pair of thick latex gloves, which frightened me a little. She saw the expression on my face and knew exactly what I was thinking.

"Well," she explained, "these chemicals eat skin."

"And you're putting this inside my body?"

She laughed and then went on to explain the process. She said the chemicals—Cisplatin, Bleomicin and Etoposide—would work like a forest fire: they would scorch everything in their path, but the healthy stuff would grow back. She said that any foreign thing that didn't belong in my forest would not be there after the fire. I didn't receive the chemicals straight up. They were mixed with a standard IV fluid to dilute the drugs so they wouldn't harm my internal organs. I would receive the Bleomicin only once a week—both in Cleveland and in Denver, where I would have to go to another clinic for the treatment. That particular drug was injected with a syringe straight into an IV line joint and it took ten to twenty minutes to empty the syringe. While the therapy sounded a little drastic, I wasn't about to argue. I had complete faith in my medical team.

As she inserted the needle, I gritted my teeth.

"Don't worry; this'll be a cinch," she said. "Your veins are like sewer pipes."

"What do you mean?" I asked.

"They're very close to the surface," she explained. "I can see them right through your skin. If you wanted to be a junkie, you could be a great one with veins like these," she kidded.

Once the needles were in I was ready to go. "Fill 'er up," I said. "With high-test."

Mary and I hit it off right away. She figured out quickly that I was thirty-eight years old going on twelve. That first week, she decorated the different chemo bags with stickers of Peanuts characters and the word *hello* spelled out in several languages. One bag of chemicals was always covered with green or purple Mylar, which I dubbed the "party bag." She made me laugh through this ordeal, and she was as essential to my recovery as any of the chemicals pouring through my body. Every patient should be blessed with a nurse like Mary.

Although the chemicals would circulate through my body six hours at a time, I was completely mobile during treatment; I could lie down, walk around my room or sit in a chair. Still, I got restless. Each day I was hooked up to that machine from 10 A.M. to 4 P.M. Then I got a seven-hour break. If my white blood cell counts were high enough, I could get permission to leave the hospital for a couple of hours. Karen and I might have dinner or take in a movie. Sometimes we went to the video store to rent some tapes or bought some CDs. I always had to be back in my room for my 11 P.M. cycle. At night while I slept, I was hooked up to the IV so fluids could be pumped through my body to keep me hydrated.

One of the hardest things about my treatment was being attached to an IV most of the time. I began to worry about getting pinched by the needle if I moved the wrong way or having the chemo tubes malfunction while I was asleep. An alarm on the IV would go off at the slightest hint of a problem, which made it difficult to get a good night's sleep. Eventually, simple complications, like air getting in the IV tube, I learned to take care of myself so I wouldn't have to wait for a nurse to fix every little thing.

The first difference I noticed in my body was an insane craving for fast food. At the end of the first day, Karen and I went out for a burger. The next day I had chicken, and on the third day I ordered Chinese. That night, I got food poisoning, but I wouldn't know it was the cause of my illness for another few days. The chemo, I thought, had to be the reason.

But it was the food, not the treatment! I got better after I took some antibiotics. Still, my doctor ordered me to go easy on the grease and fat. Actually, I never did vomit from chemo. Everyone prepares you for the worst in this department, but people respond differently to chemo, and there are medications, like Compezine, that I took to avoid getting sick. I was told it's tough to stop throwing up once you start, so I resisted the urge.

There were other side effects. Chemotherapy bloated my abdomen and I developed a paunch, just like a beer-swilling couch potato. I put on eight to ten pounds from all the liquids they pumped through me.

Despite the problems, my experience with chemotherapy was not nearly as bad as I had anticipated. I had expected I would feel sick and lethargic all the time, yet that wasn't always the case. During the first cycle, I felt well enough to leave the hospital with Karen every evening after treatment.

Karen, bless her, kept a bedside vigil. At the time she was taking singing and acting classes, but she dropped everything, came to Cleveland and was there for me twenty-four hours a day. Later, when I craved a burger and was too tired to move, she would run out and bring one back. She handled paperwork, paid bills and returned cards and calls. She was also my liaison with the doctors, and I think she knew more about my medical care than I did.

I limited the number of visitors coming through, mostly because I didn't feel my life was in peril. Still, they were an important part of my recovery and kept my spirits high during those long days wired up to an IV. My agent from Toronto, Kevin Albrecht, flew in to be with me each day for the first three rounds of chemo. He helped me set up my computer, and I watched the entire Masters Championship from start to finish for the first time in my life. Bob Kain stopped by when he was in town. My good friends Tracy Wilson, Deb Nast, Doug and Lara Ladret and Steven Cousins visited, too. Senator John Glenn called me on my first day of chemo. I got calls from a lot of friends, including IMG Chief Mark McCormack, Fox NFL producer Bob Stenner, Wayne and Janet Gretzky, and football legend Doak Walker and his wife, Skeeter.

My younger brother, Steve, came by. He was just a couple of months shy of graduation from Ohio State. While I enjoyed his visit, I resisted overtures from the rest of my family. Sue, as well as my aunt, uncle and cousins from Boston, all wanted to come out to Cleveland. I talked them out of it. For one thing, I honestly didn't think my cancer was a life-threatening illness, which may have been a little naive on my part. It just felt silly to have a long parade of people coming through the hospital. Of course, my family was upset, and they felt I was acting selfish and inconsiderate. Maybe I was. But there was another reason, one I would have denied at the time. Frankly, I wasn't looking or feeling very good after the first couple of chemo cycles, and I didn't want people seeing me at my worst. I suppose you could say I was trying to control what was out of my control. I just wanted to roll over this cancer like a small bump in the road. The fact that they were willing to make the trip to Cleveland was enough for me.

The media wanted time as well, but I chose to keep a low profile. If I had presented myself on television looking sick, pale and drawn, that would have been counterproductive. It made more sense to talk after the fact, when I could share my experiences, not my illness. So I decided only a limited number of people would deal with me while I was going through this. Look at it this way: I never saw an Olympic gold medal until I won it. And most people won't understand cancer or what you go through until they get it themselves.

But I was fascinated and flattered by the attention my illness was getting. At first it was like a fast-moving brushfire. I'd turn on the TV, and people were talking about me being sick. There were reporters in my Englewood, Colorado, neighborhood, doing live stand-ups from the street. It was bizarre.

I'm a fan of ESPN *Sports Center*, and they usually stick to covering football, baseball, basketball and hockey. But every time Michael issued a press release on my condition, they reported it. "Whoa, this is weird," I thought when I saw my face on television. I just never looked at myself as being newsworthy on such a scale.

A few days after the story broke, I got a call from Michael. The mail was arriving at his office by the bagful. The response overwhelmed me— some sixty thousand cards and letters, including a note from former first lady Nancy Reagan. People were reaching out to me from all walks of life, sending me videos, CDs and books. There was no way in the world I could individually thank all these people for what they did and what they sent. The most important thing all that mail did for me was reinforce my optimism. When anyone gets pessimistic about the state of society, I can always attest to the kindness in people. The world, I concluded, is a wonderful place filled with incredible human beings.

One of them is my good friend Bill Daniels, the Denver cable television chief who had sent his plane for me in 1984 to bring me home for my victory parade. This time he offered to send his plane from San Diego to fly me back to Denver after my first chemo treatment. I was hesitant to take him up on his generous offer because I didn't want him to go to all that trouble, but I had all this luggage from the tour and I was still in some pain, so I accepted. With all that I was going through, I can't express how much easier that plane ride made it for me. Bill was unbelievably kind. Someday I hope I can be as thoughtful and as giving to others as he is on a daily basis. He has quietly touched many lives.

After my first week of chemo, I was anxious to get home. With a few weeks off between chemo treatments, I preferred to spend as much time in Denver as possible. I went to the Colorado Cancer Center for my Bleomicin treatments. The Bleomicin made me more ill than all the other chemicals combined. Ninety minutes to the second after the injection, I got chills and a high temperature, and was bedridden for the rest of the day. The fever would subside by nighttime. Since I got Bleomicin on Fridays only, I took to calling those days "Bleo-Fridays."

Other than that, it was very relaxing. Around the house, Karen was Florence Nightingale reincarnated. She kept the medicines straight, cooked the meals, and made sure I ate, because the antinausea medication I was taking suppressed my appetite. On the bright side, the medication kept me calm and helped me sleep. I was getting eight to twelve hours a night, an amazing amount of sleep for me.

My stays in Denver lasted sixteen days, and over the next couple of months a few close friends flew in for brief visits—Katia, Kristi, Peter Carruthers. Tom Collins flew in for one day and brought me a giant indoor tree as a gift. I keep it in my living room.

My first week back home I tried to do a little business. I was helping produce an upcoming television special, "Snowden on Ice," a heartwarming children's story about a snowman who comes to life to help a young woman skate again. Several people involved with the production flew in to consult with me—producer Gary Smith, director Dwight Hemion and Gary Tobey, media consultant with Target stores, the show's sponsor. Dwight made the trip despite having recently undergone radiation treatment for prostate cancer.

Katia was my first visitor, flying in to Denver all the way from Europe. We had dinner and I told her about my first chemo. She spent the night at our house, and then she got on a plane the next morning for a trip back east to Halifax, Nova Scotia. That was a long trip for a short visit, but I appreciated it. As I was driving her to the airport, my head started to itch. I began scratching and a large clump of hair came out of my scalp. I just looked at it, then announced, "Katia, you are the last person who is going to see me with a full head of hair. Next time I see you I'll be bald."

I returned to Cleveland on April 10 for my second cycle. The first day was spent getting a CAT scan, blood work and chest X rays, which was the routine before each cycle. By this time my hair was disappearing rapidly. It wasn't that big a deal because I had cut it super short in early March. I didn't know it at the time, but it was a preview of coming attractions. The hair wasn't just falling out of my head. You lose it over your entire body. So I decided to just get it over with and shaved it all off. Karen got a pair of scissors and a razor and we did the honors together.

Going bald wasn't a big problem for another reason—I had been dealing with a receding hairline since my amateur days in Philadelphia. I first started getting concerned after the 1980 Olympics. I was at the Camps' house in Philadelphia and noticed after I was through showering and shaving one morning that there was an unusual amount of hair left behind in the sink and bathtub. It wasn't hard to miss because I was wearing my hair very long. I started keeping track of what was left behind on my brush and watching my hairline closely. It was receding, and the pace picked up noticeably as the year went on.

Most people I knew were cool about it. Kitty didn't care at all, and I think I was more preoccupied with it than other people. I had some self-image issues to deal with, and I prayed enough stayed on my head through the 1984 Olympic games so I wouldn't look like an old man compared to the young guys coming up behind me.

My friend Brent was going through the same crisis, and we even started a contest on who would keep his hair the longest. I think he won. After a while, I just kind of accepted my fate and stopped worrying about it. Then in the late 1980s, a bald spot began appearing on the back of my head. There are only so many ways you can comb your hair before reality sets in. It was easy to cover up for shows with some strategically placed eye shadow. And I did consult a doctor at UCLA Medical Center on the latest medical treatments, but they didn't feel I was a good candidate for them. Besides, there were burdensome side effects. It's like dealing with the devil a little bit. You can do it but the price could be high.

What experience taught me was that what God intends is what God intends. Respect it, deal with it and move on. If you are five-foot-two, there's nothing you can do about it. If you're six-foot-four, there's nothing you can do about it. If you're a little heavy, there's beauty in that, and if you're meant to be very thin, there's beauty in that. That image of perfection we all aspire to applies I think to one in ten thousand people. And they're the ones modeling all the clothes in fashion magazines. I don't think I've met a person who doesn't have a list of things they have to deal with. My things just happen to be that I'm short and bald.

Anyway, I noticed after I cut it all off that if I turned my head a certain way and you squinted a little, I looked like Michael Jordan.

Of course, losing your hair is the least of your worries when you're fighting cancer. At first chemotherapy wasn't the physical burden I had expected, but being cooped up in the same room for four days was driving me crazy. By the end of my second cycle, I couldn't wait to get out of the hospital to go home. Karen and I had reservations for a 6:30 P.M. flight to Chicago, so we rushed to the Cleveland airport, flew to O'Hare, and then connected to a plane to Denver. As we settled into our seats, a flight attendant gently touched my arm to get my attention. "I sent you a card. I don't know if you'll get it, but I wanted you to know we're all pulling for you."

"Thanks," I said.

After we were airborne, I began reflecting on my week. I remember thinking that the second chemo was a breeze, except for the hated

Bleomicin therapy. I looked at Karen and said, "I'm good at cancer. I can do this." I was confident that the treatment was not going to drag me down.

You get all kinds of weather in Denver during the month of April, but when we returned home from the second chemo, the weather was unseasonably warm. I spent almost every afternoon at Bear Creek Golf Club hitting some golf balls. I loved wandering over the course alone in a golf cart, playing imaginary tournaments to keep up my interest. The club is set by the foothills, with amazing views of downtown Denver. And in the middle of the week, the course was quiet and uncrowded. Sometimes I was joined by the club mascot, a golden retriever named Duffer. He was a terrific caddie, jumping into the streams and running through the sand traps. My golf pro, Dennis Murray, sometimes joined me, and there were days when I just sat in his office and talked. Golf was about all the physical activity my doctors would allow. Skating was out of the question because they feared the chemotherapy could affect my balance. So I filled myself with golf. To get out and hit balls, go for a walk or a ride and take in the beautiful surroundings, was like a mental massage. And as my strength improved, my handicap dropped from fourteen to ten.

But the nice weather that greeted us when I returned from Cleveland turned ugly, and when it started snowing in April, I got antsy around the house and decided to take a trip to Los Angeles. I needed the sunshine. I checked into a hotel by Sherwood Country Club north of Los Angeles and played many a round of golf. One day I was playing with my agent, Kevin Albrecht, producer John Brunton and actor Kevin Nealon. On the first tee, I asked Albrecht, "How many strokes are you going to give me?" He said, "The same as usual." "Kevin," I yelled, "I'm dying of cancer! You have to give me something!"

It was on that trip to Los Angeles that I stopped by a local coffee shop, ordered a cup, and found I couldn't stand the taste of it anymore. There were other changes that surprised me. Beer was out—the thought of drinking one made me sick. On the other hand, Popsicles became the greatest thing ever. Jell-O, which I had despised, turned into the greatest food in the world. I had heard women have unusual food cravings when they're pregnant, and now I completely understood what they were going through. Things I never ate in my life, I suddenly couldn't get enough of. For the most part, I tried to stick to my normal diet of meat, pasta and salads.

I also stopped by my friends' Wayne and Janet Gretzky's house. I was sitting in their living room talking about chemo when their nine-year-old daughter, Paulina, walked in and did a double take. "What happened to your hair?" she asked innocently. I laughed and thought, "Kids are so honest and forthcoming." I told her I was taking medicine that made it all fall out. Then we took turns explaining why I was sick. It was the first time I had had to explain to a child what cancer was, and it felt good educating Paulina about the disease.

When I returned to Denver after my Los Angeles trip, Karen and I changed the flower beds in the backyard and planted some shrubs. I settled into domestic life big-time. I spent time at the computer, E-mailing friends and using the Internet.

My big home improvement project was cleaning out the garage and power spraying the cement floor with a high pressure washer. Then I reorganized all the bedroom closets and the storage areas. I sent eight bags of old clothes to Goodwill—caps, shoes, T-shirts, golf shirts, pants, shorts. I found stuff I hadn't worn in ten years.

There were generous offers I had to turn down, like two play-off tickets to watch the Colorado Avalanche play the Detroit Redwings. Adam Deadmarsh, a player on the Avalanche, had invited me, but since my white blood cell counts were bottomed out by the chemo, I was susceptible to illness. Sitting in an arena with 17,000 people was an invitation to get sick if I ever saw one.

As time went by, my energy level fell off and I started feeling sick. I'd take the antinausea medication—Adivan, Compezine or Kytrol—and all I really felt like doing after that was sleeping. I also had to give myself injections of Nupogen to bring up my white blood cell count. At the end of each day, Karen or I took the medication out of the refrigerator, let it warm to room temperature and loaded up the syringe, then I injected it in my stomach area or at the top of my leg. If I did it incorrectly, it could be painful and potentially messy.

The one thing I did take advantage of during my time off was catching up on the sleep I had missed out on in the past ten years. As long as I had cancer and couldn't skate or tour, I was going to sleep in and take afternoon naps—because I knew that when it was over, I would have to work harder than ever before to get back in shape.

Kristi was my second visitor in Denver, and she arrived in late April to spend a couple of days with me and Karen. We had been talking on the phone, so I had a chance to brace her for my appearance. While I still felt strong after the second chemo and Bleomicin treatments, I wasn't sure how Kristi might react to my hairless appearance. Kristi, great friend that she is, was cool about it. We mostly hung out, watching movies, listening to music and talking about friends. After two days she was worried she might be wearing me out and wondered if she should leave. Stick around, I said, and I persuaded her to stay another day. Of course, that was Bleo-Friday, and I crashed for the entire day while Kristi and Karen went out shopping.

In the first week of May, I returned to Cleveland for the third chemo cycle. The doctors had warned me that the third treatment would be terrible, and they were right. This chemo treatment was the pits. A lot had changed in three weeks. I had left Cleveland feeling optimistic, but this time around I was tired, and it only got worse. Knowing there was one more cycle to go even after this one left me feeling depressed. It was all starting to beat me down a little. I didn't feel like doing much except lying around and watching videos. I finished on May 6 and was thrilled to fly back home.

By my last chemo, I had become a bald and bleached 135-pound slug. I flew into Cleveland on May 21 for a consultation and my usual X rays and scans. After they started up the chemo the next day, I barely moved for several days. Even on days the doctors gave me the green light to leave the hospital, I never bothered. I was absolutely drained. Fortunately it was the last time, and as I kept telling myself and Karen all week, I could do anything for the last time. On May 27, they unplugged me from the IV, Mary gave me a hug, Karen helped me pack and I left the hospital for home.

I was a happy camper flying to Denver that night. There was one last Bleo-Friday to endure on May 30, but that was it. That week I went out and had my car washed in Englewood. A lady walked up behind me and whispered, "I'm going through chemotherapy right now." Cancer survivors approached me frequently, and I was gaining a true understanding of the fear individuals go through and the camaraderie they share with other survivors.

A large part of my treatment was over, but the most difficult stage of recovery was yet to come: surgery. It was set for June 24, and would keep me laid up for several weeks. Time for more golf. Before leaving for L.A., Peter Carruthers, who was in Denver on business, came by for a day. We got some great weather and spent the afternoon just hanging in my backyard, chipping golf balls into the pool and listening to music.

A week before my operation, I packed up my golf bag and headed back to Sherwood. When I returned to Denver, I enjoyed my last decent hearty meals—burgers and Chinese—because I had to fast two days prior to surgery. Doctors feared that any food in my intestinal tract would make me really sick if they had to make an incision there. They wanted the tank completely empty, just like an airplane about to make a dangerous landing.

Two days before the operation, I flew to Cleveland and checked into the clinic. They prepped me the next day, and then the following morning at 6:30 A.M., I was wheeled into surgery. Dr. Klein had said the procedure would take four to six hours. Terrified as I was, I had confidence in Dr. Klein, and knowing I was in talented and experienced hands, and that this procedure was as routine to them as a double Axel was to me, made me feel much better.

I remember moving onto a gurney and lying in a hallway outside the operating room, feeling cold and ambivalent. I asked for some extra blankets, which warmed up my feet but not my soul. Everyone else seemed so relaxed, and then it occurred to me that this was, after all, their day job. I don't imagine they would feel comfortable skating in front of fifteen thousand people. I closed my eyes for a moment and visualized this tumor finally leaving my body. Dr. Klein came over to say hello and I was introduced to the anesthesiologist. A minute later I was in surgery, encircled by all these masked faces in blue and white. Above me were bright surgical lights, and rock music played in the background, the kind I like to hear when I psych myself up for a performance. After I was given an epidural, someone gently put a mask over my face and asked me to breathe in deeply. I pictured myself as a product on a conveyor belt, reasoning that since nothing had happened to the guys before me, there was no purpose in panicking now. I closed my eyes and stayed focused on the positive. Then I fell fast asleep.

Dr. Klein cut an incision just below my sternum to an inch above my groin, making a U turn around my navel. The doctors moved my intestines so they could get at the tumor lodged underneath. When they found it, they saw that the chemo had shrunk it to the size of a golf ball. Dr. Klein removed the tumor and my lymph nodes. A second incision was made near my appendix. From there they extracted my right testicle by pressuring it up through my inguinal canal and out the incision. Later, Dr. Klein told me that the testicle showed no sign of cancer, just scar tissue. My left testicle was in perfect condition.

When I awoke, I actually felt refreshed. "Wow," I said to a nurse. "It's over already." I wasn't hurting at all, thanks to the anesthesia. There were dressings over my incisions but I couldn't feel them. My body was numb. As they wheeled me out of recovery, I started feeling a little mischievous. I spied a doctor writing at a desk, and as we passed him, I grabbed on to his chair and started rolling him with me. He traveled backward about ten feet before he figured out what was happening.

Once I was settled in my hospital room, Dr. Klein came by and told me the surgery was a success. "That's a relief," I said. "I guess I don't have to worry about having a high singing voice anymore, right?" We had a laugh together, and it was nice to see Dr. Klein relax and smile.

The next day the nurses told me it was soon going to be time to stand up. Alone in my room, I got to my feet and felt myself tilting as everything around me started going dark. I closed my eyes, caught my breath and tried to catch my balance. A nurse came in and figured out right away what was happening, and then she let me have it, big-time. Yes, I was supposed to stand up, but not without help, she scolded.

I remained in the hospital for eight days. The anesthesia wore off after twenty-four hours, and the pain in my abdomen kicked in. Not only could I not walk; I couldn't even sit up in bed.

This was the worst of the entire ordeal. I ate no solid food for ten days. My body was essentially shut down because my intestines had been moved aside to make room to get at the tumor. It was as if my organs had gone to sleep and it was going to be a few days before they woke up and got working again. After a week, they removed thirty-eight staples from my abdomen, which made a heck of a nice-looking scar. Then I went back to Denver to rest for several weeks.

At home, my appetite continued to shrink and my energy reached an all-time low. I force-fed myself to keep up my weight, supplementing my diet with high-calorie drinks loaded with nutrients, like Ensure mixed with ice cream and chocolate. I went down to about 118 pounds, and my goal became to get back to 125 pounds of muscle weight. My stamina was gone, too. Since my body was purging itself of all the chemicals and anesthesia, my recovery was going to take some time.

This was a major setback to me, since I didn't know when my body would come around. I was trying to figure out what I was going to do for the rest of the year, and I had hoped skating would be part of the plan. Now I wasn't so sure. Finally, about three weeks after the surgery, I felt energy and mobility gradually return. It also dawned on me that despite this huge scar on my chest, I was in some ways healthier than ever before. At the very least, I was well rested, thanks to not killing myself with lack of sleep and endless travel. Ever since the 1984 Olympics, I had been going nonstop. In the fourteenth year of my career, I got cancer and took a break. That was how I looked at it.

About a month after my surgery, I was feeling up for more visitors and invited Kristi out for her second visit. I had been working on my tan, and my hair was starting to grow back, so I wasn't nearly as scary-looking as I had been in April. When I picked her up from the airport, I reached for her bags and she tried to take them away. "Don't pick up the luggage," she scolded like a mother hen. She was terrified my scar was going to split open right there in front of her. I told her not to worry, and I threw her things in my car.

We had a nice time in Denver and we did some serious talking about my future. I had decided I wanted to tour again, but the only way I wanted to skate was if I could handle a full schedule. I didn't want to do guest spots, because we had tried that before with other skaters and it was a hardship on the cast. But I also wasn't going to be content with just showing up for the sake of being there and hearing the applause. I would have hurt the tour and I'd never want to do that. It was either skate up to my standards or not skate at all.

Kristi was supportive, and spending those few days with her convinced me I needed to get back on the ice and give it a shot. I knew I couldn't rush it, but what crystallized in my mind was that skating again wasn't merely a goal to accomplish; it would be a vital part of my recovery. Not skating was conceding to the disease, and I wasn't about to let that happen. So I called my choreographer, Sarah Kawahara, and told her to be ready. I was coming out to Los Angeles to begin training on August 9.

It was probably the most painful five days of my life, but I survived. More than that, I made progress and saw there was a flicker of hope of regaining my skills. I just had to be patient. While in Los Angeles for my workouts, I did an interview with *Dateline* and Maria Shriver and she came to Simi Valley one day to watch me practice. I did some minor jumps and a few spins and she said, "Aw, you look fine; it looks great." I thanked her and appreciated the gesture, but I wanted it *all* back—triple jumps, back flip and blinding scratch spins. I wasn't settling for anything less.

In addition to working myself back into shape, I did an acting role in the "Snowden" TV special I was coproducing. I played Scootch, the elderly Zamboni driver who narrates the story. It required spending about two weeks in heavy makeup that made me resemble an old man. Katia and Daria were the stars of the show, and when Daria saw me for the first time, she didn't recognize me and refused to come near me—which was a problem, since we had to do a couple of scenes together. It took a day or two for Daria to get used to my makeup. After that, my only problem was getting used to being exhausted all the time, because that became my perpetual state, thanks to the eighteen-hour days on the set.

My close friends were worried that I was tackling too much too soon.

While people were generally supportive, there were whispers that I was crazy taking on so much after chemo and surgery. "Scott, just take the year off and get your health back," they'd say. "Take a break. No one deserves it more than you."

I wasn't going to hear of it. Tired or not, I had already made up my mind that the only way I could win my battle with cancer was to make a comeback this year. Some people were worried the cancer might return and said I shouldn't take on too much until I was 100 percent. Well, I also knew I might never be 100 percent again, so what was the point of taking the year off? I wasn't thinking about a recurrence. My mind-set was to think about what *could* happen, not what *can* happen. What *can* happen is that the cancer comes back. What *could* happen is I never see this thing again. And what *could* happen is that I work my posterior off and get back into great shape. In my view, the worst-case scenario would be doing chemo all over again. If I got through it once, I could get through it again. I wasn't going to stop living just to guard against a recurrence.

That was the attitude I took entering the 1998 season, which on paper appeared to be one of my toughest years yet. The usual pile of invitations to do pro competitions and other TV specials had been on the table, but I had to be realistic. As much as I might have wanted to, I could not physically do everything. So early on, I decided I would do no pro competitions. That was not as big a sacrifice as it might seem, since I would have had trouble beating a good six-year-old. Well, with my competition experience, I just might have been able to edge that six-year-old!

I also decided to limit my appearances to the "Snowden" show and a comeback special CBS wanted to air to honor my return to skating, and which I wanted to organize to raise money for the Cleveland Clinic's new Taussig Cancer Center. Those projects aside, I narrowed my priorities to two jobs—touring with "Stars" and covering the Nagano Olympics for CBS. Unfortunately, the Olympics would sideline me for three weeks in February, right in the middle of the tour, and once we were back, the schedule was grueling: eleven shows in the first thirteen nights. That was a potential backbreaker, especially if I couldn't get any ice time in Nagano. I decided to deal with it as it came. One day at a time.

As the "Snowden" production was winding down in late August, I was feeling so drained I wondered if I had the energy to survive a winter of touring and commentating. Yet there were worse fates than being tired all the time. While standing around on the ice one morning waiting to do a scene, I was talking with two old friends—Lisa Marie Allen and

Aimee Kravette—skaters who had come up with me in my amateur days. They were lamenting that they were on the downside of thirty, and after listening to them moan and groan for a couple of minutes, I had to interrupt. "Hey," I said. "Getting old sure beats the alternative."

Chapter Twenty-Two

Departing Neverland

On August 28, 1997, I celebrated my thirty-ninth birthday with friends at Crustacean, a nice Beverly Hills seafood restaurant. I had spent the week producing and performing in the "Snowden on Ice" TV special, and while the hours had tired me out, it had given me some hope; I was starting to feel like myself again.

And yet my good mood was tempered by sadness. I couldn't help thinking about all the others, the people who didn't survive cancer, like my mother and Dr. Klepner. I was alive and they were gone. This disease is so random and fickle. I was truly lucky to be able to celebrate my birthday five months after my diagnosis, with the relative certainty of more birthdays to come, knock on wood. Still, I felt guilty.

It was at this dinner party that it occurred to me that all the while I was fighting this disease, I never gave myself a chance to take my situation as seriously as I should have. I had cancer, for goodness' sake. Even though my cancer was curable, there was always the chance that this thing could get out of control and threaten my life, but I never allowed that thought to enter my mind. I was obsessed with getting my health and strength back to where I was before, and anything less was totally unacceptable. Maybe this state of denial was the intelligent attitude to take. But the truth was that my livelihood had been in jeopardy. I knew I could skate again, but that I might never be the same skater. There's an old saying: "You can run but you can't hide." That was my relationship with cancer. I kept trying to dodge the fact that this disease had invaded my body, but it kept hitting me over the head wherever I turned. No matter how scared I was, I was determined to put up a strong front. But there was nowhere to run anymore. Now that I was trying to get back to my old form, the toll it had taken on my body was undeniable, and that left me feeling depressed.

The main question hanging over my head was whether I could ever skate the way I wanted to again. After those first practice sessions in Simi Valley with Sarah, I had my doubts. The chemotherapy and surgery had weakened my body, and that was devastating. It had turned the clock back on my skating by a good twenty-five years, as far as my skill level was concerned, and no amount of pretending was going to change that. As a result, my practices were inconsistent. One day I would feel great and Sarah and I would get a lot done. The next day I would be horrible, and on the next, I'd perform somewhere in between. Only I was having more bad days than good, and that was freaking me out.

That was when I figured out that the cancer doesn't want you to win. And defeating it was going to take all the energy I could muster.

I didn't share these thoughts with anyone at my party. I was surrounded by a great group of friends and didn't want to dwell on the negative all night. In fact, I had much to be thankful for. When you get sick, you see things in people you never saw before. They rise to the occasion in ways even they didn't know they were capable of. There was Karen, the best nurse-in-training anyone could ever have. Kevin Albrecht, John Brunton, Jef Billings, Katia and Daria, Deb Nast, Michael Sterling, Disney executive Paul Villadolid and others—all of them were here with me tonight and all of them had come through for me in a trying year. I was touched by their care and the effort people made. But I also felt guilty; I'm a better host than a guest, and I didn't feel worthy of all this attention. But this was one time I had to let others take control and offer support, and I eventually accepted that. I believe my low point came during the third round of chemo, when I contemplated whether it was worth going through all this. I felt like unplugging the IV and walking out of there. I had turned into this bald, puffy, depressed creature, and I must have been insufferable to be around. Yet my friends hung in there with me. After I survived that week, I knew I could endure the rest of the treatment.

Hey, not everybody gets a chance to sit in the front row of their own funeral. But that was what it felt like on some days. The support and the love I received from others were every bit as healing as the chemicals swirling around in my body. People were that caring. Whether it was my good friend Steven Cousins flying in from Canada with a boxful of comic Rowan Atkinson's *Black Adder* videos for us to watch, or a sympathetic phone call from Dorothy Hamill, who reached out to me despite our differences, all of the gestures were amazing. It made me feel thankful to be alive; I got a chance to thank everyone and remember the best in them.

So on the night of my birthday dinner, I raised a glass of champagne and made a toast: "To life and great friends."

That same night, Michael Sterling gave me a special birthday present: a framed copy of the *People* magazine cover story on my cancer ordeal. It was a bit of irony that for someone who didn't want to talk at all at the beginning, I wound up telling the world about my experience. I had received a lot of support for being open, but if I had not gotten well, I never would have publicly discussed my disease. It would have remained private. I'm not one to promote myself for being sick. Reporters had been wanting to talk to me since the day I was diagnosed, and Michael suggested that I consider doing a couple of interviews, but I wanted to talk only when I was well again and could give other patients a reason to hope.

So in August, I stepped back into the public eye, did the *People* story and appeared on *Dateline*. That was the first good look people had had of me since I'd gotten sick the previous March. Of course, what little hair I had left was gone, but even worse, so was my muscle tone. Man, there were days I glanced in the mirror and didn't like what I saw. "Will this body ever be able to perform the way it did?" I wondered.

I needed to get back in shape because my comeback television special was moving full speed ahead, even if I wasn't. I had so many people to thank—the sixty thousand who sent cards and letters. I couldn't possibly write them all back personally. So we came up with the idea of doing the special. A skating show seemed like an ideal way to reach the maximum number of people and at the same time raise money for a worthy cause: fighting cancer. The Cleveland Clinic was building a new center and I wanted to help, even if I knew I couldn't deliver a perfect performance.

I set a deadline for the show—late October—and we booked the Great Western Forum in Los Angeles. Then we got to work. I was not merely going to show up and wave to the crowd. I had a clear vision of what I wanted to do on the ice, and I felt I could get there with help from Sarah. We put together a routine to the song "With One More Look at You." It was a song I felt strongly about for a long time. It's from the movie, *A Star Is Born*, which came out around the time my mother died. In the film, the character portrayed by Kris Kristofferson writes a song just before he dies and his wife, played by Barbra Streisand, finds the tape of the song, finishes writing it and then sings it in the last scene of the movie. It had always reminded me of my mother, and I'd always wanted to skate to it in her memory. Now seemed like the perfect time; I had beat the disease that took away the most important person in my life.

I asked my good friend Gary Morris to sing it so I could skate to his familiar and powerful voice. The song title said it all I wanted one more chance to see and thank those who had supported me all these years.

We titled the special *Back on the Ice,* and I invited as many close friends to skate with me as I could. We were limited by budget and airtime, so I tried not to put any pressure on anyone to perform. CBS, which was broadcasting the show, was giving us only an hour of airtime, and I warned everyone in advance that while they would each get to perform a solo, there was no guarantee CBS would air it. But the entire group— Brian Orser, Brian Boitano, Katarina Witt, Kristi, Roz, Katia, Paul and Kurt—cared enough to perform anyway.

On show night, I was a nervous wreck in a way I had never known before. I was starting over from a medical nightmare in which my body had been napalmed and undergone radical surgery. I had been off the ice for five months and had just gotten back my double Axel. And for almost the entire show—ninety minutes in all—I sat with Karen in a front row seat . . . and then had to go out and skate!

The cast of skaters opened the show with Kenny G performing live; Jane Seymour was the perfect choice as emcee, and when Kristi skated to Olivia Newton–John singing "I Honestly Love You," I nearly lost it right there.

I must admit, the highlight of the night was seeing my friends perform to many of the off-the-wall character numbers I had done, right down to the old costumes. I was forewarned that this was going to be part of the show, yet I had no clue who would do what routine. And it was hilarious. They all opened to "Hair," and then they came out one by one. Roz mimicked my Olympic exhibition routine, "You Always Hurt the One You Love," in a replica of the red, white and blue unitard I wore in Sarajevo. Good thing Roz lives on a Stairmaster, because that costume was pretty tight.

Paul did my old comedy number to "Sabre Dance"; Brian Orser did "Cuban Pete"; Katia skated to "I Love Me"; Kristi performed to "When I'm Sixty-Four"; and Kurt did "Walk This Way," the number that won me the '94 "Gold Championship." The highlight of the night was Brian Boitano doing the wacky chicken number Neil Carpenter choreographed for me back in 1977. What a gas! Mr. Dramatic Skater dressed up like a big chicken! I was amazed, but Brian had agreed to do the show only on the condition that he got to do that program—chicken costume and all.

For more than an hour, I watched from the edge of my seat, and then it was time to go backstage to change; it was my turn to skate. I tried to stay calm and focused, but I had never been so nervous. I'm usually in top form when I skate in public, but I was still only about 50 percent, and the last thing I wanted to do was embarrass myself.

After I got dressed—navy blue pants and white shirt—I made my way to the ice. There were more than ten thousand people in the audience, and I was anxious to do well. I wanted to make a statement that I was healthy again and on my way back, even after being on the ice for only two months.

As I took the ice, the audience gave me a huge lift. They were on their feet and applauding. I remembered the boisterous crowd that had un-nerved me in Sarajevo, but here it gave me strength; I was thrilled and inspired as I tried to soak up the energy. Nerves set in when I reached center ice. Then as soon as I heard Gary's voice, I relaxed and knew I could lean on Gary the rest of the way. I'm not sure what people were ex-pecting, but they were cheering every step I took. Usually I'm doing the work to reach the audience. That night I felt they were trying to inspire me. They were working as hard as they could to help me get through the program. I was able to hit two double Axels cleanly, but the triple-toe at-tempt was probably a mistake. I had been landing only one out of every two; oh well, this wasn't a night to hold back. I wanted to put it all out there. I went for it and fell. That's okay, I thought. Tonight wasn't about skating a perfect program; it was about skating, period. I could console myself knowing there was only one "first time," and the next one would be a lot easier after this. And I was determined to make sure that there would be a next time. Whew, I said to myself. I had skated respectably after all and I was fired up about that.

But that wasn't the sole purpose of the night. I was here to show how grateful I was for the love and support I received all spring and summer.

When I was finished, I was completely out of gas and my emotions just came pouring out. I looked around and everyone was on their feet and my eyes welled up with tears. I skated over to the side and grabbed a micro-phone. I knew exactly what I wanted to say.

"I win," I announced to the crowd.

My voice was quavering as I spoke. "So much tonight has been said about me, but tonight was all about *us*. Tonight was about control, and getting back on the ice so everyone sitting in a hospital right now with an IV bag hooked in their arm knows there is an end in sight. Tonight is also a thank you to all the people who worked sixteen jobs to put themselves through medical school to create the next miracle for all of us. It's all about us because with your participation and desire we can rid this planet of cancer so none of our families ever have to deal with it again."

I let out a deep breath, but I wasn't finished. Adrenaline was rushing through my body. "Tonight wasn't about being at my best, or being 100 percent—it was never about being 100 percent," I said. I pointed to the lights surrounding the rink, the ones that let skaters know where the edge of the ice is. "It was about standing between these little orange, green and red lights and having the greatest view in the world. Olivia, Jane, Kenny, Kurt, Paul, Paul, Brian, Brian, Roz, Katia, Kristi, Katarina and Gary, wherever you are, you big lug—you stuck with me all year and now I'm back. I'm in such a good mood right now! But I wouldn't be truly back"— at that moment, I began skating across the rink; I reached back and threw a back flip, hitting it cleanly with the microphone still in hand— "without this!" I yelled. Then I waved my pals onto the ice. "It's party time," I whooped.

A few weeks later, I was back in Cleveland receiving the first of my quarterly checkups—just to make sure none of those critters reappeared in my body. It was a familiar routine—chest X ray, blood workup, CAT scan, the whole deal. It was not something I would ever come to look forward to, but I decided to look upon it as a class reunion. Each time I came back I would look up the people who took care of me during the chemo treatments and surgery: Dr. Klein and Dr. Bukowski, administrator Ruth Studer and nurses Laura Wood, Mary Brinkman and Diane Shiesley. I got a clean bill of health after my first checkup, and then it was off to Lake Placid for the final rehearsals for "Stars on Ice."

One solo I was planning for the tour was giving me a little trouble— "The Show Must Go On." The theme was an actor showing up to perform in the MGM classic The Wizard of Oz and learning on the spot that no one else has shown up to work, and he must play all the parts—nine separate characters in all. It was my most ambitious program ever. We began rehearsing what I thought was a four-minute-and-thirty-second program, only it was leaving me drained after each run-through. I never did bother to time the program myself until I did a dress rehearsal under lights so Sarah could work the bugs out. I asked a crew member, Dave

Hoffis, to put a stopwatch on me. So I did the number, including costume changes, and at the end, gasping for air once more, I looked over and got the bad news. "Six-eighteen, boss," Dave said. Over six minutes? Was I crazy? I was convinced it had to be a mistake. Sarah was just as surprised as I was.

"I thought it was four and half," she said. Of course, the CD version did say 6:18, but I didn't believe the information was accurate. I was not about to gut the program, so Sarah and I decided to keep it as it was.

The tour began in earnest after Christmas, and I was pleasantly surprised that I was building my endurance at a nice pace. During the first week of January, I hit my first triple Lutz in practice. My strength was improving every day, and when we arrived in Los Angeles a week later, I felt I was on the verge of skating a clean program. While performing "With One More Look At You" at the Anaheim Pond, I did just that, nailing every jump in the program. No wobbles, no hands down on the ice. Perfectly clean. I felt like every step I took was where it was supposed to be; it came as naturally as before the cancer. Near the end of the music, my eyes welled with tears.

"I can do this. I can skate," I thought. In that moment, my confidence was restored. All the hard work, pain and frustration I had felt since returning to the ice in August were finally paying off, and I was ecstatic. The tour's costume designer, Jef Billings, was sitting in the front row, and when I looked over at him, I could tell from the joyous expression on his face that he knew exactly what was happening. It was a very emotional night. I came off the ice, and Katia and Kristi embraced me—they knew what this meant to me. It was like a rebirth, and it happened all at once. Suddenly I could skate again.

The next day we played the Great Western Forum, always one of the biggest shows on tour. My legs felt great and I hit my Lutz again. For the next couple of weeks I got stronger, and when the first leg of the tour closed in Omaha, Nebraska, I attempted every single planned triple in both of my solos. I went for broke, and while I made a few mistakes, I felt I was almost there, almost all the way back.

Then my momentum came to a halt. In the first week of February, I left for Japan to cover the Olympics. The timing could not have been worse for me. Nagano was a nice city with beautiful facilities, but there was no ice for me to skate on. The nearest available rink was two hours away, and our Japanese hosts wouldn't allow me or any other skaters covering the games to practice on the Olympic rinks because they were afraid we'd ruin the ice. The Japanese officials allowed club hockey teams and their children to use the practice ice, but the pro skaters working the games, like Roz, Kristi and me, were denied. Incredible. I had been allowed to skate a little in Albertville and had access to an outdoor rink in Norway, but in Nagano there was nothing. I got completely out of shape on the job, not a huge problem under normal circumstances, but the past year had been anything but normal

Doing the games, moreover, was exhausting. Skating events were scheduled every other day, and on those days we were working twenty-two-hour shifts. We did live reporting in the morning and covered the competition on tape delay at night. On my days off, I was going to practices and doing research. The bad weather made it even worse because the cancellation of skiing events meant more skating coverage. I was looking wan, which caused people a lot of concern. But the worst was not being able to skate, or even exercise. When I returned to the U.S. feeling jet-lagged, my legs had atrophied, and my confidence was shot. I arrived in Minneapolis on February 23, skated for the first time in three weeks on the next day, and did the first show on February 25. The topper was we were booked in eleven cities in the first thirteen days.

In Minneapolis, Kristi and I had dinner with Tom Collins and I actually mentioned the R word—retirement. I was feeling so tired in Nagano that I had brought up the possibility to IMG. Maybe it was time to kick back and lie on the beach for a while, but a lot would depend on how I finished out the tour.

In those first eleven tour dates after Japan, I worked as hard as I could, but it was a struggle and I skated far below my expectations. I was missing so many triples, I cut everything down to doubles. It came down to strength and timing, and I didn't have it. The audiences were very forgiving. They seemed to be saying, "You've been through a lot—we're going to be nonjudgmental." And that kind of support was sorely needed by me.

I got the picture that for them it wasn't about the jumps; it was about spending an evening together. I did not want to take the joy out of the experience, so I kept my head up even though I knew they deserved better. Of course, I was frustrated and wanted to perform as well as I had in January, but that goal was unrealistic after the layoff. I couldn't hold myself to that level of skating any longer. I think more than one skater caught me in the dressing room talking to myself. But the cast was cool about it. Dejected as I was backstage, I tried not to show my disappointment in front of the crowd. They were electric, and I could never allow my mediocre skating to overshadow the positive feelings I got by being able to share the night with them.

I felt that on my first day back in the United States after the Olympics. After arriving in Minneapolis, I had transformed into a walking zombie, exhausted from the flight from Nagano. I was trying to stay up to avoid sleeping all day and lying awake at night. During a stroll through the hotel lobby, I bumped into some people from ABC, who were doing a site survey for the upcoming World Championships in March. Guess who was with them, they said: ABC director Doug Wilson, my old friend who directed the coverage of the Olympics in Sarajevo. He was the same man who had warned me life would never be the same after winning a gold medal. Sure enough, back in my room, there was a message from Doug to meet him downstairs.

"I have something to show you," he said.

Doug's first wife, Debbie, had died of cancer. When I heard she passed away I sent a donation to Doug's church, and he was very touched. He knew about my mother and how important she was in my life. We had a bond—we had both lost someone we loved to cancer.

When I met him in the lobby, he had great news. "I got remarried," he said, and then held out his left hand to show me his wedding band. Have you ever gotten that feeling when you can't breathe? Where the air has gone out of the room and you literally lose your breath? That was what happened to me when I saw Doug's ring. His wedding band was a tiny gold version of the woven wristband I wore for years in memory of my mother.

"You inspired me to make it like this so I could always remember my first wife."

"Doug, I don't know what to say," I replied. A lump was stuck in my throat, and I was so overcome with emotion I couldn't speak anymore. Even though Doug had moved on to a different part of his life, he was acknowledging that Debbie would always be a part of him, even in his new marriage. It was the most beautiful compliment I ever received.

It's a funny thing about loss. It never goes away, but life does move on. Sometimes I deal with it just fine, and on other days I feel empty and depressed about the people who've left me. I miss my mother and father every day. I miss Frank McLoraine every day. I miss Sergei. And yet I think I'm one of the luckiest people on earth. I'm still skating, still making a living in a job I love and still beating cancer. I was touched by what Doug did, and flattered that something I had done had inspired him. You go through life and have no idea of the kind of impact you have on people until moments like this. So I reminded myself not to forget that no matter how bad I'm feeling, I have something to offer people beyond skating.

Part of me had wished I could come through this cancer and return to normal, just skate this season as though nothing had happened. The doctors warned me it would take time, that the damage from the chemicals and surgery would not heal overnight. But I was defiant.

I'm still defiant. But if I'm not the same skater anymore, that's okay, too. It's an incredible world out there, and I'd survive without skating. Yes, I know someday it will end. Perhaps now I'm better equipped to deal with that reality. I've reinvented myself before, and I can do it again.

Epilogue

Someday it will all be open.

Someday we will throw away the terms *sanctioned* and *nonsanctioned* competitions, and Olympic *eligible* and *ineligible* skaters. Every four years the Olympic trials will take on all comers, just like the qualifying events in track and field and skiing.

The two worlds in skating—eligible and ineligible—will merge, and then the basic question will be, Who will control the skaters and their ability to earn money? Who will govern skating? Who will make the rules and oversee the numerous competitions taking place each year?

Since the sport spans the globe, the International Skating Union would be the logical choice, but not in its current form. Though the ISU has a high regard for pro skating, I'm uncertain whether an inherently volunteer organization can handle the responsibility, especially with the lure of big money and everything that comes with it. One only need look at the International Olympic Committee scandal to size up the potential problems in all international governing bodies.

One of the solutions to restructuring organizations like the IOC and the ISU is to introduce athletes and coaches to the memberships. In the IOC, there is a great deal of reform needed for the representatives in place, including term limits, abolishing tenure of officials, and establishing a code of ethics. The volunteers should get in, do their time and pass the responsibility on to the next generation. The IOC was meant to advance Olympic ideals, like sportsmanship and the appreciation of different cultures. Who better to nurture tomorrow's champions than those who have been down the same path?

The ISU has the same responsibility for skating: to uphold the integrity of the sport. Perhaps the ISU could serve in the same capacity as the United States Golf Association, which oversees amateur golf and runs one of the premier events in the game, the U.S. Open, which allows both amateur and professional champions to compete. The ISU could keep its world championships yet open them up, in the same way the USGA opens up the U.S. Open to professionals. That way eligible skaters would explore other opportunities without having the door locked behind them for good. And an ISU membership that included more active coaches and athletes might support a change in that direction.

Of course, decisions on rules and how to judge competitions of the future should be among the issues open for discussion. One problem is that many of the best skaters around the globe are forced to miss the world championships because they don't qualify at their nationals. Why shouldn't more skaters be invited to worlds? If the United States has half a dozen men who medaled in an international competition, they all should be entitled to enter the qualifying round. It doesn't make sense for any country to be restricted to a maximum of three skaters for each discipline if they have more skaters who can be competitive. Meanwhile, other member countries get to send skaters to worlds now who can barely do triples.

Another issue is foreign skaters training in the United States and Canada for eleven months out of the year and then returning to their home countries for a month in order to represent them at worlds. I don't think that develops skating in those countries if the best skaters are gone most of the year. That type of freedom should be restricted.

Though I don't advocate any specific changes in men's skating, I must say I don't care for the emphasis on jumps—six different triples and at least one quad in a variety of combinations—at the expense of everything else. Many of today's male skaters are awesome leapers, but they don't have the audience appeal and creativity of the skaters of the past. Fine edge work, footwork, spins and audience interaction are becoming a lost art because skaters are too preoccupied with their jumps. And there are so many jumps having to be squeezed into a program, routines are starting to look the same, and the skaters are losing the individuality that makes this sport so great. The men today don't connect with audiences as they did in the past. You win by staying on your feet. Does that make the skating enjoyable to watch? Depends on the individual. But I don't believe I could have found the time to develop an individual style if I had to worry about getting a consistent triple Axel and a couple of quads.

Another development in skating that deserves watching is the representation factor. Skaters need to take more control of their future. You are responsible for your own career. Any skaters or young athletes reading this book have got to understand that an agent is not a rainmaker. You have to ask questions and know what your goals and priorities are. That's what I think is lost on a lot of these kids today. They're under a lot of pressure to sign with an agent early on or else they're left to feel nothing is going to happen for them. Whether they're better off is an open question. As they mature in the sport, representation is necessary, but I don't think it's something that should be rushed into. They should use the same care in picking an agent or manager as in picking a coach.

Nowadays it is common for an agency to pay a skater to be its client; well, that means that the relationship is in their best interest, not yours. Some of the larger agencies are offering long-term five-figure deals to skaters who haven't even won anything yet. They are gambling on the skaters' potential. If the skater hits it big, they already own the prize.

Remember, agencies are not paying you out of the kindness of their heart. It's a business deal. They may be willing to make less the first few years, but it also means they may have less to offer you than somebody of integrity who says, "All I'm going to offer you is my ability."

I'm concerned by many of the agent-skater relationships I see now. Some of the kids have put their careers totally into the hands of their agents. It's as though the skaters have said, "Here's my career; do what you want. Just tell me where to be and what time." That's a big mistake. A dangerous one.

What I've learned is that your first priority should be your skating. That's your responsibility and something you have more control over than anything else. Second, don't just turn over your career to an agent. Your career choices—such as whether to turn pro or remain "eligible"— are as significant as what you achieve on the ice. Work together as a team and you can create the best possible situation. Be specific, smart and relentless—absolutely relentless about getting what you want. And be wary of an agent who dictates your decisions and books your schedule without consulting you.

When an opportunity comes along, ask yourself, "What does that do for me?" If you're represented by IMG and want to skate with the "Champions on Ice" tour because it's better for you, IMG will negotiate that, regardless of whether it's in their best interest as operators of "Stars on Ice." And Tom Collins should have the freedom to outbid whatever "Stars on Ice" could potentially offer that client. And vice versa. Skaters on Tommy's tour should have the right to pursue a job with "Stars" if that is what they want. There should be freedom of movement and finding out what you are worth in the marketplace, and that isn't always the case.

Just how the eligible and noneligible worlds will come together remains to be seen. This past season was among the first in which amateurs and pros competed head to head in traditionally all pro events, like Dick Button's world pro competitions. Right now it appears that relationship may be short-lived, primarily because most pros don't want to skate under ISU rules, which are restrictive. I remember showing up at a Pro-Am event in New Jersey a few years back only to be told my short program music was illegal because there were vocals on the tape, so I had to switch music and had only one day to prepare the altered program. Making the world pro a Pro-Am diminished what was special about Dick's events—the best pros in the business competing against the best pros. It had luster and people had come to expect that of the world pro. As a Pro-Am, it was just another competition.

Right now there's a pretty clear division between pro and eligible skating. I won't dispute the fact that the eligible skaters are the superior athletes. The top men, for instance, are doing quadruple jumps in combination with triple jumps, and there aren't any pros even attempting to match that type of athleticism.

However, that doesn't make the eligible competitors better skaters. I will shout from the rooftops that ineligible skaters are superior all-around performers. Put the eligibles as a group up against seasoned pros and they look very awkward, the rare exception being Michelle Kwan. As a whole, eligible athletes are one-dimensional, and must be to advance in the eligible arena, where the emphasis is on jumps at the expense of almost everything else.

Not everyone agrees with me. Tara Lipinski took an enormous amount of heat for turning professional after winning the Olympic gold medal. One writer in particular, a reporter from USA Today, attacked Lipinski's decision as taking "the easy way out," and compared turning pro to "joining the circus."

Nothing could be farther from the truth.

Pros work hard, and if they want to excel they work as never before. That is what makes Kristi Yamaguchi, Kurt Browning and Brian Boitano so special. They don't have an ISU title waiting for them at the end of the year to tell them how good they are. They feed off the reaction of the audience and use it as a gauge to determine whether they are winning the larger battle, the battle for creativity and longevity. And contrary to some writers' opinions, turning pro is not about kicking back, not if you have any pride. In most cases there are growing pains to endure, and it can be an embarrassing proposition; it's like going through puberty on national television. You are maturing and changing rapidly, and it can be a very awkward process. Mistakes are made and everyone sees them. But once you develop your own style and image, you can survive as long as you have the work ethic and integrity to keep improving and sustaining an audience. In many respects, pro skating is much tougher and much less forgiving than the eligible world, but you can get out of it everything you put into it.

I don't buy this argument that a meaningful skating career is over after the Olympics. If that's the case, should we all just quit after winning our medals? Should I have retired after Sarajevo? Should Kristi have quit after Albertville, and Katarina Witt opened a skating school after Calgary? Hey, she could have coached with Brian Boitano, right? I guess Sonja Henie should never have bothered to entertain millions with her movies and touring shows. Please. The fact is, professional skating has done nothing but promote and advance the sport, artistically and technically, inside and outside the skating community. For all the technical advances of eligible skaters, the reality is the last woman to land a triple Axel in any world-class ladies' competition was by Midori Ito at the World Professional Figure Skating Championships.

That doesn't sound like "kicking back" to me.

I don't mean to denigrate the eligible world. On the contrary, some skaters may be getting out too soon before they have a chance to develop a following. Ilia Kulik is a very talented skater blessed with many of the intangibles that could make him into a bigger star. What he lacks is a world title and year-in and year-out success, and casual fans still may not know who he is. Though he won an Olympic gold medal in Nagano, it is only one win, and that absence of sustained exposure on his part means some fans may easily move on to the next champion. Men in particular can benefit from the long-term exposure amateur skating offers because they get stronger as they get older, and it takes time to match or surpass the attention given to women in the sport.

For a meaningful career, your roots have to be pretty deep—planted long ago and nourished over many seasons. What's the old saying? Time spent is time invested. I'm not criticizing Ilia; he has an Olympic title, which is plenty for skating fans. Yet it's the casual followers who give you longevity in this business. Familiarity is a huge asset to any pro career. He is now a rookie paying his dues and finding his way, putting in time and working hard. If he remains committed, people will support him. He has the opportunity to grow and mature on the professional stage. "Stars" has been a good place for that. Skaters like Kristi, Kurt Browning and Katia joined the tour with excellent credentials, but they just keep getting better and better.

I know skating will be making progress if Tara and Michelle can compete anywhere, anytime, without Michelle risking her Olympic eligibility. In Nagano, they put on one of the finest duels ever in the ladies' competition. As in 1994 with Nancy and Oksana, the outcome between Tara and Michelle could have gone either way. Two years from now, if the rules are relaxed and Tara has the option to reinstate, maybe we will see both on Olympic ice again.

Today's eligible skaters have an unprecedented opportunity. If they so choose, they can compete against pros and tour in the professional world while remaining eligible for the 2002 games. The top performers can earn millions in the process. It would not have been possible without the ascension of professional skating. So embrace the pro world. It's the best thing going, for audiences and skaters alike.

There's a saying I enjoy: God gives us only what we can endure. I believe that life was created to test us to see how much we can handle, and I believe we can endure any hardship or crisis if we put our mind and faith to it.

I've met many incredible people who have proven it to be so. I have met young people who emigrated from third-world countries not knowing a word of English and went on to graduate from college with a 4.0 GPA. I remember a young teenager who got pregnant and had a baby in high school, was disowned by her family, and yet went on to excel in school and earn a Tribute Award college scholarship—all while raising her baby and supporting herself without the aid of welfare. I think of Joel, who was burned over 85 percent of his body as an infant and yet has grown up into a charming, intelligent and very popular community leader. And Krystal, a little girl who underwent organ transplants, several at a time, not once but twice. What I remember most about our talk was that she was more concerned for her mother's welfare than her own. I met another young man who was born without a lower jaw and has been legally blind his whole life, yet he's determined to get a law degree so he can help people with disabilities. The children I have met through the Make-A-Wish Foundation are truly sensational. Their appreciation of life while overcoming huge obstacles should be an inspiration to us all. Many of these kids are suffering daily—many in fact never have known what it's like to be free of pain—and their parents have made untold sacrifices to make their lives easier. My health is nothing to write home about, but these children define the true meaning of the word *hero*.

No matter who you are, you have been given talents, and it's up to you to nurture and develop them to the best of your ability. I don't just mean something you can make your living at, but anything you enjoy. I'm not going to win any medals in golf, but I love it and work as hard as I can to improve my game. Sure, it's a lot easier to give up if you're not good at what you're trying, but no one ever accomplished anything by giving in. If you love doing something, keep at it through the hard times and you'll get over the bumps in the road.

How much longer I have in full-time skating is unclear, but even if it ended tomorrow, I will have had a heck of a run. I've gotten many more years out of skating than I ever could have hoped for. I think one reason I've lasted so long is that I've never looked back and rested on my laurels; I kept forging ahead. Careers can evaporate when the athlete gets complacent about what he's already accomplished. And of course, the only thing you build in an inactive career is an ego.

My future will always have skating in it to some degree, and I want to keep performing as long as I can. But there's so much I want to do outside the ice rink. The Cleveland Clinic Taussig Cancer Center has started a "Scott Hamilton C.A.R.E.S. Initiative" (Cancer Alliance for Research, Education and Survivorship) to develop a fund-raising and marketing program that will promote public education about cancer prevention, the myths and facts about chemotherapy, and coping skills for survivors once their disease goes into remission. I'm also busy raising money for a Target Stores program called Target House, a home for children (and their families) who are being treated for cancer at St. Jude's Children's Hospital in Memphis.

When I look at how far skating has come in fifteen years, I couldn't have imagined as much in my wildest dreams. I'm fortunate to have accomplished the goals Bob and I talked about way back in 1986—the TV specials, the broadcasting career, "Stars on Ice." As we enter the new millennium, I hope my legacy is what I have been able to create in the way of opportunities for future generations of skaters. The millennium. Hmmm. That might be a nice year to go out in. It's the end of something great and the dawn, I'm certain, of something even more spectacular.

Afterword

I would like to acknowledge the many people who were very generous with their time and who were essential to the writing of this book.

Thank you to my collaborator, Lorenzo Benet, and my editor, Tracy Bernstein; you were an indefatigable team whose insights and understanding were greatly appreciated. Thanks to all at Kensington Publishing, including Janice Rossi Schaus, Laura Shatzkin and John Masiello. I would also like to thank the wonderful professionals at International Management Group, including David Chalfant, who found the ideal publisher to tell my life story, and the indispensable Susan Lohman. Thanks also to Michael Sterling, for his friendship, help and assistance. And my gratitude goes to Karen Cover and Beth Davis of the World Figure Skating Museum and Hall of Fame, transcriber Doddie Ellis and to all the photographers whose work appears in this book.

I also want to recognize a group of special people who have made a difference in my life. Thank you to Norm and Doug Bassett; Sandra Bezic; Willie Beitak; Brian Boitano; Sam and Loyce Bornhauser; Mahlon Bradley; the Brennan Family; Kurt Browning; Pierre Brunet; John Brunton; Dick Button; Neil Carpenter; Peter and Kitty Carruthers; Kathy Casey; Tom and Jane Collins; Sam Cooper; Robin Cousins; Steven Cousins; Toller Cranston; Bill Daniels; Carlo and Christa Fassi; the Fisher Family; Jay Frye; Giuliano Grassi; the Glenn Family; Ekaterina Gordeeva; Ricky Harris; the Holding Family; Ice Capades; Jack Mack and the Heart Attack; David Jenkins; Dr. Andrew Klepner; Karen Kresge; Brent Landis; David and Rita Lowery; Verne and Nancy Lundquist; Mark McCormack; Gordon McKellen; David Meek; Nancy Meiss; Lea Ann Miller; Kevin and Linda Nealon; Rick Neilsen; Brian

Orser; Bill and Lynn Plage; Herb Plata; Jozef Sabovcik; David Santee; Evy and Mary Scotvold; F. Ritter Shumway; Janet Lynn-Solomon; Bob Stenner; Rosalynn Sumners; Charlie Tickner; Jayne Torvill and Christopher Dean; Freddie Trenkler; Paul Viladolid; Doug Wilson; Tracy Wilson; Kristi Yamaguchi; Todd, Julianne, Garrett and Hannah Zeile.

And to Sergei Grinkov, Rob McCall and Brian Pockar, three great friends who were taken at the prime of their lives.

Scott Hamilton

Index